12/93

 St. Louis Community College

Forest Park
Florissant Valley
Meramec

Instructional Resources
St. Louis, Missouri

The Other Mary Shelley

The Other Mary Shelley

Beyond *Frankenstein*

Edited by

AUDREY A. FISCH

ANNE K. MELLOR

ESTHER H. SCHOR

New York   Oxford
OXFORD UNIVERSITY PRESS
1993

Oxford University Press

Oxford   New York   Toronto
Delhi   Bombay   Calcutta   Madras   Karachi
Kuala Lumpur   Singapore   Hong Kong   Tokyo
Nairobi   Dar es Salaam   Cape Town
Melbourne   Auckland   Madrid

and associated companies in Berlin   Ibadan

Introduction: copyright © 1993 by Audrey A. Fisch,
Anne K. Mellor, and Esther H. Schor
"Mary Shelley in Transit": copyright © 1993 by Esther H. Schor
"Plaguing Politics: AIDS, Deconstruction, and *The Last Man*":
copyright © 1993 by Audrey A. Fisch
All other material: copyright © 1993 by Oxford University Press, Inc.

Published by Oxford University Press, Inc.,
200 Madison Avenue, New York, New York 10016

Oxford is a registered trademark of Oxford University Press

Library of Congress Cataloging-in-Publication Data
The Other Mary Shelley : beyond Frankenstein /
edited by Audrey A. Fisch, Anne K. Mellor,
Esther H. Schor.
p. cm.   Includes bibliographical references
(p.   ) and index.
ISBN 0-19-507740-7
1. Shelley, Mary Wollstonecraft, 1797–1851—Criticism and interpretation.
2. Women and literature—England—History—19th century.
3. Romanticism—England.   I. Fisch, Audrey A.
II. Mellor, Anne Kostelanetz.   III. Schor, Esther H.
PR5398.087   1993   823'.7—dc20
92-14568

1 3 5 7 9 8 4 6 2
Printed in the United States of America
on acid-free paper

for my parents
AAF

for Ronald Mellor
AKM

for Joseph M. Schor
EHS

ACKNOWLEDGMENTS

The editors gratefully acknowledge the generosity of A. Walton Litz, who encouraged and assisted us at an early stage. Early help also came from Alice Augenti. The preparation of the manuscript was assisted by the research of Margit Dimenti, Richard Kaye and Sarah Zimmerman; in preparing the manuscript, we were funded in part by the Department of English of Princeton University under the auspices of the John E. Annan Bicentennial Preceptorship. We also wish to acknowledge the team at Oxford—Elizabeth Maguire, Susan Chang, Stanley George and Beth Hanlon—for the professionalism and patience with which they saw our manuscript into print.

Contents

The Other Mary Shelley

Introduction

In 1979, George Levine and U. C. Knoepflmacher's *The Endurance of Franken-stein* gave serious critical attention to the metaphorical and mythical meanings of *Frankenstein*. Interpreting the novel from a variety of perspectives—biographical, social, psychoanalytic, literary historical, generic, cinematic—the essays in *The Endurance of Frankenstein* strongly suggest that *Franken-stein,* in the editors' words, "belongs to a prophetic tradition open only, one would have thought, to mature literary imaginations."[1] Despite aligning *Frankenstein* with the prophetic, philosophical fictions of *Faust, Prometheus Unbound, The Brothers Karamazov,* and *Middlemarch,* however, *The Endurance of Frankenstein* remains consistently circumspect about its claims for Mary Shelley. Though important essays by Ellen Moers and U. C. Knoepflmacher place the novel in the context of Mary Shelley's personal and intellectual experience, the essays on the whole remain oddly reticent, if not slightly embarrassed, by the matter of Mary Shelley's authorship. The murky issue of exactly how self-conscious Mary Shelley was in writing *Frankenstein*—the issue, in other words, of her responsibility for her hideously fascinating progeny—is finessed with a discreet metonymy:

> How much of the book's complexity is actually the result of Mary Shelley's self-conscious art and how much is merely the product of the happy circum-stances of subject, moment, milieu? The novel intimates that it knows little about its implications (although it seems clear enough about its literary sources in Milton, Gothic fiction and Romantic poetry). Are not its ener-gies, therefore, un-self-conscious and accidental? (xii–xiii)

A novel may certainly tell more than its author, but can it "know" more than its author? The metonymy is as prophetic as it is discreet, for during the decade that followed, the blaze of feminist interest in *Frankenstein* would throw light on the novel's darkest passages, while leaving Mary Shelley herself in her accustomed obscurity. Obscurity, at any rate, is preferable to outright occlusion; James Rieger's 1974 introduction to the 1818 *Frankenstein* an-nounces that "Shelley oversaw his wife's manuscript at every stage,"[2] a claim that has now been reexamined—to Percy Shelley's editorial detriment—by the perspicacious archival work of Anne K. Mellor.[3] Still, for an author who had been persistently overshadowed by critical and biographical attention to her illustrious husband and parents—Percy Bysshe Shelley, Mary Wollstone-craft, and William Godwin—the irony of being obscured even by her own renown is especially mordant.

Let us pause for a moment over the divergent fortunes of *Frankenstein* and Mary Shelley in the 1980s. During this decade, feminists of widely differing

3

agendas used *Frankenstein* to advance critiques of masculinist bias in literary theory. In Barbara Johnson's hands (1982), *Frankenstein* becomes a pre-text for feminist autobiography, an allegory of "autobiography as the attempt to neutralize the monstrosity of autobiography."[4] For Gayatri Spivak (1985), it becomes a novel that resists "the axiomatics of imperialism," "a text of nascent feminism that remains cryptic . . . simply because it does not speak the language of feminist individualism which we have come to hail as the language of high feminism within English literature."[5] Margaret Homans's Lacanian reading of *Frankenstein* in *Bearing the Word* (1986) defines the psychosocial predicament underlying the novel as "the self-contradictory demand that daughters embody both the mother whose death makes language possible by making it necessary and the figurative substitutes for that mother who constitute the prototype of the signifying chain."[6] According to Homans, however, *Frankenstein* allegorizes not the predicament of the Lacanian mother (or daughter) but of the Lacanian son, who "seeks figurations that will at once make restitution for the mother and confirm her death and absence by substituting for her figures that are under his control" (107). *Frankenstein*, for Homans, represents Lacan's elaboration of the oedipal crisis under the sign of romantic desire.

Reading *Frankenstein* as Mary Shelley's self-conscious revision of Percy Shelley's *Alastor* and, more generally, of his theories of love, Homans credits Mary Shelley with a coherent critique of Romantic egotism and Romantic desire; by itself, Homans's chapter suggests why *Frankenstein* has by now secured a firm place not only in courses on women writers, but also in undergraduate surveys of British Romanticism. Whereas the Keatsian ethos of negative capability was formerly regarded as the most compelling—most *teachable*—critique of Romantic egotism from within Romanticism, *Frankenstein* advances its critique in terms of an incipient feminist politics, one resonant with the revolutionary alarum sounded by the pioneeer feminist Mary Wollstonecraft a generation earlier. Furthermore, as a novel, *Frankenstein* licenses a critical examination of Shelleyan radicalism by embedding the anticommunitarian ambitions of its Shelleyan visionary within the frankly dysfunctional polity of Republican Geneva. Hence, *Frankenstein* has become a sturdy pedagogical tool for deconstructing the transcendental Romantic imagination; in the crudest terms, *Frankenstein*, by the monstrosity of the creature's body, signals the suppression of gender in the ethos of Romantic egotism.

A 1989 survey of some three hundred American universities, conducted by Harriet Kramer Linkin, reports that over half of Romantics courses now include Mary Shelley;[7] presumably, this means that one of every two students of Romanticism has read *Frankenstein*. And yet while *Frankenstein* has become canonized in the classroom, little has changed for Mary Shelley; now it is the pale face of Victor Frankenstein that obscures the pale face of his creator. Ironically, the canonization of *Frankenstein* has institutionalized the marginality of Mary Shelley, throwing her salient and central voice to the edges of Romantic discourse.

While *Frankenstein* was being recruited for poststructuralist feminism by Spivak, Johnson, and Homans, critical attention to Mary Shelley was primarily absorbed in the painstaking preparation of groundbreaking editions of her letters and journals. In her three volumes of Mary Shelley's letters (published in 1980, 1983, and 1988 respectively), Betty T. Bennett brought to light hundreds of previously unpublished letters which shed new light on Mary Shelley's thirty-year career as a writer, on her political opinions and commitments, on her family relationships, and on her personal friendships.[8] *The Journals of Mary Shelley* (1987), edited by Paula R. Feldman and Diana Scott-Kilvert, make vivid Mary Shelley's development from her early days in the flamboyant Shelley circle through the years of struggle and achievement as she continued to write, judiciously edit and publish Percy Shelley's literary remains, and support and educate her surviving son.[9]

Emily Sunstein's prizewinning biography, *Mary Shelley: Romance and Reality* (1989), assimilates and interprets these letters and journals in a biography that at long last situates Mary Shelley in her own intellectual and historical context.[10] Since the publication of Sunstein's biography, it has become redundant to observe how poorly Mary Shelley has been served by some three generations of biographers and historians of Romanticism. From even a brief sketch of Mary Shelley's life emerges the striking portrait of a woman of persistence, courage, generosity, and independence who overcame severe personal and financial hardships to achieve a full and productive life. Ten days after giving birth to Mary Wollstonecraft Godwin on August 30, 1797, Mary Wollstonecraft died of puerperal fever, leaving her husband, the anarchist philosopher William Godwin, to raise the infant Mary and her half-sister Fanny Imlay. A solicitous and conscientious father, Godwin shortly thereafter married Mary Jane Clairmont, an unmarried woman with two children; in 1805 they started the publishing firm of M. J. Godwin & Co., which produced some of the most widely read children's books of the era. As a child, Mary Godwin received an enlightened education from her father and the illustrious company of Godwin's circle, but her adolescence was strained by friction between herself and her stepmother and by the consequences of many years of financial hardship for the Godwins. When Mary Godwin was ten, M. J. Godwin & Co. published her comic poem, "Mounseer Nontongpaw," which remained in print through four British editions and two pirated American ones. After an extended, idyllic sojourn with the Baxter family in Scotland, she met Percy Shelley, a young, married disciple of her father, who prevailed upon her to elope with him (in the company of her stepsister Jane Clairmont) to the Continent in July 1814.

During her seven turbulent years with Percy Shelley, years of itinerancy, financial stress, and severe marital strains, Mary Shelley continued her writing career. She wrote a travel book based on the elopement journey, *History of a Six Weeks' Tour* (1817); two novels, *Frankenstein* (1818) and *Valperga* (1823), a historical romance set in fourteenth-century Italy; two mythological dramas, *Proserpine* and *Midas* (both written in 1820); and *Mathilda* (written in 1819), a novella of father–daughter incest, which was suppressed by Godwin. After the abandoned Harriet Shelley committed suicide, Mary Godwin and Percy Shelley were soberly married on December 30, 1816; their liaison, begun in ecstatic conviction of their mutual destiny, was increasingly strained by Percy Shelley's attachments to other women (including, among others, Jane, now Claire, Clairmont, Emilia Viviani, and Jane Williams), by the vicissitudes of Claire Clairmont's relationship with Lord Byron, and, most painfully, by the deaths of the two Shelley children who had survived infancy, Clara in 1818 and William in 1819. A third child, Percy Florence, born shortly after William's death, was the only one to survive into adulthood. Some three weeks after saving Mary Shelley from a near-fatal hemorrhage during a miscarriage in June 1822, Percy Shelley was drowned at sea along with his friend Edward Williams.

After reluctantly returning to England with Percy Florence in 1823, Mary Shelley published her edition of *The Posthumous Poems of Percy Bysshe Shelley* in 1824. Under financial threats from Percy Shelley's angry father, she agreed not to continue to publish Percy Shelley's works, thinking Sir Timothy would not live long; the "Struldbrug," as she put it, did not die until 1844. A crushing disappointment came in Jane Williams's betrayal of their intimate friendship, which had been a hope and a solace to her on first returning to England. In 1826 she published *The Last Man,* an apocalyptic novel set in the twenty-first century, in which she considers nostalgically but also skeptically the legacy of Shelleyan radicalism. During the next ten years she wrote another historical novel, *The Fortunes of Perkin Warbeck* (1830), and two domestic romances: *Lodore* (1835), her most popular novel since *Frankenstein,* and *Falkner* (1837). While she continued to publish much of her short fiction in such illustrated annuals as *The Keepsake, The Bijou,* and *Forget-me-Not,* she became convinced of her aptitude for nonfiction prose and historical research; between 1835 and 1840 she wrote the lion's share of five volumes for Lardner's *Cabinet Encyclopedia,* an anthology of biographies of Italian, Spanish, Portuguese, and French writers and scientists.

Mary Shelley's journals and letters for this period record a series of social engagements, including frequent attendance at musical, theatrical, and operatic performances; apparently, she had gained a measure of acceptance within the ranks of the gentry. She remained keenly sensitive to social opprobrium; having known the consequences of a scandalous reputation, she sought to ensure that her son's chances of obtaining a university education were never compromised. At the same time, her journals and letters record her close friendships with unconventional, iconoclastic, and even outcast women, among them Caroline Norton, Lady Morgan, and Georgiana ("Gee") Paul; she even assisted her friends Mary Diana Dods and Isabel Robinson in their plan to live in France as husband and wife under the names "Mr. and Mrs. Sholto Douglas."[11] Rejecting tentative proposals of marriage from John Howard Payne and Prosper Mérimée (and disappointed that her intimate friendship with the liberal widower Aubrey Beauclerk failed to ripen into marriage), she remained an independent, self-supporting widow until her death. With Sir Timothy Shelley's grudging permission, she published both a four-volume edition (1839) and a one-volume edition (1840) of Percy Shelley's poetry, and a two-volume edition of his *Essays, Letters from Abroad, Translations and Fragments* (1840).

During her final decade, she was beset with recurring symptoms of the brain tumor, undiagnosed until 1850, that would take her life. Perhaps these debilitating symptoms prevented her from completing her projected *Memoirs* of Godwin, who had died in 1836. Still, her final years brought the satisfactions of vigorous Continental travel with Percy Florence and his friends, including two extended sojourns in her beloved Italy. Her final publication, like her first long published work, was a travel book; *Rambles in Germany and Italy in 1840, 1842 and 1843* (1844) doubles as a travel guide and as a meticulously researched polemic on behalf of Italian nationalism. She took pleasure in seeing Percy Florence graduate from Cambridge, inherit his grandfather's estate and title, and happily marry Jane Gibson St. John; after 1844, Mary Shelley and her son enjoyed a modest increase of comfort from the Shelley estate. After months of excruciating suffering, she died in London on February 1, 1851, and was buried (along with the bodies of her unorthodox parents, recently exhumed from St. Pancras's churchyard) in St. Peter's, Bournemouth, by night, against the wishes of the scandalized rector.

With the exception of *Frankenstein* and *The Last Man* (which the University of Nebraska Press has kept in print since 1965, and which was recently reprinted by the Hogarth Press), virtually all of Mary Shelley's writings have long since gone out of print or are available only in expensive scholarly reprints. This situation is changing. Two recent paperbacks, a reprint of Mary Shelley's *Tales*, edited by Charles E. Robinson, and *The Mary Shelley Reader*, edited by Betty T. Bennett and Charles E. Robinson, have made several of her neglected works (including *Mathilda*) widely accessible once more.[12] And a complete works of Mary Shelley, under the general editorship of Betty T. Bennett, is at last in preparation.

Against the backdrop of the divergent fortunes of *Frankenstein* and Mary Shelley, a monitory image emerges. Even as *Frankenstein* has become split off from the corpus of Mary Shelley, another "Mary Shelley," intellectually formidable and remarkably accomplished, is being fashioned from the historical and biographical evidence that surrounds that corpus. What remains to be considered, clearly, is the work "beyond *Frankenstein*," the corpus of five novels, one novella, dozens of tales, sketches, essays, reviews, and stories, two mythological dramas, five volumes of biographies, two travel books, and extensive notes to Percy Shelley's works.

Amid the urgent attention to *Frankenstein* (including William Veeder's 1986 full-length study, *Mary Shelley and Frankenstein: The Fate of Androgyny*[13]) and the relative neglect of Mary Shelley's oeuvre, two critics have made notable attempts to suture *Frankenstein* to the other works of Mary Shelley, so that those works might in turn be sutured to the cultural milieu in which Mary Shelley lived and wrote. Mary Poovey, in *The Proper Lady and the Woman Writer* (1984), uses Mary Shelley's 1831 revisions of *Frankenstein* "to examine

the shadow the Proper Lady casts across the careers of . . . women who became professional authors despite the strictures of propriety."[14] For Poovey,
the 1831 revisions constitute a "retreat from unorthodoxy" which had already
motivated the ideological compromises of *The Last Man.* According to
Poovey, "*The Last Man* disavows *Frankenstein's* condemnation of the egotist
as origin and agent of destruction . . . by direct[ing] responsibility away from
the artist-protagonist to impersonal forces" (149); the late novels constitute
"rejections" of unorthodoxy within which "countercurrents" of unconventional ideas may yet be discerned. Anne K. Mellor's *Mary Shelley: Her Life,
Her Fiction, Her Monsters* (1988), the only full-length critical treatment of
Shelley's works to appear in the 1980s, argues that Mary Shelley was personally divided between a redemptive vision of the bourgeois family and a shrewd
estimation of the manner in which that family structure circumscribes the
powers, freedoms, and distinctive values of women. Mellor's readings of *Frankenstein, The Last Man,* and the later domestic fictions adumbrate "the glaring
contradiction in Mary Shelley's political ideology: the conflict between an
ethic of care and an ethic of control, between a system of justice grounded on
mutual rights and responsibilities and a system of justice grounded on the
[masculine] authority of the elders" (88). More recently, in *Romanticism and
Gender* (1993), Mellor locates Mary Shelley, along with such writers as Jane
Austen, Maria Edgeworth, Charlotte Smith, Susan Ferrier, Helen Maria Williams, and Felicia Hemans, in the context of a set of values that distinguishes
the radicalism of women writers of the Romantic period from that of their
male counterparts. Inspired by Wollstonecraft's *Vindication,* these writers ad-
vocated a "revolution in female manners," by emphasizing the rationality of
women, by celebrating community, by conceiving of nature as an ally, by
preferring gradual and evolutionary reform to revolution, and by espousing an
ethic of care rather than an ethic of individual justice.[15]

The essays in this book continue the crucial work of surveying Mary Shelley's oeuvre, of situating *Frankenstein* in that context, and of defining Mary
Shelley's career in terms of her intellectual backgrounds and political commitments. Having identified the seventeenth-century scientific revolution with
masculine hubris and an imperial colonization of nature in *Frankenstein,* Mary
Shelley turned in her other novels to a critique of imperialism in other cultural
forms: military conquest (*Valperga, The Last Man, Perkin Warbeck*), the exploration of the East (*Valperga*), the colonization of America (*Lodore*). Re-
membering her mother's identification of family politics with gender politics,
she examined domestic oppression (in *Lodore,* in *Falkner,* and in *The Last
Man*). Responding to the scientific redefinition of nature no longer as female
but as natural, "dead matter," she deftly explored the consequences of an
indifferent nature in *The Last Man.* Again and again, she sought alternatives
to the transcendental, remote, and ironic style of Romantic lyricism, nowhere
more so, as Mary Favret and Susan J. Wolfson show here, than in her prose
annotations to Percy Shelley's poetry.

By bringing Mary Shelley to the center of Romantic studies, the essays in
this book progress beyond a simple recognition of masculinism at the heart of

canonical Romanticism. What these essays discern in the "other" Mary Shelley is a writer whose resistance to Romanticism from within the discursive field we call "Romantic" is in many ways continuous with the insights of contemporary feminist analysis. In her fictions, Mary Shelley often upholds the values of domesticity and the quotidian while recognizing the ways in which a naive investment in the traditional, patriarchal, and nonegalitarian family could cripple women. Mary Shelley endorsed her mother's commitment to a politics grounded on the new female manners, but she resisted the too easy absorption of that domestic ideology into the doctrine of the separate spheres. Her novels and nonfiction prose must be read, as these essays show, as defining the precarious balance between "feminine romanticism" and the middle-class domestic ideology described by Davidoff and Hall in *Family Fortunes,* which we have since come to identify with Victorianism.[16] Mary Shelley is not so much a "transitional" figure between the early and later nineteenth century as one of the first to recognize the dangers of, and to resist, the limitation of female rationality and the ethic of care to the private sphere.

What we have in Mary Shelley is a writer who was empowered and inspired by the energies of Romanticism, but who refused to celebrate these energies in default of a coherent, communitarian ethos; a writer equally at home in the literature of the past and in contemporary politics; a writer who gave wide expression to her own talents and interests while understanding keenly the constraints of the marketplace within which she earned her living; a writer whose vision glances backward to the intellectual ferment of an enlightened Age of Revolution, and forward to the transitions and rapid changes of a doubting Age of Reform; and finally, a writer with a unique perspective on the legacy of Romanticism for us, on the perils of imaginatively remaking our minds and our world. At once mythmaker and historian, Mary Shelley understood that the intelligibility of culture depends on the myths by which we negotiate the historical. If the essays in this book enliven, rather than resolve, critical debate about Mary Shelley, they do so by demonstrating that she was an astute, informed, literate, self-conscious, imaginative, and above all courageous critic of culture.

The essays in this book attest to the variety of critical procedures that have recently been brought to bear on Mary Shelley's work. For several contributors, including Favret, Corbett, Langbauer, Ellis, Schor, Fisch, and Johnson, writing on Mary Shelley becomes the occasion for critical self-consciousness; along with Mary Shelley's works, feminism, new historicism, deconstruction, and cultural studies, among other methodologies, come under scrutiny. We have organized these essays to highlight the issues through which Mary Shelley's work compels such a variegated critical response, dividing them into two groups. Part I, "Romanticism and Resistance," considers Mary Shelley's relation to the culture of British Romanticism; part II, "Culture and Criticism," takes up Mary Shelley's considerations of the quotidian, of the routines that construct and sustain human communities over time and space. To provide an

overview of Mary Shelley's relations to Romanticism, we begin part I with
two essays concerning her crucial editions of Percy Shelley's works. Mary
Favret, in "Mary Shelley's Sympathy and Irony: The Editor and Her Corpus,"
describes a competition between "a poetic corpus"—the poetic remains of
Percy Shelley—and "a prose body"—the body of prose commentary in which
Mary Shelley situates those remains, ultimately objectifying and estranging
them from their audience. In her notes, Mary Shelley's gendering of genres
implicitly subverts the Romantic hierarchy granting lyric pride of place.
Whereas her ostensible function is to gain sympathy for Percy Shelley's writings, Mary Shelley in fact gains sympathy for her own crafted prose which,
unlike Percy's poems, claims an immediate social and ideological influence.
Susan J. Wolfson's "Editorial Privilege: Mary Shelley and Percy Shelley's
Audiences" interprets Mary Shelley's editions as an intervention in "conflicting Romantic legacies"—populist and elitist—"about the social role and potency of poetry." Wolfson defines "the master-passion of Mary Shelley's editions" as a contradiction between "the exclusionary signs that keep faith with
a select readership and the narrative of a generous and responsive poet."
Reconstructing "Shelley," argues Wolfson, ultimately enables the editor to
reconstruct "Mary Shelley" as the late poet's "ideal, best reader." Next, in
"Reading Mary Shelley's *Journals,*" Mary Jean Corbett locates "a space in
which the mutual is privileged over and above the individual, in which the self
cannot be a self without the familial context that shapes identity in particular
ways, not all of them necessarily liberating or constraining." Corbett cautions
against reading the later *Journals* as a species of Romantic confession, showing how even here Mary Shelley opens the way to a postmodernist conception
of the self as fluid and intersubjective.

While the essays by Favret, Wolfson, and Corbett consider the tense textual juxtaposition of Mary Shelley's prose and Percy Shelley's poetry, the
following three essays discuss how Mary Shelley's fictions and dramas revise
the texts and topoi of the male Romantics. First, Paul A. Cantor considers
Mary Shelley's revision of Byron's fragmentary *Deformed Transformed,*
which she herself transcribed for Byron. In "Mary Shelley and the Taming of
the Byronic Hero," Cantor demonstrates continuities between Mary Shelley's
critique of mimetic desire in *Frankenstein* and her determination to "find a
way out of the vicious circle of mimetic desire" in her short story "Transformation." According to Cantor, Mary Shelley's canny revision unmasks and cor-
rects the violence and narcissism that are constitutive of Romantic desire.
Next, Morton D. Paley's essay on *The Last Man,* "Apocalypse Without Millennium," shows how Mary Shelley undercuts, overturns, and ultimately subverts the familiar Romantic conjunction of apocalypse and millennium. Exploiting the contemporary popular topos of the last man, Mary Shelley denies
the linkage of apocalypse and millennium in a novel that laments the insufficiency of art to establish a redemptive world order. In the following essay,
Alan Richardson aligns Mary Shelley's neglected verse dramas *Proserpine*
and *Midas* with her revision of classical Prometheanism in *Frankenstein.* Moving beyond the monologism of the Romantic lyric, Mary Shelley's verse dra-

mas reach "behind Ovid to recover something of the deeper sexual/cultural tensions expressed in Greek myths and the rituals and mysteries associated with them." Mary Shelley's interests guide her in particular to the traumatic scene of Proserpine's rape, and to the cult of Demeter, whom she represents as the heart of a community of mythmaking women, quite possibly "precursors for her own revisionary project."

The final two essays in part I both focus on Shelley's *Valperga* (1823) as an example of feminine Romantic mythmaking. In "Beatrice in *Valperga:* A New Cassandra," Barbara Jane O'Sullivan interprets Beatrice in conjunction with the female literary tradition of Cassandra, a figure with whom Shelley, by her own account, identified strongly. O'Sullivan defines the novel's "Cassandra complex" as a fatalistic tradition in which women who have prophetic powers of insight are doomed to be ignored, exploited, or at worst victimized for their vision. Through figures such as Beatrice in *Valperga* and Evadne in *The Last Man,* Mary Shelley explores the creativity of women while reckoning with the forces that betray and thwart it. In "God's Sister: History and Ideology in *Valperga*" Joseph W. Lew reads the novel as "a lament for a time— simultaneously 'lost' and 'imagined'—before the differentiation of separate spheres of activity, a time when men and women could participate fully in both the private and public realms." Lew places the novel's female prophets in the context of late eighteenth-century female-dominated millenarian cults by way of exploring Shelley's difficult relationship to her mother's feminism and jacobinism. The crux of *Valperga,* Lew argues, lies in Mary Shelley's sophisticated use of historical romance to dramatize a fatal moment: a male hero, choosing among competing ideologies, yields to the seductions of tyranny. *Valperga,* in Lew's words, is "a Romantic and specifically feminist 'myth of origins' that explains how men and women came to inhabit the worlds we live in."

Part II, "Culture and Criticism," opens with Laurie Langbauer's meditation on how Mary Shelley negotiated the Romantic tension between the extraordinary and the everyday. In "Swayed by Contraries: Mary Shelley and the Everyday," Langbauer understands Mary Shelley's 1830 story "The Swiss Peasant" to debate the role of the ordinary in telling tales: "The point not just of *Frankenstein* but also of Shelley's generically mixed work (is it science fiction, gothic, domestic realism?) is the impossibility of coherence, as well as the price we pay striving for it." While Mary Shelley "shows that the greater world of the imagination is equally matched by the world of daily life," she nonetheless refuses to characterize a turn to the everyday as a subversive narrative strategy for women, preferring to leave the political status of such a gesture undetermined. The next essay suggests Mary Shelley's keen understanding of the aesthetic strategies at work in the illustrated annuals in which she published so many of her short stories. In "Disfiguring Economies: Mary Shelley's Short Stories," Sonia Hofkosh reads the relationship between Mary Shelley's fictions and the engravings that accompanied them dialectically, as a conversation (and potential conflict) between differing accounts of aesthetic production. Over the years, claims Hofkosh, the stories return obsessively to con-

cerns about tale telling, identity, and transgression; taken together, they reveal
not just the personal struggle between marketplace pragmatics and a certain
brand of Romantic idealism, but also a subversive poetics of representation.

The following two essays consider how Mary Shelley negotiates the radical
legacy of her mother, Mary Wollstonecraft. Kate Ferguson Ellis's "Subversive
Surfaces: The Limits of Domestic Affection in Mary Shelley's Later Fiction"
argues that Mary Shelley's "writing was a vehicle for a radical vision that may
even go beyond her mother's veneration of bourgeois domesticity as the
highest expression of woman's God-given rationality." In both her early
works, such as *Mathilda, Frankenstein, Valperga,* and *The Last Man,* and her
later fictions, such as *Lodore* and *Falkner,* Mary Shelley unmasks as "simply
illusory" the fictive female power that constitutes "one of the constitutive
premises of the bourgeois family." In "Mary Shelley in Transit," Esther H.
Schor argues that Mary Shelley "participates in a dialectical strain of Romantic egotism anticipated by Wollstonecraft," in whose works the discourses of
sentimentality and of Enlightenment anthropology meet. Examining Shelley's
representations of self and other in *Rambles in Germany and Italy,* Schor
argues that Shelley defines selfhood as "a process of Enlightenment, a discovery of the other; otherness makes possible the conceptualization of selfhood."
Such a dialectic enables Shelley to offer an informed, analytical polemic on
behalf of Italian nationalism, even as she writes the romance of her own
renewal and redemption in southern Italy.

The final two essays in part II consider *The Last Man,* Mary Shelley's
prophecy of the twenty-first century, from the perspective of the late twentieth century. If, as Barbara Johnson maintains, Frankenstein's monster is a
figure for the false consciousness of humanism, then Mary Shelley's last man
is a figure for the aporia that succeeds humanism. Johnson interprets the
plague—"at once that which stops all systems of meaning from functioning
and that against which those systems are necessarily erected"—as a sign of
Mary Shelley's despair of a relation between acquired knowledge and the
arena of political action. "The story of *The Last Man,*" writes Johnson, "is in
the last analysis the story of modern Western man torn between mourning and
deconstruction." In "Plaguing Politics: AIDS, Deconstruction, and *The Last
Man,*" Audrey A. Fisch elaborates on the novel's implications for a politics of
deconstruction. Fisch's discussion concentrates on the counterpoint between
the totalizing political schemes of such characters as Adrian and Raymond
and the frame narrator's "politics of imperfection." The frame narrator, argues Fisch, may well serve as a model for the deconstructive critic, "necessarily both a part of and apart from 'society,' shaping but also being shaped by
the 'materials' of his or her work, and distrusting any political agenda which,
for the sake of 'urgency,' might preclude modest, personal projects."

Mary Shelley's readings of culture—whether the culture of classical
Greece, of the Enlightenment, of British Romanticism, of Italian nationalism,
of the bourgeois family, of gender distinctions, of the literary marketplace, of
apocalypse, or even of "nature"—yet retain their impressive force and vitality
nearly a century and a half after her death. As this catalogue of her concerns

suggests, the reach of her critical inquiry is balanced by her genius for focusing it in a variety of modes and genres. But Mary Shelley reaches us in another way; if the futurism of *Frankenstein* has been overemphasized in its many cinematic adaptations, the far-seeing implications of Mary Shelley's corpus as a whole have yet to be fully appreciated. Taken together, the essays in this book make us aware that even as we read Mary Shelley, she is reading us. If it is the task of contemporary feminism to offer both genealogies of gendered consciousness and analyses of how women and men struggle for equality in families, in cities, in nations and among them, then contemporary feminism and literate culture more generally have a great deal to learn from the prescient vision of Mary Shelley.

Notes

1. George Levine and U. C. Knoepflmacher, eds., *The Endurance of Franken-stein: Essays on Mary Shelley's Novel* (Berkeley: University of California Press, 1979), xiii.

2. James Rieger, introduction to Mary Wollstonecraft Shelley, *Frankenstein, or The Modern Prometheus: The 1818 Text* (Chicago: University of Chicago Press, 1982), xviii.

3. See Anne K. Mellor, *Mary Shelley: Her Life, Her Fiction, Her Monsters* (New York: Methuen, 1988), 58–69.

4. Barbara Johnson, *A World of Difference* (Baltimore: Johns Hopkins University Press, 1987), 146.

5. Gayatri Chakravorty Spivak, "Three Women's Texts and a Critique of Imperialism," *Race, Writing, and Difference,* (Chicago: University of Chicago Press, 1986), 273.

6. Margaret Homans, ed. Henry Louis Gates, Jr., *Bearing the Word: Language and Female Experience in Nineteenth-Century Women's Writing* (Chicago: University of Chicago Press, 1986), 100.

7. Harriet Kramer Linkin, "The Current Canon in British Romantics Studies," *College English* 53 (1991): 548–70.

8. Mary Wollstonecraft Shelley, *The Letters of Mary Wollstonecraft Shelley,* ed. Betty T. Bennett, 3 vols. (Baltimore: Johns Hopkins University Press, 1980–88).

9. Mary Wollstonecraft Shelley, *The Journals of Mary Shelley: 1814–1844,* ed. Paula Feldman and Diana Scott-Kilvert (Oxford: Oxford University Press, 1987).

10. Emily W. Sunstein, *Mary Shelley: Romance and Reality* (Boston: Little, Brown, 1989).

11. A full-length account of this episode may be found in Betty T. Bennett, *Mary Diana Dods: A Gentleman and a Scholar* (New York: Morrow, 1991).

12. See Mary Wollstonecraft Shelley, *Collected Tales and Stories,* ed. Charles E. Robinson (Baltimore: Johns Hopkins University Press, 1976); and Mary Wollstonecraft Shelley, *The Mary Shelley Reader,* eds. Betty T. Bennett and Charles E. Robinson (New York: Oxford University Press, 1990).

13. William Veeder, *Mary Shelley and Frankenstein: The Fate of Androgyny* (Chicago: University of Chicago Press, 1986).

14. Mary Poovey, *The Proper Lady and the Woman Writer: Ideology as Style in the*

Works of Mary Wollstonecraft, Mary Shelley, and Jane Austen (Chicago: University of Chicago Press, 1984), x.

15. Anne K. Mellor, *Romanticism and Gender* (New York: Routledge, Chapman and Hall, 1993).

16. Leonore Davidoff and Catherine Hall, *Family Fortunes: Men and Women of the English Middle Class, 1780–1850* (London: Hutchinson, 1987).

I

ROMANTICISM
AND RESISTANCE

Mary Shelley's Sympathy and Irony: The Editor and Her Corpus

Mary Favret

> He died, and the world showed no outward sign. . . . He died, and his
> place . . . has never been filled up.
> > Mary Shelley, Preface to *The Poetical Works of Percy Bysshe Shelley*

> Any objective method, duly verified, belies the initial contact with the
> object. It must first scrutinize everything. . . . Objective thought does not
> gaze in wonderment; it must be ironic. . . . [Whereas] in the examination
> of men, equals, or brothers, sympathy is the basis of method.
> > Gaston Bachelard, *On Poetic Imagination and Revery*

In 1838, Mary Shelley wrote to publisher Edward Moxon to arrange payment
and negotiate copy rights for the forthcoming edition of Percy Shelley's *Poetical
Works*. Her letter emphasizes the difficult task of editing and her crucial involvement in the production. Indeed, Mary Shelley had taken on a formidable project. Not only does she piece together and transcribe Percy's poetry, which she
calls, elsewhere, "so confused a mass, interlined and broken into fragments,"
that "the wonder would be how any eyes or patience were capable of extracting
[a volume]" from these scattered remains.[1] This chore she had begun earlier,
with the rather flawed collection of Percy's *Posthumous Poems* (1824). But the
1839 edition is considerably more ambitious. In addition to the poems themselves, Mary Shelley presents nearly fifty pages of commentary upon the poems,
in many cases providing the first published critical assessment of Percy's works.
Most significantly, she "animates" this body of work. The woman who wrote
Frankenstein now constructs a life that holds together these scattered pieces;
these "component parts [are] . . . endued with vital warmth."[2] She circum-
vents Sir Timothy Shelley's prohibiton against a biography of his son by inserting instead "the history of those productions, as they sprang, living and warm,
from [the poet's] heart and brain" (Notes, iii). She gives the poems a story.

The ability to combine these roles—of editor, transcriber, critic, and
biographer—belongs uniquely to herself, Mary Shelley argues to Moxon. By
virtue of her exclusive relationship with the subject, more than by any objective methodology, she deserves credit:

> The M. S. from which it was printed consisted of fragments of paper, which,
> *in the hands of an indifferent person,* would never have been decyphered—
> the labour of putting it together was immense—the papers were in my

>   possession & in no other person's (for the most part) *the volume might be all*
>   *my own writing* (except that I could not write it).[3] (emphasis added)

"I will take pains," she assures the publisher, "to render [the copyright] as valuable as I can" with this edition.

To a remarkable degree, the value of *The Collected Poems of Percy Bysshe Shelley* is determined by Mary Shelley's editorial work, a work usually characterized as a wife's labor of love. The value of the work depends, in part, upon a unique emotional and almost physical tie: no "indifferent person," no less patient "eyes," would have "taken such pains" in this project. Mary Shelley writes to underscore her own sympathy with the poet, and thereby to validate her own authority as editor.

But we should remind ourselves that she herself introduces this characterization. The labor of love is also the labor (and construct) of an experienced writer of fiction. She saw the work as her own responsibility, her property, her product: "It certainly stands to reason, & I should think that it is a law that a Posthumous publication should belong to the editor," she tells Moxon (*MSL,* 2:300). To Leigh Hunt, she writes, "Thanks for your very kind offer to help me in my note. But it must rest on myself alone. The edition will be mine" (*MSL,* 2:305). In more than merely legal terms, the edition belongs to the editor, rather than the poet. I hope to complicate the notion that Mary Shelley's "loving devotion to the editing of Percy's poems displays a confidence in his work that she does not seem to have in her own."[4] Instead, we might reconsider what Marion Ross has called the woman's plan to "intertwine admiration for the poet's genius with devotion and love supposedly not predicated on genius alone"; we might read that intertwining as an effective strategy of self-promotion (Ross, 4). In her ability to temper "admiration for poetic genius" with a more prosaic "devotion and love," Mary Shelley's notes exploit the tools of her trade—prose fiction—and find an audience her husband could not previously touch.

The strategy articulated and employed in Mary Shelley's notes is one Bachelard, in the epigraph quotation, would identify as "sympathy": that appeal to "devotion and love," to personal relationship rather than "objective thought," which characterizes sentimental fiction. "This is not the time to relate the truth," she states in the preface; "and I should reject any colouring of the truth" (iii). Yet as soon as we begin to analyze the relationship between the notes and the poems, we find Bachelard's distinctions collapsing upon each other: even as we gaze in wonderment at the beloved husband whose story Mary Shelley presents, we lose that "initial contact with the object"; we detach ourselves from the poetry; we read "ironically."[5]

In this essay I want to confront the implicit irony of Mary Shelley's sympathetic method. The same strategy that draws the reader to the life of the poet(ry) and validates her editorial project also removes the poetry itself from any effective connection to the public. "I have the liveliest recollection of all that was said and done during the period of my knowing him," she claims (vi).

Thus she appears able to "fill up" his absence with her "lively" recollections, by virtue of their relationship. She has shared with the poet his most productive years, she has suffered his pains and fears, she has borne his children and transcribed his works. At the same time, the biography becomes increasingly the property of Mary Shelley (her fiction), supplanting the influence of the poetry itself. As the widow's emotional story grows more and more poignant, the poet and his work become increasingly ethereal and insubstantial. On the one hand, Percy Shelley is rendered more sympathetic—more tangible, more pitiable—through her notes; the poet's work then becomes more accessible. On the other hand, the implication grows throughout the notes that the editor *needs to* bring the poet and poetry down to earth, *needs to* draw them within the circle of our sympathies, because both poet and poetry are innately unsympathetic and inaccessible. According to the interpretive framework of the *Collected Poems,* the effectiveness of both poet and poetry depends entirely on the power of her prose to move us. Her manipulation of and emphasis upon sympathy both draw us to and separate us from Percy Shelley. The irony of *The Poetical Works* manifests itself when the editor's prose impoverishes the communicative power of the poetry. In several ways, the edition really belongs to the editor; it is her work that dictates how we read.

At stake here is not just the rhetorical posturing of one writer against the productions of another. In the very structure of the edition, Percy's work is dependent upon Mary's: we cannot connect with him unless we connect with her first, and her attachments have the advantage of appearing more solid. At stake here is the power to define and transmit literary genres. Mary Shelley's notes ultimately insist upon a profound difference between her writing and her husband's, a difference which models the definition of genres for the rest of the nineteenth century. By characterizing Percy Shelley as the very spirit of poetry, and herself as the devoted, earthbound mortal who understands us, Mary Shelley sets in motion a profound reevaluation of gender and genre. The material connectedness promoted by her notes simultaneously describes an intangibility and isolation in the poet's work. Her work appears more "real." Moreover, by wresting sympathy out of the hands of the Romantic poets and attaching it to her own work—the various modes of prose fiction— the woman writer claims for herself an immediate social and ideological influence. At the same time that her notes raise an elegy to the poetic "spirit of solitude," they supplant that "spirit." They fill up the absence with the "outward signs" of the editor's more vital sympathy.[6]

The pages that follow will trace the "outward signs" of Mary Shelley's strategy of sympathy. By means of rhetorical positioning and the figure of the body, her notes invite the reader's allegiance. At the same time, they propose a "gendering" of the distinctions between poetry and prose, a gendering which has profound implications for the ways we have learned to read genres. Finally, the fifty-odd pages of commentary on poetry become a celebration of the novelist's art and demonstrate Mary Shelley's ability to comprehend and supplant her husband's work.

The Battle over Sympathy

The notes to the *Poetical Works* introduce an editor more involved in the tangible world than her subject, who is relegated to the airy realm of "genius," of "spirit," and, she implies, of poetry. The notes, which distinguish her version of experience, are juxtaposed to the poems, which describe his. In the edition, Percy's longer pieces (with his prefaces), as well as the shorter works (arranged by year of production), are followed by his wife's notes on those poems, the pattern forming a sort of debate over the text of the poems themselves. This dialogue contrasts her tastes and his, what she calls her "reality" and his "imagination," her prosaic and his "poetic soul," her life and his death-in-life. In this debate, the editor always gets the last word.

Her "most sacred duty"—editing his poetry—gives Mary Shelley a method for writing herself away from Percy Bysshe and toward her readers:

> He loved to idealize reality; and this is a taste shared by few. We are willing to have our passing whims exalted into passions, for this gratifies our vanity; but few of us understand or sympathize with the endeavour to ally the love of abstract beauty, and the adoration of abstract good, the *to agathon to kalon* of the Socratic philosophers, with our sympathies with our kind. (iv–v)

Obviously Percy is not of "our kind." Exoticized and alienated, he becomes the object of ironic scrutiny, while she becomes the sympathetic subject.[7]

The poet she depicts is hardly "lively": his life is beset with illness, pain, and intimations of death. Only in his poems does he seem to "live." By "abstain[ing] from any remark on the occurrences of his private life," and by omitting evidence of his "early life," Mary Shelley restricts Percy's existence to the writing of poems, and more specifically, to the writing of poems during his years with her. She suggests the equation Works = Life, even as she retreats from it: Works = No Life. Her version of the poet's "life" cuts him off from his childhood, his family, and his fellow humans: he is radically, ideally, a poet.[8]

To underscore this death-in-life, the figures of physical sensation and the body measure the distance between the language of poetry and that of the editor's prose. Moving away from the poet, then, Mary Shelley aligns herself with a language of impression and inclusion. Prose, in her formulation, fills the gap left by poetry. It is circumstantial, it provides "origin and history" (vi), it "impresses," it ties words to bodies, it matters. By bearing the word between bodies and upon the body, such a language demands connection.[9] When Percy died, "the world showed no outward sign," and his work "[was] only . . . appreciated by minds which ha[d] resemblance to his own"(v). Her work, on the other hand, registers as physical, even solid matter, often eliciting our "common" sympathies. As she completes her edition, she "lay[s] the first stone of a monument" to his otherwise ephemeral "genius, his sufferings, his virtues" (vi). She asserts her ability to give weight to the blithe spirit by appealing to more than just a few "minds." She appeals to sympathy.

"Sympathy" functions as an ideological token, a word that leaps and darts all over the terrain of Romanticism like the prize in a game of "Capture the Flag." Sympathy becomes the standard for material connection—emotional, physiological, or historical connection—but it also measures influence. Percy Shelley himself praised Homer's poetry for such an influence: "the sentiments of [his] auditors must have been refined and enlarged by a sympathy with such great and large impersonations, until from admiring they imitated."[10] With sympathy you can make things *matter* to others in a palpable way.

Our reading of Romantic texts often depends upon this distinction: sympathy is brandished to attract and influence us. Mary Shelley is not alone in evoking its power. In the preface to *Lyrical Ballads,* for example, Wordsworth distinguishes "poetic" from "scientific" knowledge in these very terms. Poetic knowledge

> cleaves to us as a necessary part of our existence, our natural and inalienable inheritance; the other is a[n] . . . acquisition, slow to come to us, and by no *habitual and direct sympathies connecting us with our fellow beings.*[11] (emphasis added)

Truth for the scientist is "a remote and unknown benefactor"; but the poet, together with "all human beings," finds truth "our visible friend and hourly companion." The force of Wordsworth's argument depends upon language's potential for physical ("poetry is the *breath* . . . of knowledge") and material connectedness ("carrying sensation into the midst of the objects of science itself") (292). This potential guarantees "habitual and direct sympathies with our fellow beings." Sympathy, then, becomes the touchstone for humanity, the justification for admiration and the measure of political influence.[12]

Note Wordsworth's sympathies with an ungendered audience of "beings." Although he poses the question of influence in terms of the "Poet and the Man of science," his appeal to sympathies bears the marks of another struggle over influence: between women and men. Given their susceptibility "of the attached affections," women could, according to Mary Wollstonecraft and others, effectively civilize men and educate children.[13] And Sarah Ellis, in her ideologically proper *Wives of England,* could grant the female head of the household infinite influence, "branch[ing] off in every direction trains of thought, and tones of feeling, operating upon those more immediately around her, but . . . extending outward in the same manner, to the end of all things."[14] By virtue of sympathy, women could establish themselves as "unacknowledged legislators of the world" (Laqueur, 25).[15] Operating in a society which "naturally" assigned women the powers of sympathy, sensation, and human connection, Wordsworth had to redefine the terms as a male struggle for a sympathy which erased gender difference (Ross, 42ff).

Mary Shelley reasserts the woman writer's influence, using that "connecting" sympathy Wordsworth claimed for poetry. In doing so, she enacts the countermove as well: Percy's poems occupy the remote realm of Wordsworth's Man of Science. The markers have shifted: her prose aims to "cleave to us as a necessary part of our existence"; his poetry demands an "acquired" taste. In Mary Shelley's elegiac notes we acknowledge the "Strength in what

remains behind; / in the primal sympathy / Which having been must ever be."
Whereas, according to her characterization, in Percy's poems we follow "The
awful shadow of some unseen Power / [that] floats through unseen among
us."[16] The narrative of her attachment to his historical, biological self puts at a
distance his poetic corpus. Thus she competes with him for the reader.

She stakes that competition upon the figure of the body. With a sophisticated use of that figure, her edition of the poems becomes a contest between a
poetic corpus and a prose body. Which is livelier? Which wins our sympathy?
The problematic equation, Works = Life? / Works vs. Life?, keeps us moving
back and forth in our sympathies. It sets in motion the connections among
gender, genre, and body which problematize Mary Shelley's version of Percy
Shelley's "life," connections that structure the entire edition of *The Poetical
Works.*

Body Language

> Yesterday as I was reading I thought I heard him call me—‹I thought› *not his
> spirit*—but he my companion & *not lost Shelley*—the revulsion of thought
> agonized every nerve—& gave too much reality to the knowledge that I was
> deceived. (*MSL,* 1:312; Shelley's emphasis)

Mary Shelley's use of figurative language prompts us to feel the physical tug of
her attachments and to dismiss their object with skepticism. The paradoxes of
body and spirit evident in her letter (above) are incorporated in her editorial
notes. The poems are "productions" which "sprang, living and warm, from his
heart and brain" (iii); passions are "engendered"; generosity and heroism
"breathe throughout the poetry" (iii, iv). Yet whenever the poet's efforts
strive to overcome physical limits, the editor drags them back with an ironic
figure of speech, insisting once again on the body as ground for meaning.
Thus "the sense of mystery" in his work transforms itself into "a curious and
metaphysical *anatomy* of passion and perception" (iv). "Every *pulsation* of his
heart," she informs us, was directed "to *defecate* life of its miseries and evils"
(iii). That poems such as "Ode to a Skylark" and "The Cloud" would "*bear* a
purer poetical *stamp*" emphasizes this irony: How does one stamp an impression on the sky (iv)?

Even as they suggest these ironies, Shelley's notes nonetheless beg for
sympathy. On the one hand, she delivers a poet who transcends mortal life:
"The exalted nature of his soul would have raised him into something divine"
(iii). "His unearthly and elevated nature is a pledge of the continuation of his
being" (ix). With an "extreme sensibility," he was "too brilliant, his thoughts
too subtle" (iv). We see him as a superlative, if not superfluous, "spirit of
good" and ephemeral "genius." As such, he exists beyond our grasp—beyond
our sympathy: "to escape from [the sad vicissitudes of life], he delivered up
his soul to poetry, and felt happy when he sheltered himself, [away] from the

influence of human sympathy, in the wildest regions of fancy" (iv). Yet, on the other hand, she pulls him back to the region of the body and to sympathy:

> Through life he was a martyr to ill-health, and constant pain wound up his nerves to such a pitch of sensibility that rendered his views of life different from those of a man in the enjoyment of healthy sensations. . . . The weight of thought and feeling burdened him heavily; you read his suffering in his attenuated frame. (v)

That physical connection wins our sympathy even as it justifies his identification as "martyr," as "different."

Her notes, then, provide the earthly "frame"—"fraught with pain"—for his "unearthly and elevated" nature. She continually renders the history of the corpus in terms of the poet's distressed body.[17] We find the weight of his thoughts and words displayed upon the body she resurrects. In a sense, the editor possesses and controls the body in these notes. Through her manipulation, the figure of the body provides the warrant—a warrant won through sympathetic connection—for the poetry, a warrant which the poetry, apparently, could not win for itself. The poems depend upon external bodily evidence provided by the editor, to proclaim their inner genius:

> Perfectly gentle and forebearing in manner, he suffered a great deal of internal irritability, or rather excitement, and his fortitude to bear was almost always on the stretch; and thus, during a short life, he had gone through *more experience of sensation than many whose existence is protracted* . . . you read his sufferings in his attenuated frame, while you perceived the mastery he held over them in his animated countenance and brilliant eyes. (v; emphasis added)

This strategy is obvious, for example, in the notes to "Alastor, or The Spirit of Solitude," the poem which opens the *Poetical Works*. At first glance, the editor's rendition seems to grant the poetry great potency through recurring figures of reproduction. "Alastor" is "the outpouring of his [Percy's] own emotions, *embodied* in the purest form he could *conceive*, painted in the ideal hues which his imagination inspired"; a "solemn spirit . . . breathes throughout" (19, emphasis added). Yet simultaneously she emphasizes the self-absorption of a man inclined "to brood over the thoughts and emotions of his own soul"; clearly "the brooding of a poet's heart in solitude" breeds little connection with humanity. The contrast between this work and *Queen Mab*—Percy's most renowned and politically effective work—heightens the irony in Mary Shelley's figures of reproduction. Unlike this solitary "outpouring of his own emotion," *Queen Mab* marks the outpouring "of all the irrepressible emotions of sympathy, censure and hope, to which the present suffering and . . . the proper destiny, of his fellow-creatures, *gave birth*" (18, emphasis added). The reproductive power of *Queen Mab*, set against the opening piece of *The Poetical Works*, calls into question the effectiveness of the latter. "Alastor," the editor adds, "contains an individual interest only" (18). Yet "none of Shelley's poems is more characteristic" (19).

If, in these notes, Mary Shelley describes the poet "turn[ing] his eyes inward," she compensates by turning the reader's eyes outward to the phenomenal world. Writing the poem, she suggests, isolates and dematerializes the poet; her notes bring him back into company, into nature, into history, into the body. Matter, she emphatically claims, is her material.

Gender

> It is at least plausible to infer that the entire history of generic development and of critical response has been subtly infiltrated by this disparity [between the connotations of genre and gender]. Stuart Curran, *Poetic Form and British Romanticism*

> It may be safely affirmed, that there neither is, nor can be, any *essential* difference between the language of prose and metrical composition. . . . They both speak to the same organs, the bodies in which both of them are clothed may be said to be of the same substance, their affections are kindred, and almost identical. . . . Poetry sheds no tears "such as angels weep," but natural and human tears; she can boast of no celestial ichor that distinguishes her vital juices from those of prose; the same human blood circulates through the veins of them both. William Wordsworth, Preface, *Lyrical Ballads*

Despite Wordsworth's early gesture toward egalitarianism between the genres, we hear in his words the strains of gendered difference.[18] Poetry, he argues, is no angel; "she" is just as human as the more common, physical prose. We recognize here the language of Mary Wollstonecraft's *Vindication of the Rights of Woman,* which deplores those "weak, artificial beings, raised above the common wants and affection of their race," otherwise known as "ladies." Wollstonecraft laments the separation of "women" from "human creatures" and proposes instead that women "endeavour to acquire strength, both in mind and body," and "obtain a character as a human being" (Wollstonecraft, introd.). Unpolished prose gives weight to Wollstonecraft's efforts; proselike diction offers to anchor Wordsworth's verse.[19] In both cases, the inhuman or supernatural is labeled female and prose appears natural and human. But what is the gender of prose? Wordsworth's and Wollstonecraft's efforts to vindicate their respective interests by invoking body, strength, and common humanity give us clues to Mary Shelley's task in the *Poetical Works,* for all three writers struggle over the gendering of genre and its political effects.

The canonization of male poets has frequently led us to read poetry as a masculine form, expressive of sublime power, social efficacy, and (paradoxically) unmitigated individualism. The poets of British Romanticism no doubt played their part in thus characterizing poetic expression. Yet, read against the poetic debates of the period, Percy Shelley's defense of "the unacknowledged legislators" sounds an often unacknowledged truth: the age was not always ready to acknowledge the poet's social and political impact. Depicted as an effeminate spirit, poetry hovered outside the sphere of "real events" or "flesh and blood." In fact, as Ross has recently demonstrated, the male poets of Romanticism had to redefine poetry in order to escape its "feminizing" pressure. They resort to "masculine metaphors of power" in order to "reassert the power of a vocation that [was] on the verge of losing whatever influence it had" (Ross, 29). When the literary reviews identify "high-born dames in the bower and hall" as well as "free maids that weave their thread with bones" as the crucial audience for a collection of ballads, we can begin to understand Wordsworth's desire to "strengthen" his poetry's appeal.[20] Ross focuses on both Wordsworth and Byron, explaining how they simultaneously "remind us that women have become a primary audience for poetry and . . . target that audience as representative of the damage done to poetry" (Ross, 35). In self-defense, then,

> both Byron's and Wordsworth's strategy . . . is the same: poetry becomes a form of masculine empowerment rather than becoming, as it threatens to, a sign of "feminine" or boyish vulnerability, and it becomes a paradigmatic form of manly action in the world rather than an ineffectual and puerile preoccupation. (Ross, 40)[21]

To do so, Wordsworth, in the 1802 preface, advocates a turn from "mechanical adoption of these figures of speech" to a language of "natural connection".[22] If more natural and more real meant more bodily, as the previous quotation from Wordsworth's preface indicates, then the gender of the genre was still up for grabs. For the male poets had to reclaim that "natural connection" from the women poets who actually dominated the marketplace.[23]

It is precisely that "natural connection" that Mary Shelley wants to hold onto. But unlike the poets, who may propose images of adventure, daring, and masculine identity, the editor works for effect through her strategies of physical and emotional sympathy. She points out the poet's inability to connect the body with the body politic and claims that connection for herself and her prose. She places the edition, then, in a curious position. On the one hand, she "feminizes" the poet as a beneficent spirit, her own "angel in the house": "He walked beside [us] like a spirit of good to comfort and benefit— to enlighten the darkness of life with irradiations of genius, to cheer it with his sympathy and love" (vi). His "beauty" and his "charm" overshadow any political aspirations. It is no wonder Trelawny portrays him "gliding in, blushing like a girl, . . . [with a] flushed, feminine and artless face."[24] According to his wife's account, Percy fulfills the expectations of feminine virtue. On the other hand, she places her own writing in contrast to his: How, then, do her notes gender her? Or, to adapt Mary Poovey's formulation, how does her use of prose "disguise that aggression beneath the manners of the proper lady" (142)?

By grounding her language in the body and in sympathetic connection, Mary Shelley, I believe, strives to accomplish what her male contemporaries could not: to play the woman *and* participate in defining the "real world." As a woman, she can ally herself with that undifferentiated public which threatens to feminize the poets (Ross, 34–44; Hofkosh, 93–99). Percy, she tells us, shied away from the demands of "popularity," while she preferred "the more popular" works, "appealing at once to emotions common to us all" (iv). Moreover, by exploiting a method of self-promotion justified primarily through connection with him, she also justifies her connection with the public, as the grieving widow. But, most significantly, the prose itself redefines the female position. She composes this edition, writing not as guiding spirit but as the means of connection—the mediating body between life and death, present and past, real and ideal. It becomes a very effective position.

Margaret Homans suggests that nineteenth-century women writers, implicated in a Romantic ideology which values figural over literal representation and transcendence over immanence, devised "revisionary myths" of a language based on presence, on contact with the (mother's) body.[25] I question Homans's assumption about Romantic values, but I invoke her argument to reinforce the potent myth of affective (and effective) sympathy operating in Shelley's notes. When, as in Mary Shelley's case, "it became incumbent upon women writers to convert the writing [of male authors]"—through "translation, transmission, copying, and so forth"—the women could enact "a shift from [his] figurative to [her] literal" by means of the text itself (Homans, 31–32). Homans resigns these translations "into a version of these female duties of selfless transmission, just as, mythically, [the Virgin] Mary facilitated the transmission of Word into flesh" (Homans, 31). Yet Mary Shelley distinguishes herself from this virginal order when her notes, and the corporeality they offer, pose a genesis counter to the "productions" which "sprang, living and warm from [Percy's] brain" (iii). She switches the register, so that, by the end of the volume, we recognize that out of "so confused a mass [of papers], interlined and broken into fragments," the editor's "eyes and patience" have constructed her own progeny, using a method more congenial than Victor Frankenstein's (714n). As editor, she is no mere vessel for his words; she "gets something for her labor" (see Homans, 31). Her "translation," moving in two directions, enacts what Homans assumes: it inscribes the poetry into a spiritual, symbolic order at the same time that it substantiates her prose. Furthermore, what the editor supplies actually makes a difference to the reader.[26] In a final irony, we realize that without the notes, Percy's corpus would simply not much *matter*.

I would like to extend Homans's suggestions that these women writers "bear the word" into a more literal, maternally inflected system of representation than do men. They were trying to claim a type of influence and a genre as their own. In fact, I would argue that Mary Shelley specifically defines, then separates herself from what we now call a purely "symbolic" order, when she turns away from poetry, toward prose. As the historical debate over gendering genre shows, neither genre is essentially literal or figurative. What we witness in Shelley's account is a woman writer's reevaluation of genre and gender, along the lines of the "material" and the "immaterial," and under the aegis of affective sympathy. It is not by chance that all of the women who bear the word for Homans bear it into prose fiction.

Genre

Mr. Hazlitt says, "Poetry does not define the limits of sense, or analyze the distinctions of the understanding, but signifies the excess of imagination beyond the actual or ordinary impression of any object or feeling." What this excess is we cannot tell, but at least it must be something very unlike an impression. (*Quarterly Review* 19 [December 1818]: 429)

Could sorrow for the lost, and shuddering anguish at the vacancy left behind, be soothed by poetic imaginings, there was something in Shelley's fate to mitigate pains which yet, alas! could not be so mitigated; for hard reality brings too miserably home to the mourner all that is lost of happiness. . . .

Still, though dreams and hues of poetry cannot blunt grief, it invests his fate with a sublime fitness, which those less nearly allied may regard with complacency. (718–19)

By means of her notes, which inscribe the *Poetical Works* upon the body and into human relationship, Mary Shelley does win some sympathy from her readers for the mortal Percy. At the same time, she tells us that his poetry is not all that *impressive;* she asks us to read the poet with some detachment. The editor distinguishes a life of poetry divorced from the demands of the body and "hard reality." To this life readers bear little connection: "less nearly allied" to that sublime figure, they may contemplate it at a distance, with "complacency." If we were to appeal to the words of Gaston Bachelard which head this essay, we might say that this complacency "belies the initial contact with the object . . . [but it] does not gaze in wonderment; it must be ironic."

The "object" is poetry as much as the poet. Playing off the figure of detachment, the metaphor which trades biography for poetical works, life for corpus, Shelley asks us to scrutinize for a moment the figure of poetry. She wants us to treat poetry ironically; she keeps us at a distance from it. Following her lead, we notice that her method successfully alienates the poet and his practice from the reading public while it reinforces her own literary practice. It is a novelist's reality to which she draws her readers. The notes locate "truth" and "reality" apart from poetic imagination; they are found instead in human relationship, lived experience, dialogue, and the human body—all of which she detaches from poetry. Sympathy and irony, then, become an issue of genre. And these notes write out her defense of prose.

Elevating the poet above the demands of "hard reality," Mary Shelley simultaneously establishes poetry as an exercise in vanity: beautiful but ineffective, spiritualized but out of touch with the world. Her characterization of Percy influences the midcentury's characterization of poetry itself. Thomas Peacock, in his *Memoirs of Percy Bysshe Shelley* (1855–60), follows Mary Shelley's lead, defining poet by poetry and poetry by poet, then placing both in the same insubstantial realm: "Now I could have wished that, like Wordsworth's Cuckoo, [Shelley] had been allowed to remain a voice and a mystery; that, like his own Skylark, he had been left unseen in his congenial region" (Wolfe, 307). Edward Trelawny evidently draws on Mary Shelley's notes in his

Recollections . . . of Shelley and Byron (1858), reinforcing the dialectic at work in her edition. The following description of his first meeting with the Shelleys repeats the delineation of prosaic and poetic identities:

> "Who, Shelley?," replied Mrs. Williams. "Why, he comes and goes like a
> spirit, no one knows when or where." Presently [Percy Shelley] reappeared
> with Mrs. Shelley. She brought us back from the ideal world Shelley had left
> us in, to the real one, welcomed me to Italy, and asked me news of London
> and Paris, the new books, operas and bonnets, marriages, murders, and
> other marvels. The poet vanished, and tea appeared. (Wolfe, 172–73)

Tea and sympathy—and all the activity of the "real" world—become the domain of Mrs. Shelley, while her husband nearly disappears from reality. Later, Matthew Arnold gives the poet a similar ephemerality when he substitutes the "angel" of poetry for the living man:

> The Shelley of actual life is a vision of beauty and radiance, indeed, but
> availing nothing, effecting nothing. And in poetry, no less than in life, he is a
> beautiful and ineffectual angel, beating in the void his luminous wings in
> vain.[27]

Holding on to his angel, Arnold bemoans the appearance of Dowden's biography of Percy Bysshe Shelley (1885). He prefers "the impression, the ineffaceable impression" left by Mary Shelley's edition of 1839. "The charm of the poems flowed in upon us from that edition, and the charm of the character, . . . this rare spirit" (Arnold, 152–53). Note the paradox: her notes "impress" us with the notion of his "charm" and "spirit."

For the Victorian reader, the disembodied Percy identifies the spirit of poetry itself, and poetry becomes "a phantom-world, a place of ignes fatui and spectral illusions."[28] John Stuart Mill, in his "Thoughts on Poetry and its Varieties" (1833, rev. 1859), advocates a poetics removed from all earthly utility: any expression, once "tinged . . . by that desire of making an impression upon another mind . . . ceases to be poetry, and becomes eloquence" (Mill, 83). Percy Shelley, in his utter ineffectiveness, stands for Mill as "the most striking example of the poetic temperament":

> [He] seldom follows up an idea; it starts into life, summons from the fairy-
> land of his inexhaustible fancy some three or four bold images, then van-
> ishes, and straight he is off on the wings of some casual association into quite
> another sphere. (Mill, 93)

Both Mill's and Mary Shelley's characterizations of poetry align themselves on one side of the cultural debate over the physical nature of poetry. The *Quarterly Review* of December 1818 apparently chides William Hazlitt for promoting a poetry of intangibility, "beyond the actual or ordinary impression of any object or feeling." The result, says the *Review,* in a verdict which seems to anticipate Mary Shelley's, is "something very unlike an impression" (*Quarterly Review* 19: 429). In fact, the *Review* wanted to mark poetry as insubstantial, for Hazlitt actually argued for poetry's physical effect. For him, poetry worked like an instinctual bodily function: "Man is a poetical animal; and those of us who do not study the principles of poetry, act upon them all our lives." The body reacts to poetry, and poetry to the body:

> [Poetry is] the natural *impression* of any object or circumstance, by its vividness, exciting *an involuntary movement* of imagination or passion, and producing, by *sympathy,* a certain modulation of the voice, or sounds, expressing it. (Hazlitt, qtd. in *Quarterly Review* 19: 425; emphasis added)

The formula echoes Wordsworth's design, stated in the Preface to the Second Edition of the *Lyrical Ballads,* to enact a poetic language "more forcibly communicated," "more easily comprehended," "more durable." Such language should be "incorporated with . . . the more permanent forms of Nature," and tied to "the sympathies of men." Language is physical: "I have wished," writes Wordsworth, "to keep the Reader in the company of flesh and blood."[29] Such bodily exchanges, "proved upon our pulses," do not impress the *Quarterly Review:*

> [Hazlitt's] is an impression producing by sympathy a certain modulation of sounds. . . . In a physiological sense, [sympathy] is used to denote the fact, that, the disorder of one organ produces disorder in the function of certain other parts of the system. Does Mr. Hazlitt mean, that the impression produces the modulation of sound essential to poetry, in a mode analogous to that in which disease of the brain affects the digestive powers? (19: 426)

For physical nature is also political nature. Given the affiliations of these debators, we should be inclined to read the body as political body; and to recognize poetry's effect on "the system," as the threat of democratic revolution, or anarchy. "Thus there is nothing which is not poetry," writes Hazlitt, "and poetry is everything . . . and there is nobody who is not a poet" (*Quarterly Review* 19: 427–28).

Except the writer of prose. Mary Shelley would join with those who restrain the bodily and political power of poetry. Despite assertions that "[Percy's] influence over mankind, though slow in growth, is fast augmenting" (v), the editor refuses to give that influence any substance or content. Even as she etherealizes the poet, she voids his work of political effect. By 1817, she says, the poet had already "lost the eager spirit which believed it could achieve what it had projected for . . . mankind" (590). After his death, moreover,

> The ungrateful world did not feel his loss, and the gap it made seemed to close as quickly over his memory as the murderous sea above his living frame. . . .
> To his friends the loss is irremediable: the wise, the brave, the gentle is gone for ever! He is to them as a bright vision, whose radiant track, left behind in the memory, is worth all the realities that society can afford. (vii)

In the note following the Early Poems (1814–15), Mary Shelley makes clear that the first examples of Percy's poetry mark a retreat from society, from direct political intervention, and from prose:

> Hitherto, he had chiefly aimed at extending his political doctrines, and attempted to do so by appeals in prose essays to the people, exhorting them

> to claim their rights; but he had now begun to feel that the time for action
> was not ripe . . . and that the pen was the only instrument wherewith to
> prepare the way for better things. (567)

"The pen" must be a poet's, whose beautiful though elusive movements we
follow as a "radiant track." But we begin to perceive, apart from this "bright
vision," a body of writing composed of people, social reality, and prose.

If contemporary ideology wants to rob poetry of its force, Mary Shelley is
ready to divert that force to prose. Poetry, in this text, cannot *connect* or
impress itself upon the world without the benefit of prose. Moreover, it has no
life or truth, even, without prose. For Shelley, life and truth are the stuff of
connection, "a thousand lilliputian ties that shackle at the time," yet influence
our destiny (674). Percy continually fled such "shackles"—the ties of the body
as well as those of friendship and "sympathy." He gave up writing with Byron
and Hunt, for fear of feeling "shackled in the free expression of his opinions"
in deference to his friends (702). He gave up writing for "the People" as well.
Though the poet "loved the People" and deemed them "more deserving of
sympathy than the great," nevertheless, he found himself "shackled when he
endeavor[ed] to write down to . . . those who could not understand or feel a
highly imaginative style" (626). The notes bear a litany of Percy's flights from
social obligations into the solitude of revery and books. At the same time they
contrast the benefits of interaction with the dangers of isolation:

> [In solitude] the mind broods of its sorrows too intently; while the society of
> the enlightened, the witty and the wise enables *us* to forget ourselves by
> making *us* the sharers of the thoughts of others, which is a portion of the
> philosophy of happiness. [Percy] Shelley never liked society in numbers,—it
> usually harassed and worried him. (609; emphasis added)

The poet's alienation is reinforced by the conflicting pronouns: "it" (the mind)
versus "us" (the social). That this contrast is a function of genre is demonstrated by the notes themselves. Mary's prose denies Percy's poetry the ability
to communicate his "mind" to his readers. Only she, and those once close to
him, can fill the gaps where his works, and our imaginations, fail:

> How very few knew his worth while he lived! . . . And still less is his vast
> superiority in intellectual attainments sufficiently understood—his sagacity,
> his clear understanding, his learning, his prodigious memory. All these, as
> displayed in conversation, were known to few while he lived, and are now
> silent in the tomb. (610)

Conversation speaks, but poetry lies silent in the tomb, its evidence and
assurances inaccessible to us. We can only "share in the thoughts of others"
through the medium of the prose notes.

The editor uses the notes to discount the evidence given by poetry. In this
instance, the language of conversation provides proof unavailable in the Poems of 1818. Elsewhere, various forms of prose overshadow the messages of
the poems. The purpose of "Mont Blanc," for example, is clarified by an
extract from the Shelley's *History of a Six Weeks' Tour* (575). *The Revolt of*

Islam, the editor reports, met with little favor and still less comprehension when first published; so she inserts a letter from Percy to Godwin concerning this poem. The letter, more than the poem, is "a precious monument of his own opinion of his powers, of the purity of his designs, and the ardour with which he clung" to his views of mankind's happiness (175). In the "Note to the Poems of 1816," Montaigne's *Essays* are applauded; and Mary's account gives Percy's reading of Rousseau's *La Nouvelle Héloïse* more value than the poet's own writing, which included "Mont Blanc" and the "Hymn to Intellectual Beauty" (the note begins, "Shelley wrote little during this year"; 575). Though she insists from the outset that the poet "read few novels," novels nevertheless offer lasting images of the poet; be it Rousseau's St. Preux or Thomas Peacock's Scythrop, from *Nightmare Abbey,* the novel character provides evidence for "some points" of the poet's "personality" evidently not found in the poems (590). The proof of prose, therefore, woos our allegiance away from the specific claims of poetry, drawing connections for us while the poet remains apart, amid his "more abstract and etherealized inspiration" (174).

This sorting out of the ties that bind and the evidence that matters has political consequences, as shown in the note following *The Revolt of Islam.* Mary Shelley first offers an account of the poet's abstract musings for "forms defecated of all the weakness and evil which cling to real life" (173–74). She then provides a detailed description which does not "defecate" the poverty, illness, and political tensions that framed the poetic endeavor. The irony is potent. While Percy floated in his boat, amid a "wealth of Nature," the Poor Laws, ill-paid labor, a bad harvest, and the ravages of a long war "ground to the dust" the local population" and brought "the most heart-rending evils to the poor." The poet "afforded what alleviation he could" (174). According to the editor, Percy Shelley's "active sympathy" with the suffering poor— evident only through her account—alone lends "a thousand-fold interest" to these "speculations" in verse; only her anecdotes and contextualization "stamp with reality his pleadings for the human race" (174). Sympathy and material concerns ground her method, make the argument, and win an audience for the poetry. But her effectiveness serves to point out the inadequacy of the unannotated verse. Percy, she explains, "did not expect sympathy and approbation from the public; but the want of it took away a portion of the ardour that ought to have sustained him." Her note, with its persistent turning from abstract ideas to material suffering, from the poet to his relationships, detaches the poetry from the realm of emotional or political effect. Yet she plants her own writing firmly in that realm. She wants and gains "the sympathy and approbation of the public."

Romantic Fiction

It is Mary Shelley's own writing that shackles our sympathy with innumerable "lilliputian ties." As Matthew Arnold acknowledges, her writing leaves "the impression, the ineffaceable impression." Accordingly, the final note to the poems asserts her prominence as a writer, as a prose writer and novelist. Gone are Percy's reading lists, enumerating the classics and the legacy of great poets. Gone too are references to the poet's ailing body. Instead, Shelley gathers all our sympathies unto herself in a virtuoso performance of her own writing talent. As the notes develop into a progressively explicit performance of fiction writing, Mary Shelley demonstrates her comprehension and control of the various techniques of editor, biographer, novelist, . . . and poet.

"I dislike speaking of myself," she writes in the final note, "and cannot help apologizing to the dead, and to the public, for not having executed in the manner I desired the history I engaged to give of Shelley's writings" (714). Indeed, the notes, having won our sympathy, award that sympathy to the editor's own history. She writes now, in this last note, as the stricken body, and its demands for our sympathy are forceful: "I began with energy, and a burning desire to impart to the world, in worthy language, . . . the virtues and genius of the beloved and lost; my strength has failed under the task" (714). Language, then, resorts to another task—communicating the gifts of the novelist and editor. The "Note to the Poems of 1822," by far her longest and most elaborate, makes Mary Shelley herself and her mode of writing the objects of our attention; we follow her sensations and reactions more closely than before. Her inner life, not Percy's, is on display. Suddenly, the romantic fiction which had been unfolding throughout the edition reaches full bloom.

More explicitly now, the setting (the northern Italian coast) enters into the mood and activity of the story: "Had we been wrecked on an island of the South seas, we could scarcely have felt ourselves further from civilization and comfort." "The beauty of the place seemed unearthly in its excess," as did the "brilliant spirits" of their company (1716–17). Moreover, Mary Shelley sketches in the company, peopling her account with a cast of characters— Williams, Byron, Trelawny, an old Italian proprietor, a young sailor, a local official—who bustle about in a manner unprecedented in the earlier notes. Thus she sets the stage for her story, creating a world around her husband's death. Her preface to Percy's *Posthumous Poems* (1824) had begged that "a veil . . . be drawn" over her own misery after her husband's death. "The real anguish of these moments transcended all the fictions that the most glowing imaginations ever portrayed" (ix). No such qualms seem to inhibit the practiced fiction writer in 1839.

With a certain justification, then, she paints this final episode in the glowing colors of Radcliffean gothic romance—perhaps to draw attention to the connections between body and spirit, perhaps to impress us with the special effects of fiction. We discover the exotic setting, disturbingly reminiscent of home: a house on the ruined estate of a crazed Italian, with a plantation "more in the English taste than I ever elsewhere saw in Italy" (715). We recognize the chiaroscuro scenery, "such as one sees in Salvator Rosa's landscapes only" (716). The threat of sensual excess extends from the scenery to the indigenous population, who are "wilder than the place," and whose "singing, or rather howling" echoes as the waves crash on the beach (716). Radcliffe's Emily St. Aubert would have found the locale uncannily familiar.

This gothic apparatus (not unfamiliar to the creator of *Frankenstein*) allows her to focus the entire episode upon her own sensibility. Mary Shelley herself plays both author and heroine. We watch the approaching tragedy not just through her eyes, but through her feelings and very body as well:

> During the whole of our stay at Lerici, an intense presentiment of coming evil brooded over my mind, and covered this beautiful place and genial summer with the shadow of coming misery. I had vainly struggled with these emotions—they seemed accounted for by my illness; but at this hour . . . they recurred with renewed violence. I did not anticipate danger for them [Percy and Williams], but a vague expectation of evil shook me to an agony. (717)

Not only does the writing wed feeling to the body and to the "outer world," it also connects thought with physical effect. Thus causality falls subject to uncanny sympathies. We know her premonitions will result in Percy's drowning, not just because history has already scripted his death, but also because gothic conventions allow forebodings of evil to materialize. "If ever fate whispered of coming disaster," writes Mary Shelley, "such inaudible but not unfelt prognostics hovered around us" that summer (717). Moreover, the gothic mode forges that connection between the real and the transcendent which Shelley has denied to poetry: "[A]ll these things led the mind to brood over strange thoughts, and, lifting it from everyday life, caused it to be familiar with the unreal. A sort of spell surrounded us" (718).

Given the spellbinding tale, we may understand why Mary Shelley felt obliged to apologize to the dead: indeed, she has converted his history into a fiction of her own. We may also perceive why she complains/insists that no "poetic imaginings" could mitigate her "shuddering anguish" (718). The juxtaposition of this final note with Percy's fragmentary "Triumph of Life" makes the contrast obvious: "the most mystical of his poems" was written when the poet "could not bend his mind away from the broodings and wanderings of thought, divested from human interest, which he best loved." Mary Shelley prefers shared to solitary "brooding."

Not only does she supplant Percy's history with her own story, she also reorders the structure of the edition, so that poetry is put to the service of prose. Earlier, as I mentioned, the poet's prefaces and the editor's notes framed the text of the poems themselves, thereby performing a sort of dialogue of interpretation over the poem. This last prose note, the finale of the volume, is introduced by one poem by Mary and concluded by a portion of Percy's *Adonais*—as if, indeed, it were a chapter in a novel by Charlotte Smith or Ann Radcliffe. As if, indeed, this were the text to be interpreted.[30]

The two commentaries in verse reenact the dialogue between Percy's version of experience and Mary's, although now we see the distinctions of genre momentarily blurred. The editor's introductory lyric on the death of her husband both echoes and condenses Percy's *Adonais:*

> This morn thy gallant bark
> Sailed on a sunny sea:

> 'Tis noon, and tempests dark
>   Have wrecked it on the lee.
>   Ah woe! ah woe!
> By Spirits of the deep
>   Thou'rt cradled on the billow
> To thy eternal sleep.
> Thou sleep'st upon the shore
>   Beside the knelling surge,
> And Sea-nymphs evermore
>   Shall sadly chant thy dirge.
>   They come, they come,
> The Spirits of the deep,—
>   While near thy seaweed pillow
> My lonely watch I keep.
> From far across the sea
>   I hear a loud lament,
> By Echo's voice for thee
>   From Ocean's caverns sent.
>   O list! O list!
> The Spirits of the deep!
>   They raise a wail of sorrow,
> While I forever weep.

The presence of her own lyric serves several functions here. It announces that Mary Shelley is not only able to assemble and comprehend her husband's work; she can herself produce poetry. She can, in fact, choose between genres. This poem, moreover, signals the shift in sympathies to which all of the notes point: from the dead poet our attention turns to the grieving widow. Furthermore, she positions herself once again as the medium between two worlds. The echoing songs of unworldly Spirits she alone hears and attempts to translate—"O list! O list!"—as if some obstruction blocks communication between the realm of the lost beloved and the reader. The spiritual "wail of sorrow" must be converted into her language and its more physical register: "I forever weep." The poem makes Mary Shelley herself the eternal Echo, both receiving and repeating the songs of mourning from Nature. In this sense, the lyric explicitly reverses Percy's elegy for Keats, which transforms the dead poet (and his corpus) into the undying voice of Nature. "He is made one with Nature: there is heard / His voice in all her music, from the moan / Of thunder, to the song of the night's sweet bird; / His is a presence to be felt and known" (*SPP*, 402). Whereas Percy rushed to join his colleague in death (" 'Tis Adonais calls! O hasten thither, / No more let Life divide what Death can join together"), Mary Shelley situates herself as a survivor, in the land of the living.

Yet again, in the debate, Mary Shelley gets the last word. Again she depicts her prose as the medium for making sense of and giving life to the fragments of Percy's corpus. When she does quote from the elegy, near the end of her note, she excerpts only bits and pieces. She first drains *Adonais* of mystical optimism by selecting the description of the sepulcher, the cold, physical marker of the dead (lines 424–25, 442–50). Thus she echoes her promise "to lay the first stone of a monument due to Shelley's genius" (vi). This comment follows:

> Could sorrow for the lost, and shuddering anguish at the vacancy left behind, be soothed by poetic imaginations, there was something in Shelley's fate to mitigate pangs which yet, alas! *could not be so mitigated;* for hard reality brings too miserably home to the mourner all that is lost of happiness. . . . *Though dreams and hues of poetry cannot blunt grief,* it invests his fate with a sublime fitness. (718–19; emphasis added)

She then converts the very subject of the poem, incorporating its fragments into the fullness of her story. When we read the final stanza of *Adonais* in light of her alternative verse, and in light of her sensational gothic tale, we read the poem as prophecy, not elegy. "Who but will regard as a prophecy the last stanza of the 'Adonais'?" she asks, in conclusion, before giving the stanza.

Unlike the poet, the editor has no desire to join the dearly departed in death. She has made her husband's poem *come true,* but her strategies differ markedly from his. Percy would reanimate the dead poet through poetry and join him in the infinity of death, in the celebration of that male bond (" 'Tis Adonais calls! . . ."). Mary, on the other hand, will reanimate the poet only to draw attention to her—and our—distance from him. She incorporates *Adonais* into this prose finale as the final movement in her interplay of gender, genre, and body. By doing so, she usurps the position of the poetic subject and restores experience to the realm of body, not spirit. She also revises the poem, forcing it to bear the weight of her story. Her writing, not his, has made the corpus materialize as body. By insisting upon connection, relationship, history, and the body, the strategies of her prose have the effect of making poetry matter, even as they emphasize the poet's death.

Notes

1. Mary Wollstonecraft Shelley, preface and notes, *The Poetical Works of Percy Bysshe Shelley,* 1839, rpt. *Complete Poems of Keats and Shelley with Mrs. Shelley's Notes* (New York: Random House, n. d.), 714n. Unless otherwise noted, excerpts frrom both Mary Shelley's preface and notes and Percy Shelley's poetry are drawn from this edition and cited in the text. For earlier work on the connection between the edition and biography, see Paula R. Feldman, "Biography and the Literary Executor: The Case of Mary W. Shelley," *Papers of the Bibliographical Society of America* 72 (1978): 287–97.

2. See Mary Shelley's introduction to the third edition of *Frankenstein or The Modern Prometheus: The 1818 Text,* ed. James Rieger (Chicago: University of Chicago Press, 1974), 222–29; after discussion of Dr. Darwin's experiments in galvanism, the author wonders, "Perhaps a corpse would be re-animated; . . . perhaps the component parts of a creature might be manufactured, brought together, and endued with vital warmth" (227). It is worth noting that she wrote the second volume of Lardner's Literary *Lives* (1838–39) while working on this edition.

3. See Mary Wollstonecraft Shelley, *Letters of Mary Wollstonecraft Shelley,* ed. Betty T. Bennett, 3 vols. (Baltimore: Johns Hopkins University Press, 1980–88), 2:300. Cited in text as *MSL.*

4. Marlon B. Ross, "Romantic Quest and Conquest: Troping Masculine Power in the Crisis of Poetic Identity," *Romanticism and Feminism,* ed. Anne K. Mellor (Bloomington: Indiana University Press, 1988), 4.

5. For epigraph quotation, see Gaston Bachelard, *On Poetic Imagination and Revery,* trans. Colette Gaudin (Dallas: Spring Publications, 1987), 2. I use the word "irony" in two senses here. The first is our conventional sense of irony, in which the explicit meaning of a verbal expression suggests an opposite or contrary meaning; the second, referred to in Bachelard's quotation, becomes an actual mode of apprehension. Paul de Man's discussion of irony correlates with my use of Bachelard's term by emphasizing detachment. De Man writes that irony divides "the subject into an empirical self, immersed in the world" and "a self that becomes like a sign in its attempt at differentiation and self-definition"; see Paul de Man, *Blindness and Insight: Essays in the Rhetoric of Contemporary Criticism,* 2nd ed., rev. (Minneapolis: University of Minnesota Press, 1983), 213. Poetry, if we participate in Mary Shelley's irony, distinguishes the poet himself as a sign, opposed to the sentient being to whom she feels related.

6. "Alastor, or the Spirit of Solitude" is the first of Percy Shelley's poems presented in the 1839 edition.

7. For a more detailed discussion of sympathy in the literature of the period, see David Marshall, *The Surprising Effects of Sympathy: Marivaux, Diderot, Rousseau and Mary Shelley* (Chicago: University of Chicago Press, 1988); and Roy Male, Jr., "Shelley and the Doctrine of Sympathy," *Studies in English* 29 (1950): 183–203.

8. As she constructs the *Poetical Works,* Mary Shelley aligns Percy with an idealized language which cannot refer beyond itself; it is a language of isolation and depopulation. Elaine Scarry stresses the relation of this "matterness" with human life when she writes, "The human voice, the written word, continually regulates the appearance and disappearance of the human body"; see Scarry, introduction to *Literature and the Body: Essays on Populations and Persons,* ed. Elaine Scarry (Baltimore: Johns Hopkins University Press, 1986), ix. She elaborates "a materialist conception of language" that "is capable of registering in its own contours the contours and weight of the material world" and that can also "enter, act on, and alter the material world" (xi). Mary Shelley, I argue, participates in a similar "materialist" conception of language, which contrasts with her notion of poetry. One of her letters to Leigh Hunt makes clear the evanescent, if transcendent, qualities of her husband's work: "I fear that if he [Percy] cd send us any of his Poetry from where he now is, the world wd find it [even] more unintelligible & elementary than that which we have"; see letter to Leigh Hunt, 5 Aug. 1823, *MSL,* 1:360.

9. For an elaboration of an alternative, Lacanian approach to language, see Jacques Lacan, "The Mirror Stage" and "The Signification of the Phallus," in *Ecrits: A Selection,* trans. Alan Sheridan (New York: Norton, 1977), 1–7 and 281–91, and *Feminine Sexuality: Jacques Lacan and the Ecole Freudienne,* ed. Juliet Mitchell and Jacqueline Rose, trans. Jacqueline Rose (New York: Norton, 1982).

10. Percy Bysshe Shelley, *Defence of Poetry* in *Shelley's Poetry and Prose,* ed. Donald Reiman and Sharon Powers (New York: Norton, 1977), 486. Cited in text as *SPP.*

11. William Wordsworth, *Selected Prose,* ed. John O. Haydon (New York: Penguin, 1988), 292.

12. Clearly, the presence of sympathy is debatable in any work. With the same argument, for example, William Hazlitt turns the tables on the poet, who, he says, has "a fastidious antipathy to immediate effect"; "However we may sympathize with Mr. Wordsworth in his attachment to groves and fields, we cannot extend the same admiration to their inhabitants. . . . There is nothing which excites so little sympathy in our minds, as exclusive selfishness"; see Hazlitt, *Complete Works,* ed. P. P. Howe, 21 vols. (London: Dent, 1930), 4:114, 4:121. Elsewhere, Hazlitt castigates the typical "Lake District Poet." "He tolerates only what he himself creates; he sympathizes only with what can enter into no competition with him. . . . This is the reason that so few people take an interest in his writings, because he takes an interest in nothing that others do!"; see "On the Living Poets," 5:163.

13. Mary Wollstonecraft, *The Female Reader; or Miscellaneous Pieces, in Prose and Verse* (London: Joseph Johnson, 1789; rpt. New York: Scholars' Facsimiles and Reprints, 1980), vii.

14. Quoted in Thomas Laqueur, "Orgasm, Generation and the Politics of Reproductive Biology," *Representations* 14 (Spring 1986): 24.

15. On the ideologies of female "influence" and "sympathy" in this period see also Mary Poovey, *The Proper Lady and the Woman Writer: Ideology as Style in the Works of Mary Wollstonecraft, Mary Shelley, and Jane Austen* (Chicago: University of Chicago Press, 1984), 27–30; and Mitzi Myers, "Reform or Ruin: A Revolution in Female Manners," *Studies in the Eighteenth Century* 11 (1982): 199–217.

16. William Wordsworth, "Ode: Intimations of Immortality," *Poems,* ed. John O. Hayden, 2 vols. (New Haven: Yale University Press, 1981), 1:529; and Percy Bysshe Shelley, "Hymn to Intellectual Beauty," *Poetical Works,* 569.

17. In her note on 714, Shelley reverses this image, depicting herself as the body in pain. I discuss this switch later in this essay.

18. Epigraphs to this section are drawn from Stuart Curran, *Poetic Form and British Romanticism* (New York: Oxford University Press, 1986), 9; and William Wordsworth, Preface to *Lyrical Ballads* in *Poems* 1:875–76.

19. See Mary Wollstonecraft, introduction, *Vindication of the Rights of Woman,* ed. Carol H. Poston (New York: Norton, 1988), 9. Wollstonecraft's writing emphasizes this point: "I shall disdain to cull my phrases or polish my style;—I aim at being useful . . . wishing rather to persuade by the force of my argument, than dazzle by the elegance of my language" (10).

20. "Review of *Old Ballads, Essays on Song-Writing,* etc." *Quarterly Review* 3 (May 1810): 481.

21. Sonia Hofkosh pursues a similar logic, using Byron and Keats as her examples in "The Writer's Ravishment: Women and the Romantic Author—The Example of Byron" in Mellor, 93–114.

22. William Wordsworth, *Poetical Works,* ed. Ernest de Selincourt (Oxford: Oxford University Press, 1944), 2:405.

23. On the prominence of women poets, see Curran, "Romantic Poetry: The 'I' Altered," in Mellor 185–207; and Ross, 50n, 186–231.

24. See Edward John Trelawny, *The Recollections of the Last Days of Shelley and Byron* in Humbert Wolfe, ed., *The Life of Percy Bysshe Shelley as comprised in "The Life of Shelley," by Thomas Jefferson Hogg, "The Recollections of the Last Days of Shelley and Byron," by Edward John Trelawny, and "Memoirs of Shelley," by Thomas Love Peacock,* 2 vols. (London: Dent, 1933), 2:172. Memoirs by Hogg, Trelawny, and Peacock are cited in the text as Wolfe.

25. Margaret Homans, *Bearing the Word: Language and Female Experience in*

Nineteenth-Century Women's Writing (Chicago: University of Chicago Press, 1986), 1–39.

26. Indeed, as subsequent editors have remarked, her textual labor was significant, and not just for the remarkable feat of collection and correction: "What her changes reveal is that, so far from careless copying, she used her intelligence to correct . . . [his] solecisms"; see Neville Rogers, introduction to *Complete Poetical Works by Percy Bysshe Shelley* (Oxford: Oxford University Press, 1972), 1:xxiii. Furthermore, her work "was a constant revision and improvement. . . . Mary Shelley looks beyond the words to the mind of the poet. . . . She releases a fine poetic image that *had* been hidden amid uncertain cancellations" (Rogers, 398–99). For other assessments, see Susan J. Wolfson's essay in this volume.

27. Matthew Arnold, "Shelley," *Works* (London: Macmillan, 1903), 2:184–85.

28. John Stuart Mill, "Thoughts on Poetry and its Varieties," in Robert L. Peters, ed., *Victorians on Literature and Art* (Englewood Cliffs: Prentice-Hall, 1961), 90.

29. Ross comments on the Preface of 1802: "Wordsworth's task is to return the language, and by extension the feeling and thought, to its aboriginal source in the 'real events,' to embolden the language and re-empower the influence of the poet . . . [as] the natural man of action" (39).

30. Like other women novelists of the period, Radcliffe and Smith often introduced or concluded their chapters with excerpts from their own poems, or from favorite poets such as Cowper or Thompson. Normally these verses stood as introduction to or summary of the events to come. Nor was it unusual for these novelists to integrate original poetry into the story itself, usually as the creations of the heroine.

Editorial Privilege: Mary Shelley and Percy Shelley's Audiences

Susan J. Wolfson

> I am to justify his ways; I am to make him beloved to all posterity.
> Mary Shelley, quoted by Thomas Jefferson Hogg,
> "The Life of Shelley"

> Mrs. Shelley [was] . . . in every respect, a congenial companion for Mr.
> Shelley. She has acquired great literary celebrity by her "Frankenstein,"
> and other works, which evince the power and depth of her imagination.
> *The Drama,* 3 Dec. 1822

> But this is for myself; my readers have nothing to do with these associations.
> Mary Shelley, "Author's Introduction" to *Frankenstein*

Poems "Divided into Two Classes"

In assembling her husband's works—*Posthumous Poems* in 1824, and in 1839 two editions of *Poetical Works* and one of essays and letters—Mary Shelley conceived of two classes of readers. The first, as she names it in the Preface of 1839, was "the world" to whom she would give "the productions of a sublime genius . . . with all the correctness possible."[1] With this "perfect edition"—the "first stone of a monument due to Shelley's genius, his sufferings, and his virtues" (xvi)—she hoped to diminish the aura of his unintelligibility, quell the controversies over his conduct and political opinions, and solicit the favor of "any one newly introduced" (viii). In this editorial capacity, she acts as mediator, offering herself as a model of perfect sympathy for and understanding of the poet. Yet simultaneously and more subtly, she was representing herself as the synecdoche of another kind of audience and with a somewhat contradictory agenda. Motivated by the charge—self-generated as well as held by some of their friends—of her having failed the poet spiritually and emotionally in his last years, the editor, in view of "the public" whom she purports to serve, displays herself in a position of unique, and at times hermetic, readerly privilege: a singular Shelleyan audience, the intimate who is the poet's ideal, best reader.

This gesture of discriminating two audiences—popular and elite—is not particular to Mary Shelley's volumes, of course; its double view reflects conflicting Romantic attitudes about the social role and potency of poetry: To whom does a poet speak? How is he heard? Such questions, which extend to the construction of a posthumous reputation, are informed by what we call today a consciousness of the reader as "a function: the repository of the codes

which account for the intelligibility of the text."[2] Mary Shelley is not only alert
to this function but aggressive in managing it. Eager to associate Shelley with
poems of a "more popular nature for the most part tha[n] his former productions,"[3] she uses her preface of 1839 to distinguish "two classes." The first, of
limited appeal she concedes, are "purely imaginative": "curious and metaphysical" poems such as *The Witch of Atlas, Adonais,* and *The Triumph of
Life* (*PW,* 1:x), given to "huntings after the obscure" or to "mystic subtlety"
(xiii).[4] Having admitted these curiosities, which she still attributes to Shelley's
overall "struggle for human weal" (ix), she advertises the "more popular"
appeal of a "second class" with a Wordsworthian vocabulary that by 1839 was
both legible and legitimating: "sprung from the emotions of his heart" (x),
these poems speak "to the many" (xiii), "to emotions common to us all . . .
the passion of love . . . grief and despondency . . . the sentiments inspired by
natural objects" (x).

This solicitation is furthered in her series of explanatory notes (an innovative format imitated in the 1840s both by Wordsworth and by one of Shelley's
Cambridge Apostles, R. M. Milnes, in his edition of Keats's *Life, Letters and
Literary Remains*). Strategically constructing the poet by constructing his
reader, the "Note on the Mask of Anarchy" is typical:

> Shelley's . . . warmest sympathies were for the people. He was a republican,
> and loved a democracy. . . . His hatred of any despotism . . . was in-
> tense. . . . [T]he news of the Manchester Massacre . . . roused in him vio-
> lent emotions of indignation and compassion. . . . Inspired by these feel-
> ings, he wrote the *Mask of Anarchy* . . . for the people, and . . . in a more
> popular tone than usual. (*CW,* 373–74)

Portraits such as this, shadowed by the highly politicized and tenacious controversies over Shelley's poetry and personality, are mobilized by a tactical effort
to rescue a "republican" Shelley from the radicals (he was a Chartist champion by the 1830s) and cleanse him of the taints of sedition and revolution that
would harm his reception by genteel readers. His politics are thus sentimental-
ized: personal rather than collective, self-sacrificing rather than violent.
Hence, "Note on The Revolt of Islam" reports that "while bringing out his
poem, Shelley had a severe attack of ophthalmia, caught while visiting the
poor cottages," and it urges us to see how "this minute and active sympathy
with his fellow-creatures gives a thousand-fold interest to his speculations,
and stamps with reality his pleadings for the human race" (*PW,* 1:377).

In this palpable design to portray an idealist of Christian aura, Shelley's
ideal readers are cast accordingly: "Those who have never experienced the
workings of passion on general and unselfish subjects," the editor suggests,
will not understand his dedication to "political freedom" or "the persecutions
to which [such as he] were exposed" (Preface, 1:viii–ix). This idealism is so
integral to the poet's imagination, argues the first note of 1839, on the
Chartists' darling, *Queen Mab,* as to justify its more abstruse poetics and
deserve our sympathetic latitude:

Shelley possessed a quality of mind which experience has shown me no other human being as participating, in more than a very slight degree: this was his *unworldliness*. The usual motives that rule men, prospects of present or future advantage, the rank and fortune of those around, the taunts and censures, or the praise of those who were hostile to him, had no influence whatever over his actions, and apparently none over his thoughts. . . . He was animated . . . by compassion for his fellow-creatures. His sympathy was excited by the misery with which the world is bursting. He witnessed the sufferings of the poor, and was aware of the evils of ignorance. He desired to induce every rich man to despoil himself of superfluity, and to create a brotherhood of property and service, and was ready to be the first to lay down the advantages of his birth. . . . In this spirit he composed QUEEN MAB. (*PW,* 1:99–100)

It is also in this spirit, another note tells us, that Shelley wrote *The Cenci,* "urged on by intense sympathy with the sufferings of the human beings whose passions, so long cold in the tomb, he revived" (2:274)—the image drawing its power, in part, from an ethically efficacious revision of the story of Frankenstein's perverse endeavors.

Interacting with this narrative of the poet's common sympathies, however, is another story: Shelley's apparent disdain for gaining an audience on such terms. Commenting that he shrugged off her entreaties "to write . . . in a style that commanded popular favour," the editor regrets that "the bent of his mind went the other way," drawn to "fantastic creations of his fancy, or the expression of those opinions and sentiments with regard to human nature and its destiny; a desire to diffuse which, was the master passion of his soul" (*PW* 2:280). The syntax almost has the effect of saying that Shelley's passions did not distinguish one from the other, its fantastic creations and its noble sentiments. The confusion is pertinent, for the editor means to redeem the "fantastic" Shelley canon by proposing an integral relation between its inclinations and those of the more popular poetry. Recalling the road not taken by the dominant "bent" of the poet's mind, she draws a different outline, its fulfillment impeded only by Shelley's sensitivity and lack of confidence in his readers. Although "Shelley did not expect sympathy and approbation from the public," she writes in a subsequent note,

> the surpassing excellence of the Cenci, had made me greatly desire that [he] should increase his popularity, by adopting subjects that would more suit the popular taste, than a poem conceived in the abstract and dreamy spirit of the Witch of Atlas. It was not only that I wished him to acquire popularity as redounding to his fame; but I believed that he would obtain a greater mastery over his own powers, and greater happiness in his mind, if public applause crowned his endeavours. . . . Even now I believe that I was in the right. . . . I had not the most distant wish that he should truckle in opinion, or submit his lofty aspirations for the human race to the low ambition and pride of the many, but, I felt sure, that if his poems were more addressed to the common feelings of men, his proper rank among the writers of the day would be acknowledged. (*PW* 4:51–52)

Yet as the editor argues this case, the paradoxes shimmer into ideological contradictions that disclose a more elitist poetics of audience. The accommodation she urges above, for instance, "adopting subjects to suit a popular taste," flirts with the truckling she disdains, while its images of adaptation make Shelley seem unnaturally constrained in such regard. It is, after all, "unworldliness" which distinguishes him from "the usual motives that rule men." A writer is "always shackled" when he "endeavours to write down" to his audience, she says elsewhere (*PW*, 3:207), and in other notes she shows Shelley sensing this keenly, at times with unsocial consequences. While Hunt and Byron were collaborating on *The Liberal,* he demurred, she reports sympathetically, "partly from pride, not wishing to have the air of acquiring readers for his poetry by associating it with the compositions of more popular writers; and, also, because he might feel shackled in the free expression of his opinions, if any friends were to be compromised" (4:154). The idealism of audience so claimed for the poet also serves the editor's more worldly motive: divorcing Shelley from the offensiveness of *The Liberal* without portraying him as deserting his friends or lacking their courage. By rendering him sensitive to the harm that might be done to *others* by his putative radicalism, she clears him, but only at the cost of divesting him of engagement with the political and historical world within which he wrote. This oddly double narrative intrudes even in the midst of documents sometimes cited (along with "Note on Queen Mab") for Shelley's liberal, class-conscious, even proto-Marxist, principles—such as the "Note on Poems of 1819."[5]

> Shelley loved the People. . . . He believed that a clash between the two classes of society was inevitable, and he eagerly ranged himself on the people's side. He had an idea of publishing a series of poems adapted expressly to commemorate their circumstances and wrongs. He wrote a few; but, in those days of prosecution for libel, they could not be printed. (*CW*, 626; cf. *PW*, 3:206–7)

Prosecution did not stop William Hone or Richard Carlile; Georgian England had a notoriously active libelous press. The more evident fact is that Shelley remained an aristocrat averse to political association with anyone lower than Hunt; even then, as his delicacy about *The Liberal* suggests, he hesitated. Mary Shelley evades these facts in a sentimental narrative of altruism: the poet's bold severing of class affiliation to ally with "the people," a romance thwarted only by a repressive legal system and booksellers' legitimate self-concern. Yet having cast this noble figure, she muddies its lines by then suggesting that Shelley, under the sway of such sympathies, violated his talent: the works so inspired "are not among the best of his productions. . . . [H]e had meant to adorn the cause he loved with loftier poetry" (*CW*, 626; *PW*, 3:207).

The mythology of this shackle-shy Shelley (predicting Arnold's ineffectual angel) is keyed in the edition's first note, on the much abused *Queen Mab:* he is "like a spirit from another sphere, too delicately organised" for the contentions of worldly life (*PW*, 1:97). Her Preface to *Essays, Letters from Abroad, Translations and Fragments by Percy Shelley,* in fact, concludes with a figure of the poet radically "unshackled," released in death from everything "which hedged him in on earth."[6] With this map of earthly and eternal spheres, the editor attempts to make a coherent narrative out of Shelley's widely fluctuating attitudes toward his audience: alternately messianic and hostile, selective and solicitous, at times simply dismissive. Some works, such as *The Cenci,* he claimed to have composed "with a certain view to popularity" in an idiom calculated "for the multitude."[7] With a more idealistic vision of public responsibility, he could project an ideal popularity, calling Poets "the institutors of laws and the founders of civil society" (*A Defence, EL,* 1:28), and in this spirit wrote some "*popular songs* wholly political, & destined to awaken & direct the imagination of the reformers" (*PSL,* 2:191; his emphasis). But he had no illusions about influence in his particular historical moment. "I have the vanity to write for poetical minds, and must be satisfied with few readers," he tells Trelawny.[8] Idealizing a spiritual integrity, these expectations also rationalize a material fact: during his lifetime, Shelley was a coterie poet, not widely published and even then, not widely appreciated or understood.[9]

A sense of this audience—elite, select, and slender— frequently enters into the rhetoric of the poems. If the editor's note suggests that *Alastor* holds "an individual interest only" (*PW,* 1:139), this modifies for her gentle reader the bluntness with which the poet's own preface distinguishes those of "too exquisite a perception" from all "meaner spirits" comprising the world's "unforeseeing multitudes" (1:110). The sorting is nearly perpetual. His preface to *The Revolt of Islam* projects the poem's success in "the public mind" only "among the enlightened and refined" (1:145) and, to fix such odds, greets its readers here and elsewhere with untranslated foreign languages. *Epipsychidion* was written "simply for the esoteric few" with no desire that "the vulgar should read it," he informs his publisher (16 Feb. 1821, *PSL,* 2:263–64), and its advertisement guards the gate. Readers are faced not only with the obstacle of Italian and an unelaborated allusion to Dante but also by blatant discrimination: "The present Poem, like the Vita Nuova of Dante, is sufficiently intelligible to a certain class of readers . . . and to a certain other class it must ever remain incomprehensible, from a defect of a common organ of perception" (*PW,* 4:59). The preface to *Prometheus Unbound*—also a poem "written only for the elect" (*PSL,* 2:200)—appeals to "the highly refined imagination of the more select classes of poetical readers" able to appreciate the "beautiful idealism of moral excellence" (*PW,* 2:6).

On some occasions, exclusion replaces tests of adaptation. At the end of *Julian and Maddalo,* this gesture is coded into the very narrative as Julian withholds the outcome of the sensational story of the lovelorn maniac that he has been retailing for several hundred lines and which outcome he himself has learned from Maddalo's daughter: "I urged and questioned still: she told me how / All happened—but the cold world shall not know"—the blank sense of these final lines reinforced in Mary Shelley's first edition of 1839 by closing volume 3 (314).[10] This poetics of exclusion could aspire to registers in which all audience is cast as eavesdroppers on a purely self-involved discourse: "A poet is a nightingale, who sits in darkness and sings to cheer his own solitude," radically unconscious of any wider sphere of influence—so argues Shelley's *Defence*.[11] At best, he reaches a Miltonic elite of fit audience though few: "the jury which sits in judgment upon a poet . . . must be composed of his peers . . . impanelled by time from the selectest of the wise" (*EL,* 1:4). In her Preface to the edition in which the essay was first published, Mary Shelley extends this myth: here is "a work whence a young poet, and one suffering from wrong or neglect, may learn to regard his pursuit and himself" under the aspect of "genius" elevated above "the mire of the earth . . . into those pure regions" inhabited by "the holy brotherhood, whose vocation it is to divest life of its material grossness" (1:6).

This editorial narrative of historical versus eternal audiences, or popular versus elite reception, in fact serves a second purpose for her: not only does it draw Shelley's peculiar aspects into the orbit of higher human sympathies, but the very production of this reading demonstrates the editor's refined sympathy with her subject, and so implicitly defuses the impression that she may have failed him in sympathy or understanding. This self-defense is explicit in her "Note on Poems of 1820" (quoted above), where she answers the poet's gentle mocking of her in the dedicatory stanzas of *The Witch of Atlas* for being too "critic-bitten" in worrying about a lack of "human interest" in his "visionary rhyme"; she insists that she was eager for his fame only as a resource for his self-confidence. And she subscribes to Shelley's elite poetics. Her Preface of 1839, for instance, flatly states that some poems require "a taste shared by few" (*PW,* 1:xii)—so few, that these perhaps will be "only appreciated by minds who have resemblance to his own" (xiii). Even within his circle, reports one note, he was "looked up to . . . by the few who knew him well, and had sufficient nobleness of soul to appreciate his superiority" to "his fellows in intellectual endowments and moral worth" (3:163). She has no qualms displaying Shelley in Byronic postures of disdain, reprinting a letter in which he says matter-of-factly, "I am formed, if for anything not in common with the herd of mankind, to apprehend minute and remote distinctions of feeling" (1:379). When she gets to *Prometheus Unbound,* although she provides a lengthy explanation of its allegory, she does not apologize for the "abstruse and imaginative theories" rendered in its lyrics, remarking only that it "requires a mind as subtle and penetrating as his own to understand the [poem's] mystic meanings. . . . They elude the ordinary reader by their abstraction and delicacy" (2:135).

Another way she preserves this standard is by retaining the key textual signifiers of Shelley's barriers to ordinary understanding. She leaves all the foreign languages in his titles, epigraphs, and notes unannotated by translation,[12] and follows suit in her own texts, assuming literacy in Greek in her Preface (1:xii) and "Note on The Prometheus Unbound" (2:136–37), and featuring untranslated, unspecified verse from Petrarch's *Rime sparse* in both the 1824 and 1839 prefaces, as well as at the close of "Note on Poems of 1818" (3:164). The 1839 preface does not even cite Petrarch, but merely appends an unattributed verse, as if in code:

> Se al seguir son tarda
> Forse avverrà che 'l bel nome gentile
> Consacrerò con questa stanca penna.[13]

Each title page of the four volumes of the first 1839 edition, moreover, bears a tercet of the *Rime,* with only the author identified:

> Lui non trov'io, ma suoi santi vestigi
> Tutti rivolti alla superna strada
> Veggio, lunge da'laghi averni e stigi—PETRARCA

After the final note, she reprints the Preface of 1824 (4:237–40), along with the title page's epigraph from Petrarch, as if to reinscribe this circle of literary and cultural knowledge:

> In nobil sangue vita umile e queta,
> Ed in alto intelletto un puro core;
> Frutto senile in sul giovenil fiore,
> E in aspetto pensoso anima lieta—PETRARCA[14]

In these quotations, there is one interesting editorial alteration: the pronouns are regendered so that the poet is addressed in the role of the absent Laura and the editor speaks as the devoted earthbound survivor. About this conversion and its implications there is more to say; what concerns us now is how these ritual consecrations via Petrarch at once write a public hagiography of Shelley and employ a somewhat inaccessible mode of representation. This uncompromising contradiction—the exclusionary signs that keep faith with a select readership, set against the narrative of a generous and responsive poet advanced in the prefaces and several notes—constitutes the master passion of Mary Shelley's editions.

Constructing "Shelley"

The contradictory poetics of audience in Mary Shelley's editions are deeply implicated in the public reception of Shelley during his life and for several years after his death.[15] The arena was highly charged—given to extreme representations, attracted to scandals, fixated on Shelley's repute as an immoral, self-indulgent man, of exotic, often revolutionary, ideas. The Tory stance is epitomized by *The Investigator*'s relentless flogging of "that most execrable publication, Queen Mab," for arousing "unmingled horror and disgust. . . . Our blood curdled in our veins as we waded through nine cantos of blasphemy and impiety."[16] Such a poet was a lightning rod in the England to which his widow returned in the summer of 1823 with plans for a posthumous edition. In a country agitated by economic upheaval and still given to fears of foreign invasion, publishers were not eager to option a property susceptible to legal harassment or, at best, a coterie sale and hostile reviews. Subsidized by Shelley's friends, *Posthumous Poems* finally found a sponsor in the radical publisher John Hunt (*MSL,* 1:384, 386n). An edition of five hundred came out in June, 1824, but by August, with about three hundred sold and about a dozen reviews, Shelley's father, intent to salvage the family name, bought up the rest and required his daughter-in-law, as a condition of

her annuity (she reports to Leigh Hunt on August 22), to refrain from bringing Shelley's name "before the public again" during his lifetime (1:444).

This emphatic suppression registers the scandal of Shelley's reputation,
especially in the 1820s, and Mary Shelley's chief hope, early and late, was to
dispel this atmosphere. In her penultimate note of 1839, she anticipates a time
when Shelley's "calumniators . . . and the poison breath of critics" will have
"vanished into emptiness before the fame he inherits" (*PW,* 4:150). It was this
vitriol, this edition suggests more than once, that forced Shelley's retreat into
his famously abstruse and exclusivist idioms:

> An exile, and strongly impressed with the feeling that the majority of his
> countrymen regarded him with sentiments of aversion, such as his own heart
> could experience towards none, he sheltered himself from such disgusting
> and painful thoughts in the calm retreats of poetry, and built up a world of
> his own." (*PW,* 2:139)
>
> Had not a wall of prejudice been raised . . . between him and his country-
> men, how many would have sought [his] acquaintance. (3:183)
>
> [P]opularity as a poet . . . would enable his countrymen to do justice to his
> character and virtues; which, in those days, it was the mode to attack with
> the most flagitious calumnies and insulting abuse. (4:52)

One crucial omission of these interventions is that even countrymen prepared
to acknowledge Shelley's virtues had walls to scale. To readers of *The Edinburgh Review,* Hazlitt complained of this volume's "dark sayings, . . . allego-
ries and riddles," especially in new poems such as *The Witch of Atlas, The
Triumph of Life,* and *Marianne's Dream,* which he found "difficult to read
through, from the disjointedness of the materials, the incongruous metaphors
and violent transitions. . . . [I]t is impossible, in most instances to guess the
drift or the moral".[17] He was not alone.[18]

The political fallout was just as difficult. In its otherwise rhapsodic notice
of *Posthumous Poems, Knight's Quarterly* lamented the "leaden" effect of the
poet's "theory" and his "wretched" reasoning, while the review in Constable's
Edinburgh Magazine nearly canceled its case for "a mind singularly gifted
with poetical talent" with the addendum, "however it may have been obscured, and to many, we doubt not, absolutely eclipsed by its unhappy union
with much that is revolting in principle and morality."[19] This rhetoric had
reached lurid extremes of summary judgment with Shelley's death by drowning in 1822, an event which made the passionately controversial discourse as
much an issue as its referent. From the right, Shelley was ritually paraded as
the epitome of obscurity or, when intelligible, the justly punished enemy of
orthodoxy; from the left, he was eulogized as a divine messenger and mar-
tyred champion. As *The Investigator* makes clear, the incendiary *Queen Mab*
was the designated synecdoche of the canon.[20] The hotly Tory *John Bull*'s
initial notice, on August 12, is symptomatic: "Mr. Bysshe Shelley, the author
of that abominable and blasphemous book called *Queen Mab,* was lately
drowned in a storm somewhere in the Mediterranean." Although a follow-up
a week later claimed "no wish to review his past life and conduct nor . . .

allude to his published productions," it quoted lavishly from *Queen Mab,* nicely reminding its readers that Shelley wrote verse of "appalling" atheism, "blasphemy," "treason," and "abuse of Monarchs and their Governments." The left, meanwhile, rushed to the defense. On August 4, *The Examiner,* addressing "those who know a great mind when they met with it, and who have been delighted with the noble things in the works of Mr. Shelley," played up the tragedy, announcing that readers "will be shocked to hear that he has been cut off in the prime of his life and genius." Subsequent notices took a cue from *John Bull* or *The Examiner,* according to disposition, and declaring these alliances soon became as important as the news at hand.[21]

Shelley emerged from the obituaries newly refurbished as a weapon in political and cultural skirmishing—a role whose potency may be measured by its endurance. Hunt is still busy at damage control in 1828, insisting that "with all his scepticism, Mr. Shelley's disposition may be truly said to have been any thing but irreligious. . . . The leading feature of [his] character, may be said to have been a natural piety."[22] The last term, a calculated Wordsworthian gloss on the question, perhaps inspired Mary Shelley to list in her "Note on Queen Mab" the "love and knowledge of nature developed by Wordsworth" as among the poet's "favourite reading" (*PW*, 1:102), tacitly recuperating the poem's canonization by a coterie in the 1820s that was not Shelley's chosen elite, but a "small group" of "unliterary radical admirers [who] considered him a prophet" and whose enthusiasm, assisted by pirated editions from radical booksellers, was responsible for a portion of his fame.[23] Lewes found it worth saying in his review of the 1839 volumes that he would gladly "give up the political parts" of the poetry for more verse about "the power and loveliness of human affection."[24] And as late as 1870, Rossetti felt it advisable before ending his introductory memoir to address "Shelley's opinions."[25] These sensitivities spell the force of the controversies with which Mary Shelley had to contend in undertaking to rehabilitate Shelley as a poet and political thinker. Her challenge was to represent the humanitarian passion for reform that was the basis of the idealism without provoking the political storms of the obituaries. Wondering in 1823 "whether to reprint a Vol. of unpublished" poems only, or "the whole together," she tells Leigh Hunt that she "encline[s] to the former—as it w^d be a specimen of how he could write without shocking any one—and afterwards an edition of the whole might be got up inserting any thing too shocking for this Vol." (*MSL*, 1:396–97).

When Arnold praised "Mrs. Shelley's representation" of the poet in the "delightful volumes of the original edition of 1839" for revealing a "rare spirit—so mere a monster unto many," the latter term had resonance.[26] Her most famous work, *Frankenstein,* was its mirror image, a shocking story of a rare spirit creating a monster. "Perhaps a corpse would be reanimated; . . . perhaps the component parts of a creature might be . . . brought together, and endued with vital warmth," was the tenor of the conversation by which she was inspired, so reports the "Author's Introduction" to the 1831 edition.[27] In rescuing the spirit of Shelley with a new gathering of his works from the monster pieced together by a hostile press, Mary Shelley revisits and revises this earlier story of creation, enacting as textual work the twin dramas of production represented in its introduction. There, she described both how she as "Author" invented her work from fragments of inspiration, struggling to reverse the "mortifying negative" of "blank incapability" (x) with the "progeny" that is her story (xii); and how its eponym, also an "author" (87, 96), animated a corpse from the scraps and fragments he gleaned from the dead, "bestowing animation" by "collecting and arranging . . . materials" (52).

These allied acts of creation are evoked by the preface she writes at the other end of this decade, to the 1839 edition of Shelley's *Works,* as she reworks the metaphors to tell a story of producing a posthumous literary corpus.[28] If Frankenstein "put together" a body of work, hoping to "communicate" life to dead matter and sensing success as his materials "show signs of life and stir with an uneasy, half-vital motion" (xi), an analogous process brings the poet to life. Calling on "liveliest recollection" (*PW,* 1:xvi), the editor will detail "the history of those productions, as they sprung, living and warm, from his heart and brain" (vii), and she renders the poet's "character" in appropriately revivifying terms: his "animated" social relations, his "warm affection," "pulsation of his heart," his "internal sensations," his capacity for "new-sprung hope" and "a joy and an exultation . . . intense and wild" (viii; xi). "These characteristics breathe throughout his poetry," she insists (ix), and she implicitly refuses to concede their death: "his influence over mankind, though slow in growth, is fast augmenting"; indeed, he "now exists where we hope one day to join him" (xv). Reversing the trajectory of his death and her loss is the early and recurring narrative of these prefaces. The one for the 1824 *Poems,* in fact, makes the poet's death seem less a loss than a translation along the proper path for one too refined for this world: "his unearthly and elevated nature is a pledge of the continuation of his being, although in an altered form. Rome received his ashes."[29]

The continuation of a poetic being required some intervening resuscitation, however, in the form of editorial labor, and Mary Shelley could draw readily on the resources of her intimacy with the poet during the period of his greatest productivity, her credit as an educated and sympathetic reader of his poetry, and not the least, her "sole access to many of his unpublished literary manuscripts."[30] "Invention," the author of *Frankenstein* "humbly admit[s]" in the Introduction, "does not consist in creating out of void, but out of chaos; the materials must, in the first place, be afforded: it can give form. . . . [I]t consists in the capacity of seizing on the capabilities of a subject and in . . . moulding and fashioning ideas" (x). This description of engendering her novel also applies, in the mode of Petrarchan *Rime sparse,* to fashioning her editions. Many of the poems "collected," she says in the Preface of 1824 (the year after she began revising *Frankenstein*), were rescued from chaos, "scattered in periodical works" (*PW,* 4:240). Or worse: the manuscripts from which some were gleaned, reports a footnote in 1839, were barely viable, "so confused a mass, interlined and broken into fragments, . . . that the sense could only be deciphered and joined by guesses" (4:226); a postscript to the second edition's preface refers to yet more "scattered and confused papers" and "fragments" (*CW,* vi).[31] In a revealing condensation, this last term had, by the production of *Essays, Letters,* become equivalent in her imagination to the poet himself: "fragments of Shelley" its preface calls the contents (*EL,* 1:13). Motivating her editorial assembly is a Petrarchan sense of fidelity to a divine authority contrasting the pride-sotted work of a Frankenstein. She is certain that "a mind so original so delicately and beautifully moulded, as Shelley's . . . would never be shattered and dispersed by the Creator; . . . the qualities and consciousness that formed him, are not only indestructible in themselves, but in the form under which they were united here, and to become worthy of him is to assure the bliss of a reunion" (1:12).

We can see how this creative assistance and its myth of humble service yield an unequal, hierarchical economy in which "women are overshadowed (and overshadow themselves) by the men they see as poetic geniuses," so Marlon Ross analyzes Mary Shelley's editorial function. Yet we might modify the density of this shadow by noting the considerable authority, at times co-creation, that her editing involved.[32] This is clear even on the most literal level. The "fragments" Mary Shelley gathered are now part of the Shelley corpus: these include not only the several major poems designated as "Fragment" but also a wealth of manuscript "fragments," which, "broken and vague as they are," the editor urges, "will appear valuable to those who love Shelley's mind, and desire to trace its workings" (*PW,* 3:68–69).[33] By fragments and wholes, she virtually produced the basic "Shelley" texts and canon. *Rosalind and Helen* and *Lines written among the Euganean Hills,* reports her 1839 Preface, "I found among his papers by chance; and with some difficulty urged him to complete" (xi; cf. 3:159). It was under her supervision, too, that his essays were published together (*A Defence* for the first time, and newly edited texts of the fragments, *On Life* and *On Love*); it was she who gave *Queen Mab* a reputable imprimatur (it was the leading poem, albeit expurgated, in the first 1839 edition); and, as Hazlitt immediately recognized, it was she who introduced *Julian and Maddalo, The Triumph of Life, Letter to [Maria Gisborne], The Witch of Atlas, Swellfoot the Tyrant, Peter Bell the Third,* and two of the lyrics to Jane Williams.[34] She also was the first to refine a canon, featuring principal works before a chronological record.[35] Moreover, the now-standard practice of using editor's notes "to relate a poet's creative work to the relevant circumstances of both time and stress may be said to originate with [these editions]," claims Sylva Norman, adding that "any full edition of Shelley's works that should now appear without her annotations would seem truncated and outrage our sense of unity."[36] The last image nicely chimes with Shelley's editorial project: not only did it unify a fragmented poetic corpus but it made her restoration integral to the poet's reception.

One crux in this reconstruction was the all-too-durable *Queen Mab:* reviled by the Tory press in its own day, it had gone on to acclaim in the working-class and radical press in the 1830s.[37] This mattered, because the 1839 "Shelley" was being issued by Edward Moxon, an establishment publisher whose list included Wordsworth, among other notables.[38] That John Hunt, intermittently imprisoned adversary of the throne, had printed *Posthumous Poems* made Moxon's imprint especially important to the rehabilitation of Shelley, and his cautions demanded respect: he would print *Mab,* but he wanted to drop "the 6th & 7th parts as too shocking & atheistical." This plan bothers Mary Shelley, even as she sees its merit: "I dont like mutilations—& would not leave out a word in favour of liberty. But I have no partiality to irreligion & much doubt the benefit of disputing the existence of the Creator," she tells Hogg (11 Dec., *MSL,* 2:301). She airs this debate to Moxon himself (303) and Leigh Hunt, insisting to the latter that she herself has "a great love" for the poem because Shelley "was proud of it . . . & it is associated with the bright young days of both of us" (12 and 14 Dec., 2:304, 305). Her plural is crucial, for it discloses a personal as well as professional stake in preserving the poem's integrity from mutilation. Moxon prevailed for the first edition, and she cooperated, her note emphasizing that this was a juvenile production which Shelley "never intended to publish" (*PW,* 1:103), that he was distressed by the piracies and had said as much in a letter to *The Examiner,* which she reprints entire (105–6).[39] When Moxon relented for the second edition, agreeing to the whole, she was vigilant. Noticing some endnotes dropped in proofs, she protests, "the omissions only render our editions imperfect & mutilated" (8 Sept. 1839, *MSL,* 2:324). No matter how "peculiar," she writes of another provocative piece, "[t]he world has a right to the entire compositions of such a man" (*CW,* 416). And when she "scratched out a few lines which might be too shocking" in the essay "On the Devil and Devils," she tells Hunt, "I hate to mutilate."[40]

The defense against mutilation and the production of a perfect "Shelley" from confused masses, fragments, and scatterings is not just a matter of editorial principle for Mary Shelley; it is fundamental to her narrative of Shelley's endurance. Her citation of Petrarch's *Rime sparse* in each edition of the poems is involved with this myth and her role in sustaining it. That the loss of Laura's body "constitutes the intolerable absence, creates a reason to speak, and permits a poetic 'corpus,' " Nancy Vickers argues, casts the *Rime* as "a poetry of tension, of flux, of alternation between the scattered and the gathered."[41] Gathering Shelley's scattered verse, Mary Shelley enacts this drama, with a key reversal of gender roles. If "Petrarch's particularizing mode of figuring that body, the product of a male-viewer / female-object exchange, . . . goes to the heart of his lyric program" (Vickers, 107), Mary Shelley's editorial program, her review of her husband's body of work, involves similar authority—one enhanced by its inversion of the structure of mentorship in her first real experience as author, writing *Frankenstein.* This initial state of affairs is recalled in her "Author's Introduction" (the novel's "real" introduction, she emphasizes [*MSL,* 2:129], referring to Shelley's ghosting her voice for the preface to the first edition of 1818): "My husband . . . was for ever inciting me to obtain literary reputation. . . . [H]e desired that I should write, not so much with the idea that I could produce any thing worthy of notice, but that he might himself judge how far I possessed . . . promise" (viii). In this story, as Mary Poovey remarks, Mary

Shelley depicts herself "as a creation of others."[42] Editing Percy Shelley, paradoxically, promotes her to creator.

Invested with this authority, she fashions the volume, constructs its subject, and looks out for her own interests. If in her Introduction to *Frankenstein* she claimed to be "infinitely indifferent" to her "literary reputation," compared to when she first wrote the novel (viii), her work as an editor recovers some of her original spirit. Negotiating her fee with Moxon, she insists that her labors on *Posthumous Poems* grant a claim of property: "I feel sure . . . the copy right . . . must be entirely mine," she writes on December 7, 1838: "The M.S. from which it was printed consisted of fragments of paper which in the hands of an indifferent person would never have been decyphered—the labour of putting it together was immense—the papers were in my possession & in no other person's (for the most part) the volume might be all my writing (except that I could not write it)." Despite the demurral, the editor M. S. clearly regards herself as a kind of co-author of the newly coherent "MS" she delivered to the publisher, and hence, co-owner: "it certainly stands to reason, & I should think that it is law that a Posthumous publication must belong entirely to the editor, if the editor had a legal right to ‹poss› make use of the MS."[43] With this sense of legal right, she also deals ably with Sir Timothy's refusal to let her "publish Shelley's Poems." His injunction already violated by "[m]any pirated editions," she argues, the only result is that she herself has been "prevented . . . any benefit."[44] When he agrees to an edition but no memoir, she resourcefully applies a loose construction. If "Sir Tim forbids biography," she tells Hogg on December 11, she means "to write a few notes appertaining to the history of the poems" (*MSL*, 2:301)—a history which in aggregate, as Newman Ivey White remarks, all but constitutes a "subterfuge" (*Shelley*, 2:401).

Along with an exercise of authority, editing *Posthumous Poems* gave Mary Shelley a practical alertness to market conditions and commercial necessity. Having asked Leigh Hunt for a memoir and guessing his reluctance to forsake the role of liberal point man he had eagerly played in the obituary battles, she urges him not to "excite inimical feelings" (11 Dec. 1823, *MSL*, 1:409). She also presses the value of timeliness: "Shelley has celebrity even popularity now—a winter ago greater interest would perhaps have been excited than now by this volume—but who knows what may happen before the next. . . . send me what you prepare; for it is not yet too late—but if you wait . . . it will be" (9 Feb. 1824, 1:411). Hunt never did send a notice, but by 1839, Mary Shelley was ready to produce this text herself. When he offered help then, she politely protected her authority, insisting that "our notes must be independant [*sic*] of each other": "Thanks for your very kind offer. . . . But it must rest on myself alone. . . . The edition will be mine" (2:305).

Reconstructing "Shelley"

In the volatile political and cultural atmospheres of 1824, Mary Shelley decided to win readers for Shelley both by domesticating him and then, tactfully, insisting on the legitimacy of the challenges he posed to popular understanding. Her Preface to *Posthumous Poems* thus depicts a character of peculiar, but worthy enthusiasms: "His life was spent in the contemplation of nature, in arduous study, or in acts of kindness and affection. He was an elegant scholar and a profound metaphysician" (*PW*, 4:238). She locates his inspirations, especially for those "purely imaginative" poems, not in abstruse and unorthodox ideas but in various natural settings, to which she gives the reader imaginative access: " 'Prometheus Unbound' was written among the deserted and flower-grown ruins of Rome; and when he made his home under the Pisan hills, their roofless recesses harboured him as he composed 'The Witch of Atlas,' 'Adonais,' and 'Hellas.' . . . [H]e often went alone in his little shallop to the rocky caves that bordered [the sea], and sitting beneath their shelter, wrote 'The Triumph of Life' " (238–39). By this shimmer of description, which reviewers began to reflect, the editor turns earlier charges of indistinction and remoteness into truth to nature: the language of Shelley's poems is otherworldly because these places are.[45]

And so is Shelley: in order to insist on the special stance of his poetry toward mankind, the Preface lifts him from the world of common humanity. The dominant image is the Christian martyr, a figure to be appreciated by those who read aright:

> [H]is fearless enthusiasm in the cause which he considered the most sacred upon earth, the improvement of the moral and physical state of mankind, was the chief reason why he, like other illustrious reformers, was pursued by hatred and calumny. No man was ever more devoted than he, to the endeavour of making those around him happy; no man ever possessed friends more unfeignedly attached to him. The ungrateful world did not feel his loss, and the gap it made seemed to close as quickly over his memory as the murderous sea above his living frame. (*PW*, 4:237–38)

Presenting this noble figure of self-sacrifice, Mary Shelley splits an ungrateful hegemony in two: the calumniators, no less murderous than the obliterating sea, and the potential converts. It is the latter to whom she appeals for a sense of the real worth of Shelley's poetry and a vindication of his memory: "the wise, the brave, the gentle, is gone for ever! He is . . . as a bright vision, whose radiant track, left behind in the memory, is worth all the realities that society can afford" (238).

This recuperation of Shelley both within and beyond this world—as, paradoxically, the uncommon property of common idealism—influenced the course and discourse of reception. Many reviews of the 1824 *Poems*—such as those in Constable's *Edinburgh Magazine*, *The Literary Gazette*, and Hazlitt's for *The Edinburgh*—although still equivocal, refrained from the obituary extremes, and others overtly disseminated Mary Shelley's terms.[46] *Knight's* found the *Poems* "a work upon which the genuine mark of intellectual greatness is stamped" and deemed themselves "ennobled by our relation to a superior mind"—all said in defiance of those who reviled Shelley as "an Atheist . . . a man of flagitious character" and his poems as "nothing more than a heap of bombast and verbiage" (182–83). As a measure of sympathy, it urged a liberal view of the "peculiar opinions in politics and theology" as mere "excrescences on the surface" of his poems, "disfiguring them" (186). Even Hazlitt's review conceded that Shelley was "with all his faults . . . a man of genius," "an honest man . . . sincere in all his professions": "He thought and acted logically, and was what he professed to be, a sincere lover of truth, of nature, and of humankind" (495–96).

The road to recuperation was not entirely smooth, however. In the same year as *Posthumous Poems,* Medwin's *Conversations* appeared. On the helpful side, he echoed Mary Shelley's praises and took her cue in noting Shelley's Wordsworthian "deifi[cation] of Nature." He even outdid her on *Alastor,* calling it "one of the most perfect specimens of harmony in blank verse" and stressing the positive influence of such poems, as well as Shelley's "critical judgment," on Byron's works.[47] Shelley, in turn, benefitted from the record of Byron's judgment that he had "more poetry in him than any man living" (235). At the same time, however, Medwin retailed the scandals recently heated up by the obituaries, and publicized Shelley's expulsion from Oxford for the pamphlet on atheism, his break with his father, his leaving England to avoid creditors, Harriet's suicide, and his loss of their children's custody "in consequence of his atheistical opinions" (248). He ended, moreover, rehearsing the complaints of inaccessibility: "Even if Shelley had not set himself up as a reformer, his poetry was never calculated to be popular. His creations were of another world . . . clothed in too mystical a language; his allusions are too deep and classical for many minds" (250).

It is a significant register of the force of Mary Shelley's "Shelley" that Leigh Hunt used it against Medwin's in the portrait he drew in *Lord Byron and Some of His Contemporaries.* Persevering in her project of reconstruction, he broadcasts the terms of her Preface, a document dismissed by *Literary Gazette* as "panegyric"[48] and merely tolerated by Hazlitt as "imperfect but touching" (499). Hunt quoted it lavishly and developed its themes, polemicizing Shelley as a champion of the "improvement of the moral and physical state of mankind" (168). In more moderate tones, he elaborated and added his testimony to her image of the poet as a scholar, a disciplined and serious man, and he rehearsed her canny alliance of otherworldliness and political fate: "this spirit, not sufficiently constituted like the rest of the world, to obtain their sympathy . . . a misunderstood nature, slain by the ungenial elements" (157). This reading was virtually canonized in Lewes's influential review of the 1839 volumes: against "another dark instance of the world's ingratitude," Shelley displayed "the obduracy and strength of a martyr; an angel-martyr, however, not a fanatic" (304, 307). In the same year as this review, *The National* was drawing on both Mary Shelley's earlier account and Hunt's to construct its own "Life of Shelley."[49]

This reconstructed Shelley, partly by force of historical distance, proved steadily attractive in the 1830s, and Mary Shelley began to supplement her initial hagiography with some worldly refurbishing. She placed three minor poems and the fragment *On Love* in one of the highly popular, commercially

successful annuals, *Keepsake for 1829*. The essay in particular was warmly
received in middle-class parlors and contributed to the growing acceptability of
Shelley by the social mainstream.[50] She polishes this appeal in the notes of 1839,
courting new appreciation while sustaining the figure cherished by the converted. Following Hunt, she emphasizes the poet's learning, scholarship, and
intellectual maturity. He "possessed two remarkable qualities of intellect—a
brilliant imagination and a logical exactness of reason," she asserts in the first
sentence of "Note on the Revolt of Islam" (*PW,* 1:374), and elsewhere he is
nearly a Victorian sage: "he was clear, logical, and earnest, in supporting his
own views; attentive, patient, and impartial, while listening to those on the
adverse side" (3:163). Her chief narrative, increasingly influential in the reading public, represented Shelley as a martyr to his ideals, enhancing the glow by
casting him as a figure of the lost age of idealism and passion that was emerging
as the elegiac, or at least tolerant, Victorian reading of the Romantic poets. In
fact, the "keynote" of early Victorian criticism of Shelley—certainly in the
expanding liberal press—was "apologetic appreciation."[51] The time was ripe
for reassessment, announced *The Monthly Chronicle* in its review of "Shelley's
Poems": "public opinion has at no former period had larger indulgence for
error, enthusiasm, or the fanaticism of elevated sentiment."[52]

Mary Shelley, remarking that the 1830s, versus the years when Shelley
wrote, have "seen the rise and progress of reform" (*PW,* 2:344), exploits this
shift of opinion in her first note of 1839, on the "atheist" *Queen Mab.* Shelley's political enthusiasms are cast in the mode of literary romance, overlaid
with an aura of Christian idealism and martyrdom:

> At the age of seventeen, fragile in health and frame, of the purest habits in
> morals, full of devoted generosity and universal kindness, glowing with
> ardour to attain wisdom, resolved at every personal sacrifice to do right,
> burning with a desire for affection and sympathy,—he was treated as a
> reprobate, cast forth as a criminal.
>
> The cause was that he was sincere. . . . he loved truth with a martyr's
> love; he was ready to sacrifice station and fortune, and his dearest affections
> to its shrine. (*PW,* 1:99)

This Shelley is a figure of Romantic myth, embellished with the vocabulary
that, by the 1830s, was being codified as the character of the Romantic poet:

> The solemn spirit that reigns throughout, the worship of the majesty of
> nature, the broodings of a poet's heart in solitude—the mingling of the
> exulting joy which the various aspects of the visible universe inspires, with
> the sad and struggling pangs which the human passion imparts, give a touch-
> ing interest to the whole. The death which he had often contemplated during
> the last months as certain and near [In the spring of 1815, an eminent
> physician pronounced that he was dying rapidly of a consumption], he here
> represented in such colours as had, in his lonely musings, soothed his soul to
> peace. (*PW* 1:141 [140])

This "Note on Alastor" was so impressive to Lewes that he cited its authority
in his lengthy review, quoting it entire (325). Ironically, where Mary Shelley

apologized for the poem's "individual interest only" (1:139), Lewes was prepared to suggest that this "is perhaps of all his poems that which pleases the generality of people most, because it contains nothing of his peculiar views" (324).

If she couldn't quite make this case with *Alastor,* Mary Shelley found other ways to frame her Romantic portrait of "Shelley" with appeals to Victorian tastes. One was to repair his inclination (as she says offhandedly in the Introduction to *Frankenstein*) "to embody ideas and sentiments in the radiance of brilliant imagery, and in the music of the most melodious verse that adorns our language, than to invent the machinery of a story" (ix). Her notes remedy this lack even more than the Preface of 1824, and having written *Frankenstein,* oddly, provides a resource. Its most influential review, a leading essay by Scott for *Blackwood's,* praised its author for ideas "clearly as well as forcibly expressed" and for "descriptions of landscape" infused with "the choice requisites of truth, freshness, precision, and beauty"; "the work impresses us with a high idea of the author's . . . happy power of expression," he said in summary.[53] This author now puts such talents to work in Shelley's behalf. We hear about the social and political contexts of his work as a poet; there are also domestic details: homes, haunts, and jaunts; Shelley's anxieties for his children and his grief at their deaths; the pains, pleasures and anxieties of fatherhood; his generosity to friends and family. Many of these stories are interwoven, as before, with picturesque, accessible accounts of poetic origins: "It was on a beautiful summer evening, while wandering among the lanes, whose myrtle hedges were the bowers of the fire-flies, that we heard the carolling of the sky-lark, which inspired one of the most beautiful of his poems" (*PW,* 4:50). In the manner of much English travel-writing, Mary Shelley depicts the inspiration of various locales—such as the view from Shelley's study window in Italy:

> it looked out on a wide prospect of fertile country, and commanded a view of the near sea. The storms that sometimes varied our day showed themselves most picturesquely as they were driven across the ocean; sometimes the dark lurid clouds dipped towards the wave, and became water-spouts, that churned up the waters beneath, as they were chased onward and scattered by the tempest. . . . In this airy cell he wrote the principal part of the Cenci. (*PW,* 2:275–76)

She is especially conscientious about applying these frames to poems which the reviewers had found fanciful, abstract, incomprehensible:

> He visited some of the more magnificent scenes of Switzerland, and returned to England from Lucerne, by the Reuss and the Rhine. The river navigation enchanted him. . . . he visited the source of the Thames, making the voyage in a wherry from Windsor to Crichlade. His beautiful stanzas in the churchyard of Lechlade were written on that occasion. "Alastor" was composed on his return. He spent his days under the oak shade of Windsor Great Park; and the magnificent woodland was a fitting study to inspire the various descriptions we find in the poem. ("Note on Alastor," *PW,* 1:140–41)

> The house was cheerful and pleasant; a vine-trellised walk, a Pergola, as it is
> called in Italian, led from the hall door to a summer-house at the end of the
> garden, which Shelley made his study, and in which he began the Prome-
> theus; a slight ravine, with a road in its depth, divided the garden from the
> hill, on which stood the ruins of the ancient castle of Este. ("Poems of 1818,"
> *PW,* 3:160)

Beyond their scene-painting, these tourist notes also involve a private circuit
of significance for the editor: she attempts to refresh interest in Shelley's
poetry by means of the very genre in which they had collaborated for her
earliest publication, *History of a Six Weeks' Tour.*[54]

It is thus no small consequence that this literary as well as recollective
reunion shaped a reception for the editor as well as the poet. Lewes found Mary
Shelley's notes "most interesting, sympathising, and affectionate" (310), a response shared even by those such as Arnold inclined to resist their idealizing:
notwithstanding his view of the poet as an "ineffectual angel," he praised the
editor for giving "the very picture of Shelley to be desired," detailing the "soul
of affection, of 'gentle and cordial goodness,' of eagerness and ardour for
human happiness"; indeed, her intimacy with her subject uniquely authorized
those defenses which, voiced by biographers such as Dowden, could breed only
"impatience and revolt" (306). For overt partisans such as Rossetti, the notes
constituted an authoritative resource for any interest in the poet's life; his own
174-page memoir rivaled them in self-admitted "reverence" for their subject:

> Any judgment pronounced upon Shelley ought to be that of a sympathizing
> and grateful as well as an equitable man; sympathizing, for history records
> no more beautiful nature,—grateful, for how much do we not all owe
> him! . . . After everything has been stated, we find that the man Shelley was
> worthy to be the poet Shelley,—and praise cannot reach higher than that;
> we find him to call forth the most eager and fervent homage, and to be one
> of the ultimate glories of our race and planet. (1:clxxvii–clxxix)

What Rossetti is praising, in effect, is a second creature produced by the
author of *Frankenstein,* a "Shelley" whose appeal as "one of the ultimate
glories of our race and planet" claims a victorious success over the earlier
monstrous constructions of others.

Reconstructing "Mary Shelley"

Prior to this apotheosis, however, assessment of her labors was divided, its
welter of conflicting voices leaving Mary Shelley with a sense of the radical
privacy of her recollections and their incommensurability with any coherent
public reception, either of the poet or his editor. Not only did several of
Shelley's friends berate her for cowardice in marring *Mab* and suppressing
other works, but the reviews were not as supportive as she had hoped, often
contradicting one another in their complaints and grudging in their praise.[55]
And in others, she laments to Hunt, her work "met with no remark," and
"like all else I do, attracted no attention" (20 July 1839, *MSL,* 2:318). Integrat-

ing the poet's works was taking an inverse toll on the editor: "publishing the book writing the notes & receiving disagreable [*sic*] letters had so violent an effect on my health that I really felt in danger of losing my senses" (ibid.). Earlier this year, in the midst of "editing Shelley's Poems, and writing notes for them," she had confessed in her journal: "I am torn to pieces by memory. Would that all were mute in the grave!"[56]—a strikingly poignant inversion of her initially unifying and revivifying agenda for him.

This double process of restoring Shelley by fragmenting her own existence compels her to assimilate herself to his story, specifically within the textual circuit of reading and writing. Although this gesture begins in a radical and tortured privacy, it ultimately issues in a figure of mutual and shared vocation. The original pain of mourning that composing the notes had reanimated was deeply involved with writing as a way to retain a relationship with Shelley, making him her ideal audience. In her grief, she summoned this correspondence by imagining herself as a compatible figure of death-in-life, her life entombed with his—"Now I am alone—oh, how alone! . . . my thoughts are a sealed treasure, which can confide to none" (2 Oct. 1822, *MSJ*, 180)—or disintegrating as he had: "I am a wreck. By what do the fragments cling together? Why do they not part, to be borne away by the tide to the boundless ocean, where those are whom day and night I pray that I may rejoin?" (26 Oct. 1824, 196). Her only consolation is fixating her present life on this past life. This is partly material—"being permitted to live where I am now in the same house, in the same state"—and partly textual: "collecting His manuscripts—writing his life." It is these identifications ("he is with me, about me") that sustain her: "were it not for the steady hope I entertain of joining him what a mockery all this would be. Without that hope I could not study or write" (27 Aug. 1822; *MSL*, 1:252, 253). They also sharpen her appeal to Shelley as her necessary audience: "I write, at times that pleases me; though double sorrow comes when I feel that Shelley no longer reads and approves of what I write; besides I have no great faith in my success" (3 Sept. 1824, *MSJ*, 195).

That this appeal is voiced in writing is important, however, for as Mary Shelley regenerates her identity as author, her rhetoric of vulnerable private dependence modulates into one of privileged, authorizing audience. Even as she closes a letter to Maria Gisborne just after Shelley's death with a sigh, "Well here is my story—the last story I shall have to tell," she begins to develop the Petrarchan trope that will sustain her as editor: she means to become "worthy to join him. Soon my weary pilgrimage will begin" (15 Aug. 1822, *MSL*, 1:250). Regenerating her life becomes synonymous with writing his. "Tomorrow I must begin this new life of mine," she pledges to herself in October (*MSJ*, 183), and the next day this "new life" beckons as the production of Shelley's: "I shall write his life, and thus occupy myself in the only manner from which I can derive consolation" (185). In this occupation, she begins to apostrophize him, as if to animate him in figures of writing and feel a generative force in so doing: "I was occupied by reflection—on those ideas you, my beloved, planted in my mind" (188).

Shelley's "life" never came to fruition, except by other hands, an event suggesting to some that the widow was incapacitated by "feelings of guilt,

shame, and remorse" for having been "unworthy to have been his wife."[57]
Ironically victimized by her own monstrous idealization of the poet, Mary
Shelley was inhibited further by the prospect of herself as a text for others. This
anxiety plagued her reluctance to finish a biography of her father in the late
1830s, just before she decided to devote herself to producing Shelley's *Poetical
Works,* and it erupted forcefully in 1829, in consequence of Trelawny's pester-
ing her for assistance with his own biography of Shelley. Her response to him
reflects as much self-concern as concern for Shelley's memory:

> Could you write my husband's life, without naming me it were something—
> but even then I should be terrified at the rouzing the slumbering voice of the
> public—each critique, each mention of your work, might drag me for-
> ward. . . . to be in print—the subject of men's observations—of the bitter
> hard world's commentaries, to be attacked or defended! . . . Shelley's life
> must be written—I hope one day to do it myself, but it must not be pub-
> lished now—There are too many concerned to speak against him—it is still
> too sore a subject . . . I pray for omission . . . I seek only to be forgotten—
> (*MSL,* 2:72; Shelley's emphasis)

The issue is deeply agitated by a strong desire for protection—for both herself
and Shelley—from a world of unsympathetic, or even hostile, readers:

> the truth—any part of it—is hardly for the rude cold world to handle—His
> merits are acknowledged—his virtues—to bring forward actions which right
> or wrong, and that would be a matter of dispute, were in their results
> tremendous, would be to awaken calumnies and give his enemies a voice—
> For myself—am I to be left out in this life?—if so half my objections, more
> than half, would disappear—for with me would depart that portion which is
> most painful—I do not see what you could make of his life without me—
> but . . . leave me out . . . I fear publicity. . . . it would destroy me to be
> brought forward in print. (15 Dec. 1829; *MSL* 2:94).

The widow in effect writes herself into the narrative of the bitter, hard, rude,
cold world that shaped her discourse of the poet's abuse and victimization,
and in this shared misery she sustains a relationship with him.

   This emotional turmoil, as Mary Poovey notes, also involves social constraints, ones whose register on Mary Shelley made her think it "unwomanly
to print and publish"; economic necessity alone, a friend surmised, compelled
her to "come before the world as an authoress."[58] That she would figure in a
biography not only as "authoress" but also, necessarily, as a character might
compromise her hopes of getting her son Percy Florence socially established;
reviving old scandals would be embarrassing or worse, given the catastrophe
to her mother's reputation wrought by Godwin's *Memoirs of the Author of a
Vindication of the Rights of Woman.*[59] Convinced by 1838 that "the greatest
happiness of woman was to be the wife or mother of a distinguished man"
(*MSL,* 2:306), Mary Shelley adopted a role in Shelley's posthumous existence
that was a tactical concession both to propriety and greatest happiness. "The
Poetical Works of Percy Bysshe Shelley. Edited by Mrs. Shelley" reads the
title page of each of the four volumes of 1839, with the initial inscription: "To

Percy Florence Shelley, The Poetical Works Of His Illustrious Father Are Dedicated, By His Affectionate Mother, Mary Wollstonecraft Shelley (*PW*, 1:v). This compromise of bringing the poet to life under the aspect of motherly and editorial service begins to unfold in the mid 1830s: "You know how I shrink from all <u>private</u> detail for the public," she stresses to Maria Gisborne, "but Shelley's letters are beautifully written, & every thing <u>private</u> could be omitted" (9 Feb. 1835, *MSL*, 2:221).

At the same time, however, to name bonds of domestic affection publicly is to signal a private privilege. As Mary Shelley puts this etymologically bound compound under conscious rhetorical control—announcing a private life without specifying its terms—she constructs the special authority of her intimacy. In her role as editor, she converts the irreducible privacy of her inability to write Shelley's "life" into a public discourse of her privilege as his reader. "I abstain from any remark on the occurrences of his private life; except, inasmuch as the passions which they engendered, inspired his poetry. This is not the time to relate the truth. . . . No account of these events has even been given at all approaching reality in their details," she states at the opening of her Preface of 1839 (vii). This contradictory stance, first pointedly concealing "the truth" then complaining of its absence, announces a complicated investment: as editor, Mary Shelley attempts to turn the anguish of her journals and letters into a display of a life and a truth that is her property alone. This discourse begins to develop in the 1830s with the gesture that sends her newly refurbished *Frankenstein* into the world at the close of the "Author's Introduction":

> I have an affection for it, for it was the offspring of happy days, when death and grief were but words which found no true echo in my heart. Its several pages speak of many a walk, many a drive, and many a conversation, when I was not alone; and my companion was one who, in this world, I shall never see more. But this is for myself; my readers have nothing to do with these associations. (xii)

This inscription of a privacy veiled from the reading public will enter Mary Shelley's subsequent editorial discourse in more crucial hints of her privileged status as the poet's truest audience.

Scott's assumption in 1818 that the author of *Frankenstein* was Percy Shelley uncannily predicts this epipsychic self fashioning, for the effect was to compound the Shelleys into one authorial identity.[60] A minor theme throughout Mary Shelley's notes of 1839, in fact, is her advertisement of her own talents as vital to her sympathetic support of Shelley's. Shelley "conceived that I possessed some dramatic talent, and he was always most earnest and energetic in his exhortations that I should cultivate any talent I possessed, to the utmost," she reports in "Note on the Cenci" (*PW*, 2:272). Even if she demurs, the point is there to appreciate, as well as her judgment: "We talked over the arrangement of the scenes together. I . . . triumphed in the discovery of the new talent brought to light from that mine of wealth" (274); "The Fifth Act is a masterpiece. It is the finest thing he ever wrote, and may claim proud comparison not only with any contemporary, but preceding poet" (279). In such narratives, the editor casts herself in the role of the ideal partner that she says the poet created for Laon: "a woman such as he delighted to imagine— full of enthusiasm for the same objects" (1:376).

This shared enthusiasm gets troped throughout the notes in her assimilation of his poetic mythology into her commentary. There is a double performative value. First, she proves her worth as a reader of Shelley by giving him the benefit of his own ideals: " 'Gentle, brave, and generous,' he describes the Poet in Alastor: such he was himself" (*EL*, 1:19). Just as significantly, in speaking this language as a writer herself, she moves into his earthly place, assuming his poetic postures beckoning to the world beyond. Lamenting in the final paragraphs of her 1839 Preface, "He died, and the world shewed no outward sign. . . . He died, and his place among those who knew him intimately, has never been filled up" (xv), she writes herself into the voice of the poet at the end of *Alastor*. Such also is her gesture in the Preface to *Essays, Letters:* "the pang occasioned by his loss can never pass away" (1:19). His mythology becomes the lens through which she reads her loss, a transfer overt in her final commentary, on *Adonais*. At the close of the last and longest of all her narratives in the Notes, about Shelley's death, she initiates what would become a favorite nineteenth-century trope: "—who but will regard as a prophecy the last stanza of the 'Adonais?' "[61]

> The breath, whose might I have invoked in song,
> Descends on me; my spirit's bark is driven,
> Far from the shore, far from the trembling throng,
> Whose sails were never to the tempest given;
> The massy earth and sphered skies are riven!
> I am borne darkly, fearfully, afar;
> Whilst burning through the inmost veil of Heaven,
> The soul of Adonais, like a star,
> Beacons from the abode where the Eternal are.
>
> (*PW*, 4:236)

By quoting this stanza in her note, Mary Shelley joins her voice, in a spectral temporality, to Percy Shelley's. His yearning after Adonais becomes, in the context of her narrative, her yearning after him; she speaks his voice and performs his role, and so, in the rhetoric of her edition, becomes one with him.

The editor's assimilation of her life to the poet's becomes the dominant narrative of her last two notes. These texts adhere little to the previous protocol of detailing the circumstances and inspirations of the poems. What they unfold instead is nearly autobiographical, her recollection of her premonitions of disaster and her enduring grief. "Note on Poems of 1821" opens in this personal mode: "My task becomes inexpressibly painful as the year draws near that which sealed our earthly fate; and each poem and each event it records, has a real or mysterious connexion with the fatal catastrophe." Even as she cannot imagine herself able to repeat her agony "to the public ear" (*PW*, 4:149), this is her occupation and her inspiration. If the death of Shelley was a radical rift in her material existence, the narrative yields an opportunity for spiritual and, just as significantly, textual correspondence with him. Her last text, "Note on Poems Written in 1822," is framed by mutually implicated poems by both Shelleys. At its close, Mary Shelley reads herself into *Adonais;* at its head, she places a revision of a poem she wrote soon after Shelley's death, published some years later, and regarded as one of her best works.[62] Introducing it into her edition integrates it, in effect, into his *Poetical Works,* where it appears untitled and unsigned:

> This morn thy gallant bark
>   Sailed on a sunny sea,
> 'Tis noon, and tempests dark
>   Have wrecked it on the lee.
>   Ah woe! Ah woe!
> By spirits of the deep
> Thou'rt cradled on the billow,
> To thy unwaking sleep.
>
> Thou sleep'st upon the shore
>   Beside the knelling surge,
> And sea-nymphs evermore
>   Shall sadly chant thy dirge.
>   They come! they come,
> The spirits of the deep,
> While near thy sea-weed pillow
> My lonely watch I keep.
>
> From far across the sea
>   I hear a loud lament,
> By echo's voice for thee,
>   From ocean's caverns sent.
>   O list! O list,
> The spirits of the deep;
> They raise a wall of sorrow,
> While I for ever weep.
>
>   (*PW*, 4:225)

In this new text, not only has Mary Shelley polished her poem, tightening its rhythms, but she has also altered both its mythology and its rhetoric in significant ways. In her first version, "spirits" in the third-to-last line and "echo," three lines above, were capitalized personifications, marked as sentient figures of nature, singing the dirge in symphony with her. Deleting these allegorizing capitals, she internalizes what had been external, making the echo seem the effect of her own voice populating the world with a private grief, as if "the spirits of the deep" were primarily forces in the isolated depths of self. This intensification is also the effect of her other crucial revision, her conversion of all third-person pronouns ("He's cradled"; "his unwaking sleep"; "his sea-weed pillow") to second-person addresses. This shift completes the turn of the rhetorical axis away from her readers, who in her first version were also told of this absent "he" of address. As much attention as such readers get now is the exhortation, "O list!"—a sign that they are not hearing what the poet hears. Despite her invitation to better attention, then, the effect is to cast her readers, in Mill's paradigm, as overhearers, witnesses only of their exclusion by a poet who devotes her voice to an eternity of attention to her absent correspondent: "By echo's voice for thee . . . I for ever weep." Yet, as isolating as this inscription is for its author, its gesture is subtly instructive for Percy Shelley's readers, for the figure of the unseen addressee evokes his most fundamental poetics of audience which, as Culler remarks, "display a considerable interest in a pervasive unseen power" (140), an interest, moreover, frequently troped in apostrophe. The editor who addresses an absent poet—in effect, her muse—dramatizes and powerfully recapitulates this generative situation for the reader of Shelley's verse.

The symbolic gesture drawing this circuit of communication is replayed less melodramatically, but no less significantly, in the formal contours of the last edition that Mary Shelley produced, Shelley's *Essays, Letters*. Its first piece is a republication of their collaboration, *History of a Six Weeks' Tour*, which the editor claims to offer merely for the sake of "some of the most beautiful descriptions ever written" (Preface, 1:15). Yet its presence also reminds readers of the life the Shelleys shared in its high romantic phase, their elopement to the Continent. Significantly, Mary Shelley now makes this collaboration part of the canon.[63] The implicit story, a public display of privileged intimacy, persists in a slight textual drama concluding this last edition. She ends volume 2, an assemblage of fifty-six letters, with one from Shelley to her, beginning "My dearest Mary." Although it is full of depressing news about Hunt and Byron, it ends with his promise to write to her, "my best Mary," again by the next post, and signs off

> Ever, dearest Mary,
>   Yours affectionately,
>   S.

Preserving this signature of affection as essential to the record of Percy Shelley's works, Mary Shelley inscribes herself into his story. Quietly but significantly, she summons editorial privilege to define her status, for herself and for the world, as Shelley's enabling and loving reader—his best, and last, audience while he lived. Resurrecting him, she also finds a way to resurrect herself, both as private correspondent and as public authority.

Notes

For valuable advice on this essay, I thank my own sympathetic editors: first and foremost, Ronald Levao, but also Peter Manning, William Galperin, Esther Schor, and Neil Fraistat.

1. Mrs. [Mary] Shelley, ed., *The Poetical Works of Percy Bysshe Shelley,* 4 vols. (London: Edward Moxon, 1839), 1: vii. Quotations of her notes and prefaces, and of his poems, notes, and prefaces, follow this edition, hereafter cited parenthetically and as *PW,* where necessary.

2. Jonathan Culler, *The Pursuit of Signs: Semiotics, Literature, Deconstruction* (Ithaca: Cornell University Press, 1981), 38; hereafter cited parenthetically.

3. Mary Wollstonecraft Shelley, *The Letters of Mary Wollstonecraft Shelley,* 3 vols., ed. Betty T. Bennett (Baltimore: Johns Hopkins University Press, 1980–1988), 1:430; hereafter *MSL,* cited parenthetically.

4. In this class, too, are *Peter Bell* and *Swellfoot the Tyrant,* both described in the second edition of 1839 as expressions of "Shelley's peculiar views"—the former a satire on the laureate-apparent, the latter a satire on a relative of the present queen. Both were withheld from the first edition of 1839 but published, with slightly defensive notes, in the second. See Mrs. [Mary] Shelley, ed., *The Poetical Works of Percy Bysshe Shelley,* rev. 2nd ed. (London: Edward Moxon, 1839, d. "1840"), rpt. *The Complete Works of Percy Bysshe Shelley* in *The Complete Poems of Keats and Shelley with Mrs. Shelley's Notes* (New York: Random House, n.d.), 393, 416; hereafter *CW,* cited parenthetically. Her adjective *peculiar* is carefully nuanced. In the 1830s, its senses ranged from "individually characteristic, distinctive," to "strange, odd, eccentric," and she was likely evoking all these shades, perhaps with a slight tilt to the latter, in light of the "Peculiars," a religious sect founded in 1838 and "most numerous around London" (*Oxford English Dictionary* [1971], P: 602).

5. See, for example, William A. Walling, *Mary Shelley* (New York: Twayne, 1972), 141. To Shaw, *Queen Mab* anticipated "modern" socialist analyses; quoted in Kenneth Neill Cameron, *The Young Shelley: Genesis of a Radical* (New York: Macmillan, 1950), 241. The paragraph in *CW* that comprises the "Note" from which I quote was embedded in a considerably longer note in the first edition of 1839; Shelley subsequently distributed its earlier and later paragraphs to other notes, isolating this emphatic paragraph.

6. Mrs. [Mary] Shelley, ed., *Essays, Letters from Abroad, Translations and Fragments by Percy Bysshe Shelley,* 2 vols. (London: Edward Moxon, 1840 [1839]); quotation follows the American edition (Philadelphia: Lea and Blanchard, 1840; rpt. 1841), 1:19; hereafter, *EL,* cited parenthetically.

7. Percy Bysshe Shelley, *The Letters of Percy Bysshe Shelley,* 2 vols., ed. Frederick L. Jones (Oxford: Clarendon Press, 1964), 2:190, hereafter *PSL,* cited parenthetically.

8. E. J. Trelawny, *Recollections of the Last Days of Shelley and Byron* (Boston: Ticknor and Fields, 1858), 80.

9. Of the two poems he regarded as his most perfect, he tells his publisher that he expects neither *Prometheus Unbound* nor *Adonais,* which "is little adapted to popularity," to "sell"; see letters of March 6, 1820 and June 11, 1821 (*PSL,* 2:200, 2:299). The prediction was accurate. Save some piracies of *Queen Mab,* his poems came out in small editions, and even these moved slowly; see Ollier's report, *MSL,* 1:401n. That only *The Cenci* had a second edition in Shelley's lifetime (James E. Barcus, ed., *Shelley: The Critical Heritage* [London: Routledge and Kegan Paul, 1975], 3–4) credits Timothy Webb's surmise of some defensiveness in Shelley's pronouncements to publishers and friends (*Shelley: A Voice Not Understood* [Atlantic Highlands: Humanities Press International, 1977], 92). Elise Gold also sees "self-defensive" posturing, arguing that Shelley was "more often than not . . . resigned . . . to finding few qualified readers, using his prefaces as screening devices not only for defining but for reducing his readership" ("Touring the Inventions: Shelley's Prefatory Writing," *Keats-Shelley Journal* 36 [1987]: 73–74). My thinking about Shelley's construction of his audience has been assisted by Webb and Gold, by Stephen Behrendt's detailed study (*Shelley and His Audiences* [Lincoln: University of Nebraska Press, 1989]), especially of Shelley's wavering between a sense of political mission and his concentration on "a dis-

tinctly elite audience" toward the end of his career, and by William Keach's consideration of the issue of the *sunetoi*—a term Shelley sometimes used for this elite (*PSL*,
2:363). Keach explores this notion in relation to the political projections of certain of
Shelley's works, his negotiations with his publishers, and his reactions to radical-press,
cheap-edition piracies ("Knowing Readers: Shelley and the 'Sunetoi' " [Lecture,
MLA Convention, 1985]).

10. Shelley's gesture gained a material result in the fact that *Julian and Maddalo*
was not published in his lifetime; it reached the world for the first time as the first
poem in *Posthumous Poems of Percy Bysshe Shelley,* ed. Mary W. Shelley (London:
John and Henry L. Hunt, 1824).

11. The essay was composed in 1821; by the time it was published in 1839, this
view of a poet's audience had already received influential articulation from J. S. Mill
("What is Poetry?," *Monthly Repository* [Jan. 1833]) "Eloquence is *heard,* poetry is
*over*heard. Eloquence supposes an audience; the peculiarity of poetry appears to us to
lie in the poet's utter unconsciousness of a listener. Poetry is feeling confessing itself to
itself" (*John Stuart Mill: Autobiography and Other Writings,* ed. Jack Stillinger [Bos-
ton: Houghton Mifflin, 1969], 195).

12. Some of Shelley's foreign-language inscriptions are simply dropped in the first
edition of 1839; all are restored in the second. These include the French, Latin, and
Greek epigraphs for *Queen Mab* (*CW*, 804) and the foreign languages in his notes to
the poem; by contrast, popularizing editions of *Queen Mab* drop the epigraphs and
translate all the foreign languages in the notes. For a late example, see *Queen Mab, A
Philosophical Poem. With Notes* (London: James Watson, 1841).

13. See Francesco Petrarch, *Petrarch's Lyrical Poems: The "Rime Sparse" and
Other Lyrics,* trans. Robert Durling (Cambridge: Harvard University Press, 1976).
The text is *Rime* 297 ("if I am slow to follow, perhaps it will happen that I shall
consecrate her lovely noble name with this weary pen"). Thanks to David Quint for
helping me to identify this verse.

14. The verses are from *Rime* 306 ("Him I do not find, but his sacred footsteps /
All turned to the highest road / I see, far from the avernian and stigian lakes"; Durling
notes that Lake Avernus, near Naples, was thought to lead to the underworld) and 215
("In noble blood, humble and quiet life, / And in lofty intellect a pure heart; / The fruit
of age in a youthful flower / And in aspect thoughtful, [in] soul light"). The sustaining
force of this Petrarchian mythology is suggested by the frequency with which Shelley
summons it. She writes to someone who had admired *Posthumous Poems,* "I wish that
the preface had [in the absence of Hunt's notice] been longer and better, but

> Trovaimi all' opra via piu lento a frale
> D'un picciol ramo cui gran fascio piega
> Adunque
> Beati gli occhi che lo vider vivo."

She is quoting from *Rime* 307 ("I found myself much more slow and frail in my work /
Than a little branch bent by a great burden") and 309 ("Therefore / Blessed are the
eyes that saw him alive"), once again masculinizing the pronoun (*MSL,* 1:430).

15. Instead of poetic values, Shelley's reputation fastened on "biography, ethics
and politics," remarks Webb (op. cit., 4). A generous compendium of contemporary
reviews and obituary notices is assembled by Newman Ivey White, *The Unextinguished
Hearth, Shelley and His Contemporary Critics* (Durham: Duke University Press,
1966); hereafter *UH.* Some of these, as well as subsequent items, are summarized in

Karsten Engelberg's *The Making of the Shelley Myth: An Annotated Bibliography of Criticism of Percy Bysshe Shelley, 1822–1860* (London: Mansell, 1988; Westport: Meckler, 1988).

16. "Licentious Productions in High Life," *The Investigator, or Quarterly Magazine* 5, 10 (Oct. 1822); except in *UH*, 98–104.

17. William Hazlitt, rev. of *Posthumous Poems*, in *The Edinburgh Review* 40 (July 1824), 494, 452; hereafter cited parenthetically.

18. *The Honeycomb* registered similar complaints, suggesting that Shelley "should have written intelligibly to common understandings if he wished to be popular" (12 Aug. 1820; Barcus, *Critical Heritage*, 272–73). Even as *London Magazine* warmed to Shelley—after ruing his scorn of religion and morality in an earlier review (April, 1820), it now appreciated the poet's idealism, his effort to restore religion to primitive purity, and his "benevolence toward mankind"—it could not overcome this difficulty. The praise was prefaced with a judgment that, "all the combined attractions of mind and verse" notwithstanding, "Mr. Shelley can never become a popular poet . . . he is too visionary for the intellect of the generality of his readers" (Feb. 1821, *UH*, 262).

19. " Shelley's Posthumous Poems," *Knight's Quarterly Magazine* 3 (Aug. 1824), 187; hereafter cited parenthetically. Constable's *Edinburgh* is quoted in Theodore Redpath, *The Young Romantics and Critical Opinion, 1807–1824: Poetry of Byron, Shelley, and Keats as seen by their contemporary critics* (New York: St. Martin's Press, 1973), 396.

20. Next in line of attention was *The Cenci*. In the sample of obituary notices that White reprints, *Queen Mab* is cited in nine, *The Cenci* in five; see *UH*, 321–28. Other poems mentioned, much less frequently, are *Prometheus Unbound, Alastor, Hellas, Rosalind and Helen, The Revolt of Islam*, and *Adonais*.

21. *Examiner* 758 (4 Aug.), 489. *John Bull*'s first notice appears on August 12; its follow-up of August 19 was a reaction to the high praise of Shelley in *The Morning Chronicle* of August 12. On August 18, *The British Luminary* quoted the entire first notice, offering it as "a pure specimen of the cant which [*John Bull*] affects to despise." For the texts, see *UH*, 321–25. On the bullish side, *The Courier* virtually hooted that "Shelley, the writer of some infidel poetry, for the republication of which a man of the name of Clarke either has been, or is about to be, prosecuted, is dead"; somewhat more decorously, *Gentleman's Magazine* joined the chorus in September, noting that "Mr. Shelley is unfortunately too well known for his infamous novels and poems. He openly professed himself an atheist." See the obituary notices in *The Courier* 9616 (5 Aug.), 3, and *The Gentleman's Magazine*, Part 2, 92 (Sept.), 283.

22. Leigh Hunt, "Mr. Shelley, With a Criticism on His Genius, and Mr. Trelawney's [*sic*] Narrative of His Loss at Sea," *Lord Byron and Some of His Contemporaries: With Recollections of the Author's Life, and of His Visit to Italy* (London: Henry Colburn, 1828; Philadelphia: Carey, Lea & Carey, 1828), 155; hereafter cited parenthetically.

23. See Newman Ivey White, *Shelley*, 2 vols. (New York: Knopf, 1940), 2:395. Although only seventy copies of the first edition of 250 of *Queen Mab* had been disposed of by 1822, when Carlile bought up the remainder, the piracies made it the most widely read, widely sold, and widely reviewed of Shelley's works. At least nine such editions appeared between 1822 and 1841 (*UH*, 45; *Shelley*, 2:397), Carlile himself publishing four between 1823 and 1826. It was this poem that, "for at least twenty years after his death," remarks White, was "the largest single factor in the vitality of Shelley's reputation" (*Shelley*, 2:406–8).

24. G. H. L[ewes]., rev. of *Poetical Works of Percy Bysshe Shelley* (1839); *Letters*

and Essays from Abroad (1840); a German translation of *The Cenci* (1838); and an Italian translation of *Adonais* (1830), in *The Westminster Review* 35 (1841): 303–44; hereafter cited parenthetically. I quote from 329.

25. William Michael Rossetti, ed., *The Poetical Works of Percy Bysshe Shelley; Including Various Additional Pieces from Ms. and Other Sources. The Text Carefully Revised, With Notes and a Memoir*, 2 vols. (London: E. Moxon & Son, 1870). Rossetti focused on "three principal topics": "the Existence or Nature of a Deity"; "the Immortality of the Soul"; and "Political Institutions. " For the first, he urges regard for the atheism of *Queen Mab* as juvenile and of other such pronouncements as a defiance of established religion, not of the Deity; Shelley was "pantheistic" rather than atheistic. For the second, he cites the discourse of the "One Mind" to argue for Shelley's belief in a general, if not individual, immortality. For the last, he insists that Shelley was an intense "lover of freedom" and cherished the ideal of "the democratic state." Rossetti concedes Shelley's indifference to the British constitution, his contempt of some of its rulers, and his occasional fancy that the oppressed were entitled to violent retaliation; but he echoes Mary Shelley's notes in representing him as one who "looked on political freedom as the direct agent to effect the happiness of mankind"; "He loved and respected the people" (1: clxv–clxxiii); hereafter cited parenthetically.

26. Matthew Arnold, "Shelley" (rev. of Dowden's *Life of Percy Bysshe Shelley* in *Nineteenth Century* [Jan. 1888]), *The Complete Prose Works of Matthew Arnold*, 11 vols., ed. R. H. Super (Ann Arbor: University of Michigan Press, 1960–77), 11:306; hereafter cited parenthetically.

27. Mary Wollstonecraft Shelley, *Frankenstein: Or the Modern Prometheus*, (London: Henry Colburn and Richard Bentley, 1831; New York: New American Library, 1965), x; hereafter cited parenthetically.

28. In a different line of argument, Mary Favret's essay in this volume briefly but suggestively engages some of these affinities, finding the editor trying to broaden Shelley's readership by evolving an ironic perspective on some of his mythology. P. D. Fleck summons *Frankenstein* in a similar vein, discovering the critique of Promethean Romanticism embodied in Victor to be perpetuated in "Mary's portrait of Shelley" in the notes ("Mary Shelley's Notes to Shelley's Poems and *Frankenstein*," *Studies in Romanticism* 6 [1967]: 226–54); I quote from 252.

29. The reprinting of the 1824 Preface in the 1839 editions (in the first, it follows the last note in vol. 4; in the second, it follows the Preface and Postscript [vii–ix]) itself constitutes a significant textual feature, making Mary Shelley's earliest memorial part of the accreting reception of Shelley's poems. Quotations follow the text in *PW* (4:237–40).

30. Paula R. Feldman, "Biography and the Literary Executor: The Case of Mary Shelley," *The Papers of the Bibliographical Society of America* 72 (1978), 287; hereafter cited parenthetically.

31. Her representation of these manuscripts is confirmed by both Trelawny (op. cit., 78) and Richard Garnett, who brought to light new pieces of composition in *Relics of Shelley* (London: Edward Moxon, 1862), xi–xii.

32. Marlon B. Ross, *The Contours of Masculine Desire: Romanticism and the Rise of Women's Poetry* (New York: Oxford University Press, 1989), 4. Jack Stillinger (*Multiple Authorship and the Myth of Solitary Genius* [New York: Oxford University Press, 1991]), in fact, lists "Mary Shelley's editing of her husband's posthumous poems" as an example of multiple authorship (206).

33. In addition to the major works titled or subtitled "Fragment"—*Prince Athanase. A Fragment; The Daemon of the World. A Fragment; Fragments of an*

Unfinished Drama—and the unfinished *Triumph of Life* ("a glorious fragment," a later editor, Harry Buxton Forman, calls it), the second edition of 1839 assembles eighty-five pieces titled in the table of contents as "Fragment" or denoting a similar mode: "Cancelled Stanza," "Cancelled Passage," "Original Draft," "Variation," "Another Version." For Forman's remark, see *The Poetical Works of Percy Bysshe Shelley,* 4 vols. (London: Reeves and Turner, 1876), 3:226; hereafter cited parenthetically.

34. If Emily Sunstein perhaps too enthusiastically declares that these editions "established" Shelley, who otherwise "might have remained little known" (*Mary Shelley: Romance and Reality* [Boston: Little, Brown, 1989], 345, 5), the fact is that Shelley's "reputation as one of England's half-dozen greatest poets," as White writes, "can hardly be regarded as general or reasonably secure before 1839–40"—before, that is, Mary Shelley's editions "received wide-spread and practically unanimous recognition" (*Shelley,* 2:394); Lewes's essay in *The Westminster Review* (1841) is indicative. Although some of Shelley's editing falls short by modern standards, and like most nineteenth-century efforts, has been superseded, her editions were important. Rossetti, the next major editor of Shelley, relies on them to construct his edition (see Donald H. Reiman, *Romantic Texts and Contexts* [Columbia: University of Missouri Press, 1987], 60), in which he cites her authority and reprints her prefaces and notes. Often reprinted in the nineteenth century, her notes were virtually canonized by Thomas Hutchinson in the Oxford edition of 1904, itself reprinted several times in this century (*Shelley: Poetical Works* [Oxford: Oxford University Press, 1904, 1905, 1934, 1965, 1971]); when not so privileged, the notes were quoted frequently and generously by other editors, including George Edward Woodberry for the Cambridge Edition (*The Complete Poetical Works of Percy Bysshe Shelley* [1892; Boston: Houghton Mifflin, 1901]).

Mary Shelley's appreciative-biographical principles of editing were rejected by Forman, however. A textual scholar, he was determined to remedy the "very corrupt" posthumous editions, convinced that "more service was to be done to the cause in this way" than by "unscrupulous remodeling of the text and a free addition of expository or explanatory notes." Although he does not name Shelley, the charge is transparent—and extends to Rossetti as well. Forman also rejects her effort to devise a canon, opting for a more rigorous historicism that presents the poet's "various volumes in chronological order, with the contents arranged as issued in his lifetime," then the posthumous publications and all the "distinctly immature work" (including *Queen Mab*—"the climax of the juvenile period") in a "separate chronology." When he eventually cites "Mrs. Shelley's edition" in his Preface, he does so merely with nothing to say "derogatory to the admiration and gratitude which we all owe her" and suggests that, given both the less developed state of editorial scholarship in previous decades and her intimacy with her subject, it is "not surprising that—she should have seen no need for studying minutely the details of a series of texts" (1: xv, xviii, xix–xx, xxxiii).

Even so, that his textual notes retain a dialogue with her readings confirms some of their value, despite methodological flaws. Although Charles H. Taylor, Jr. details the corruptions introduced by her reliance on error-ridden base texts, he credits her overall accomplishment, as does Irving Massey; see Taylor, *The Early Collected Editions of Shelley's Poems: A Study in the History and Transmission of the Printed Text* (New Haven: Yale University Press, 1958) and "The Errata Leaf to Shelley's Editions," *PMLA* 70 (1955): 408–16; Massey, "The First Edition of *Shelley's Poetical Works* (1839): Some Manuscript Sources," *Keats-Shelley Journal* 16 (1967): 29–38. For a more stringent criticism, see Joseph Raben, "Shelley's 'Invocation to Misery': An Expanded Text," *Journal of English and German Philology* 65 (1966): 65–74. Like

Forman, Donald Reiman (the best informed modern editor of Shelley) refers to Mary Shelley's editions for "authoritative variant readings," ascribing her lapses to an age of editing when the aim was not to establish accurate texts and scholarly apparatus but to present a full record of a writer's career for the general reader (op. cit., 35, 91). Other such productions, Reiman notes, include John Murray's edition of Byron, H. N. Coleridge's and Sara Coleridge's editions of Samuel Taylor Coleridge, R. M. Milnes' *Life, Letters, and Literary Remains of John Keats,* and Moxon's and Macmillan's midcentury editions of Wordsworth's *Prelude* and *Poetical Works.*

35. The first section of *Posthumous Poems* introduced *Julian and Maddalo, The Witch of Atlas,, Letter to [Maria Gisborne], The Triumph of Life, Fragments from an Unfinished Drama, Prince Athanase, Ode to Naples, Marianne's Dream,* and *Alastor.* This last and *Mont Blanc* were reissued ("the difficulty" of obtaining them justifying "republication," Shelley explains [ix]); all these poems were distinguished with separate title-pages. In the first edition of 1839, the "principals" were *Queen Mab* (bowdlerized), *Alastor, The Revolt of Islam, Prometheus Unbound, The Cenci,* and *Hellas.* In the second edition, also in chronological order, they were *Alastor, The Dæmon of the World* (an extract from *Queen Mab* previously published with *Alastor*), *The Revolt of Islam, Prince Athanase, Rosalind and Helen, Julian and Maddalo, Prometheus Unbound, The Cenci, The Mask of Anarchy, Peter Bell the Third, Swellfoot the Tyrant, Charles the First, Letter to Maria Gisborne, The Witch of Atlas* (now with the dedicatory stanzas to Mary), *Epipsychidion, Adonais, Hellas, Fragments of an Unfinished Drama,* and *The Triumph of Life.* Forman regretted the intermediate demotion of *Letter to Maria Gisborne,* thinking it "second in importance" in the 1824 *Poems* only to *Julian and Maddalo* (3:226).

36. Sylva Norman, "Mary Wollstonecraft Shelley," *Romantic Rebels: Essays on Shelley and His Circle,* ed. Kenneth Neill Cameron (Cambridge: Harvard University Press, 1973), 82–83.

37. The poem was often cited in the journals of British working-class radicalism, and within twenty years of its initial publication, at least fourteen "separate editions were issued by piratical radical publishers" (*Shelley,* 2:304). Cheaply available, it became "part of socialist culture" and "a weapon in the battle of ideas"; see Michael Henry Scrivener, *Radical Shelley: The Philosophical Anarchism and Utopian Thought of Percy Bysshe Shelley* (Princeton: Princeton University Press, 1982), 67. J. Watson was still selling a one-shilling edition in 1841 in its series of "Cheap and Valuable Works," a list also featuring works by Thomas Paine and Robert Owen, Byron's *Cain,* Volney's *Law of Nature, William Tell,* and volumes with such intriguing titles as *Socialism Made Easy* and *The Right and Expediency of Universal Suffrage* (see the back leaves, after p. 112).

38. The front and back leaves of Mary Shelley's first 1839 edition advertised, and thus placed it in the respectable company of, other "Just Published" works on Moxon's list, including the complete works of Charles Lamb; a six-volume *Poetical Works of William Wordsworth,* as a well as *The Sonnets of William Wordsworth* in one volume; *The Poetical Works of Samuel Rogers, Esq.,* along with one-volume pocket editions; *The Poetical Works of Thomas Campbell; The Poems of R. M. Milnes, Esq. M. P.; Letters, Conversations and Recollections of Samuel Taylor Coleridge;* various works by I. Disraeli, Esq.; as well as works by other MPs (Sergeant Talfourd), baronets (Henry Bunbury, John Hammer), reverends (R. C. Trench), esquires (Henry Taylor, John Sheridan Knowles, John Kenyon), and lords (Leigh). Moxon's establishment credentials, Mary Shelley may have thought, would immunize him against prosecution for publishing all of *Queen Mab.* Although she initially resisted doing so for fear of

harming sales, by the second edition of 1839, she tells Moxon, "I think it would improve the sale" (4 March 1839, *MSL,* 3:311).

39. The first edition deleted IV:203–20 ("Then grave and hoary-headed hypocrites . . . the mockeries of earthly power"), all of VI:53 *ff,* and VII—the denunciation of Kingcraft and Priestcraft so admired by the radicals. Also dropped were the dedicatory verses to Harriet, a potential reminder of the scandalous elopement and divorce. Mary Shelley believed that Percy would have wanted these omitted, recalling his pleasure on hearing (erroneously) thus of Clarke's 1821 piracy; see the note in *MSL,* 2:310. Yet because the piracies had already circulated the poem unexpurgated, her bowdlerization was not only obvious but drew attention to what was cut. Stung by negative reviews on this issue and, more personally, by the wrath of Trelawny and Hogg, she persuaded Moxon to print it all in the second edition of 1839, along with a Postscript to the Preface announcing the "restored" passages and, in consequence, "a complete collection of my husband's poetical works" (*CW,* vi). Her new note (which, as before, stressed the poem's youthfulness and concluded with Shelley's letter of protest) called attention to the emendation and her earlier conflict: "In the former edition certain portions were left out, as shocking the general reader from the violence of their attack on religion. I myself had a painful feeling that such erasures might be looked upon as a mark of disrespect towards the author, and am glad to have the opportunity of restoring them" (850). Moxon's instincts were more prudent than prudish: other publishers had suffered legal reprisal, and a judgment of blasphemy could cost him his copyright; see *MSL,* 2:302 n. 3. When the second edition appeared, in fact, some radical publishers forced his indictment and trial for blasphemous libel, "and by the threat of compelling equal justice helped abolish" the repressive legislation (he was convicted but not punished); see White, *Shelley,* 2:167, 407–8.

40. 6 Oct. 1823, *MSL,* 2:326, her emphasis. For the early plans to publish this essay, see her letters to Leigh Hunt (1:384, 393). Despite her feeling that, as she says to him in 1839, "it is my duty to publish everything of Shelley," she is concerned for reception (6 Oct., 2:326); two days later, she tells Moxon to cancel the essay, explaining, "I think it would excite a violent party spirit against the volumes which otherwise I believe will prove generally attractive" (327). The poem to which I allude is *Oedipus Tyrannus, or Swellfoot the Tyrant,* a satire on the trial of Queen Caroline, which, Shelley's note reports, was "published anonymously; but stifled at the very dawn of its existence by the Society for the Suppression of Vice, who threatened to prosecute it, if not immediately withdrawn" (*CW,* 415).

41. Nancy J. Vickers, "Diana Described: Scattered Women and Scattered Rhyme," in Elizabeth Abel, ed., *Writing and Sexual Difference* (University of Chicago Press, 1982), 106–7.

42. Mary Poovey, *The Proper Lady and the Woman Writer: Ideology as Style in the Works of Mary Wollstonecraft, Mary Shelley, and Jane Austen* (Chicago: University of Chicago Press, 1984), 141; hereafter cited parenthetically.

43. *MSL,* 2:300. Moxon initially proposed a fee of £200 for an edition of 2,000; offering to sell her copyright, Shelley asked for £500, a sum to which Moxon agreed and paid in installments as each of the four volumes of the first edition appeared in the early months of 1839 (see her letters to him: 2:300, 311, 313, 316).

44. 3–4 August 1839, *MSL,* 2:298–99. Not only were there several unauthorized editions of poems (thirteen between 1826 and 1835) but the scandals had been retailed by Thomas Medwin in a series of publications throughout the 1820s and early 1830s (see White, *Shelley* 2:397, and Feldman, op. cit., 291). Hunt's *Lord Byron* had also provoked attention to the scandals by its patent sanitizing—the claim, for instance,

that Percy and Harriet Shelley "separated by mutual consent" and that he was devastated by the news of her suicide (163). Hunt "has slurr[ed] over the real truth," in effect "writ[ing] fiction," Mary Shelley herself complains to Trelawny (*MSL,* 2:94).

45. See, for instance, the reviews of *Posthumous Poems* in *The News of Literature and Fashion,* which declared that Shelley's poetry owed "more to the power of nature than the teaching of other men" (vol. 1:2 [19 June 1824], 29; Engelberg, 138); and in *The New Monthly,* which admired the poems' "faithful and glowing pictures" of nature (N. S. vol. 12, 43 [July 1824]: 316–17).

46. Constable's *Edinburgh* welcomed this "memorial of a mind singularly gifted with poetical talent, however it may have been obscured, and to many, we doubt not, absolutely eclipsed by its unhappy union with much that is revolting in principle and morality" (Redpath, 396). *The Literary Gazette and Journal of the Belles Lettres, Arts, Sciences, &c.,* overcoming an inclination to retreat from its liberal stances when faced with radicalism and atheism, attempted a truce in the politics of the earlier reviews with a nearly metaphysical conceit: the poems are "a blend of beauty and blasphemy, trash by the side of some fine poetry" (391 [17 July 1824]: 451–52). This compound also dominates the opening paragraph of Hazlitt's review: "Mr. Shelley's style is to poetry what astrology is to natural science—a passionate dream, a straining after impossibilities, a record of fond conjectures, a confused embodying of vague abstractions,—a fever of the soul, thirsting and craving after what it cannot have, indulging its love of power and novelty at the expense of truth and nature, associating ideas by contraries, and wasting great powers by their application to unattainable objects" (494).

47. *Medwin's "Conversations of Lord Byron"* (1824), ed. Ernest J. Lovell, Jr. (Princeton: Princeton University Press, 1966), 248; hereafter cited parenthetically.

48. Quoted in Sylva Norman, *Flight of the Skylark: The Development of Shelley's Reputation* (Norman: Oklahoma University Press, 1954), 53.

49. *The National: A Library for the People* 6 (9 Feb. 1839): 76–78.

50. *The Keepsake for* MDCCCXXIX, ed. Frederic Mansel Reynolds (London: Reynolds, 1829); the essay appears on 47–49. The poems were "Summer and Winter," "The Tower of Famine," and "The Aziola" (160–62). The press on the left warmed especially to *On Love. London Magazine* quoted it approvingly ("The Editor's Room: No. IX"; 3rd ser. 2, 9 [Dec. 1828], 696–97; Engelberg, 171); *The Monthly Review* called it an "exquisite morceau," a "rhapsody" (N.S. 3, 10 [1829]: 95); *The Athenæum* declared that it demanded atonement from those who have "wronged [Shelley's] memory" with the brand of "infidel," for it revealed him as "one of the most earnest, affectionate, truth-seeking, humble, and self-denying men that ever lived on this earth" (55 [Nov. 12, 1828], 864). Thanks to Peter Manning for telling me about the last two reviews. This middle-class, female-oriented, gift-book marketing of Shelley was plumped by *The Beauties of Percy Bysshe Shelley, Consisting of Miscellaneous Selections from His Poetical Works: The Entire Poems of Adonais and Alastor, and a Revised Edition of Queen Mab Free from All the Objectionable Passages,* ed. C. Roscoe (London: Stephen Hunt, 1830)—a piracy that enjoyed four editions between 1830 and 1836 (see Taylor, *Early Collected Editions,* 94–95, and Engelberg, 180). The polite freedom from objectionable passages was appreciated by *The Mirror of Literature, Amusement, and Instruction* ("Notes of a Reader: Beauties of Shelley," vol. 15 422 [3 Apr. 1830]: 231; Engelberg, 181); and *The Athenæum* praised its biographical memoir for confirming an image of Shelley as an idealist charmed by bad ideas (128 [10 Apr. 1830]: 218). Further to the left, and probably unbeknownst to middle-class sentimentalists, *The New Moral World: Or Gazette of the Universal Community Society of Rational Reli-*

gionists praised and reprinted "On Love" for exemplifying socialist doctrinne ("Shelley on Love," 3rd ser. 3, 15 [25 Sept. 1841]: 99).

51. White, *Shelley,* 2:415.

52. *The Monthly Chronicle* 3 (Apr. 1839): 340–48; its review of *Essays, Letters* praised the "moral grandeur" of Shelley's prose (5 [Feb. 1840]: 179–82). See also Engelberg's summary of the reviews (58 nn. 48, 49); "After 1830," he remarks, "an increasing number of critics refrained from drawing the conclusion that Shelley was a thoroughly immoral man and poet" and were inclined to speak of him "as a benevolent and unselfish man."

53. [Walter Scott], "Remarks on Frankenstein, or the Modern Prometheus; A Novel," *Blackwood's Edinburgh Magazine* 12 (March 1818), 619–620.

54. This work—in full-dress title, *History of a Six Weeks' Tour Through a Part of France, Switzerland, Germany, and Holland; With Letters, Descriptive of a Sail Round the Lake of Geneva, and of the Glaciers of Chamouni*—was first published in 1817 (in London by T. Hookham and the Olliers); it contained a journal to which they both contributed and four descriptive letters (two by each), as well as *Mont Blanc*.

55. She was stung by the reviews in *The Examiner* (1618 [3 Feb. 1839]: 69–70, and 1634 [26 May 1839]: 323–24; rpt. in *UH,* 321) and *The Spectator* (12, 252 [26 Jan. 1839]: 88–89, and 598 [14 Dec. 1839]: 1186–87)–the former calling her notes affected, "cold and laboured," failing to convey any sympathy for the vision of Shelley's poetry; the latter accusing her of partiality, and then of crass trading on Shelley's name, by publishing everything without discrimination, "the circumstance of her taste harmonizing with the weakest and most defective parts of his mind." *Table Talker, or Brief Essays on Society and Literature* (2 vols. [London, 1840], 2:274–79; summarized by Engelberg, 269), complained of overkill (an infatuated editorial enthusiasm rendered the collection of essays incoherent), while *The Athenæum* (600 [27 Apr. 1939]: 313) carped of her having been too selective when a complete record was due and not informative enough about Shelley's intellectual development; the letters, moreover, should not have been issued separately from the poems (it was more appreciative of the second edition and *Essays*). *The Cambridge University Magazine* (1, 1 [March 1839]: 78–79) valued the sanitized *Mab,* while *The Monthly Review* regretted its "broken or imperfect representation" as well as the notes' failure to illuminate his intellectual life (N. S. 1, 3 [March 1839]: 445–48). For a fuller account of these and related documents, see Norman, *Flight,* 146; Bennett in *MSL,* 2:333; and Engelberg, 248–77.

56. Mary Shelley, *Mary Shelley's Journal,* ed. Frederick L. Jones (Norman: University of Oklahoma Press, 1947), 12 Feb. 1839, 206–7; hereafter *MSJ,* cited parenthetically.

57. Feldman, op. cit., 296–97.

58. The remark, by Eliza Rennie, is quoted by Poovey (op. cit., 171). Walling surmises that in the years immediately following Shelley's death, his widow felt "two responsibilities which, in her psychological reaction to them, far transcended any literary ambitions of her own: the vindication and enlargement of her husband's memory; and the care, maintenance, and advancement of her infant son" (op. cit., 15). Poovey sees Shelley as more habitually conflicted: "On the one hand, she repeatedly bowed to the conventional prejudice against aggressive women by apologizing for or punishing her self-assertion; she claimed that her writing was always undertaken to please or profit someone else [and] she dreaded exposing her name or personal feelings to public scrutiny. . . . On the other hand, both in her numerous comments about her profession and by her ongoing literary activity, Mary Shelley demonstrated that

imaginative self-expression was for her an important vehicle for proving her worth and, in that sense for defining herself" (115). It is clear that editing Shelley would satisfy both these impulses as well as those Walling discusses.

59. For a brief account of the reception of these *Memoirs,* see R. M. Janes, "On the Reception of Mary Wollstonecraft's *A Vindication of the Rights of Woman,*" *Journal of the History of Ideas* 39 (1978); rpt. Carol H. Poston, ed., *A Vindication of the Rights of Woman,* 2nd ed. (New York: Norton, 1988), especially 302–4.

60. This may have been the general assumption until the second edition. *The Keepsake for 1829,* for instance, cites in its "List of Contributors," "The Authors of Frankenstein" (op. cit., 15).

61. Although Mary Shelley was preceded in this reading by reviews of *Adonais* in *The Literary Register* and *Fraser's,* it is clear from her letters that her own sense of this prophecy is original. Engelberg (64 n. 6) lists a bibliography of comments on *Adonais* in these terms following the publication of her 1839 notes.

62. The earlier version, titled "A Dirge," appeared in *Keepsake for 1831* (85). The syntax in which Shelley reports her esteem of this poem as "the best thing I ever wrote in the Keepsake" (*MSL,* 2:246) is ambiguous: this is either a summary evaluation with an incidental location, or a specific evaluation of her *Keepsake* publications. She copies the *Keepsake* version in a letter to Maria Gisborne (2:247–48).

63. It also represents, once again, Mary Shelley's status as companionable author: its opening pages refer to its characters as "the author, with her husband and friend" (*EL,* 2:11). She took personal as well as editorial pride in this republication. Hoping to convince Moxon to publish a journal of her tour of Italy in the early 1840s, she tells him that "my 6 weeks tour brought me many compliments" (*MSL,* 3:96). As for the effect of *Essays, Letters* in establishing her place in Percy Shelley's affections, *The Monthly Chronicle* reviewer thought that this was one of the things that the volume confirmed (5 [Feb. 1840]: 179–82; Engelberg, 266).

Reading Mary Shelley's
Journals: Romantic Subjectivity
and Feminist Criticism

Mary Jean Corbett

"For the master's tools will never dismantle the master's house": Audre Lorde's classic cautionary to white middle-class feminists should continue to have a particular resonance for all those working to "dismantle the master's house."[1] Even as we have embarked on building new houses, the tools we have used, the paradigms we have taken over from masculinist discourse, are not themselves innocent. Critical analysis has exposed the racist, sexist, and heterosexist logic of what once must have seemed the product of a process as "natural" as natural selection, yet some of the academy's assumptions about literature have remained undisturbed. If we fail to attend to the persistence of some very basic dichotomies that still seem to structure our collective thinking, even our new centers could unwittingly reproduce some features of the older consensus about what counts as literature and what does not, what deserves attention and what can be ignored. I want to suggest here that what winds up at the center still depends, to an alarming extent, on the privileging of the "literary" over the nonliterary, the "extraordinary" over the everyday, the subject of writing over the subject of experience.

My case in point will be the respective positions of Dorothy Wordsworth's *Journals* and Mary Shelley's *Journals* within new feminist Romanticist studies. Along with Austen and Wollstonecraft, these two writers have received the lion's share of the attention feminist critics have paid to literature by women in this period: Margaret Homans's pathbreaking study of Dorothy Wordsworth in *Women Writers and Poetic Identity* (1980) and, more recently, Susan Levin's *Dorothy Wordsworth and Romanticism* (1987) have given her work central status; Mary Shelley and especially *Frankenstein* have become equally important to our feminist canon, and the very publication of this book suggests an effort to bring more of her oeuvre into the light of feminist critical analysis.[2] Yet texts by the two have been differentially valued, differentially positioned within feminist Romanticist discourse: while Wordsworth's *Alfoxden* and *Grasmere Journals,* along with her poetry, have become especially germane texts for the study of subjectivity, Shelley's *Journals* have not. I want to suggest that the "unliterariness" of Shelley's *Journals* accounts in part for their absence from feminist Romanticist discourse: the *Journals* are unreadable to those feminist critics who still hold implicitly masculinist premises about literary subjectivity. Because the *Journals* deny those premises, both

Shelley's subjectivity and the *Journals* remain marginal to the new feminist Romanticist canon.

I will begin by examining the terms under which Wordsworth has been appropriated by feminist critics in order to illustrate how these terms reproduce rather than critically interrogate a certain version of literary subjectivity; then I will read Shelley's *Journals* as a countertext to that mode of understanding the writing subject. To explicate why the subjectivity of and in her early journals—those written before Percy Shelley's death—appears not to appear at all, I will also analyze Mary Shelley's tentative effort to adopt an individualist idiom as a means of self-expression. In concluding with an analysis of "the way in which [the *Journals'*] character changed as time passed," as their editors frame it, I will argue that the later *Journals* yield a kind of introspective reflection that is easier for contemporary feminist critics to read because the later texts adopt a subjective confessional mode more assimilable to our conceptions of the deep psychological subject.[3] Yet I want to suggest, too, that for Mary Shelley, the intimate turn of the later journals signifies not the gain of a new voice for experience, but the loss of the dream of intersubjectivity that had structured her life with Percy Shelley.

One of "the master's tools" for keeping women inmates of houses—not their makers—has been the inscription of the "literary" as the primary and privileged locus of writing. Defined at least in part by what it is not, the "literary" manifests itself in the unique productions of genius, which transcend the literal ground of everyday life and make any one-to-one correspondence between poetic text and experience seem reductive. But the fixity of these oppositions—art against life, genius against the ordinary and literal—ought to be undermined from a class-conscious feminist perspective. As both Regenia Gagnier and Mary Poovey have shown in a more properly Victorian context, the creation of both the "literary standard" and the privileged category of the "man of letters" depends on the institution of particular barriers which separate "real" writers from amateurs, true literary genius from inferior hacks and scribblers.[4] That such oppositions construct and are constructed by gender and class polarities should be no surprise: with few exceptions, only middle-class men (and some "exceptional" middle-class women) produce the nineteenth-century "literary," while all working-class women and men, and most middle-class women, are represented as incapable of doing so.[5] We may ascribe the "failure" of these latter groups to produce high art to culturally imposed norms and definitions that keep women and workers more closely aligned with nature and give them only object status, but we should not forget that the "literary" is an ideological formation which reinscribes a center–margin dynamic. Uncritical use of such a category, even by feminists who seek to dismantle what Margaret Homans labels "the masculine tradition," does little to undermine the stability of the categories themselves, as I now wish to demonstrate in reading Homans's own chapter on Dorothy Wordsworth in *Women Writers and Poetic Identity*.

Summarizing her argument, Homans contrasts the "centrism" and unity of

William Wordsworth's poetic vision with the fragmentation of Dorothy Wordsworth's textual works: "Whereas Wordsworth makes separation and continuity indivisible parts of a unified myth, Dorothy's alternate myths of origins . . . preclude the possibility of a unified identity. . . . Dorothy leaves
herself out of every center she proposes."[6] Lacking the "strong sense of identity" necessary to writing Romantic poetry, Dorothy Wordsworth is also said
to lack subjectivity, and so to be "incapable of self-representation, the fundamental of masculine creativity" (17). As Susan J. Wolfson notes, Homans
makes of William Wordsworth's works too stable a center, but we might also
note how she disallows particular strategies within Dorothy Wordsworth's
own writing.[7] Since Romantic poetry is seen to require "a unified identity,"
what Dorothy Wordsworth writes cannot be Romantic poetry; indeed, at one
point Homans claims that "the result" of her "reunion with nature . . . is not
poetry" at all, but rather serves to "[avoid] conflicts" (57). Although Homans
qualifies this reading at another moment by asserting that Wordsworth's "refusal to risk that break with [maternal] nature prevents her from being a poet,
at least from being a poet in her brother's mode" (56), Homans generally
naturalizes that mode as the only available poetic position. Thus while she
begins the book with a critique of "the masculine tradition," Homans's argument gradually comes to accept its terms.

Reading Dorothy Wordsworth in relation to Romantic poetics thus inscribes her on the margins of Romantic discourse; Homans's reading implicitly and explicitly underwrites a center–margin polarity that makes sexual
difference the determining factor in poetic production. But while she dismisses "cultural differences" (42) between women and men as "external factors" that "cannot be ultimate causes" (43) of poetic differences, Homans also
makes an effort to redeem some of Wordsworth's writings from the charge of
being unliterary. While "the letters and journals that form the bulk of Dorothy's writings are informal and might seem to be transparent expressions of
lived experience rather than literary texts" (43), she writes, thus invoking the
split between the literary and the experiential, she goes on to argue that the
written, and even the writing of ordinary events, is not equivalent to actual
experience: "anything represented in words has to some degree, however
small, departed from experience and entered the realm of the imaginative"
(44). Yet the defense ultimately accepts the masculinist distinction between
the literal and the figural, the experiential and the literary: while "large sec-
tions of the letters and journals contain family news and domestic details,"
this writing is dismissed as "part of her evasion of traditional poetic powers"
(44). And this "evasion," which Homans equates with a "habitual fragmentation of identity" (70–71) and a concomitant lack of subjectivity, can be viewed
only negatively within Homans's framework; because she "[wants] to assess
Dorothy Wordsworth's writing as an end in itself," as Kurt Heinzelman puts
it, Homans finds that "the subjectivity that [Wordsworth] has is the devalued
fancy that flits from one vantage point to the next" (81).[8]

"Subjectivity" is perhaps the most problematic term in Homans's analysis
because it is the least well-defined. She associates the lack of it with the

condition of women as "others" to male creators in Western discourse: "to be for so long the other and the object made it difficult for nineteenth-century women to have their own subjectivity" (12). But to understand the term only within a subject–object dyad discounts numerous other possibilities of conceiving the cultural construction of subjectivities: to say that Dorothy Wordsworth is "other" to William Wordsworth's "self," and to leave it at that, radically underestimates the extent to which subjectivity is contingent not only on one's position in the sex–gender system, but also on one's class position and one's family or community identification, to name just two other potential matrices. Speaking of subject positions, as recent feminist postmodernist analysts of subjectivity have done, avoids the reinscription of a center-margin, subject–object binary while also respecting the possibilities of being multiply interpellated within diverse discursive and experiential networks.[9] Rather than claim as one recent critic does, following Homans, that "for all the selves that Dorothy became for William—child, parent, servant, observer, recorder, amanuensis—a terrible price was exacted: the loss of any firm sense of personal identity," and so suggesting that "personal identity" should be a fixed essence, we need to understand it as constituted in and by social relations, social constructs, and social contexts.[10]

One such context for reading Dorothy Wordsworth's life and work emerges in Susan Levin's important book, *Dorothy Wordsworth and Romanticism,* which swerves from Homans's model by situating Wordsworth's work within what we have come to call "women's culture." Levin's primary claim—that "Dorothy's writing organizes traditionally female realms of concern in its concentration on the domestic, on family, and on community"—provides a necessary corrective to Homans's positing of "the masculine tradition" as a monolithic force even as her argument draws on some of Homans's insights.[11] Expanding Homans's somewhat tentative claim that Dorothy Wordsworth's "selflessness almost seems to be a deliberate refutation of Wordsworthian egotism" (Homans, 75), Levin argues that hers is "writing characterized by refusal" to "engage the world in the usual [i.e., masculine Romantic] manner" (4); she sees Wordsworth's subjectivity as shaped in and by the Grasmere community she inhabits as sister and neighbor, and presents her "writing as a family matter, a community product" (36–37). And in noting how Wordsworth "[projects] the continuous presence of an already situated reader, William" (30–31), Levin also suggests that the intersubjective character of the *Journals,* their existence as a record of a collective vision and a shared enterprise, accounts in part for their silences as well as their profusion of descriptive detail.

In reading the *Grasmere Journals,* we can see the value of Levin's approach, for the text begins as a response to a temporary loss of community for Dorothy Wordsworth: "my heart was so full that I could hardly speak to W when I gave him a farewell kiss," and she starts writing as a means of easing that full heart until her brothers come back to Grasmere.[12] The act of writing the journal itself is designed to maintain the existence of that community and also to prevent a fall into the isolation that could potentially turn Wordsworth back on herself: "I resolved to write a journal of the time till W & J return, & I set about keeping my resolve because I will not quarrel with myself, & because I shall give Wm Pleasure by it when he comes home again" (1). In the absence of the brothers who partially compose her world and her sense of herself, Wordsworth wants to keep her own composure: not to "quarrel with myself"—not to be introspective, not to be internally divided—is as important as to "give Wm Pleasure," and indeed the two imperatives may be closely linked. For if we take seriously, as the Wordsworths did, the notion that their Grasmere home was to provide "Perfect Contentment, Unity entire," we must also realize that such unity depended on creating and maintaining intimate bonds between and among individuals, bonds so intimate that what we today understand as zones of privacy—the written space of a journal, one's own unspoken thoughts—must have been differently and perhaps less rigidly demarcated.[13] Wordsworth imagines her journal-writing in terms that value community over isolation, intersubjective connection over subjective musings; writing redeems absence but only because it seeks to conserve the valued qualities of interpersonal interaction. Wordsworth's *Grasmere Journals* suggest that rather than reify the notion of the individual as writer, we should attempt to imagine the community that provides the context for writing—for in the case of Mary Shelley, to which I'll now turn, the pleasure and power of journal-writing both proceed from and depend on the participation of another reader and writer.

What we call Mary Shelley's *Journals* also open with the absence of a loved one, but in this case, only fictively absent and with reunion imminent and immanent. The first words are not Mary Godwin's, but Percy Shelley's:

> July 28. The night preceding this morning, all being decided—I ordered a chaise to be ready by 4 o clock. I watched until the lightning & the stars became pale. At length it was 4. I believed it not possible that we should succeed: still there appeared to lurk some danger even in certainty. I went. I saw her. She came to me. Yet one quarter of an hour remained. Still some arrangements must be made, & she left me for a short time. How dreadful did this time appear. It seemed that we trifled with life & hope. a few minutes past she was in my arms—we were safe. we were on our road to Dover.— (6)

Written at least a day after the events and emotions the entry recounts in full—their flight to Dover, their trip to Calais, their fear of pursuit—Shelley's dramatic reading of danger, deferral, and eventual safety traces the coming together of the pair, the transformation of "I" and "she" into a united "we," pronominally marked if not legally or patriarchally sanctioned. This entry of several hundred words concludes with both voices, each marking the presence of the other: "Mary was there. S.helley was also with me" (7). Like the *Grasmere Journals,* then, this first segment of the Godwin–Shelley *Journals* devotes itself not to the history of a single individual, but to the "pleasure and security" (6), in Shelley's words, that two lovers—who are also two readers and two writers—seek and find in each other. Written among notes on Swiss currency on the journal's title page in Mary Godwin's hand is the appellation she—or they—gave it: "Shelley and Mary's journal book" (5).

Later Mary Shelley was to name the journal in other terms and to begin and end new books with different emotions as her marital and familial relationships underwent further transformations. The second surviving journal book frames itself in terms of loss:

Journal
1816
Begun July 21—1816
Ended with my happiness June 7th 1819 (112)

Itself buried beneath pages that record three years' worth of reading lists, this epitaph ironically echoes a standard journal form used by middle-class mothers of the period, the "baby book" (of which the most famous example is Elizabeth Gaskell's *My Diary: The Early Years of My Daughter Marianne*) so commonly used by women to record the growth and progress of their infants.[14] But in marking the end of her happiness with the death of her son William, and so retroactively imposing a period to and on her life, Mary Shelley also marks other losses, among them the gradual withdrawal of Percy Shelley as co-producer of the journal. The epitaph thus not only puts a period to "my happiness" by showing the process by which the text came to be, as she put it after Clara's death in September 1818, "the Journal book of misfortunes" (226), but it also cites that loss in the radical diminution of the plural "our" to the singular "my." Appropriating a poem by Percy Shelley to open the next journal book (and writing on his birthday), she refigures their relationship as a mutual death in which only a shared past remains to unite them: "We two yet stand, in a lonely land, / Like tombs to mark the memory / Of joys & griefs" (293).[15] And the *Journals* themselves, taciturn and unrevealing as they often are, similarly mark "the memory / Of joys & griefs," inscribed with the writing of both Shelleys.

Percy Shelley's writerly participation in the journal project was extensive only for the first few months, becoming sporadic thereafter. Almost the whole of the record of their first two weeks together is in his hand; Mary Godwin continues one of his sentences on August 11, 1814 (12), and so begins a pattern of alternating entries which lasts until their return to England in mid-September of that year. Perhaps because Percy Shelley was being pursued by creditors and consequently lodged elsewhere, she takes primary responsibility for keeping the journal from this point on, although he did continue to make entries periodically, most notably two concerning Claire Clairmont, one describing a fit of terrors that she suffered (32–33), the other complaining of "Janes insensibility & incapacity for the slightest degree of friendship" (35). And the decreasing frequency of his writing over the next year need not suggest that he was no longer involved with the journal as a reader: that he wrote in it on occasion also implies that he read in it at his pleasure. But this sexual division of writerly labor corresponds to a now-familiar division of household tasks along gender lines: Mary Godwin, later Mary Shelley, is charged with the keeping of the domestic record just as she and other nineteenth-century middle-class women were given and accepted responsibility for maintaining domestic order as agents of moral and affective ties.

Only Claire—the placeless third—seems to have been excluded from this reading and writing yet present to both as the person against whom they define their own mutuality. "Jane very gloomy—she is very sullen with Shelley," Mary Godwin writes in November 1814, and in admonishing Percy to think no more of it, she addresses him directly in writing: "Well, never mind, my love we are happy" (43–44). As the textual space they share, the journal constitutes a realm of conjugal privacy secure from what was construed, in the early part of their relationship, as Claire's intrusion. Yet the shared journal also represented the lack of barriers between them: as the editors of the *Journals* note, this first journal book "has a special quality of its own, because the early months of her life with Shelley seem to have been the only period of her life during which Mary's habitual reserve was temporarily dormant" (xvi). And given Percy Shelley's emphatic ideal of heterosexual love as unreserved communion between like souls, we can speculate that the journal in some way emblematized for both the completeness of their trust in each other: rather than understanding the journal form as a place for private thoughts and individual introspection, they both generally refuse that mode and fix on the representation of daily life—visits, readings, letters received and sent—as their subjects.

The early journal characteristically mixes and intermixes all kinds of family events, yet its entries impose a pattern on the randomness of experience; in reading it, we not only get a sense of how the Shelley–Godwin household passed its days and evenings, but we also see the way in which the recording of everyday events defines the contours of a shared existence:

Sunday 16th [April 1815]
Rise late—a parcel from Fanny in which is a letter from Christy Baxter received last september in which she professes friendship—but such friendship—we see how much worth it is. Miss smith calls & gossips for above an hour—draw and read a few lines of Ovid—After dinner S & J.[ane] walk—read a scene or two out of "As you like it"—go upstairs to talk with Shelley—Read Ovid (54 lines only) Shelley finishes the 3d canto of Ariosto

Monday 17th
Rise at ½ past 8—Hogg goes to the courts—Read Ovid—Peacock comes—tells us of his plan of going to Canada & taking Marrianne—talk of it—after dinner walk out to Piccadilly—After tea Read Ovid 83 lines—Shelley two or three cantos of Ariosto with Clary & plays a game of Chess with her Read Voltaire's Essay on the spirit of the Nations

Teusday 18th [by Percy Shelley]
Rise late—S. reads Aristo—the Maie Ovid—S.& C. go out. C. makes S. a present of Seneca. buy Good's Lucretius—Jefferson [Hogg] & the Maie go for bonnets after dinner with Clara. S. reads Ovid—Medea & the description of the Plague—After tea M reads ovid 90 lines—S & C. read Ariosto—7th Canto. M reads Voltaire p. 126 (75)

The pattern of daily life that emerges from these few entries depends in part on the simple repetition of elements common to each day—the approximate time of waking, what each one is reading, who comes to visit, who goes out and at what time—and each day's entry mimes the temporal progression from morning to night. Events that might occasion further reflection or signal emotional tensions—such as a letter from the faithless Christy Baxter, or the substance of Mary's talk "upstairs" with Shelley—are only alluded to rather than exhaustively discussed. And Percy Shelley's entry takes almost exactly the same form as Mary Godwin's: in limiting itself to the properly common account of their ordinary shared and separate activities, his writing departs not at all from the format she had established over the previous six months. This joint method of "marking time" underwrites the household and helps to constitute it as a site of value; the journal gives shape and form to the experience of a shared daily life as much by what it excludes—the interior or psychological realm, for example—as by what it reports.

Since the journal covering the period from May 1815 to July 1816 is lost, it is impossible to trace an evolution in Mary Godwin's mode of journal-keeping, or to know the extent to which Percy Shelley continued to fill a role as sometimes reader and writer during that year; what Feldman and Scott-Kilvert see as a "marked change in the content of the entries" (xvii) when they resume may have been much less abrupt than it appears in the absence of that year's record. What they do see in the second extant journal, however, is that "Mary's discretion is much more in evidence"; they assert that "she has accepted the need for circumspection and concealment" (xvii). Various textual absences tend to confirm this reading: Fanny Imlay's suicide in October 1816, for example, is marked only by the insertion of a single sentence that records the day of her death and Mary Godwin's notation of the day she heard the news as a "miserable" one on which they bought mourning wear (141). Increasing tensions with Claire Clairmont in that same month and later on, in May 1817, are documented through shorthand symbolism used again in June 1820 with apparent reference to Paolo Foggi's blackmail attempt.[16]

Even the deaths of Clara and William provoke no textual outpouring but the briefest; indeed, the six years from 1816 to 1822 covered by the two journals consist mainly of very regular entries (some written four or five at a time, no doubt) that chart reading and writing, but with much less specific attention to household activities. Here are some entries from May 1817 that represent the paring down of the journal to its barest bones:

Friday 9th
Read Pliny—transcribe—read Clarke's travels—Shelley writes and reads Apuleius and Spencer in the evening.

Saturday 10th

Teusday 13th
Finish transcribing—read Pliny & Clarke's travels—Shelley writes his poem—reads Hist. of Fr. Rev. and Spencer aloud in the evening.

Wednesday 14th
Read Pliny and Clarke—walk in the garden—S. reads Hist of Fr. Rev. and
walks. he reads Spencer in the evening (169)

The severely factual mode has clearly taken hold here: Mary Shelley gives
very little attention to the activities of the household, and the earlier commitment to communicating a sense of or fashioning a shape to any particular day
has almost entirely dropped out. What remains are accounts of readings and
writings, not only Mary Shelley's, but her husband's, too, even though his
writerly participation in the journal has all but ceased. The journal thus seems
to function almost solely as a record of reading and writing, a log of books
perused and manuscripts transcribed.

Yet the very ordinariness of the journal—as testimony to the Shelley's
working lives that refuses introspection or speculation about the realm of the
personal—may signify not just "discretion" or "concealment," but a desire to
conserve textually the record of a shared life: just as Wordsworth determines
not to "quarrel with myself," Shelley's silences could also represent her desire
not to be divided either from her husband or within herself. Concentrating on
the common and the communal, the journal generally excludes any kind of
self-centeredness. And in keeping her commitment to the journal, even in the
minimalist form she adopts for most of the second and third journal books,
Shelley expresses what Anne K. Mellor identifies as her obsessive and continually frustrated need for a stable bourgeois family life: more and more assigned
to be the silent mediator of familial relations in flux, Shelley more and more
relies on representing the relatively few constants in her life, and especially
the still-shared endeavor of their writing and reading lives.[17] Rather than
succumb to the temptation of "[reading] too much into Mary's silences"
(xviii), which the *Journals'* editors warn against, and thereby ignoring the
surface of the text while imagining the depths it conceals, I suggest that it is in
the texture of this mundane surface—in the literal account of the Shelleys' life
that it offers, and even as the barest record of mutual readings—that much of
its meaning inheres.

The concrete regularity of the journal's order breaks down three times in the
few months preceding Percy Shelley's death in July 1822, once (understand-
ably enough) because of Mary Shelley's severe illness following her miscarriage in June of that year. As biographers of both Shelleys have established,
the final months of their marriage were a period of acute distress for both;
under the strain of Percy Shelley's increasing involvement with other women
and Mary Shelley's growing withdrawal from him, the two grew even further
apart. Ironically, Percy Shelley attributed to her the "insensibility" he had
once seen in Claire Clairmont, and he found in the closeness of their familial
ties a potential explanation for their alienation from one another:

I only feel the want of those who can feel, and understand me. Whether
from proximity and the continuity of domestic intercourse, Mary does not.
The necessity of concealing from her thoughts that would pain her, necessi-

tates this perhaps. It is the curse of Tantalus, that a person possessing such
excellent powers and so pure a mind as hers, should not excite the sympathy
indispensable to their application to domestic life.[18]

His perception that she lacked sympathy with him was matched by her recognition that the failure cut both ways: the division Mary Shelley begins to figure in
her journal in the last few months of Percy Shelley's life draws its terms from his
work, particularly the fragment "On Love," suggesting the extent to which she
lacked the language of self and other, the language of individuation that would
have enabled her to speak and write herself as an independent agent. I want to
look now at these textual moments in the *Journals* as an important transitional
space between the Shelleys' life together and Mary Shelley's life alone in light
of her search for a new vocabulary of and for self-representation.

The two earliest moments of disturbance in the otherwise deliberately
uneventful record foreshadow the change in Mary Shelley's journal practice
after her husband's death. The first of these, a series of two entries written
during Percy Shelley's absence on a househunting trip with Edward Williams,
is incomplete—with a leaf torn from the book—and describes, in uncharacteristically abstract terms for Mary Shelley, a mood familiar to us from Percy
Shelley's poetry. Using the impersonal "you," she considers the interrelation
of memory, time, and sorrow:

> During a long—long evening in mixed society, dancing & music—how often
> do ones sensations change—and swift as the west wind drives the shadows of
> clouds across the sunny hill on the waving corn—so swift do sentiments
> pass . . . You remember what you have dreamt—yet you dwell on the shadowy side and lost hopes, and death such as you have seen it seems to cover
> all things with a funeral pall. The Time that was, is, & will be presses upon
> you & standing [in] the centre of a moving circle you "—slide giddily as the
> world reels." You look to heaven & would demand of the everlasting stars,
> that the thoughts & passions which are your life may be as everliving as
> they—You would demand from the blue empyream that your mind might be
> as clear as it—& that the tears which gather in your eyes might be as the
> shower that would drain from its profoundest depths the springs of weakness
> and sorrow. But where are the stars? Where are the blue empyreams? a
> cieling clouds that & a thousand swift consuming lights supply the place of
> the eternal ones of heaven. The Enthusiast suppresses her tears—crushes
> her opening thoughts and—
>
> But all is changed—some word some look exite the lagging blood. laughter
> dances in the eyes & the spirits rise proportionably high— (395–96)

The Shelleyan trope of inconstancy dominates this representation, yet Mary
Shelley refrains from adopting the poet's "I" even as she directly echoes his
words and works. Like the poet watching the skylark, Shelley here asks for
some permanence in a world of change; looking up to the heavens, she wishes
that the human mind "might be as clear" as the empyrean, and that her own
tears would be as a cleansing "shower." But the heavens and stars are themselves blotted out, and as the metaphorical sky clouds over, both "tears" and

"thoughts" are suppressed, only to be forgotten in the next passing mood, replaced by "laughter." Yet the reference to the "opening thoughts" which "the Enthusiast"—the creature of moods—"crushes" is ambiguous here. Are they the thoughts the passage expresses in its appropriation of Percy Shelley's poetic idiom, or are they some other thoughts, self-suppressed and perhaps inarticulable, "opening" but swiftly closed? The fortuitous turn away from thought, sanctioned by the very theme of mutability that provokes the meditation, itself serves as but a temporary brake on Shelley's effort to make an idiom for herself as a solitary speaker.

From the impersonal poetic of this entry we move directly into the entry of the next day, February 8, 1822, in which Mary Shelley literally cancels out the impersonal and attempts to replace it with a first-person voice:

> Sometimes ~~one~~ I awaken from ~~ones~~ my ordinary monotony & my thoughts flow, until as it is exquisite pain to stop the flowing of the blood, so it is painful to check expression & make the overflowing mind return to its usual channel—I feel a kind of tenderness to those whoever they may be (even though strangers) who awaken this train & touch a chord so full of harmony & thrilling music—When I would tear the veil from this strange world & pierce with eagle eyes beyond the sun—when every idea strange & changeful is another step in the ladder by which I would climb the— (396)

This entry, too, is a fragment, but it is broken off by Shelley herself, broken off, moreover, at the moment it has moved into Percy Shelley's metaphors— "veil," "eagle eyes," "the ladder by which I would climb"—and away from the first-person voice of overflowing emotion she so hesitantly adopts. Having "[awakened] from my ordinary monotony," she halts the "flow" of emotion by eventually "[returning] to [the mind's] usual channel": the final detour into poesis that stops the movement of the passage seems almost to prove that she has no language for self-expression at this point apart from Percy Shelley's own—and it is perhaps this recognition, rather than any desire to avoid self-revelation, which pulls her up short. Taken together, the two entries illustrate the difficulty with which Shelley sought a voice for one where once there had been two voices blended in a single strain.

In an entry from about two weeks later, in late February 1822, Shelley again resorts to metaphor as a means of expressing both her disgust with what is—"What a mart this world is!"—and her own determination not to make "coin" of "sentiments more invaluable than gold or precious stones" (399). Refusing the model of exchange, she settles instead on a plan of individual existence that includes love of nature, just estimation of other people, and mature self-consciousness in a manner that suggests that she is coming to understand herself as a solitary:

> The most contemptible of all lives is where you live in the world & none of your passions or affections are called into action—I am convinced I could not live thus—& as Sterne says that in solitude he would worship a tree—so in the world I should attach myself to those who bore the semblance of those qualities which I admire—But it is not this that I want—Let me love the

trees—the skies & the ocean & that all encompassing spirit of which I may
soon become a part—let me in my fellow creatures love that which is & not
fix my affections on a fair form endued with imaginary attributes—where
goodness, kindness & talent are, let me love & admire them at their just rate
neither adding or diminishing & above all let me fearlessly descend into the
remotest caverns of my own mind—carry the torch of self-knowledge into its
dimmest recesses—but too happy if I dislodge any evil spirit or ensh[r]ine a
new deity in some hitherto uninhabited nook— (399–400)

As Feldman and Scott-Kilvert note, Shelley's reference to Sterne recalls Percy
Shelley's previous mention of him in the essay "On Love," where Sterne's
power of loving even a cypress in the desert is said to maintain in him the
power of having and giving affection: "So soon as this want or power is dead,"
Percy Shelley continues, "man becomes the living sepulchre of himself, and
what yet survives is the mere husk of what once he was"; man becomes, in
short, his own tomb.[19] In using the same image, Shelley suggests her resistance to the fate Percy Shelley unfolds for the individual cut off from sympathy. However, her self-imposed imperative to "love the trees—the skies & the
ocean" also echoes "On Love," and Percy Shelley's text supplies the unspoken dimension that motivates it: "in solitude, or in that deserted state
when we are surrounded by human beings and yet they sympathise not with
us, we love the flowers, the grass and the waters and the sky" (474). Perceiving herself as wholly isolated, her sense of "that deserted state" produces in
Shelley "above all" an inward turn, and unlike the poet-traveler of *Alastor,*
she vows self-consciously to "carry the torch of self-knowledge into [the
mind's] dimmest recesses." For Shelley, then, the Romantic impulse to look
within the self arises only through the breakdown of the kind of mutuality
Percy Shelley had described in "On Love" and that she herself had defined
through her representation of the De Lacey family in *Frankenstein.* And the
consequences of that impulse, along with the fact of Percy Shelley's death,
make the later journals the very obverse of what had come before.

The third extant journal book breaks off at Percy Shelley's death on July 8,
1822; the fourth begins about three months later; the fifth opens in September
1826 and covers the next twenty-two years of Shelley's life, until she quit
writing in it more than six years before her own death. The material differences between those volumes written before and those after her husband's
death are very striking: while the journals of their lives together functioned
not only as a record, but also as a catch-all space for household notations—
lists of expenses for clothing, prescriptions for ailments, reading lists, mathe-
matical computations—Shelley's properly private journals include no such
signs of domestic negotiations. And whereas the earlier journals are written
regularly, typically with brief citations of the Shelleys' activities, the later ones
are kept only at intervals, with longer entries but none of the signs of routine
that the earlier texts display. These differences suggest, I think, the larger loss
of the coherent if monotonous rhythm of family life that the earlier journals so
painstakingly recorded: in turning to the journal in the years after Percy

Shelley's death, Shelley made only a brief effort to frame a life in writing. And if the journal of domestic order had underwritten the Shelley household even in the midst of emotional disorder, then "The Journal of Sorrow," as she named the fourth journal book, became to her by the time she concluded it in January 1825, "trash nobody will read . . . future waste paper" (489).

What the actual loss of her husband (as opposed to the period of their emotional estrangement) means for her journal is a complete shift in tone and content. While she had once used epitaph to indicate real and metaphorical deaths, this journal represents itself as the sole living tomb: like the last date the third journal book records—July 8, 1822, Shelley's death-day—this book stands as "a monument to shew that all ended then" (429). Taking on Percy Shelley's "Epipsychidion" metaphor for her, she presents her identity as wholly contingent on his, even more true in his death than in their life: "I am then moonshine, having no existence except that which he lends me, & through his influence glimmering on the earth, known & sought through the light he bestows upon me. Thus I would endeavour to consider my self a faint continuation of his being, & as far as possible the revelation to the earth of what he was" (436). More succinctly, and with an eye toward the past rather than the future, she makes memory of her former self the ground of her present identity: "So may it be said of me that I am nothing, but I was something and still I cling to what I was" (443). In the absence of "the intercourse I once dayly enjoyed" (474), in the loss of the roles and practices that helped her to define her position, Shelley finds no substitutes other than the mode of the grieving widow.

The only concerted effort to use the journal as a means of reconstructing the self proceeds through her imagining the space of writing as itself a potentially intersubjective one. Imagining her private consciousness as "a sealed treasure" that "now no friend" can open, she begins the fourth journal book by making an intimate of it: "I will trust thee fully, for none shall see what I write" (429). This conventional use of the journal as a diary—a private textual account of emotions and feelings—works for her at various moments, as when she feels "urged to recur to the relief of this book from the extreme melancholy that oppresses me" (474). Yet almost from the first, writing is concomitantly constructed as an inadequate replacement for the interpersonal: revising her relationship to Percy Shelley as one in which she was "united to one to whom I could unveil myself, & who could understand me" (430), Shelley finds self-expression without the possibility of response from another a futile exercise. "I am now reduced to these white pages which I am to blot with dark imagery" (430): the blankness of the journal mirrors back to her what she construes as the emptiness of her dark existence.

Shelley's mode of recording the grieving self exposes what we might think of as the "plotlessness" of female dysphoria: the death of the beloved reader makes the effort to textualize her experience seem to her a vain endeavor. Although I do not mean to suggest that the loss of the privileged male reader inevitably imposes silence on the female writer—Charlotte Brontë's fictional Lucy Snowe, for example, produces her self-representation under similar circumstances of literal and figurative shipwreck—it seems clear that for Shelley, writing the self outside the context of a specific and personalized reading community proves an act that she cannot value in and of itself. Even the fictional narrator of *Villette,* in her negotiation of what can and cannot be told and in her commitment to the material and professional legacy M. Paul has left her, makes of her tragic experience a kind of anticonfession, a narrative that refuses to posit self as the sole value while still managing to construct a self as subject-of-experience; Shelley's final journal, on the other hand, as a text more open than even the radically inconclusive *Villette,* refuses to turn the past into narrative in the interests of situating the present or imagining the future. The therapeutic value critics have so often assigned to the great fictional autobiographies of the Victorians—*David Copperfield, The Mill on the Floss,* or even such earlier works as *The Prelude* or *Sartor Resartus*—has inscribed a centering authorial self as the locus of the proper subjectivity literary texts should display; Shelley's later journal, equally drawn to such fictions, yet refuses to work through its materials in that fashion. Placing the *Journals,* themselves constructed in relation to norms for femininity, domesticity, and subjectivity, alongside their fictional counterparts should thus reveal a broader range of subject positions for nineteenth-century middle-class writers, male and female, than we have yet been able to imagine.

All in all, however, the later journals "reveal" more of Mary Shelley than the earlier ones, and as such, are more accessible to the kind of subjectivity analysis some feminist critics might want to practice. One could argue on the evidence they provide that Shelley comes to define herself as silent and private, fractured and fragmented, yet I want to stop short of representing these texts as her confessions. To reinscribe the confessional as the subjective mode par excellence of the Romantic period would marginalize what I see as the equally crucial construction of Shelley's *Journals* as a space in which the mutual is privileged over and above the individual, in which the self cannot be a self without the familial context that shapes identity in particular ways, not all of them necessarily either liberating or constraining. If we are to break the association among subjectivity, centrism, and individualism that dominates critical practice, we need to hold on to some part of the feminist ideology that values community over isolation and that recognizes, in Susan Stanford Friedman's words, that *"identification, interdependence,* and *community . . .* are key elements in the development of a woman's identity."[20] Relocating our critical vision on the intersubjective in Shelley's work may not make her fully legible, but it can open a new direction in our writing of the history of women's subjectivity.

Notes

1. Audre Lorde, "The Master's Tools Will Never Dismantle the Master's House," *This Bridge Called My Back,* ed. Cherríe Moraga and Gloria Anzaldúa (New York: Kitchen Table: Women of Color Press, 1981), 98–101.

2. At one level, my analysis here, my central focus on these two writers, may reproduce the very center–margin polarity I am trying to critique: by claiming that Mary Shelley's journals have remained beyond or outside the powers and preoccupations of feminist literary criticism, I may be entirely erasing others from the map. Why not Mary Shelley and Mary Hays, or Hannah More, or Felicia Hemans? This is a question I cannot long evade—it will continue to haunt this text throughout—but I hope that in posing the questions of why and how the Wordsworth journals have been appropriated by feminist critics while the Shelley journals have not, I will justify (if not wholly authorize) my own engagement in the institutional discourse I am criticizing.

3. Paula R. Feldman and Diana Scott-Kilvert, introduction to *The Journals of Mary Shelley: 1814–1844,* 2 vols. (Oxford: Oxford University Press, 1987), 1:xv; all further references to the *Journals* are to this edition and are cited in the text by page number. In most instances, I have omitted all crossed-out words in citing from the *Journals,* but I have allowed punctuation, capitalization, and spelling to stand.

4. For further discussion of "the literary," see Regenia Gagnier, *Subjectivities: A History of Self-Representation in Britain, 1832–1920* (New York: Oxford University Press, 1991); Mary Poovey, *Uneven Developments: The Ideological Work of Gender in Mid-Victorian England* (Chicago: University of Chicago Press, 1988); and Mary Jean Corbett, *Representing Femininity: Middle-Class Subjectivity in Victorian and Edwardian Women's Autobiographies* (New York: Oxford University Press, 1992), esp. Chapter 2.

5. Julia Swindells argues this point persuasively in *Victorian Writing and Working Women* (Cambridge: Polity Press, 1985).

6. Margaret Homans, *Women Writers and Poetic Identity* (Princeton: Princeton University Press, 1980), 70; all further page references are cited in the text. See as well Homans's chapter on Wordsworth in *Bearing the Word: Language and Female Experience in Nineteenth-Century Women's Writing* (Chicago: University of Chicago Press, 1986), 40–67, which expands the earlier reading via Lacan and Chodorow.

7. See Susan J. Wolfson, "Individual in Community: Dorothy Wordsworth in Conversation with William," *Romanticism and Feminism,* ed. Anne K. Mellor (Bloomington: Indiana University Press, 1988), esp. 144–47, for a useful and sensitive revision of Homans's work.

8. Kurt Heinzelman, "The Cult of Domesticity: Dorothy and William Wordsworth at Grasmere," in Mellor, *Romanticism and Feminism,* 55. Heinzelman's work, like Wolfson's, stresses the communal and intersubjective character of Dorothy Wordsworth's writerly and domestic labor.

9. In the growing literature on postmodernism and subjectivity, see especially Donna Haraway, "A Manifesto for Cyborgs," *Socialist Review* 50 (March–April 1985): 65–107, and "Situated Knowledges: The Science Question in Feminism and the Privilege of Partial Perspective," *Feminist Studies* 14, 3 (Fall 1988): 575–99; Teresa de Lauretis, "The Technology of Gender," *Technologies of Gender* (Bloomington: Indiana University Press, 1987), 1–30; and Nancy K. Miller, "Changing the Subject: Authorship, Writing, and the Reader," *Subject to Change* (New York: Cambridge University Press, 1988), 102–21.

10. James Holt McGavran, Jr., "Dorothy Wordsworth's Journals: Putting Herself Down," *The Private Self: Theory and Practice of Women's Autobiographical Writings,* ed. Shari Benstock (Chapel Hill: University of North Carolina Press, 1988), 232.

11. Susan M. Levin, *Dorothy Wordsworth and Romanticism* (New Brunswick: Rutgers University Press, 1987), 1; all further page references are cited in the text.

12. Dorothy Wordsworth, *The Grasmere Journals,* ed. Pamela Woof (Oxford: Clarendon Press, 1991), 1; all further page references are cited in the text.

13. William Wordsworth, *"Home at Grasmere"*: *Part First, Book First, of "The Recluse,"* ed. Beth Darlington (Ithaca: Cornell University Press, 1977), ms. B:170.

14. Gaskell's diary was privately printed by Clement Shorter in 1923. For another related kind of text, see Mary Martha Sherwood, *The Life of Mrs. Sherwood,* ed. Sophia Kelly (London, 1857).

15. Feldman and Scott-Kilvert note that the draft version Mary Shelley cites here differs from her notebook copy and Percy Shelley's own version. See their note (293).

16. See Feldman and Scott-Kilvert's appendix on "Mary Shelley's Use of Symbols" (579–81) for an analysis of their possible meanings.

17. See Anne K. Mellor, *Mary Shelley: Her Life, Her Fiction, Her Monsters* (New York: Methuen, 1988), esp. Chapter 1.

18. In *The Letters of Percy Bysshe Shelley,* 2 vols., ed. Frederick L. Jones (Oxford: Clarendon Press, 1964), 2:434–36.

19. "On Love," in *Shelley's Poetry and Prose,* eds. Donald H. Reiman and Sharon B. Powers (New York: Norton, 1977), 474; all further references are cited in the text.

20. Susan Stanford Friedman, "Women's Autobiographical Selves: Theory and Practice," in Benstock, *The Private Self,* 38; see as well in the same book Elizabeth Fox-Genovese, "My Statue, My Self: Autobiographical Writings of Afro-American Women," 63–89, for an exemplary effort to create a medium for looking at "individual" texts within the frame of a shared context.

Mary Shelley and the Taming of the Byronic Hero: "Transformation" and *The Deformed Transformed*

Paul A. Cantor

Having long been viewed as peripheral to the study of Romanticism, *Franken-stein* has been moved to the center. Critics originally tried to assimilate Mary Shelley's novel to patterns already familiar from Romantic poetry. But more recent studies of *Frankenstein* have led critics to rethink Romanticism in light of Mary Shelley's contribution. Gradually emerging from the shadow of her husband, she is increasingly being recognized as a distinct voice within Romanticism, a distinctly feminine voice within what seems to be a male-dominated movement.[1] The trend of recent studies of *Frankenstein* has been to view it as a critique of Romanticism, particularly as developed in Percy Shelley's poetry. Critics have argued that *Frankenstein* is a protest against Romantic titanism, against the masculine aggressiveness that lies concealed beneath the dreams of Romantic idealism. They characterize Victor Frankenstein as a man claiming to be acting for the benefit of humanity but in his egotism only succeeding in destroying himself and all those he loves.[2] As a story focusing on an aggressively male attempt to displace the female from her role as creator and nourisher of human life, *Frankenstein* embodies on several levels Shelley's distinctive concerns as a woman in the early nineteenth century. Above all, the novel can be viewed as a protest in the name of domesticity against the destructive effects of the Romantic heroic ideal.[3]

As Shelley's most powerful work, *Frankenstein* has inevitably played the most important role in helping reshape our notions of Romanticism. But *Frankenstein* is not unique among Shelley's works in providing a critique of male Romanticism. In 1822–23, she transcribed Byron's *The Deformed Transformed* at his request with a view to publication.[4] This unfinished poetic drama involves a bizarre twist on the Faust legend, telling the story of a tormented hunchback who invokes the devil's aid to give his spirit a new lodging in a scaled-down version of Achilles' body. In 1830, Shelley published in *The Keepsake* annual a story called "Transformation," which clearly constitutes a rewriting of Byron's work. First published in 1824, *The Deformed Transformed* has never received much attention from critics, partly because as a fragment it is hard to analyze, partly because in conception it is derivative from Goethe's *Faust,* and partly because its poetry is uneven in quality.[5] "Transformation" has lived largely in the shadow of *Frankenstein,* which it resembles in its use of the *Doppelgänger* motif and its treatment of the body as

the prison of the soul. Read separately, *The Deformed Transformed* and
"Transformation" may seem relatively unimportant to our understanding of
Romanticism. But viewing "Transformation" as a feminist revision of *The
Deformed Transformed* does allow us to see this confrontation as a significant
episode in the history of English Romanticism. I want to use "Transformation" to help reread its precursor text in Byron, and at the same time use *The
Deformed Transformed* to help rethink a central pattern in Byron's poetry, the
relation of love and aggression. This rereading of Byron should have implications for our understanding of *Frankenstein* as well.

What works like *Frankenstein* and "Transformation" call attention to in Romantic literature in general and in Byron's poetry in particular is the remarkable prevalence of aggression and violence in a movement that claimed to
promote peace and love. In many ways Wordsworth shaped the image of
Romanticism that traditionally prevailed in the Anglo-American world, with
the result that critics tended to picture the Romantic poet typically at peace
with nature. This characterization is in fact inadequate to the complexity of
Wordsworth's poetry; it cannot account for the massive scenes of warfare
throughout Blake; and it certainly gives a false impression of the second
generation of the English Romantics. It is indeed hardly surprising to find so
much violence in Romantic literature, given the fact that it was a product of a
revolutionary age. It would in fact be strange if the violence of the French
Revolution and the Napoleonic Wars were not somehow reflected in Romantic literature. Even though the Romantics typically posited nonviolent goals
for humanity, like liberty and equality, they did not always advocate nonviolent means to those ends. To the extent that the Romantics supported the
cause of political revolution, they often found themselves in the position of
portraying and even celebrating political violence.

But Byron goes a step further: he seems fascinated with violence per se,
especially with the crime of murder. And Byron does not confine himself to
political violence: the murders he portrays often grow out of disputes between
men competing for women and thus could be classified as domestic violence.
But in fact in Byron, it is not always possible to draw a clear line between
domestic and political violence. In a series of works beginning with the Oriental tales, such as *The Giaour* and *The Corsair,* and continuing on through
poems such as *Parisina,* Byron seems to dwell obsessively upon a pattern
which has many variations but in some ways stands most clearly revealed in
Mazeppa. A younger man wins the love of a beautiful woman away from an
older man; the older man, who is somehow socially and politically superior to
the younger, metes out a dreadful punishment to him; out of the depth of his
defeat, the younger man somehow reconstitutes his strength and lives to exact
a terrible vengeance upon the older man and anyone associated with him.
This narrative pattern is of course not unique to Byron: in its outline it
provides the staple of romantic plots in all ages. But what is peculiar to Byron
is the proportions of his narratives. For a Romantic poet, he seems curiously
to downplay the role of romance in his poetry. One might expect the love

element in these stories to be primary and the revenge element to be secondary, but exactly the reverse happens. The imaginative core of these poems—the most fully realized moment poetically—is almost always a scene of brutal and devastating violence: an army wiped out, a castle obliterated, an enemy savagely cut down. Whereas Byron presents the love that provokes the violence in shadowy terms, sometimes merely alluding to it elliptically, he dwells in paradoxically loving detail on the violence itself and the hate it expresses. And if one steps back from these poems to survey their pattern, one cannot help being struck by the disproportion of the violence they portray. A comparatively isolated incident of domestic violence triggers an outpouring of community-wide violence that may eventually lay an entire kingdom waste.

It is this pattern in Byron which struck Mary Shelley, this interweaving of love and hate, romance and war, a pattern in which the aggressive elements tend to predominate. As Mazeppa speaks of his beloved, we see how love and hate blend in his mind:

> I loved her then—I love her still;
> And such as I am, love indeed
>   In fierce extremes—in good and ill.
> But still we love even in our rage.
>   (225–28)[6]

In *The Giaour* the equivalence of what appear to be opposite emotions is suggested by the poetic symmetry of a single line: "The maid I love—the man I hate—" (1018). The first in this series of poems, *The Giaour* is the most explicit in portraying hate as an emotion deeper than love:

> But Love itself could never pant
> For all that Beauty sighs to grant,
> With half the fervour Hate bestows
> Upon the last embrace of foes,
> When grappling in the fight they fold
> Those arms that ne'er shall lose their hold;
> Friends meet to part—Love laughs at faith;—
> True foes, once met, are joined till death!
>   (647–54)

The relationship of the Giaour and his enemy, Hassan, is in fact presented as a kind of marriage (line 718), while the feminine element in the poem is literally and figuratively occluded and suppressed (in terms of the narrative, the hero's beloved, Leila, is placed in a sack and drowned). *The Giaour* appears to be a romantic poem, in which the love of man and woman ought to be at the center. But in practice Byron pushes the love story to the margins, while he focuses on the hate of man for man, which is paradoxically presented as a kind of love. In general, Byron's poetic tales present a hypermasculine world, in which women function largely as pawns in the power struggles of men.

One can readily see why Shelley might have reacted negatively to the portrayal of women in Byron's Oriental tales, but before discussing her revision of Byron, it is important to analyze this pattern in greater depth. It is only when we read his works in conventionally romantic terms that the violence in them seems disproportionate. Our first impression in the Oriental tales is that romantic love is the cause and violence is the effect, and in that case the effect does seem out of proportion to the cause. At first sight Byron seems to be portraying situations in which men become rivals because they have fallen in love with the same woman. But the poems suddenly appear in a new light if we experiment with reversing our sense that love is the primary phenomenon and aggression the derivative. Suppose for a moment that in Byron's poetry the men fall in love with the same woman because they are rivals. Then the violence would no longer seem as peculiar, for the love conflict would merely be providing the excuse for a more basic hostility that was already latent in the situation.

Readers familiar with the writings of René Girard will recognize that I am applying his theory of mimetic desire and mimetic violence to Byron.[7] Girard's reconception of the nature of desire is best understood in terms of his polemic against Freud and specifically the idea of the Oedipus complex.[8] In Freud's conception of the oedipal triangle, the primary fact is the son's desire for his mother, from which his hostility to his father as his competitor is derived. More generally, for Freud the foundation of all explanation is the fact of human desire, and he views aggression as a derivative phenomenon.[9] Girard, by contrast, treats desire as learned rather than spontaneous. For Girard the primary fact is the son's identification with his father; wanting to be like his father, he comes to desire what his father desires, namely, his mother. Thus Girard views the rivalry between father and son as the cause rather than the effect of the son's desire for his mother. Byron's poetry offers unusually fertile ground for applying Girard's theories. To be sure, at first glance the poetic tales seem to be readily explicable in Freudian terms. The basic situation repeatedly seems oedipal: a younger man in conflict with an older over a woman who is usually midway between them in age and sometimes related to the younger man (in *Parisina,* for example, the younger man is the illegitimate son of the older, and falls in love with the woman who becomes his father's wife). In *The Bride of Abydos* the language becomes pointedly oedipal, as Old Giaffir speaks with contempt for his nephew-son Selim in clearly phallic terms:

> But if thy beard had manlier length,
> And if thy hand had skill and strength,
> I'd joy to see thee break a lance,
> Albeit against my own perchance.
>
> (I.122–25)

But as the inversion of Freud's theory of the Oedipus complex, Girard's theory of mimetic desire can explain these patterns in Byron's poetry equally well. The question becomes, Where does the emphasis fall in Byron's poetic tales: on the sexual aspects or the aggressive behavior?

I would argue that what energizes these poems is Byron's portrayal of masculine rivalry and specifically the way mimetic desire leads to violence. At one point Byron even speaks of "mimic slaughter" (*Abydos,* I.247). He constantly dwells upon how protagonist and antagonist, despite their apparent differences in age, nationality, and faith, are mirror images of each other. Consider the striking moment when the Giaour stands over his defeated foe:

> Fall'n Hassan lies—his unclos'd eye
> Yet lowering on his enemy,
> As if the hour that seal'd his fate,
> Surviving left his quenchless hate;
> And o'er him bends that foe with brow
> As dark as his that bled below.—
>
> (669–74)

Thus what seems to draw Byron's characters into conflict is not the accidental conjunction of their desires but some fundamental similarity in their natures that from the beginning sets them on a collision course of imitation.

The advantage of a Girardian rather than a Freudian reading of Byron's poetic tales is that it allows us to see the hidden agenda of the Byronic hero. At first sight the characters in the poetic tales seem to stumble into criminality. Because their desires are for one reason or another illicit, they end up at odds with society. But a Girardian reading suggests that something deep within these characters makes them antisocial to begin with, and the desires that ostensibly ruin their lives paradoxically serve the function of bringing about the break with society they secretly crave. Along with such writers as Kleist and Dostoevsky, Byron must be credited with discovering what might be called the metaphysics of criminality as a theme for literature.[10] Byron's characters are not antisocial because their desires are criminal; they generate criminal desires because they are by nature antisocial. Something in them cannot stand ordinary contentment and a peaceful life within society, and thus they in effect seek out a way of life that will prevent them from becoming trapped in a conventional existence. What seems to be merely the result of fatal accidents in their lives turns out to correspond to their deepest longing.

This approach helps account for the fact that, despite the way the violence is generated domestically in Byron's poetic tales, he supplies a political dimension to the stories. Mazeppa's tale is doubly framed by political events: it is narrated in the context of Peter the Great's victory over Charles XII of Sweden at Pultowa, which is in turn associated with Napoleon's later defeat at Moscow. The Oriental tales all take place against the background of Greek–Turkish conflicts, and specifically the issue of Greek independence. In *The Giaour* Byron harks back to the great battles of Thermopylae and Salamis and hence to the conflicts between the ancient Greeks and Persians. Thus the domestic violence in these poetic tales takes place within a larger political context, which suggests that aggression is a pervasive phenomenon in human life. Once again, what is characteristic of Byron is the way the domestic violence tends to spill over into political. If as I have been arguing Byron's heroes are in effect looking for a fight, then we can understand why what initially seems like a limited occasion for conflict in his poetry swiftly generates uncontrollable violence. Feeling at odds with the fabric of society, his heroes seize upon the first excuse to tear it down. What is most modern in Byron's poetry is his portrayal of violence as a symptom, a symptom of a root dissatisfaction with human existence driving his heroes into an escalating pattern of aggression and destruction that ultimately aims at nothing less than dislodging the frame of the universe.

Though incomplete as a poem, *The Deformed Transformed* provides the fullest realization in Byron of the pattern of mimetic desire and mimetic violence. The hero of the play, Arnold, is a hunchback, who as a result of his ugliness is rejected by everyone, even by his own mother. As a result Arnold becomes a creature of pure negation: he wishes to be anything other than what he is (I.i.347–48). When he reaches the point of attempting suicide, a stranger who we gradually learn is the devil appears to offer Arnold his aid. Conjuring up the shades of some of the greatest heroes of the ancient world, the devil makes Arnold an offer he cannot refuse: he can have the bodily form of anyone he desires. Notice how this differs from the normal scene of satanic temptation. Byron's devil does not corrupt Arnold with promises of worldly goods, with visions of wealth or sexual temptations. He seems to understand that what ultimately motivates human beings is not their appetites but their will to power. If they crave the objects the devil traditionally dangles before their eyes, the reason is that they associate those objects with higher states of being. Byron's devil goes right to the heart of the matter: he knows that what Arnold really wants is to be someone other than himself.

In a curious way Byron has captured in the opening scene the great heritage of Romanticism for modernity, the dream that human beings can be whatever they want to be. The devil gives Arnold a chance to act out the Romantic fantasy of complete autonomy: "You shall have no bond / But your own will" (150–51). At the beginning Arnold's body seems to be his fate, condemning him to a life of tortured isolation, but the devil makes it possible for Arnold's body to become a matter of free choice, as if he could shape his physical being to suit his fancy. This opening scene suggests why Girard's theories are particularly applicable to Byron and Romantic literature. At no point has the ideology of human freedom and equality been stronger than in the Romantic era, and this ideology is the strongest provocation to mimetic desire. Though Girard has increasingly tried to universalize his theories, it is no accident that his studies originally focused on the nineteenth-century novel, which is to say, on the world of postrevolutionary France (Balzac, Stendhal, Flaubert). In an aristocratic and strictly hierarchical society, human beings tend to view their positions in life as natural or divinely ordained, and hence are less prone to dream of rising above their given stations. In a democratic society, by contrast, with the traditional supports of social privilege weakened if not entirely undermined, the barriers to mimetic desire dissolve. In his quixotic wish to become one of the heroes he has read about in books, Arnold is in a sense the perfect embodiment of Romantic-democratic man: the only limits he recognizes are the limits of his aspirations and imagination.

But in a strange twist of plot—one of the most original aspects of the play— Arnold finds he cannot simply leave his old body behind. The devil decides to adopt the body Arnold has abandoned, and thus the transformed hero is shadowed by an image of his former self throughout the play as we have it. Thus the idea of the deformed transformed allows Byron to probe the mysteries of the Romantic self. Is a man's sense of identity bound up with his sense of his body? Is he free to shape a new identity for himself? Or is his destiny linked to the body in which he was created? *Mutatis mutandis,* these are the same questions Shelley explores in *Frankenstein,*[11] which might have borne the subtitle *The Deformed Not Transformed.* The creature Frankenstein creates comes to shadow him in much the same way the devil shadows Arnold. And both works focus on the question of whether human beings can find a way to transcend their physical limitations. Critics are used to speaking of the way Romantic poetry influenced the genesis of *Frankenstein,* but in the case of *The Deformed Transformed* we may be witnessing a flow of influence in the opposite direction. When Byron's devil speaks of those "who make men without women's aid" (I.i.436), he could almost be referring to Frankenstein. Shelley's novel may very well have helped to shape Byron's conception of a creature so deformed that he can find no place in society and above all no one to love him.

Unfortunately the first scene is the high point of *The Deformed Transformed,* and the play thereafter declines in quality.[12] Nevertheless, the way Byron develops the action in *The Deformed Transformed* reveals a great deal about the relation of romance and aggression in his work. Love and war are the explicit themes of the play. When Arnold, like Faust, asks the devil to show him the world, his shadow tells him: "That's to say, where there is War / And Woman in activity" (I.i.495–96). But once again the proportion of the two motifs is unbalanced. This may be only an accidental result of the unfinished character of the work, but in what Byron chose to write of *The Deformed Transformed* war occupies center stage and romance is merely hinted at. What constitutes the heart of the play is the story of Arnold's participation in the siege of Rome in 1527; we see only the bare beginnings of the development of a romance between Arnold and Olimpia.

The fact that Byron places the early sixteenth-century French attempt to conquer Rome at the center of his poem allows him to dwell upon masculine aggressiveness at its most brutal. When Olimpia first appears in the play, she is threatened with rape by a group of pillaging soldiers who clearly are in competition to see who can win her as his prize (II.iii.58–60). Byron heightens the sense of the all-pervasiveness of violence by the historical perspective he creates on the action. He scatters reminders of ancient Rome throughout the play. When the devil takes over Arnold's body, he adopts the name of Caesar. The would-be heroes of the play clearly are acting in imitation of ancient greatness. When Bourbon seems daunted by a vision of the real Julius Caesar, Philibert tells him to copy his model and thus surpass him: "Then conquer / The walls for which he conquered, and be greater!" (I.ii.212–13). Byron repeatedly refers to the legend of the foundation of Rome in an act of mimetic rivalry and violence. The devil reveals:

> I see your Romulus (simple as I am)
> Slay his own twin, quick-born of the same womb,
> Because he leapt a ditch ('twas then no wall,
> Whate'er it now be;) and Rome's earliest cement
> Was brother's blood.
>
> (I.ii.80–84)

As a story of twins—mirror images—engaged in fratricidal strife, the Romulus and Remus myth is one of Girard's examples of how mimetic violence stands at the basis of social organization.[13]

By means of his range of historical reference, Byron develops a strong sense of how mimetic violence breaks down hierarchy and social categories. The conquered are always threatening to turn the tables on their masters and become the conquerers: " 'Twas *their* turn—now 'tis ours" (I.ii.283).[14] In particular, family relationships are constantly being subverted by the power of ambition and aggression:

> Rome's sire forgot his mother,
> When he slew his gallant twin.
> (II.i.74–75)

> Yield not to these stranger Neros!
> Though the Son who slew his mother,
> Shed Rome's blood, he was your brother:
> 'Twas the Roman curbed the Roman.
> (II.i.106–9)

In the chaos of mimetic violence, even sexual differentiation begins to break down. In a remarkable passage, Rome itself switches gender:

> now to be
> Lord of the city which hath been Earth's lord
> Under its Emperors, and—changing sex,
> Not sceptre, an hermaphrodite of empire—
> *Lady* of the Old World.
> (I.ii.6–10)

The fact that when Rome becomes the object of rival heroes, the city becomes figured as symbolically female is one of the most telling moments in the play, another sign of how the feminine tends to be equated with the oppressed in Byron and of how romance tends to be subordinated to aggression.

The fragmentary part III of the play opens with the promise of a reversal of this pattern:

> The wars are over,
> The spring is come;
> The bride and her lover
> Have sought their home.
> (III.i.1–4)

But like much else in this play, the promised triumph of domesticity over warfare was likely to prove abortive. Though part III was going to be devoted to the love of Arnold and Olimpia, that story was almost certainly going to end in violence, probably at least one act of murder. It is of course impossible to come to any firm conclusions about the unwritten ending of the work. Mary Shelley reports that Byron knew how he was going to end the play,[15] but he left no more than hints of what he had in mind. Various attempts have been made to figure out how *The Deformed Transformed* would have ended, based largely on the study of proven and hypothetical sources of the play.[16] Whatever the exact shape of the ending, one thing seems clear: part III was to tell a story of mimetic desire. Arnold, Olimpia, and Caesar were to become involved in a Girardian love triangle, reflecting the underlying tension between the two males. Byron was preparing for this outcome, as Caesar learns to imitate Arnold in his love for Olimpia in part II:

> *Caes.* I am almost enamoured of her, as
>   Of old the Angels of her earliest sex.
>
> *Arn.* Thou!
>
> *Caes.*   I. But fear not. I'll not be your rival!
>
> *Arn.* Rival!
>
> *Caes.* I could be one right formidable.
>
>   (II.iii.177–80)

In fact, as early as the beginning of the second scene of the play, Arnold has begun to sense that the devil is chafing under his position of servitude and hoping to reverse their positions:

> *Caes.*   Your obedient humble servant.
>
> *Arn.* Say *Master* rather.
>
>   (I.ii.18–19)

Too proud to accept a position of inferiority vis-à-vis a mortal, the devil was evidently going to reassert his superiority by accepting a remarkable challenge, to win Olimpia by getting her to fall in love with him in Arnold's old body.

This is the brilliant direction in which Byron hoped to develop *The Deformed Transformed* according to a note he left:

> Mem. Jealous—Arnold of Caesar. Olympia [*sic*] at first not liking Caesar— then?—Arnold jealous of himself under his former figure, owing to the power of intellect, etc., etc., etc.[17]

The one substantial fragment we have of the dialogue between Arnold and Caesar in part III confirms that jealousy was going to be the focus of the last section. Arnold has become disillusioned with the deal he made with the devil. Originally his desires were purely other-directed: he wanted the beautiful appearance of somebody else so that he could be the envy of all eyes and above all be attractive to women. But now he has come to sense the absence of integrity in his situation and feels dissatisfied with being loved on the basis of externals, loved for anything other than his innermost self. As the devil explains to him:

> you would be *loved*—what you call loved—
> *Self-loved*—loved for *yourself*—for neither health
> Nor wealth—nor youth—nor power—nor rank nor beauty—
> For these you may be stript of—but *beloved*
> As an Abstraction—for—you know not what—
>
> (III.61–65)

Arnold is on the verge of realizing the irony of the situation he has brought upon himself. His original wish was based on the premise that the self is wholly separable from the body, that he could maintain his identity in somebody else's form. But if that is so, when Olimpia falls in love with him in Achilles' form, then she is not falling in love with *him,* but in effect with someone else. In articulating a truly Romantic sense of self—that the human spirit transcends any concrete embodiment of it—the devil condemns Arnold to a perpetual sense of self-alienation in his newfound body and hence to a life of frustration in love.

This frustration was evidently to be compounded by the spectacle of the devil proving that Olimpia could have learned to love Arnold in his original deformed appearance. From Byron's comment "owing to the power of intellect," we may surmise that Caesar was to play a kind of Richard III to Olimpia's Anne, and win her despite his ugliness by the strength and daring of his spirit.[18] Arnold himself had earlier claimed that virtue is independent of physical appearance. When the devil offered to go beyond giving him a new body and include some new virtues in the bargain, Arnold refused, saying: "I ask not / For Valour, since Deformity is daring" (I.i.312–13). Citing the case of Timor the lame Tartar, Arnold claims that he already has the valor of Achilles, though not the beauty; indeed he argues that his ugliness acts as a spur to his virtue. In trying to distinguish the quality of his soul from his outward appearance, Arnold echoes Frankenstein's monster.[19] But if his assertions are correct, then there is no reason why Caesar in Arnold's old form should not be able to woo Olimpia with a demonstration of the superior quality of his intellect, thus leaving Arnold to curse his fate in bargaining away his chances for true love. How exactly the story was to end we cannot be sure—if tragically, either Arnold or Caesar might have accidentally or deliberately killed Olimpia. The most probable scenario for the denouement was for Arnold to attempt to kill Caesar, only to discover that in slaying his double he had slain himself. This ending would have provided a powerful image of the self-destructive character of mimetic desire.

Even though a fragment, *The Deformed Transformed* provides a relentless working out of the self-defeating logic of mimetic desire. In a variant of the proverb "the grass is always greener in someone else's yard," in the world of mimetic desire the pole of satisfaction always remains elusively in the Other. If one somehow gets one's wish and becomes the desired Other, the positions of superiority and inferiority are reversed and one finds oneself jealous of one's original self. Arnold is drawn into an increasingly destructive—and ultimately self-destructive—world of violence because of his nagging sense that his life is governed by a defective providence, that he was not made to be happy (see especially I.i.35–37). Out of this frustration, which is only increased by attempts to overcome it, Arnold is driven to strike out in hopes of bringing the world around him down in ruins.

Having transcribed *The Deformed Transformed* for Byron, and perhaps in the process even influenced in minor details the way the work appeared in print,[20] Shelley had a special interest in the work, which culminated in her attempt to rewrite it in "Transformation." And the phenomenon she chose to focus on is the triangulation of desire. This should not be surprising, since she shows interest in the subject as early as *Frankenstein*.[21] The monster is in fact a veritable case study in mimetic desire. As the book makes clear, his spontaneous desires are few and simple, based in his physical needs and thus involving food and shelter. The monster's desires begin to get complicated only when he starts observing and imitating human beings. It is from watching the De Lacey family that he learns to desire human companionship and love. In his variant of the Quixote syndrome, the monster gets his idea of what he wants to be from reading books, in his case not *Amadis of Gaul* but *Plutarch's Lives, Paradise Lost,* and *The Sorrows of Young Werther* (all three of which, incidentally, deal with the issue of heroism and mimetic desire in one form or another).

The logic of mimetic desire explains why the monster gets locked into a life-and-death struggle with his creator. In some sense the monster's desire for a mate reflects his rivalry with Frankenstein: if his creator is going to have a bride, then the monster should have one, too. His fundamental desire is not for any particular object but for a certain state of being. What he wants above all is to be human, or at least as human as possible, and as he learns from observing the De Laceys, for a male that state requires female companionship. As the monster comes to understand, his sense of his own identity ultimately rests on his ability to define himself in relation to another being of his own species. That consideration explains the seemingly curious fact that he does not desire a beautiful mate, but rather one who would be a mirror image of himself: "one as deformed and horrible as myself would not deny herself to me. My companion must be of the same species and have the same defects" (137).[22]

When Victor destroys the bride intended for the monster, he replies with mimetic violence: Frankenstein's bride must be destroyed on their wedding night. As in Byron's poetic tales, the females in *Frankenstein* become pawns in the power struggles of the males. The murder of Elizabeth precipitates a mortal conflict between Frankenstein and the monster, in which they keep exchanging roles; we cannot tell from one moment to the next who is the hunter and who the hunted, who is the master and who the slave. *Frankenstein* is in fact filled with examples of masculine rivalry and aggression. Frankenstein seeks to create life very much out of a spirit of rivalry with his scientific predecessors and colleagues. Similarly, in the frame tale, Walton hopes to become preeminent among polar explorers. Wherever one turns in the book one finds masculine pairs, men who are in some way bonded together but in some way torn apart by a spirit of competition (Frankenstein and Walton, Frankenstein and his father, Frankenstein and Clerval, Frankenstein and the monster, and so on). Well before she read *The Deformed Transformed,* Shelley shows her awareness of the potentially destructive effects of a masculine ethos so strong that it tries to displace women even from their role in the creation of life.[23]

What is distinctive about Shelley's rewriting of *The Deformed Transformed* in "Transformation" is her attempt to shape a happy ending to the tale, to find a way out of the vicious circle of mimetic desire. Like *Frankenstein,* "Transformation" is a retrospective narrative, but unlike the novel, the story is told solely by its hero, who in this case has survived and learned to reform his character. Again as in *Frankenstein,* to understand her principal character Shelley goes back to his childhood. Like Victor Frankenstein, Guido is an only child, and even more explicitly than his counterpart, he is corrupted by overindulgence: "I became a spoiled child" (123/887).[24] Guido grows up in an even more exclusively masculine world than Frankenstein does. Both his father and his father's one friend, the Marchese Torella, are widowers. It is no accident, then, that masculine aggressiveness becomes the hallmark of Guido's character:

> I was born with the most imperious, haughty, tameless spirit, with which ever mortal was gifted. I quailed before my father only; and he, generous and noble, but capricious and tyrannical, at once fostered and checked the wild impetuosity of my character, making obedience necessary, but inspiring no respect for the motives which guided his commands. To be a man, free, independent; or, in better words, insolent and domineering, was the hope and prayer of my rebel heart. (121–22/886)

We can observe here the fruits of Shelley's reading of Byron: "generous and noble, but capricious and tyrannical" is an apt characterization of the typical Byronic hero. In the words "fostered and checked" Shelley captures the double bind mimetic rivalry inevitably produces. Guido's father both wants his son to resemble him and does not want him to. The rivalry between father and son leads to the development of an extreme masculinity which Shelley calls into question (notice her equation of "to be a man" with to be "insolent and domineering").

Into this hypermasculine world, Shelley introduces a single female, Juliet, the daughter of Torella, who is left in the care of Guido's father when her own father is banished from Genoa. Guido becomes her protector, but he does not begin to love her until a rival for her affections intervenes:

> When I was eleven and Juliet eight years of age, a cousin of mine, much older than either—he seemed to us a man—took great notice of my playmate; he called her his bride, and asked her to marry him. She refused, and he insisted, drawing her unwillingly towards him. With the countenance and emotions of a maniac I threw myself on him—I strove to draw his sword—I

clung to his neck with the ferocious resolve to strangle him: he was obliged
to call for assistance to disengage himself from me. On that night I led Juliet
to the chapel of our house: I made her touch the sacred relics—I harrowed
her child's heart, and profaned her child's lips with an oath, that she would
be mine, and mine only. (122/886)

This passage betrays all the familiar signs of mimetic desire. Guido is
prompted into falling in love with Juliet by observing the attentions of an
older male and indeed we get the impression that Guido feels that in order to
prove himself a man, he has to win a woman for himself, preferably one
already shown to be desirable in the eyes of another male.[25] The outbreak of
mimetic violence is sudden and powerful, thus presaging the destructive behavior Guido exhibits later in life. From the very beginning his love for Juliet
is bound up with his will to power; he regards her as a possession: "she would
me mine, and mine only." Here Shelley gives Guido exactly the same words
she gave Frankenstein in his account of his childhood bond with Elizabeth
(who like Juliet also grows up in the same household as her lover): "since till
death she was to be mine only" (35).

As he matures, Guido's possessiveness continues to dominate his love for
Juliet. When he finally decides to ask for her hand in marriage, his sense of
masculine triumph overwhelms his initial appreciation of her beauty: "Admiration first possessed me; she is mine! was the second proud emotion, and my
lips curled with haughty triumph" (124/888). (The curled lip is of course
another trademark of the Byronic hero.) Threatened with losing Juliet, Guido
is less troubled by the thought of being deprived of her beauty than by the
prospect of another man enjoying it:

And Juliet!—her angel-face and sylph-like form gleamed among the clouds
of my despair with vain beauty; for I had lost her—the glory and flower of
the world! Another will call her his!—that smile of paradise will bless another! (126/890)

More concretely, Guido's love for Juliet becomes bound up with his rivalry
with her father Torella. After Guido's father dies, Torella becomes his guard-
ian and hence his symbolic father ("Torella was to be a second parent to me";
122/887). Guido's sense of competition with his own father thus gets transferred to Torella, and winning the daughter away from him becomes Guido's
way of triumphing. In an odd twist of plot, at one point he kidnaps both
Torella and Juliet, as if conquering the father were as significant to him as
conquering the daughter. At the culminating moment of Guido's mad aggressiveness, his real motive in possessing Juliet comes to the surface: "To bring
Torella to my feet—to possess my Juliet in spite of him" (130/894). In effect
Juliet has no intrinsic value for Guido; what matters to him is that she is a
prize to be won away from a masculine rival.

Thus in "Transformation" Shelley recreates the typical configuration in
Byron's poetic tales: a younger man in competition with an older man for a
woman's affections, with the characters tangled in a web of real and symbolic
ties that gives a vaguely incestuous aura to the situation. Like Byron, Shelley

even gives a political dimension to the story by sending Guido to Paris at one point and associating him with dynastic intrigue in France, a struggle within the royal family, who are "alternating friends and foes—now meeting in prodigal feasts, now shedding blood in rivalry" (122–23/887). This "savage strife" culminates in a moment of mimetic violence: "The Duke of Orleans was waylaid and murdered by the Duke of Burgundy" (123/887). Up to this point, Shelley could be imitating many of Byron's works, but in the crucial plot development of "Transformation," she focuses on *The Deformed Transformed*. In the depths of his despair over losing Juliet, Guido observes a storm and a shipwreck. Only one person survives the shipwreck: Shelley's equivalent of Byron's Arnold: "a misshapen dwarf, with squinting eyes, distorted features, and body deformed" (127/891).[26] The dwarf offers to exchange bodies with Guido for a period of three days; in return he will give Guido a chest filled with treasure which will allow him to buy his revenge against Torella. Thus Shelley refashions the central motif of the exchange of bodies in *The Deformed Transformed*.

Shelley develops a number of interesting variations on her central Byronic theme. She hints at the undercurrent of homosexuality that always seems to lie just beneath the surface in these intense male relationships.[27] The dwarf tells Guido: "something does please me in your well-proportioned body and handsome face" (128/892). And in one of the most emotionally charged moments in the story—Guido shivers—the dwarf replies to the question, What can he possibly desire of a man who has lost all his possessions?: "Your comely face and well-made limbs" (129/893). In view of the fact that the dwarf is clearly Guido's *Doppelgänger,* or shadow, and hence a reflection of part of his self, one could also read these passages as an expression of the hero's narcissism. The dwarf gives voice to Guido's love of his own "comely face and well-made limbs," which is at the root of all his problems. His pride, vanity, and self-centeredness make it impossible for him to love another human being as anything other than an extension of his self, which explains why he treats Juliet as a possession. Guido's narcissism is in many respects the keynote of his character. Even after his destructive encounter with the dwarf, he does not fully renounce his narcissistic tendencies: "my first broken request was for a mirror" (134/897). Shelley seems to dwell upon this aspect of his character, even at the end of the story:

> I thought myself a right proper youth when I saw the dear reflection of my own well-known features. I confess it is a weakness, but I avow it, I do entertain a considerable affection for the countenance and limbs I behold, whenever I look at a glass; and have more mirrors in my house, and consult them oftener than any beauty in Venice. Before you too much condemn me, permit me to say that no one better knows than I the value of his own body; no one, probably, except myself, ever having had it stolen from him. (134–35/897)

If "Transformation" is a commentary on Byron, then this is a telling passage, revealing the narcissistic tendencies that shadow the Romantic self, even—

and perhaps especially—in its moments of greatest self-consciousness (a theme Shelley had already explored in *Frankenstein*).[28] And the importance of mirrors and reflections in "Transformation" is another sign of the centrality of mimetic desire in the story.

Shelley's rewriting of Byron is most evident in the way she inverts the pattern of *The Deformed Transformed*. In Byron's play, the hero begins as ugly, and becomes handsome as a result of his meeting with a demonic figure. In "Transformation" just the opposite happens: the hero begins as handsome, and becomes ugly as a result of the bargain he makes. Indeed, Shelley might have entitled her story "The Transformed Deformed." The psychological implications of these contrasting patterns are interesting. Byron's story seems to reflect a typical masculine fantasy: "Despite appearances, I am not ugly: inside me is a handsome man just waiting to get out." Shelley's story seems to reflect the corresponding feminine fear: "The handsome appearance of this man conceals an inner ugliness: inside is a hideous demon just waiting to get out." "Transformation" repeatedly suggests that the hidden ugliness of the male is his aggressiveness and will to power. In that sense, Guido's transformation is in fact a revelation of his inner character. As in *Frankenstein,* Shelley imaginatively depicts the release of a man's dark, violent urges in the form of a shadowy companion. Guido even thinks of himself in terms reminiscent of Frankenstein's creature: "I was not quite sure that, if seen, the mere boys would not stone me to death as I passed, for a monster" (131/895).

Thus "Transformation" appears to be headed for the kind of tragic conclusion we have seen in all the other tales of mimetic desire we have examined. The dwarf violates his bargain with Guido and uses his newly acquired body to win Juliet for himself. Guido thus experiences the horrible emotion Arnold has to live with: in the purest distillation of mimetic desire, he becomes jealous of himself: "But it was not I—it was he, the fiend, arrayed in my limbs, speaking with my voice, winning her with my looks of love" (130/894). One might expect Guido's sense of rivalry with himself to result in the kind of self-destruction that Byron was evidently going to portray in *The Deformed Transformed*. But Shelley was out to revise the Byronic myth, not repeat it. In her variation, the release of Guido's aggressive impulses in the hideous form of the dwarf turns out to be purgative, a way for Guido to get them out of his system. In fact, the dwarf points the way to Guido's salvation: he wins Juliet precisely by swallowing his pride and humbly begging Torella for forgiveness. Guido's realization—"O! had an angel from Paradise whispered to me to act thus!" (132/896)—suggests how to interpret the climax of "Transformation." When Guido murders the dwarf he is in effect killing the "demoniac violence and wicked self idolatry" (131/895) within himself, which have come to be crystallized and externalized in this hideous form. Only by destroying part of himself—his masculine pride—can Guido be freed to experience true love with Juliet.

Shelley thus tells the story of the taming and domestication of the Byronic hero (in some ways resembling what Charlotte Brontë does in *Jane Eyre*). Leaving behind the hypermasculine world to which he was attracted, Guido becomes *il Cortese,* the "courteous one," now fit for the society of women. Shelley is aware of the price Guido must pay for his transformation but suggests that the result makes the bargain worthwhile:

> I have never, indeed, wholly recovered my strength—my cheek is paler since—my person a little bent. Juliet sometimes ventures to allude bitterly to the malice that caused this change, but I kiss her on the moment, and tell her all is for the best. I am a fonder and more faithful husband—and true is this—but for that wound, never had I called her mine. (135/898)

Here the domestic world finally triumphs over the heroic, as Guido loses his aggressiveness and settles down to a peaceful life within society, for the first time speaking of his "fellow-citizens" (135/898). To be sure, Juliet must settle for something less of a man: Guido no longer has the same strength. But in return for accepting a diminished version of her lover, she wins his undying loyalty. With characteristic sobriety and restraint, Shelley carries out her struggle with Byron and reshapes one of the central myths of his poetry. As in *Frankenstein,* she exposes the dark side of Romanticism, the destructive potential of the egotism and narcissism that lies barely concealed beneath the new Romantic premium on the self. However one may side in the quarrel between Shelley and Byron, one must acknowledge that "Transformation" displays remarkable insight into the pattern embodied in its precursor text. And in helping to uncover the centrality of triangulated desire and mimetic rivalry in Byron, Shelley once again, as in *Frankenstein,* provides a profound clue as to the character of Romanticism in general.

Notes

1. To survey developments in the contemporary criticism of *Frankenstein,* see the excellent collection of essays, edited by George Levine and U. C. Knoepflmacher, *The Endurance of Frankenstein* (Berkeley: University of California Press, 1979), which contains several feminist essays on the novel. For further feminist approaches, see, among others, Sandra M. Gilbert and Susan Gubar, *The Madwoman in the Attic: The Woman Writer and the Nineteenth-Century Literary Imagination* (New Haven: Yale University Press, 1979), 213–47; Mary Poovey, "My Hideous Progeny: Mary Shelley and the Feminization of Romanticism," *PMLA* 95 (1980): 332–47; and Gayatri Chakravorty Spivak, "Three Women's Texts and a Critique of Imperialism," *"Race," Writing, and Difference,* ed. Henry Louis Gates, Jr. (Chicago: University of Chicago Press, 1986), 262–80.

2. For an example of this approach, see my book, *Creature and Creator: Mythmaking and English Romanticism* (Cambridge: Cambridge University Press, 1984), 103–32.

3. For an approach to Shelley which focuses on her concern for the integrity of the family, see Anne K. Mellor, *Mary Shelley: Her Life, Her Fiction, Her Monsters* (London: Methuen, 1988). For a contrary view—that *Frankenstein* constitutes a critique of the bourgeois family—see the essay by Kate Ellis, "Monsters in the Garden: Mary Shelley and the Bourgeois Family," in Levine and Knoepflmacher, *Endurance,* 123–42.

4. Shelley's letters indicate that she had an unusually high opinion of the drama. See, for example, her letter to Byron of February 2, 1823: "The more I read this Poem that I send, the more I admire it. I pray that Your Lordship will finish it. . . . You never wrote any thing more beautiful than one lyric in it—& the whole, I am tempted to say, surpasses 'Your former glorious style'—at least it fully equals the very best parts of your best productions." See *The Letters of Mary Wollstonecraft Shelley*, 3 vols., ed. Betty T. Bennett (Baltimore: Johns Hopkins University Press, 1980–88), 1:311.

5. For such judgments, see George Steiner, *The Death of Tragedy* (New York: Hill and Wang, 1963), 211; and Leslie A. Marchand, *Byron's Poetry: A Critical Introduction* (Cambridge, Mass.: Harvard University Press, 1968), 94.

6. All quotations from Byron are taken from Jerome J. McGann, ed., *Lord Byron: The Complete Poetical Works* (Oxford: Clarendon Press). All poems cited appear in volume 3 (1981), except *Mazeppa* (volume 4, 1986) and *The Deformed Transformed*, ed. Barry Weller (volume 6, 1991).

7. See, for example, René Girard, *Deceit, Desire, and the Novel*, trans. Yvonne Freccero (Baltimore: Johns Hopkins University Press, 1966), esp. chapter 1, " 'Triangular' Desire," 1–52; *Violence and the Sacred*, trans. Patrick Gregory (Baltimore: Johns Hopkins University Press, 1977); and *Things Hidden Since the Foundation of the World*, trans. Stephen Bann and Michael Metteer (Stanford: Stanford University Press, 1987).

8. See especially *Violence*, 169–92.

9. In his later writings, in particular, *Beyond the Pleasure Principle*, Freud did come to recognize two basic drives, but it is significant that even here he chose not to call the second drive *aggression* but to reinterpret it in negative terms as the *death instinct*.

10. For a more general discussion of this point in Byron, with particular regard to *Cain*, see the chapter "The Metaphysical Rebel" in my *Creature and Creator*, esp. 144–45.

11. For a brief comparison of *Frankenstein* and *The Deformed Transformed*, see Daniel P. Watkins, "The Ideological Dimensions of Byron's *The Deformed Transformed*," *Criticism* 25 (1983): 31.

12. See Charles E. Robinson, "The Devil as Doppelgänger in *The Deformed Transformed*: The Sources and Meanings of Byron's Unfinished Drama," *Bulletin of the New York Public Library* 74 (1970): 177.

13. On the importance of Romulus and Remus in *The Deformed Transformed*, see Robinson, 195–96. For Romulus and Remus in Girard, see *Violence*, 61–65, and *The Scapegoat*, trans. Yvonne Freccero (Baltimore: Johns Hopkins University Press, 1986), 91–94.

14. See also Caesar's comment: "Aye, slave or master, 'tis all one" (II.iii.137).

15. In the flyleaf of her copy of *The Deformed Transformed*, Shelley wrote: "I do not know how he meant to finish it; but he said himself that the whole conduct of the story was already conceived." See Ernest Hartley Coleridge, ed., *The Works of Lord Byron* 7 vols. (London: John Murray, 1898–1904), 5:474.

16. For the most plausible account, see Robinson, 194–96.

17. Coleridge, 5:531.

18. For an extended comparison of *The Deformed Transformed* and *Richard III*, see G. Wilson Knight, *Byron and Shakespeare* (New York: Barnes & Noble, 1966), 155–59.

19. See *Creature and Creator*, 127–28.

20. See Emily W. Sunstein, *Mary Shelley: Romance and Reality* (Boston: Little,

Brown, 1989), 229. In their comparison of Byron's autograph manuscript with the first printed text of *The Deformed Transformed,* Weller and McGann speak of Byron's "tacit sanction of changes, which Mary Shelley may have introduced in the process of transcription" (McGann, 6:727).

21. For a Girardian reading of *Frankenstein* from a feminist perspective, see Mary Jacobus, "Is There a Woman in This Text?" *New Literary History* 14 (1982): esp. 127–37.

22. All quotations from *Frankenstein* are taken from Harold Bloom's edition (New York: New American Library, 1965).

23. We can only speculate as to the extent to which Shelley's awareness of the phenomenon of masculine rivalry was based on her experience of the relationship of her husband and Byron. Certainly there is much evidence of triangular desire in the Shelley–Byron circle.

24. I quote "Transformation" from *Mary Shelley: Collected Tales and Stories,* ed. Charles E. Robinson (Baltimore: Johns Hopkins University Press, 1976). But since the story is at the moment most readily available in M. H. Abrams, ed., *The Norton Anthology of English Literature,* 5th ed., vol. 2, (New York: Norton, 1986), I give two page references, the first to Robinson's edition, the second to the Norton.

25. The phallic dimension of this incident is hinted at in Guido's reaching for his rival's sword, and perhaps even in his forcing Juliet to touch the "sacred relics." Later in the story, Guido's phallic anxiety becomes evident when he worries about the length of his weapon: "I had no sword—if indeed my distorted arms could wield a soldier's weapon—but I had a dagger, and in that lay my every hope" (132/896).

26. This shipwreck scene recreates a passage from Calderón's *El mágico prodigioso,* which Percy Shelley had translated into English (ii.23–61). The way the dwarf appears before Guido parallels the way Calderón's Daemon appears before his hero, Cyprian. Shelley's reference to a "wizard's wand" (126/890) in her tale reinforces the parallel. The Calderón play is another story of mimetic desire. Two men, named Floro and Lelio, are in love with the same woman (Justina); when Cyrpian tries to mediate the dispute, he ends up falling in love with Justina himself. Robinson proposes *El mágico prodigioso* as a source for *The Deformed Transformed* as well (187–89).

27. Here I touch on the work of Eve Kosofsky Sedgwick, who in her book *Between Men* (New York: Columbia University Press, 1985) reinterprets what Girard calls mimetic desire as what Sedgwick calls homosocial bonding (see esp. 16–17, 21–24). Despite the fact that Sedgwick appears to be presenting a revisionary account of Girard, in many respects her theory is less radical than his. Instead of presenting aggression as a genuinely independent drive, she maintains the monolithically erotic bias of Freudian thought. She may be looking at a different kind of eros than Freud did, but her analysis still privileges eros over all other drives. For that reason, whatever the general cogency of her theory may be, I find Girard more relevant to the analysis of Romantic literature, and especially to the relation of Byron and Shelley.

28. See *Creature and Creator,* 124.

The Last Man: Apocalypse Without Millennium

Morton D. Paley

Early in 1826 appeared a book advertised as a "new Romance, or, rather Prophetic Tale"[1]—Mary Shelley's novel *The Last Man*. It was published at just the wrong time. Since 1823 the literary world had been preoccupied with a controversy about just who had invented the Last Man, beginning with the publication of Thomas Campbell's poem "The Last Man" and Francis Jeffrey's suggestion in *The Edinburgh Review* that Campbell was indebted to Byron's "Darkness" for the idea.[2] Campbell was moved to print an open letter to Jeffrey asserting his own priority and claiming that it was he who at least fifteen years before had suggested to Byron the subject of "a being witnessing the extinction of his species and of the creation, and of his looking, under the fading eye of nature, at desolate cities, ships floating with the dead."[3] According to Campbell, the publication of "Darkness" had discouraged him from pursuing the theme, but "I was provoked to change my mind, when my friend Barry Cornwall informed me that an acquaintance of his intended to write a long poem entitled the Last Man."[4]

Barry Cornwall's acquaintance was Thomas Lovell Beddoes, who had been projecting a play on the Last Man, but who now gave up on the subject at least temporarily. "Meanwhile let Tom Campbell rule his roast & mortify the ghost of Sternhold," he wrote acerbically to his friend Thomas Forbes Kelsall. "It is a subject for Michael Angelo, not for the painter of the Marquis of Granby on the sign-post."[5] Beddoes's withdrawal may have been prompted by the mirth Campbell's claims had elicited from the literary press. "—How could he submit, in short, to produce a *last* Last Man, when the *first* conception was his?" asked *The London Magazine*.[6] The anonymous author went on to recall the first of all Last Man narratives, published anonymously in London as *Omegarus and Syderia, a Romance in Futurity* in 1806.[7] Campbell's claim was ridiculous, "the idea of the Last Man being most particularly obvious, or rather absolutely common-place, and a book with the taking title of *Omegarius* [sic], or *The Last Man,* having gone the rounds of all circulating libraries for years past."

By 1826 the subject of the Last Man had come to seem not apocalyptic but ridiculous. Behind the ridicule, however, there is a suggestion that the imagination resists the idea of Lastness, an idea that presupposes a recipient or reader whose very existence negates the Lastness of the narrating subject. This supposed unimaginability is the theme of an essay published by *The Monthly Magazine* entitled "The Last Book: with a Dissertation on Last Things in General."[8]

The word "last," it is to be lamented, is not sufficiently final to preclude the emulative subsequency of all we leave behind: we cannot close the doors of language on the thousand little beginnings that tread on the heels of the safest conclusion. A term should be invented comprehensive enough to include those superlatively late comers that usually follow the last. . . . But, as words are at present, last things are generally the last things in the world that are last.

The Lay of the Last Minstrel and *The Last of the Mohicans* are among the instances that illustrate "the inadequacy of the word to include contingencies and possibilities," and the existence of more than one Last Man—"Mr. Campbell's prior and poetical candidate" and "Mrs. Shelley's subsequent and sibylline one"—demonstrates the self-contradictory nature of the subject. "In short, there is no getting at the last of our never-ending, still-beginning language."

We can see that in the year that Mary Shelley's novel was published, its very subject seemed to invite derision, although behind that derision one senses a certain eschatalogical anxiety that may account for the virulence of some of the reviews. "A sickening repetition of horrors," said *The Literary Gazette and Journal of Belles Lettres, Arts, Sciences, &c.;* "The offspring of a diseased imagination, and of a most polluted taste," said the *The Monthly Review.*[9] *Blackwood's* cruelly called it an "abortion."[10] A writer in *The Literary Magnet,* without even having seen the book, condemned it as "another Raw-head-and-bloody-bones," presumably referring to *Frankenstein*. This reviewer also recalled *Omegarus and Syderia:* "There is, we believe, a novel already published, entitled Omegarius [*sic*], or the Last Man, a bantling of the Leadenhall press; a fact which might have spared Mr. Campbell the trouble of writing his long letter to the editor of the Edinburgh Review, on the subject of the originality of the conception of *his* Last Man."[11]

It's as if the critics were trying to annihilate with their rhetoric the very possibility of writing a novel on this subject. The author's gender was of course not spared. In a mock announcement *The Wasp* published the title as *The Last Woman,*[12] while two publications combined misogyny with the now familiar play on Lastness: "Why not *the last Woman?*" asked *The Literary Gazette and Journal of Belles Lettres*. "She would have known better how to paint her distress at having nobody left to talk to."[13] (Actually, this last point touches inadvertently on an important point to be considered later.) Although the novel was reprinted in Paris by Galignani (1826) and then in Philadelphia (1833), it was not a success, and it may be for this reason, as Elizabeth Nitchie suggests, that its author "avoided the unnatural"[14] in her subsequent novels.

One theme sounded in some of the humorous and satirical essays already discussed appears in a number of reviews of *The Last Man*—the supposed impossibility of representing the subject:

This idea of "The Last Man" has already tempted the genius of more than one of our poets, and, in truth, it is a theme which appears to open a magnificent and boundless field to the imagination. But we have only to consider it for a moment, in order to be convinced that the mind of man might as well endeavour to describe the transactions which are taking place in any of the countless planets that are suspended beyond our own, as to anticipate the horrors of the day which shall see the dissolution of our system.[15]

Even a sympathetic critic could reach the same conclusion. Reviewing Mary Shelley's *Lodore* in 1835, *The Literary Gazette* said *The Last Man* had "passages of great power," but continued:

> Details, which usually strengthen, here weaken the general effect. "Of that day no man knoweth." The imagination penetrates the unknown by dint of its own strong sympathy: and with that terrible future we have nothing in common; ere it arrives all the usual emotions must have perished.[16]

The conviction shared by most of the book's early critics, whether reflective or vituperative, is of the impropriety of the subject. In "Darkness," Byron had envisaged apocalypse without millennium;[17] Mary Shelley made this, for the first time since *Omegarus and Syderia,* and subject of a novel and moved almost the entire critical establishment to deny the possibility of imagining Lastness.

The Last Man was the first ambitious work undertaken by Mary Shelley after her husband's death and her consequent return to London. Almost everyone who has written about this novel adverts to the personal element of isolation in it and cites Mary's journal entry for May 14, 1824: "The last man! Yes I may well describe that solitary being's feelings, feeling myself as the last relic of a beloved race, my companions extinct before me."[18] This feeling is amplified in a letter dated October 3, 1824, while her novel was being written:

> The happiness I enjoyed and the sufferings I endured in Italy make present pleasures & annoyances appear like the changes of a mask—. . . . My imagination is not much exalted by a representation mean & puerile when compared to the real delight of my intercourse [with] my exalted Shelley . . . and others of less note, but remembered now with fon[dness] as having made a part of the Elect.[19]

This dark weather of the heart may also, as Brian Aldiss suggests,[20] have recalled to her the extraordinary meteorological events of the summer of 1816, called "the year without a summer," causing her to include these as well as the "Elect" in her work-in-progress.

As the autobiographical aspect of *The Last Man* is widely recognized,[21] it requires only brief mention here. Percy Bysshe Shelley is resuscitated (only to be drowned at sea in the end) as Adrian, earl of Windsor, who would have been king of England had not England become a republic in the year 2073. He is a beautiful if not ineffectual angel, his mind "frank and unsuspicious . . . gifted . . . by every natural grace, endowed with transcendant powers of intellect, unblemished by the shadow of a defect (unless his dreadless independence of thought was to be construed into one)."[22] He is, needless to say, a republican and opposes the revanchist plans of his mother, the dour Countess of Windsor. Byron, who died while the novel was in its early stages, appears as Lord Raymond, at times the Bad Lord B., whose countenance is convulsed by a spasm of pain as he says "Even the ghost of friendship has departed, and love"—only to break off and curl his lip in disdain (34). As for the author, she divides herself into two characters: Lionel Verney, the Last Man and narrator, and Lionel's sister Perdita, who is also compounded of Mary's stepsister, friend, rival, and thorn-in-the-flesh, Claire Clairmont. Perdita is allowed to realize Claire's fantasy of marrying Byron/Raymond, but she must suffer his infidelity with the Greek princess Evadne and then commit suicide after her husband's death. Thus Mary Shelley in *The Last Man* reconstituted in an idealized form her little band of the Elect and killed them off again except for her narrating self.

The Last Man is nevertheless more than a roman à clef. Two of its most important aspects have been so expertly discussed as to allow me to concentrate upon a third. Lee Sterrenburg has viewed this book's political—or counterpolitical—nature as a reaction to the state of Europe after the failure of the French Revolution, the defeat of Napoleon, and the Congress of Vienna.[23] (As all these events took place during the lifetime of Percy Shelley and tempered but failed to obliterate his revolutionary hopes, the despair of *The Last Man* is in some sense a repudiation of his politics as well.) In her recent literary biography of Mary Shelley, Anne K. Mellor fruitfully explored the theme of the nuclear family in *The Last Man,* arguing that in social terms, the novel pits her personal ideology of the nuclear family as the source of psychological fulfillment and cultural values against those human and natural forces which undermine it: male egoism, female self-destruction, and death.[24] My own concern is the manner in which *The Last Man,* culminating a tradition in which *Omegarus and Syderia* and "Darkness" are prominent, denies the linkage of apocalypse and millennium that had previously been celebrated in some of the the great works of the Romantic epoch, perhaps most fully in *Prometheus Unbound.*

In contrast to the universe of Cousin de Grainville, Mary Shelley's has no sovereign God and no supernatural agency. However, although eschatology has been secularized[25] to a great degree, there remain ghosts of a former paradigm and any rational explanation of the destruction of humankind is conspicuously absent—the plague that kills everyone in the world save four people and then stops remains at least as arbitrary as Calvinist predestination. As in both *Omegarus and Syderia* and "Darkness," signs of a millennium appear only to be dissipated. And like these preceding works and Campbell's "Last Man" as well, *The Last Man* is presented as an indirect narrative. In this instance, it is the "Author's Introduction" that displays that "buffering" that the subject seems to demand.

The introduction recapitulates an excursion to the supposed Cavern of the Sibyl on the Bay of Naples. In reality, that trip, made by Mary and Percy Shelley with Claire Clairmont on December 8, 1818,[26] had proven disappointing. In *The Last Man,* the date is preserved, but the nameless and genderless narrator reduces the participants to herself and her companion, and she makes it the occasion of a marvellous discovery. While exploring the sibyl's cave, the author and her companion, like Grainville's narrator, desert their guides, and like him they are consequently initiated into the history of the future. First they enter "a wide cavern with an arched dome-like roof" (2), a setting worthy of a painting by John Martin. There they find "piles of leaves, fragments of bark, and a white filmy substance, resembling the inner part of the green hood which shelters the grain of the unripe Indian corn"(3). (In *The Madwoman in the Attic* Sandra Gilbert and Susan Gubar call attention to the specifically female associations of this debris as well as of the "dim hypaethric cavern" in which it is discovered.)[27] On the leaves they find inscriptions in many languages, ancient and modern.

" 'This *is* the Sibyl's cave; these are Sibylline leaves,' " exclaims the author's companion (3). His exclamation has several associations. There is book VI of the Aeneid, alluded to on the same page, where the Cumaean Sibyl, wielding the talismanic Golden Bough, leads Aeneas underground to his vision of the afterlife. There is also Michelangelo's powerful representation of her, which Shelley would have seen while in Rome during the spring of 1819. A further, modern dimension is provided by Coleridge's *Sibylline Leaves* of 1817, in the title of which is implicit the same play of meaning suggested by Shelley's authorial persona, self-characterized as the "decipherer" of these "discoveries in the slight Sibylline pages" (3, 4). The line of vision thus passes from the ancient embodiment of female vatic power to the modern imagination, coming to reside in the author. Indeed, in a letter written at the time that the novel was published, Shelley refers to it as "my Sibylline leaves."[28] Thus the introduction to *The Last Man* has a function similar to that of the beginning of *Omegarus and Syderia* and to the first line of "Darkness." We are to be told the history of the Last Man before he exists, and we are therefore relieved of the anxiety of imagining a world in which there are no readers.

The human world projected in the early parts of Lionel Verney's ensuing narrative may at first seem like a realization of the archetype of human development propounded in the works of Blake, Wordsworth, and Coleridge and amplified in those of Keats and Percy Bysshe Shelley. In these Romantic mythologies, the history of the race is repeated in the individual, beginning in primal innocence, experiencing a "fall," and eventuating in a higher innocence.[29] The integrating factor in this process is the human imagination, which brings into play all the energies of the psyche, harmonizing knowledge and power. These terms—especially imagination and power—recur throughout the novel, but in such contexts as to make us aware of enormous fissures between them. Ultimately *The Last Man* is a repudiation of what might simplistically be termed the Romantic ethos as represented, for example, in the poetics and politics of Percy Bysshe Shelley.

The "Romantic" ethos characteristically involves a search for the actuation of true power. At first it seems as if Lionel Verney will be an exemplification of this process, growing up as a boy-shepherd in the Wordsworthian territory of Cumberland. But Lionel, unlike the boy Wordsworth portrays himself as having been, is rough and uncouth. When he says "my chief superiority consisted in power," he is speaking of mere brute force. Young Lionel is if anything a travesty of the Wordsworthian ideal of power. It is only by the civilizing influence of Adrian that Lionel's conception of himself changes. He is then able to look back upon his past self as one who "deified the uplands, glades, and streams" (22) and to quote from "The World Is Too Much with Us," but power no longer seems to be one of his attributes, except perhaps close to the very end where the Last Man regresses to his former propensities of "robber and shepherd."

In Lord Raymond—at least in that part of the novel written before Byron's death—we see the embodiment of the will-to-power. Returning from the Greek wars, where he has been a victorious general, Raymond inherits a fortune and dedicates himself to becoming Lord Protector. He will rule those who he thinks despised him before he became famous and rich and who now adulate him. "If the acquisition of power in the shape of wealth caused this alteration, that power they should feel as an iron yoke. Power therefore was the aim of all his endeavours" (27). Raymond enjoys the exercise of power and is both enlightened and intelligent enough to employ it benevolently, but he is not self-disciplined enough to continue long to do so, and he returns to the Greek wars to die in empty, plague-ridden Constantinople.

When Adrian falls in love with the Greek princess Evadne, we are told that his heart "had power, but no knowledge." The result of such division is described in *Prometheus Unbound:*

> The good want power, but to weep barren tears,
> The powerful goodness want—worse need for them,
> The wise want love, and those who love want wisdom;
> And all best things are thus confused to ill.
>   (I.625–28)[30]

The conjunction of these separated human qualities is achieved at the end, when Demogorgon can speak of "Love from its awful throne of patient power/ In the wise heart" (IV.557–58). Likewise Wordsworth desires (in a passage not known to the Shelley circle) "Knowledge not purchased by the loss of power."[31] Such a synthesis seems not to be attainable by Adrian or by anyone else in *The Last Man,* however much it may be wished for or simulated. "We aided the sick," says Verney "and comforted the sorrowing; turning from the multitudinous dead to the rare survivors, with an energy of desire that bore the resemblance of power" (230).

At first it may seem that Adrian's imaginative qualities may offer compensation for his inability to unite knowledge and power. Indeed he is given a speech that sounds something like a statement by Percy Bysshe Shelley:

> "Look into the mind of man, where wisdom reigns enthroned; where imagination, the painter, sits, with his pencil dipt in hues lovelier than those of sunset, adorning familiar life with glowing tints. What a noble boon, worthy the giver, is the imagination! it takes from reality its leaden hue: it envelopes all thought and sensation in a radiant veil, and with an hand of beauty beckons us from the sterile seas of life, to her gardens, and bowers, and glades of bliss." (53)

However, one need only compare the idea of imagination in *A Defence of Poetry* to see the difference. For example, in discussing the heroic aspect of ancient Rome, Shelley says: "The imagination beholding the beauty of this order, created it out of itself according to its own idea: the consequence was empire, and the reward ever-living fame" (494). For Shelley, the imagination moves from the individual to society; Adrian's conception is in contrast solipsistic, offering only an escape from a grim reality.

Other characters either exemplify Adrian's limited view of imagination or, worse, find imagination a torment. Raymond is "one who seemed to govern the whole earth in his grasping imagination, and who only quailed when he attempted to rule himself" (40). Lionel, searching for Raymond's body in the ruins of Constantinople, says, "For a moment I could yield to the creative power of the imagination, and for a moment was soothed by the sublime fictions it presented to me." Perdita, who is characterized by "active fancy," "visionary moods," and "creative imagination" (10, 92), finds no constructive outlet for her powers (unless it be in copying Old Master paintings); but after the death of Raymond, Lionel finds her to be "influenced by passionate grief and a disturbed imagination" (152) and says, "Nor do I wonder that a feeling akin to insanity should drive you to bitter and unreasonable imaginings" (153). Terrified in plague-stricken London, Idris (Lionel's wife and Adrian's sister), "with all the vividness of imagination with which misery is always replete . . . poured out the emotions of her heart" (219).

The nature of imagination in *The Last Man* is teasing. It presents itself as a savior only to be revealed as a creator of phantasms. This is nowhere so much evident as in two episodes involving Lionel Verney. When Lionel visits a hospital in London, "The tormentor, the imagination, busied itself in picturing my own loved ones" (203). He looks for relief by going to a play, which turns out to be *Macbeth*. He does find a temporary respite when the setting for the witch scene "permitted the imagination to revel, without fear of contradiction, or reproof from the heart" (204), but the fancy does not cheat so well as she is famed to do: at Macduff's "All my pretty ones" speech, "I re-echoed the cry of Macduff, and then rushed out as from a hell of torture, to find calm in the free air and silent street."

Verney's last attempt to find salvation through the imagination is ultimately no more successful. Alone in Rome, he thinks of the city as "the wonder of the world, sovereign mistress of the imagination, majestic and eternal survivor of millions of generations of extinct men" (335). This leads him to continue:

> The romance with which, dipping our pencils in the rainbow hues of sky and transcendent nature, we to a degree gratuitously endow the Italians, replaced the somber grandeur of antiquity. I remembered the dark monk, and floating figures of "The Italian," and how my boyish blood had thrilled at the description. I called to mind Corinna ascending the Capitol to be crowned, and, passing from the heroine to the author, reflected how the Enchantress Spirit of Rome held sovereign sway over the minds of the imaginative, until it rested on me—sole remaining spectator of its wonders. (336)

This passage sounds very much like an illustration of Adrian's escapist fantasy, and one need only contrast the statement about Rome already cited from *A Defence of Poetry* to see the difference. Critics who find Lionel a newborn poet in the last pages of the novel[32] ignore the irony of his conjuring up novels by Anne Radcliffe and Mme. de Staël to create a ghostly community. Indeed, the personification of Rome here seems to mask only for a moment the female personification of Plague, although Verney doesn't seem to realize it.

The failure of imagination in *The Last Man* is linked to a theme also prominent in *Omegarus and Syderia:* the failure of art. The imaginative Perdita is described in terms of one of the artistic touchstones of the era and Mary's personal favorite:[33] "she was like one of Guido's saints" (9), and she paints copies after Raphael, Correggio, and Claude (35). However, it seems significant that these *are* copies and that the only creative artist in the book is Evadne, Perdita's unsuccessful rival for Raymond's love. Raymond sponsors an international competition for a design "characterized by originality as well as by perfect beauty" for his projected national gallery of art; the only entry that fits this bill is Evadne's anonymously submitted. The consequence is estrangement between Raymond and Perdita, but Evadne's artistic gift brings her not happiness but suffering; she will die in Turkey of unrequited love for Raymond.

Later in the book, after Lionel Verney becomes the Last Man, art takes on a sinister aspect. In the Vatican Gallery Verney looks upon the statues in a paroxysm of frustration:

> Each stone deity was possessed by sacred gladness, and the eternal fruition of love. They looked on me with unsympathizing complacency, and often in wild accents I reproached them for their supreme indifference—for they were human shapes, the human form divine was manifest in each fairest limb and lineament. . . . Often . . . I clasped their icy proportions, and coming between Cupid and his Psyche's lips, pressed the unconceiving marble. (338).

In the world of the Last Man, these masterpieces appear not as bringers of solace but as self-born mockers of man's enterprise, and, as in Yeats's poem, they too break hearts. The ultimate verdict on the Romantic ethos of redemption through art is expressed by Verney: "Farewell to the arts . . . farewell to poetry and deep philosophy, for man's imagination is cold" (234).

Countering the insufficient artistic imagination in Mary Shelley's novel is the power of prophecy. Here as elsewhere the author's theme is in direct contrast to the politics and poetics of her late husband. There are no unacknowledged legislators here, enlarging the sense of human community through their poems. Instead, prophecy is seen as entirely divorced from human ends—impersonal, inexplicable. We see this from the very beginning in the novel's epigraph from Milton:

> Let no man seek
> Henceforth to be foretold what shall befall
> Him or his children.[34]

Adam says this after he has been vouchsafed a vision of futurity up to the Flood. In context, it has a particular bearing upon *The Last Man:* Michael has in Adam's view shown him disasters he cannot prevent, the knowledge of which can only torment him. This terribly pessimistic coloring given to prophetic vision is, later, reinforced by another text. After his first premonition that he will be the Last Man, Verney asks, "Were these warning voices, whose inarticulate and oracular sense forced belief upon me?" (192) only to recall a passage from Coleridge's translation of Schiller's *Wallenstein:*

> Yet I would not call *them*
> Voices of warning, that announce to us
> Only the inevitable.

The inevitable is also voiced by the dying Evadne, who prophesies the death of Raymond in terms that seem borrowed from the Book of Revelation: "fire, and war, and plague, unite for thy destruction—O my Raymond, there is no safety for thee!" (131). Far from agreeing with Verney that these prophecies are "the ravings of a maniac, Raymond accepts them fatalistically: "Fire, the sword, and plague! They may all be found in yonder city; on my head alone may they fall" (134). After it becomes clear that these apocalyptic visitations will fall on all humanity," Verney hears "an internal voice" say:

> Thus from eternity, it was decreed: the steeds that bear Time onward had this hour and this fulfillment enchained to them, since the void brought forth its burthen. Would you read backwards the unchangeable laws of Necessity? (290)

These words have a curious relation to several passages in *Prometheus Unbound.* In act III, scene i, Demogorgon, who may be said to incarnate Necessity, arrives in the car of the Hour to dethrone Jupiter and make possible the freeing of Prometheus and the instauration of a new age. Then, just after the beginning of act IV, "A Train of dark Forms and Shadows" sings:

> Spectres we
> Of the dead Hours be,
> We bear Time to his tomb in Eternity.
> (11–13)

This is of course a prelude to the millennial transformations that are the subject of act IV. Verney's internal voice seems to have taken the images of steeds, chariot, and Time along with the idea of Necessity derived from William Godwin and to have inverted the meanings Percy Shelley gave them. No longer part of a millenarian conception of history, they are now associated with the destruction of humankind. Verney addresses Necessity as a kind of Norn, blind to human concerns and female as is the Plague itself: "Mother of the World! Servant of the Omnipotent! eternal, changeless Necessity! who with busy fingers sittest ever weaving the indissoluble chain of events!"

The idea of a Millennium does surface repeatedly in *The Last Man,* but it always turns out to be a will-o'-the-wisp. This is nowhere so evident as in the speculations of the astronomer Merrival, whose views seem ironically compounded of the most perfectibilian aspects of William Godwin's and Percy Bysshe Shelley's.[35] Before the plague has left the East, Merrival asserts that "in an hundred thousand years . . . the pole of the earth will coincide with the pole of the ecliptic, an universal spring will be produced, and earth become a paradise" (159). When news is received of the spread of the plague westward from Turkey, however, Merrival concedes "that the joyful prospect of an earthly paradise after an hundred thousand years, was clouded to him by the knowledge that in a certain period of time after, an earthly hell or purgatory would occur, when ecliptic and equator would be at right angles" (160). After England is ravaged by the plague, the astronomer reappears as a caricature of millenarian expectation, having completed his Essay on the Pericyclical Motion of the Earth's Axis:

> Merrival talked of the state of mankind six thousand years hence. He might with equal interest to us, have added a commentary, to describe the unknown and unimaginable lineaments of the creatures, who would then occupy the vacated dwellings of mankind. (210)

The reality principle breaks upon his consciousness only after Merrival's wife and children die and he goes mad. "Among the victims of His merciless tyranny," he then says, "I dare reproach the Supreme Evil" (221).

Merrival is not the only character who mistakenly foresees a millennium. After the Greek victory over the Turks, there is universal peace, and Adrian makes a speech that recollects "The world's great age begins anew" at the opening of the final chorus of *Hellas:*

> "Let this last but twelve months and earth will become a Paradise. The energies of man were before directed to the destruction of his species; they now aim at its liberation and preservation. Man cannot repose, and his restless aspirations will now bring forth good instead of evil. The favoured countries of the south will throw off the iron yoke of servitude; poverty will quit us, and with that, sickness. What may not the forces, never before united, of liberty and peace achieve in this dwelling of man?" (159)

To this the radical Ryland ripostes: "Dreaming, for ever dreaming, Windsor! Be assured that earth is not, nor ever can be heaven, while the seeds of hell are natives of her soil." This exchange brings out a fundamental ambivalence in the novel, for the wholly admirable Adrian will be proved wrong and the scoundrel and coward Ryland right, although of course Ryland does not understand the true import of his words and securely believes the plague will never reach England.

The hope of a millennium persists even when it should long have been abandoned. The English dream that they could be "a nook of the garden of paradise" (180) is dissipated by the plague's penetration of London. Idris's dream "of a tranquil solitude, of a beauteous retreat, of the simple manners of our little tribe, and of the patriarchal brotherhood of love, which would survive the ruins of the populous nations which had lately existed" (252) is belied by her death a few pages later. Verney proposes that all survivors leave the north—"We must seek some natural Paradise, some garden of the earth" (226). This is strange because the plague abates in *winter;* they really should seek the ice-pack like Frankenstein's monster. But it presents another opportunity to demonstrate the failure of the paradise of imagination.

Close to the end, Adrian, sailing with Lionel and Clara toward Greece, imagines an island paradise of the sort Percy Shelley created for himself and Emilia Viviani in *Epipsychidion.* Since this fantasy is Mary's, however, it would reunite her, as Lionel Verney, with Adrian-Shelley and their own lost Clara. "We would make our home of one of the Cyclades, and there in the myrtle-groves, amidst perpetual spring, fanned by the wholesome sea-breezes—we would live long years in beatific union—" (321). Here once more we see the rhythm by which the author raises the possibility of millennial bliss only to brutally disappoint both herself and the reader. Immediately a storm breaks, the ship is swamped, Adrian and Clara are drowned, and Lionel Verney survives to be the Last Man.

Another aspect of *The Last Man*'s ambivalence toward millenarianism is seen in two episodes involving religious movements. Both are probably derived from a scene in John Wilson's verse drama *The City of the Plague,* which Mary Shelley read in 1817.[36] In the first (190–91), a mechanic whose wife and child are dead harangues a crowd at Windsor town hall. "His diseased fancy made him believe himself sent by heaven to preach the end of time to the world." After he gazes at a peasant in the front rank, the man falls down in convulsions, and the "maniac" announces, "That man has the plague." The curious thing is that maniac or not the preacher appears to be right—at least the man is dead. And his "ravings" about the last days of humankind are about to be proved right as well.

The second episode is more fully developed. Here the "self-erected prophet" is referred to as "the methodist," and the doctrine of reprobation and election is attacked. "His father had been a methodist preacher, an enthusiastic man with simple intentions; but whose pernicious doctrines of election and special grace had contributed to destroy all conscientious feeling in his son" (274). Can it be coincidence that Mary Shelley's father had been raised as a strict Calvinist and was for a time deeply influenced by his teacher Samuel Newton, a member of the Sandemanian sect, known for its especially rigorous views on divine election?[37] The preacher, also called "the methodist," gathers around him a following that contemporary readers might have thought typical of Calvinist Methodism—mostly from "the lower rank of society" plus "a few high-born females" (282). These people are denominated the Elect and accept a quasi-Manichaean doctrine. "Now, at the time of the Flood, the omnipotent repented him that he had created man, and as then with water, now with the arrows of pestilence, was about to annihilate all, except those who obeyed his decree" (295–96).

The methodist's teaching is a ghastly parody of the Prophetic idea of the Saving Remnant, but he himself, like the prophet in Wilson's *City of the Plague,* is a charlatan. He thinks that if a few survive, "so that a new race should spring up, he, by holding tight the reins of belief, might be remembered by the post-pestilential race as a patriarch, a prophet, nay a deity." Self-interested though his motive may be, the readiness of his followers to accept his doctrine seems psychologically credible. (When cholera actually did come to England only five years after Mary Shelley's novel was published, Thomas Arnold, neither a madman nor a charlatan, wondered whether it might be a sign of the Last Days.)[38] The episode of the preacher, like the earlier one of the maniac, seems designed to show that one can neither have one's eschatological cake nor eat it: the religious paradigm is shown to be irrelevant even when when the conditions it prophesies are brought forth.

It is consistent with the greater distance of *The Last Man* from traditional religious beliefs that, although Mary Shelley's novel has, like Grainville's, echoes of the Bible and of Milton, these are fewer and more peripheral than those in *Omegarus and Syderia*. Verney sees the vision of man in Psalm 8 as "a little lower than the angels" (229) as irrevocably past. His characterization of the survivors who reach Switzerland in book III as a "failing remnant" is perhaps an ironical allusion to the idea of the Saving Remnant in Isaiah; and the drowning of the invading Irish, who go down in their ships "to rise only when death loosened their hold," seems to parody the prelude to resurrection in Revelation 20:13 when "the sea gave up the dead which were in it." Certainly ironical is the attempt to bring in Biblical typology when Adrian, Clara, and Verney set sail for Greece. "Ocean, we commit ourselves to thee—even as the patriarch of old floated above the drowned world, let us be saved, as thus we betake ourselves to thy perennial flood" (320). In this doomed world, no antitype can find its type.

Paradise Lost is likewise an ironical presence, limited to the epigraph and several memorable similitudes. The advance of the plague to England is likened to Satan's "one slight bound" in book IV (lines 181–84): "the earth's desolator had at last, even as an arch-fiend, lightly over-leaped the boundaries our precautions raised" (177); the sound of the wind in the sails of the invading Irish fleet is "such whir as may have visited the dreams of Milton, when he imagined the winnowing of the arch-fiend's van-like wings, which increased the uproar of wild chaos" (214). When at the beginning of book III Lionel Verney declaims a long eulogy for humanity, he figures it in terms of the expulsion from Paradise (XII.632–40) but transforms Milton's Eastern Gate into "the high walls of the tomb" and the angels' flaming sword into "the flaming sword of plague" (234). The last lines of *Paradise Lost* are reshaped with bitter irony: "Like to our first parents, the whole earth is before him, a vast desert." *Him* is radically different from *them,* and the analogy of Adam and Eve only intensifies our sense of the ultimate failure of humankind.

These references to a sacred order no longer believed to exist are among the ghosts that haunt Mary Shelley's narrative. In *Omegarus and Syderia* supernatural beings freely roamed the earth; in *The Last Man* we encounter their afterimages, sometimes momentarily terrifying, more often ludicrous. Raymond enters Constantinople on his charger, but his officers hang back, "as if they expected some Mighty Phantom to stalk in offended majesty from the opening" (144). The mourners of the dead killed by the plague look up, "fancying they could discern the sweeping wings of angels, who passed over the earth, lamenting the disasters about to fall on man" (163). The band of refugees from England hears "wailing and cries in the air . . . as if spirits above sang the requiem of the human race"—but "What was this, but the actions of diseased imaginations and childish credulity?" Later, a "Black Spectre" who dogs the refugees on a coal-black steed turns out to be a French nobleman, who then dies of the plague. Such ghostly manifestations seem introduced not only for the purpose of demonstrating that there is no supernatural explanation but also in order to produce natural ones so trivial as to bring out the insufficiency of all natural explanations.

Of special interest is an episode in Switzerland, when, passing through Ferney, the refugees suddenly find the atmosphere transformed:

> The peal of an organ with rich swell awoke the mute air, lingering along, and mingling with the intense beauty that clothed the rocks and woods, and, waves around. . . . The air was Haydn's "New-Created World," and, old and drooping as humanity had become, the world yet fresh as at creation's day, might still be worthily celebrated by such a hymn of praise. (306).

The "air" is actually part of a chorus in Haydn's *Creation.* As Jean de Palacio points out in his invaluable discussion of the the function of music in this novel, this detail reveals the influence of Mary's friend Vincent Novello, organist and Haydn enthusiast, who had, she declared, made her "a convert to Haydn."[39] However, the incident cannot support the optimistic construction that de Palacio gives it. The situation in *The Creation* occurs close to the beginning of the oratorio. After God divides the light from darkness, the spirits of hell flee to the abyss, and the chorus, as rendered in Novello's vocal score, sings:

> Despairing cursing rage attends their [hell spirits'] rapid fall,
> A new-created world springs up at God's command.[40]

In *The Last Man* the occurrence of this passage is a cruel joke by author upon reader. It turns out that a young woman already dying of plague is playing to her blind father, who dies soon after her. The effect can be compared to the episode of the radio message from North America in *On the Beach,* where the crew of the submarine discovers no living explanation. In *On the Beach,* however, the cause of disaster is at least known; in *The Last Man* it remains chillingly indeterminate.

That indeterminacy is itself masked in ghostly reflections of a former paradigm. In *Omegarus and Syderia* Death walked about, leaned on his scythe, and killed with his dart. In *The Last Man* he appears only as a personification, first in the description of a picture:

> All the inhabitants of earth were drawn out in fear to stand the encounter of Death. The feeble and decrepid fled; the warriors retreated, though they threatened even in flight. Wolves and lions, and various monsters of the desert roared against him, while the grim Unreality hovered shaking his spectral dart, a solitary but invincible assailant. (139)

Later Death is described by Verney as "rising from his subterranean vault, girt with power, with dark banner flying" (197). This presence is regarded by some as directed by Providence, by others as a pre-Hardyan "passing casualty," but it never crosses the threshold from personification to literal being. This makes its effects more rather than less mysterious; we are reminded of the fictive nature of Grainville's paradigm and are at the same time conscious of a void in its place.

The ultimate mysterious personification in *The Last Man* is the Plague itself. Mary Shelley must have created this mythological being out of reports of the great cholera pandemic that began in 1817, and that had spread north to the Caspian region almost as far as Astrakhan in Russia by 1823,[41] only months before she began writing her novel. In *The Last Man* Plague is always female, a powerful goddess whom Adrian seems to identify with the Hindu Kali when he says " 'I have hung on the wheel of the chariot of plague; but she drags me along with it, while, like Juggernaut, she succeeds in crushing out the being of all who strew the high road of life' " (289). To Lionel she is a snow queen, who, after seven years, "abdicated her throne and despoiled herself of her imperial sceptre among the ice rocks that surrounded us" (310). Why this powerful and remorseless empress should give up her power is never explained, nor is the reason for her reigning for seven years (unless it be the prevalence of sevens in the Book of Revelation). Like Death she exists somewhere between personification and myth in a borderland where causality seems nonexistent.

These personifications of Death and of Plague made by Lionel Verney in the course of his exposition make the reader aware of Verney's role as a literary artist. His authorial identity (which at least two critics have seen as a positive, virtually redemptive feature)[42] manifests itself in other ways as well, increasingly as the human race wears toward its end. Sometimes, as in *Omegarus and Syderia,* this is merely a matter of the narrator's addressing the reader directly (56, 300) or interrupting his account of the past for his "present" reality (as on 173). As the novel goes on, however, there is more emphasis on the act of writing and also on the problem of finding a readership when the author is the last man on earth. For although earlier on Lionel thinks "To read were futile—to write, vanity indeed" (223), as humanity thins out, both writing and the reader become more important. Verney decides to write a book and begins:

DEDICATION
TO THE ILLUSTRIOUS DEAD.
SHADOWS, ARISE, AND READ YOUR FALL!
BEHOLD THE HISTORY OF THE
LAST MAN. (339)

But, as Verney says, "for whom to read?" Not really content with the illustrious dead, at times he imagines a live reader for his narrative. At the same time he feels he must warn this putative "tender offspring of a re-born world" (318) of the terrible effects that reading this book will have. In another mood, he thinks of himself in a pedagogical role in relation to the future reader, who will be "a solitary being" and "young"; "It is right" says he, "that I should erect for thy instruction this monument of the foregone race" (291). Elsewhere he casts himself in the role of historian to "the children of a saved pair of lovers, in some to me unknown and unattainable seclusion, wandering to these prodigious relics of the ante-pestilential race, [who will] seek to learn how beings so wondrous in their achievements, with imaginations infinite, and powers godlike, had departed from their home to an unknown country" (339).

It's as if Verney were fulfilling the reviewer's misogynistic fantasy about the author's fear of having no one left to talk to. However, the authenticity of Verney's narrative is predicated on his being *Last,* a condition that precludes by definition his having readers. It's true that by an unknown process his account has somehow been transformed into the shape it assumes in the Cumaean cave, to be spelled from Sibyl's leaves by the author. This may alleviate the reader's anxiety at having to imagine Lastness and the void that must follow Lastness, but it isn't what Verney himself has in mind. He wants readers as a guarantee of the survival of the race in the *future* and also as a testimony to his own existence. It is also for these reasons that he sets out to sea at the end of the book.

"I shall read fair augury in the rainbow" (342), says Verney in the last paragraph. Far from being a triumphant indication of self-transcendence and poetic imagination, his closing statement indicates he has failed to understand the condition of his Lastness. The rainbow allusion makes us recall God's covenant with Noah ("I do set my bow in the cloud, and it shall be for a token of a covenant between me and the earth" [Gen. 9:13]) and how Adrian attempted to invoke it with catastrophic results. Without being aware of it, Verney places himself very much in the situation of the Ancient Mariner in saying, "While the sun is high, and the moon waxes or wanes, angels, the spirits of the dead, and the ever-open eye of the Supreme, will behold the tiny bark, freighted with Verney—the LAST MAN" (342). Verney can no more become an antitype of Noah than he can realize God's injunction in Genesis 9:7: "And you, be ye fruitful, and multiply; bring forth abundantly in the earth, and multiply therein." This failure of typology, inescapably attached to the presentation of apocalypse without millennium, is the last frightful irony of *The Last Man.*

Notes

The author gratefully acknowledges the Keats-Shelley Memorial Association's permission to use material that previously appeared in the *Keats–Shelley Review.*

1. See Jean de Palacio, "Mary Shelley and the 'Last Man,' " *Revue de la littérature comparée* 44 (1968): 40. The precise date of publication was January 23, 1826. See *The Letters of Mary Wollstonecraft Shelley,* 3 vols. ed. Betty T. Bennett (Baltimore: Johns Hopkins University Press, 1980–88), 1:512 n. 8.

2. *Edinburgh Review* 61 (1824–25): 284.

3. Campbell's widely circulated response is reprinted in Cyrus Redding's *Literary Reminiscences and Memoirs of Thomas Campbell* (London: Charles J. Skeat, 1869), 304–8.

4. Ibid., 305.

5. Letter postmarked March 25, 1825, *The Works of Thomas Lovell Beddoes*, ed. H. W. Donner (London: Oxford University Press, 1935), 600. Donner (753–54) points out that Thomas Sternhold's translations of the Psalms had been satirized by Dryden in *Absalom and Achitophel*.

6. *The London Magazine*, N.S. 1 (1825): 284–86.

7. Although several contemporary reviewers noticed resemblances among *The Last Man*, Byron's "Darkness," and the novel known as *Omegarus and Syderia*, this subject was not further explored until 1896, when Eugen Kölbung discussed it extensively in his edition of *The Prisoner of Chillon and Other Poems* (*Lord Byrons Werke in kritischen Texte mit Einleitung und Anmerkungen*, vol. 2 (Weimar: Emil Ferber, 1896). Kölbung evidently did not realize that *Omegarus and Syderia* was a translation of *Le dernier homme* by Jean-Baptiste François Xavier Cousin de Grainville (1746–1805), privately published in Paris in 1805. On the original novel, which has the distinction of being the first Last Man narrative, see my article "*Le dernier homme:* The French Revolution as the Failure of Typology," *Mosaic: A Journal for the Interdisciplinary Study of Literature* 24 (1991): 67–76.

8. *The Monthly Magazine*, N.S. 2, 8 (1826): 137–43.

9. *Literary Gazette*, no. 474 (18 Feb. 1826): 103. *Monthly Review*, N.S. 1 (1826): 333–35.

10. *Blackwood's Edinburgh Magazine* 21 (1827): 54.

11. *The Literary Magnet*, N.S. 1 (1826): 56. The *London Magazine* writer on the Campbell controversy (see note 6 above) misspelled Omegarus in the same way. One wonders whether either had actually seen the book.

12. *The Wasp* 1 (1826): 79 (from Jean de Palacio, *Mary Shelley dans son oeuvre: Contribution aux études Shelleyennes* [Paris: Editions Klincksieck, 1969], 664).

13. *The Literary Gazette*, no. 949 (1835): 194. Elizabeth Nitchie reports a similar gibe in the *St. James Royal Magazine;* see *Mary Shelley: Author of "Frankenstein"* (New Brunswick: Rutgers University Press, 1953), 151.

14. Nitchie, *Mary Shelley*, 152.

15. *The Monthly Review*, 334.

16. *The Literary Gazette*, no. 949 (1835): 194.

17. A reviewer of the first American edition called *The Last Man* "a sort of detailed and prose copy of Byron's terrible painting of darkness." *The Knickerbocker Magazine* 2 (1833): 315; qtd. by W. H. Lyles, *Mary Shelley: An Annotated Bibliography* (New York: Garland, 1975), 175.

18. *The Journals of Mary Shelley*, 2 vols. ed. Paula R. Feldman and Diana Scott-Kilvert (Oxford: Oxford University Press, 1987), 2: 476–77.

19. *The Letters of Mary Wollstonecraft Shelley*, 1:450.

20. See his introduction to *The Last Man* (London: Hogarth Press, 1985), giving as examples the appearance of a black sun and a four-month windstorm in volume III.

21. See Walter E. Peck, "The Biographical Element in the Novels of Mary Shelley, *PMLA* 38 (1923): 196–219; Edmond Gosse, "Shelley's Widow," *Silhouettes* (New York: Charles Scribner's Sons, 1925[?]), 231–38; Nitchie, *Mary Shelley*, 15–16, 68–75, 94–95, 102–4, 109, 110–17; Ernest J. Lovell, "Byron and Mary Shelley," *Keats-Shelley Journal*, 2 (1953): 36; Angela Leighton, rev. of *The Last Man*, *Keats-Shelley Review*, no. 2 (1987): 144–48.

22. *The Last Man* (London: Hogarth Press, 1985), 30. Subsequent page references are cited in the text.

23. *"The Last Man:* Anatomy of Failed Revolutions," *Nineteenth Century Fiction* 33 (1978): 324–47.

24. Anne K. Mellor, *Mary Shelley: Her Life, Her Fiction, Her Monsters* (New York: Methuen, 1988).

25. See Arthur McA. Miller, *The Last Man: A Study of the Eschatological Theme in English Poetry and Fiction from 1806 Through 1839* (diss., Duke University, 1966), esp. 134–77, and W. Warren Wagar, *Terminal Visions* (Bloomington: Indiana University Press, 1982), 16.

26. See *Journal,* (1:242) and Muriel Spark, *Child of Light: A Reassessment of Mary Wollstonecraft Shelley* (Hadleigh, Essex: Tower Bridge Publications, 1951), 195.

27. New Haven: Yale University Press, 1979, 95–99.

28. Letter to John Howard Payne, 28 Jan. (7 Feb.) 1826, *Letters,* 508.

29. See Hugh M. Luke, Jr., introduction, *The Last Man,* by Mary Shelley (Lincoln: University of Nebraska Press, 1965), xvii–xviii.

30. Citations from the works of Percy Bysshe Shelley refer to *Shelley's Poetry and Prose,* ed. Donald Reiman and Sharon Powers (New York: Norton, 1977).

31. *The Prelude, 1799, 1805, 1850,* ed. Jonathan Wordsworth, M. H. Abrams, and Stephen Gill (New York: Norton, 1979), 174, line 425 [1805].

32. See Hartley S. Spratt, "Mary Shelley's Last Men: The Truth of Dreams," *Studies in the Novel* 7 (1975): 526–37; Robert Lance Snyder, "Apocalypse and Indeterminacy in Mary Shelley's *The Last Man," Studies in Romanticism* 17 (1978): 435–52. I should emphasize that I have profited from both these generally excellent essays.

33. See de Palacio, *Mary Shelley dans son oeuvre,* 568, n. 181.

34. *Paradise Lost,* XI.770–72.

35. Earl R. Wasserman compares Merrival's speeches with Percy Shelley's optimism in *Queen Mab,* VI.45–46n about the plane of the ecliptic disappearing. See *Shelley: A Critical Reading* (Baltimore: Johns Hopkins University Press, 1971), 262n.

36. London, 1817 [Edinburgh, 1816], I.ii, 21. De Palacio, pp. 376–77 n. 91, calls attention to Mary Shelley's *Journal* entry dated 27 May 1817.

37. On Godwin and Newton, see Peter H. Marshall, *William Godwin* (New Haven: Yale University Press, 1884), 17–29.

38. See G. Kitson Clark, *Churchmen and the Condition of England 1832–1885* (London: Methuen, 1973), 74.

39. See *Mary Shelley dans son oeuvre,* 333–34; *Letters,* 1:408.

40. *The Creation* ["Reprint from Novello's Original Octavo Edition"] (Boston: White, Smith & Co., n.d.), 1.

41. See Michael Durey, *The Return of the Plague* (London: Gill and Macmillan, 1979), 8.

42. See Spratt, "Mary Shelley's Last Men," and Snyder, "Apocalypse and Indeterminacy in Mary Shelley's *The Last Man."*

Proserpine and *Midas:* Gender, Genre, and Mythic Revisionism in Mary Shelley's Dramas

Alan Richardson

In 1820 Mary Shelley began studying Greek. The previous year she had been at work transcribing the manuscript (now lost) of *Prometheus Unbound,* Percy Shelley's revisionist response to Aeschylean drama. Now, in the midst of her Greek studies, she wrote two revisionist mythological dramas of her own, *Proserpine,* which she eventually published in the *Winter's Wreath* for 1832, and *Midas,* which apparently remained in manuscript until 1922. Both works were written in partial collaboration with Percy, who supplied two lyrics for each; as a result, Mary Shelley's plays have held a marginal reputation among critics who, more interested in the poetry of her husband, have seen them (to the disparagement of her other works) as catching "something of the pure Shelleyan limpidity."[1] The two plays have fared no better in critical studies of Mary Shelley, which often neglect even to mention them; Elizabeth Nitchie writes that the plays are "distinguished only by the lyrics that Shelley wrote for them"; Sylva Norman flatly states that they "do not really call for analytical and comparative study."[2] On the contrary, a careful and sympathetic examination of Mary Shelley's poetic dramas is long overdue. *Proserpine* and *Midas* are of great interest on several fronts: as a woman writer's innovative assault on classical mythology; as generic experiments; and as unusual collaborative ventures which raise questions regarding the differences between female and male approaches to poetic invention in the early nineteenth century.

The questions concerning gender and the subject of genre are closely related and must be addressed first, especially in light of the odd reception history of the plays as "pretty" containers for Percy Shelley's "limpidity." Margaret Homans, in her important study of women writers and poetic identity in the nineteenth century, argues that the Romantic tradition in poetry is a "masculine" one: "In Romantic poetry the self and the imagination are primary. . . . Where the male self dominates and internalizes otherness, that other is frequently identified as feminine." The equation of woman with "otherness" is doubly reinforced in the male Romantic canon, by "her association with nature and her exclusion from a traditional identification of the speaking subject as male."[3] Homans's thesis that nineteenth-century women writers are effectively excluded from the "strong" voice of lyric subjectivity seems qualified rather than contradicted by Stuart Curran's recent survey of women poets in the Romantic period. For Curran, women like Mary Robinson and Anna Letitia Barbauld reject the "visionary flight" and "investment in symbols" characteristic of male Romantic verse, with "imaginative projection as an end in itself," for a contrary "actual vision" concerned with the quotidian, the fragmented or decentered, "discriminating minute objects or assembling a world out of its disjointed particulars."[4] Or, as in the signal case of Joanna Baillie, ranked in her time with Shakespeare and all but forgotten since, women poets could turn to the dramatic mode.

This schema fits neatly with the gendered division of literary labor in *Proserpine* and *Midas,* with Percy supplying the visionary lyrics and Mary the dramatic exchanges with their emphasis on quotidian particulars, especially flowers (a key object of "actual vision" in Curran's analysis). The fit is, if anything, too neat. As Tilottama Rajan argues in an essay entitled "Romanticism and the Death of Lyric Consciousness," the Romantic movement as a whole was concerned with "making the lyric interdiscursive, by intertextualizing it, narrating, or dramatizing it." *Prometheus Unbound,* characterized by its "movement . . . from lyric to drama," represents the mingling of lyric and dramatic modes in what, following Byron, has been called "mental theater," a salient instance of how male poets in the period invented their own formal and generic strategies for evading or at least complicating the "monological" character of the single-voiced lyric.[5] And lyrical drama, or "mental theater," with its emphasis on character over plot, on reaction over action, and its turn away from the theater is the genre to which *Proserpine* and *Midas* most nearly belong.

Nevertheless, Mary Shelley's dramatic poems differ significantly from those of Byron and Percy Shelley, in ways that seem to support an interrelation between gender and genre. In works like *Manfred* and *Prometheus Unbound,* lyric and dramatic modes are not so much fused as dialectically juxtaposed, and soliloquy becomes a central and pervasive device for exhibiting the isolated subjectivity of their "visionary" protagonists. In *Proserpine,* on the other hand, there is virtually no soliloquy, and the element of lyric subjectivity is provided mainly by the presence of Percy's two songs; in *Midas,* soliloquy is resisted in the first act and exposed in the second act as a questionable and implicitly masculine mode. In both plays, Percy's lyrics function through their difference from the dramatic passages into which they are spliced, and the disequilibrium which critics persist in remarking on between the two Shelleys' contributions is almost certainly intended. It is in describing that disequilibrium in terms of quality, rather than in terms of poetics, that most of what little commentary there is on the mythological dramas has proved so disappointing.

In *Proserpine* the tension between female and male poetic modes is underscored by its subject, a rape. With one exception, all the characters who appear in the drama are female; the significant male characters, the rapist-god Pluto and his brother, the Olympian patriarch Jupiter, remain offstage throughout. As Susan Gubar states in her brief but brilliantly suggestive discussion of *Proserpine,* the first act (which takes place before the rape) "represents a time of nurturing sisterhood between mother and daughter, a pastoral time of communality between all women, young and old."[6] This

communitarian atmosphere translates into poetic terms in that, as opposed to
the detached, even solipsistic set speeches characteristic of *Manfred* or act I of
Prometheus Unbound, nearly all the dramatic verse in *Proserpine* is other-
directed, composed in what might be termed (in Mitzi Myers's phrase) a
"relational literary mode."[7] Nearly every speech is directed feelingly toward
another character and is typically as concerned with describing another's emotional state, and/or eliciting an emotional reaction, as with expressing the
speaker's subjectivity:

> Sweet Ino, well I know the love you bear
> My dearest Mother prompts your partial voice,
> And that love makes you doubly dear to me.
>
> (17)

Discursive exchange in *Proserpine* is based not, as is usual in drama, on
conflict, but on empathy: "let thy words be poured / Into my drooping soul,
like dews of eve / On a too long parched field" (32).

Ino's song "Arethusa," supplied by Percy, represents feeling and feminine
experience in a quite different manner, one that brings out the usually repressed connotation of "licentious" in the term "poetic licence." While the
play in which it is set portrays rape in terms of its disastrous effects on
Proserpine, on Ceres, and on their attendant nymphs, Percy's interpolated
song lyrically abstracts rape from both its social context and dramatic consequences, idealizing Alpheus's violation of Arethusa as amorous pursuit resolved in erotic union: it moves from "Alpheus rushed behind / An eagle
pursuing / A dove to its ruin" to "Like friends once parted / Grown single
hearted / They ply their watery task" with neither transition nor comment.
This song, incidentally, of which the quoted lines are not an unfair sample,
makes one think twice about the stock comment that the presence of Percy's
lyrics in the two plays "reveals unmistakably that the pleasant lines on either
side of them belong to a competent versifier rather than a poet";[8] "Arethusa"
is not one of Percy's best efforts, and the nymph Eunoe's comment that
"Proserpine's tale / Is sweeter far than Ino's sweetest song" (8) does not seem
ironically intended. The relationality of *Proserpine* is manifested as well on
the level of plot, in Shelley's many departures from her source in Ovid.
Whereas Ovid, for example, portrays Proserpine as an unreflective child,
willfully straying after flowers in infantile abandon, Shelley portrays Proserpine as a thoughtful, empathetic adolescent, seeking flowers not for herself
but in order to "twine a blooming wreathe / For [her] dear Mother's rich and
weaving hair" (16). Shelley's revisions of Ovid are worth insisting upon, since
it has been regularly, and quite wrongly, stated that Shelley "stuck to her Latin
source as closely as she could."[9] But a discussion of Shelley's critical relation
to Ovid, which seems needed at this point, should begin by acknowledging the
problematic status of classical mythology for a woman poet working within
the Romantic tradition.

I began this essay by noting that Mary Shelley was engaged in learning
Greek when she wrote *Proserpine* and *Midas,* and her interest at this time in

writing on mythological subjects might be taken as her asserting a claim on the classical tradition considered in her age and place as the exclusive heritage of upper-class males. Like Keats, who throughout his poetry is drawn to classical mythology while famously relying on Chapman's translation for Homer's pure serene, Mary Shelley, essentially self-educated, could be seen as an outcast from the British system of classical education, belatedly approaching the Greek myths via Ovid.[10] But an acknowledgment of Mary Shelley's relatively alienated position in regard to the classical tradition should not lead us back to the standard view of her mythological dramas as schoolgirlish copy-book exercises (their editor characterizes the manuscript itself as "a cheap exercise book").[11] Rather, Shelley's approach to mythology should be seen in terms of the revisionist attitude with which most writers in the period approached classical myth, and of the particular dilemma which taking up what has been aptly termed a "mythology of rape" entailed for nineteenth-century women writers.[12]

In her essay on women poets and "revisionist mythmaking," Alicia Ostriker remarks that whereas myth is used "ornamentally" by Augustan writers, Romantic writers take myth both seriously and critically, characterizing the prevailing Romantic practice as "mythic revisionism."[13] For the male Romantic poet, particularly the generation of Byron, Shelley, and Keats, this practice often involves revitalizing the classical tradition by challenging its ruling codes, as Percy Shelley does, on political, philosophical, and ethical grounds, in *Prometheus Unbound*. But women writers had in addition to be wary of the profound patriarchal bias of traditional myths which, in Gubar's phrase, are "male-devised stories which invariably pattern woman as the Other."[14] The view of classical culture and its mythologies as what would now be termed "patriarchal" is one we can attribute to Mary Shelley without fear of anachronism. In the "Discourse on the Manners of the Ancient Greeks Relative to the Subject of Love," written to accompany the translation of Plato's *Symposium* which Percy Shelley undertook in 1818 "to give Mary some idea of the manners and feelings of the Athenians," the two great cultural failures of Greek civilization are described as the twin institutions of "personal slavery" and the "inferiority of women, recognized by law and opinion": among the Athenians, "the male sex, one half of the human race, received the highest cultivation and refinement; while the other, so far as intellect is concerned, were educated as slaves and were raised but few degrees in all that related to moral or intellectual excellence above the condition of savages."[15] It is not going far to imagine Mary Shelley extending this critique to the Athenian mythology taken up and codified by Ovid. And it is certain that she viewed Ovid not as the true Hippocrene but as a secondary, only somewhat reliable, transmitter of Greek myth. In her fragmentary essay, begun as an ironic rejoinder to Byron's defense of Christianity, on the equal claim to authenticity of "Heathen Mythology" with that of the Bible, Shelley sketches the following notion: "Vergil & Ovid not truth of the heathen Mythology, but the interpretation of a heathen—as Milton's Paradise Lost is an interpretation of a Christian religion of the Bible" (xxv).[16] In addition to the evidence from the plays themselves, then, there is ample reason to view Shelley's relation to Ovid as a profoundly critical one; her mythological dramas are anything but the "essentially close adaptations of the corresponding tales in Ovid's *Metamorphoses*" they are usually taken for.[17]

The myth of Demeter and Persephone has held a great deal of significance for feminist writers. In "Demeter Revisited," the introduction to *Women and Madness,* Phyllis Chesler invokes the rites of Demeter and Persephone as archetypal "celebrations of mothers and daughters" tragically displaced by the rise of monotheism; analyzing the Homeric *Hymn to Demeter,* the classicist Marilyn Arthur sees Demeter's dilemma as "that of all women, who must struggle to achieve self-definition in a social and psychic world which values male attributes more highly and depreciates females"; Susan Gubar describes Demeter as the "central mythic figure for women," a female counterpart to the figure of Oedipus in representations of male psychic life.[18] The particular association of Demeter and Persephone (or Kore) with women's experience is, of course, a rich and ancient one: the Demeter–Kore legend was the central cultic myth both of the Thesmophoria, an Athenian ritual festival held exclusively by and for women, and of the Eleusinian mysteries, thought to be originally an "Earth-mother fertility religion," associated especially with women and administered by priestesses; in ancient Athens the mother–daughter pair were "the divinities most often invoked by women, who alone swore by the 'twain goddesses.' "[19] The worship of Demeter was revived in Roman times in the Hellenized cult of Ceres and Proserpine; aspects of both the Thesmophoria and the Eleusinian mysteries were revived as well, and the story of Demeter and Kore was ritually reenacted by Roman matrons and virgins.[20]

Before writing *Proserpine,* Mary Shelley had already called upon the myth in her unpublished novel *Mathilda* (written in 1819). When the heroine's incestuous father grows jealous of a young gentleman's attentions, he becomes harsh and distant in a manner at first inexplicable to Mathilda: "Often, when my wandering fancy brought by its various images now consolation and now aggravation of grief to my heart, I have compared myself to Proserpine who was gaily and heedlessly gathering flowers on the sweet plain of Enna, when the King of Hell snatched her away to the abodes of death and misery."[21] (Interestingly, Chesler also sees in the myth a fable of paternal incest: "Afterward, the three sisters agreed that he was old enough to be Persephone's father. Perhaps he was: who else could he be?")[22] *Proserpine* is also concerned with male tyranny, both that of Pluto and of the father-god Jove, but here the dramatic emphasis is placed on the community of women—goddesses, nymphs, and naiads—victimized by patriarchal tyranny and eventually united against it.

Significant in this regard is Shelley's decision to take Pluto out of the action altogether; as Gubar points out, the rape occurs "in the silence between the acts."[23] Here Shelley departs not only from Ovid, whose version features a brief but incontestable display of Pluto's infernal power, but from

most later literary and operatic versions as well, which tend to expand the
abduction and rape into a scene of courtship, what Jean de Palacio, in a
comparative study of the play, calls the "élément galante" of the typical adaptation.[24] For example, in a more conventional version published the same year
as Shelley's composition of *Proserpine,* Bryan Waller Procter's "dramatic
scene" *The Rape of Proserpine,* the heroine is portrayed as immediately attracted to Pluto ("Terribly lovely"), flirting with him and coyly leading him
on, and protesting rather unconvincingly when she is finally carried away ("O
fraudful King!").[25] Instead of celebrating or romanticizing rape (an attitude
firmly established in Attic mythology and all too prevalent today),[26] Shelley
condemns it through emphasizing Ceres' bereavement, the heartsickness of
Proserpine's nymphs, and Proserpine's own desire to escape "from hateful
Tartarus" (34).

Nor does Shelley portray the female characters in her drama as passive
sufferers. While Ovid's Arethusa, for example, simply catches sight of
Proserpine in Hades and reports back to Demeter, Shelley's Arethusa witnesses the rape and actively tries to prevent it; Pluto escapes through an act of
phallic violence symbolically directed against the earth:

> I hastened at her call—
> But Pluto when he saw that aid was nigh,
> Struck furiously the green earth with his spear,
> Which yawned,—and down the deep Tartarian gulph
> His black car rolled—the green earth closed above.
>
> (31)

Shelley also anticipates a tradition of women writers portraying Demeter as
less passive, more aggressive in her response to her daughter's abduction:
winter arises not from Ceres' despondency but from her "rage" (26).[27] Nor
does Shelley's Ceres simply wait upon and then accept Jove's absolute decree.
When she learns of her daughter's fate, her response is to threaten Olympus—
"Restore my child, or let all heaven sink, / And the fair world be chaos once
again!" (31)—an ultimatum no sooner uttered than powerfully felt: "The
Thunderer frowned, & heaven shook with dread" (32). When Jove's unilat-
eral, monological decree ("'tis fixed by fate, / Nor prayer nor murmur e'er can
alter it") dooms Proserpine to live forever as "The wife of Pluto and the Queen
of Hell" (32–33), Ceres, Arethusa, and the nymphs vow to "descend with
her":

> We will all leave the light and go with thee,
> In Hell thou shalt be girt by Heaven-born nymphs,
> Elysium shall be Enna,—
> . . . .
> I will sink down with thee;—my lily crown
> Shall bloom in Erebus, portentous loss
> To Earth, which by degrees will fade & fall
> In envy of our happier lot in Hell.
>
> (39)

The allusion to Milton's Satan ("The mind is its own place, and in itself / Can make a Heav'n of Hell, a Hell of Heav'n") both elicits a favorite Romantic precedent for resistance to divine tyranny and points up, by implicit contrast with Satanic solipsism, the communitarian nature of the female deities' resolve. Proserpine, for her part, laments less her exile from the earth than her separation from her mother and her beloved nymphs:

> Oh! Mother, dearer to your child than light,
> Than all the forms of this sweet earth & sky,
> Though dear to me, and dear are my poor nymphs,
> Whom I must leave.
>
> (38)

This powerful display of female solidarity forces Jove to compromise on his "fixed" decree, and Proserpine is granted half of each year on Enna with her mother and her companions. Proserpine's response allows the drama to end with a final gesture of moral defiance directed toward the Olympian patriarch:

> Six months together we shall dwell on earth,
> Six months in dreams we shall companions be,
> Jove's doom is void; we are forever joined.
>
> (42)

Where Ovid's version of the myth confirms the male pantheon's ascendancy, and blandly presents rape as an Olympian prerogative, Shelley's version restores something of Demeter's pre-Olympian power as Earth goddess, translated into the ethical and political force of women united as a community.

In *Proserpine* Shelley revises a myth of particular significance to women both in classical and more recent times; her interest in writing a poetic drama on the subject of Midas seems at first puzzling. Two other questions suggest themselves in addition to that of Shelley's decision to take up the subject at all: How does Shelley bring together the two Midas stories that she appropriates from Ovid—the unfortunate decision in the singing contest between Pan and Apollo and the equally unfortunate gift of the golden touch—in her own version; and how (if at all) can *Midas* be related thematically to *Proserpine*, its companion piece? These questions will again be pursued in terms of gender, genre, and mythic revisionism.

In *Midas* one is at first struck not so much with Shelley's departures from Ovid (which in this play are more subtle than in *Proserpine*) as with her reaction against a prior revision of Ovid within the English tradition. Chaucer retells the story of Midas's ears (Apollo turns them into those of an ass as a punishment for the judgment against him) and his ultimately futile attempt to hide them as one of the antifeminist topoi in *The Wife of Bath's Tale*. Whereas in Ovid it is a stereotypically loquacious barber who is unable to keep the king's secret, in the Wife of Bath's version (perhaps included in her fifth husband's "book of wikked wyves"), it is Myda's wife who whispers the scandal to the water (not the reeds) of a marsh: "Heere may ye se, thogh we a tyme abyde, / Yet out it moot; we kan no conseil hyde." Dryden retains (and somewhat augments) the Wife's misprision of Ovid in his version of her tale in the *Fables:* "Like leaky Sives no Secrets we can hold: / Witness the famous tale that *Ovid* told."[28] In Shelley's version it is neither Ovid's stock barber nor Chaucer's wicked wife who blurts out the secret, but Midas's prime minister, with his comic (and, in the context of lyrical drama, significant) inability to speak in soliloquy; when the reeds whisper back his words, Midas is certain he hears "a woman's voice / That dares belie her king," but a courtier answers, contra Chaucer and Dryden, "There is no woman here" (67).

This bit of intertextual play, however, is fairly incidental to Shelley's purpose in *Midas.* In approaching nearer to the heart of the drama, Susan Gubar's reading of the Proserpine myth again proves extremely helpful, particularly her remark that "male domination in sexual relationships becomes a synecdoche for a culture based on acquisition and brutality, a culture that justifies (when it does not overtly celebrate) male mastery."[29] If the rape of Proserpine is an archetypal instance of brutality, the Midas touch is an equally powerful myth of acquisition. *Midas* begins, as does *Proserpine,* in an atmosphere of pastoral harmony; the king himself is a kind of shepherd ("Our rural tasks begin" [48]). But the touch of gold, which Bacchus reluctantly grants Midas in return for his care of Silenus, is prompted by a wish to break with and dominate over nature: "Nature shall bend her laws at my command" (68). It is at this point in the drama that Midas takes visionary flight, turning to the subjective, univocal mode of soliloquy: "wrapt / In golden dreams of all that I possess" (76–77). Shelley links Midas's sudden delight in capital accumulation to the acquisitiveness of contemporary England, racing headlong into its new identity as an industrialized, consumerist society financed by political and mercantile imperialism:

> Now I am great! Innumerable armies
> Wait till my gold collects them round my throne;
> I see my standard made of woven gold
> Waving o'er Asia's utmost Citadels,
> Guarded by myriads invincible.
> Or if the toil of war grows wearisome
> I can buy Empires:—India shall be mine.
>
> (72)

Metal is here linked, as in *Proserpine* (where Pluto is characterized by his "iron hoofed steeds" [30]), to the male pantheon, the "Olympian gold" of Jove (73), Vulcan's forge, and the "Tartarian Gold" of Pluto's mines (80), as opposed to the maternal nature evoked in the drama's opening. Where Demeter's green world is life-giving, gold is shown to be "life-killing" (77), "its aspect hard and cold" (80), a "metallic curse" (82).

How does this critique of male acquisitive culture, figured by Midas's deathly touch and with its poetic equivalent in soliloquy, relate to the singing contest between Pan and Apollo represented in the first act? Douglas Bush's linkage of the two plots in the play's "moral . . . that only a man who pre-

ferred earthly to divine music would be fool enough to crave unlimited gold,"
could not be more misleading.[30] In fact, the Apollonian principle is firmly
rejected in *Midas;* as the sun god, Apollo is gold incarnate:

> *Asphalion:* They say Apollo's sunny car is gold.
> *Midas:*   Aye, so it is for Gold belongs to him—
>   But Phoebus is my bitterest enemy.
>   *(87)*

Apollo's beautiful song, written by Percy Shelley, is one of mastery and
domination—"Whatever lamps on Earth or Heaven may shine / Are portions
of one power, which is mine"—very much in the egotistical sublime register
identified by Homans with the "masculine tradition":

> I am the eye with which the Universe
>   Beholds itself & knows it is divine.
> All harmony of instrument or verse,
>   All prophecy, all medicine is mine;
> All light of art or nature;—to my song
>   Victory and praise, in its own right, belong.
>   (52–53)

Significantly, Pan's song (also by Percy Shelley) is not much less "masculine"
than Apollo's lyric of power; although it begins in the first person plural
rather than singular ("From the forests and highlands / We come, we come"),
it soon takes on its own visionary burden and (like Percy's "Arethusa") includes the pervasive Attic rape motif, in this case adding the more modern
corollary of denigrating the victim:

> I sang of the dancing stars,
>   I sang of the daedal Earth—
> And of heaven—& the giant wars—
>   And Love, & death, [&] birth,
>   And then I changed my pipings,
> Singing how down the vale of Menalus,
>   I pursued a maiden & clasped a reed,
> Gods and men, we are all deluded thus!
>   (54–55)

In fact, the more telling opposition in *Midas* is not that between Pan and
Apollo but one between Apollo and Dionysus. It is Bacchus who provides
the drama's resolution by freeing Midas—"Bacchus, O pity, pardon, and
restore me!" (80)—and it is as a devotee of Bacchus, "crowned with flowers,
ivy & Bacchic vine" (88), that Midas recovers his communal identity as
shepherd-priest-king:

> Oh Bacchus, thanks! for this to thee
> Will I each year offer three sucking lambs—
> Games will I institute—nor Pan himself
> Shall have more honor than thy deity.
>   (81–82)

Midas errs not in rejecting Apollo's song, but in failing to reject as well his element and all it stands for: power, acquisition, the golden crown of empire. By divesting himself of these through the power of Bacchus, Midas is able by the drama's end to become once more a member of the "festal band" escorting "Silenus to his woods again" (62).

The dynamic opposition in *Midas* between Apollonian and Dionysian modes, along with the Bacchic revival at its close, also suggests some more esoteric links between this play and Shelley's *Proserpine*. Midas's first food after being restored by Bacchus is, appropriately, a bunch of grapes, associated implicitly with Bacchic wine and in the drama explicitly with the fruits of the earth goddess, "the gifts of rich-haired Ceres" (86). The intimate connection of Demeter and Dionysus in the juice and pulp of the grape brings out their twin function as deities of nourishment and festivity, touched on early in *Proserpine* as Ceres leaves for a divine banquet: "They drink, for Bacchus is already there, / But none will eat till I dispense the food" (6). But there are cultic as well as mythological connections between the two divinities that seem equally relevant to Shelley's revisionist project. As Froma Zeitlin argues in her essay "Cultic Models of the Female," Dionysus and Demeter are "closely connected at many points both in myth and cult," and in their cultic function both were particularly associated with women. Comparing the Bacchic rites to the Thesmophoria, Zeitlin writes that "both rituals were confined mainly or only to women. . . . Dionysus is sometimes a child and they his nurses, and sometimes he himself is a bisexual figure who crosses the strict dividing line between the sexes. . . . Both rites emphasize the connection of women and nature. . . . In both, the women participants manifest 'subversive' traits in acts of aggression or self-assertion."[31] In Rome also, the Hellenized mysteries of Ceres were confined to women, while the cult of Bacchus was initially exclusively female as well; the admission of men led to a "national scandal," and the Bacchanalia became again primarily a women's festival.[32]

In writing one dramatic poem based on the cult legend acted out in the Thesmophoria, "a festival that combined elements of a fertility cult with those of a rite of rebellion," presented in a ritual "dramatic performance" by the priestess at Eleusis, and later enacted by women in the rituals of Ceres at Rome; and in ending her other dramatic poem in a return to the Bacchanalian rites represented at its midpoint—

> 'Tis he surrounded by a jocund throng
> Of priests and bacchant women, bearing spears
> Blunted with pine cones & with ivy wreathed,
> And here and there they cry, "Bacchus! Evoe!"
> As if the Nysian impulse just began
>
> (65)

—Shelley seems less engaged in versifying Ovid than in recovering the ritualistic beginnings of Greek drama, with its roots in Dionysian cult worship and earth goddess fertility rites.[33] One might object that such a conception of classical myth would be unavailable to Mary Shelley, in part because the "myth of matriarchy" and its emphasis on pre-Olympian mother-goddesses and fertility cults would not be established for another forty years (with the publication of Bachofen's *Das Mutterrecht* in 1861).[34] But in fact, following a series of archaeological discoveries, developments in classical scholarship, and changing attitudes in the comparative study of religion, there was a great deal of interest in Greek and Roman ritual in the late eighteenth and early nineteenth centuries, and among the new syncretic systems proposed to ground classical mythology in cultic practices or fertility rites, several suggested (in their quite different manners) important links between Demeter and Dionysus. Jacob Bryant, for example, whose exhaustive treatise *A New System* (1774–76) was read eagerly by Blake, proposed that the meanings of myths were to be found not in their literary aspect but in the "part that relates to . . . rites and religion"; in a chapter on the "Rites of Damater, or Ceres," he remarked on the once "dreaded" aspect of the later "innocent and rural goddess," and on the similarly "formidable" aspect of her daughter-avatar Proserpine; Demeter was ultimately for Bryant "Da Mater," *"the mother of the gods,"* and identified with the Ark, while Dionysus was the *"Ark-born Deity,"* identified with Osiris and Noah.[35] Richard Payne Knight, in *A Discourse on the Worship of Priapus* (1786), argues that Greek myths should be approached not through the "wild and capricious stories of Ovid's *Metamorphoses*" but through studying the "first principles of ancient religion" which were "the subjects of the ancient mysteries"; he follows Apuleius in identifying "the Eleusinian Ceres, Celestial Venus, and Proserpine" with the Near Eastern mother goddess Isis, and he discusses Ceres, Proserpine, and Bacchus together as personifications of the "two great attributes of creation and destruction."[36] Charles Dupuis, in the "Traité des Mystères" of his massive *Origine de tous les cultes* (1794), identifies Ceres and Bacchus with Isis and Osiris, "unis par un culte commun" at Eleusis and elsewhere; Proserpine and Bacchus are, in addition, compared as deities of the afterlife who descend to the underworld and reascend.[37]

All this is not meant to suggest that Shelley was directly "influenced" by any one of these treatises, but rather that the cultic connections between Demeter and Dionysus could as readily be perceived in her time as in ours, perhaps more readily. There was much both in extant Greek and Roman texts (the Homeric hymns, the choral songs of the Greek tragedies, Apuleius, Plutarch) and in recent mythographical speculation to suggest that "rich-haired Ceres" was once a powerful mother goddess, and that her cult as well as that of Bacchus was administered by priestesses and celebrated particularly by women. In *Proserpine* itself Demeter's identity as earth goddess and primal mother is the theme of Proserpine's song to Ceres, contributed by Percy Shelley and reminiscent of the Homeric "Hymn to the Earth: Mother of All," which he had translated in 1819:

> Sacred Goddess, Mother Earth,
>   Thou from whose immortal bosom
> Gods, and men, and beasts have birth,

> Leaf, and blade, and bud, and blossom,
> Breathe thine influence most divine
> On thine own child Proserpine.

(18)

It should be noted also that the Dionysian aspect of Greek culture, popularized by Nietzsche in the late nineteenth century, was known much earlier among German authors read by the Shelleys. Wieland was fascinated by Dionysian mystery cults and described what he could discover about them in a series of novels published in the late eighteenth century; Schiller enthusiastically depicted a Bacchic procession in his poem *The Gods of Greece* (1788).[38] Schlegel, in his *Course of Lectures on Dramatic Literature and Art* (read by Mary Shelley in John Black's 1815 translation) notes that the chorus in Greek tragedy "had a local origin in the feasts of Bacchus," and that "Bacchus, and not Apollo, was the tutelary deity of tragic poets . . . we must remember that Bacchus was not merely the god of wine and joy, but also the god of all higher kinds of inspiration."[39] There was also, of course, the evidence from the tragedies of Euripides; ritual connections between Demeter and Dionysus can be seen, for example, in *The Bacchae,* in which "the chorus of maenads . . . invoke the Earth Mother [as Demeter] even before their own patron god, Dionysus."[40]

In her mythological dramas, Mary Shelley seems able to reach behind Ovid to recover something of the deeper sexual/cultural tensions expressed in Greek myths and the rituals and mysteries associated with them. The legend acted out by the priestess at Eleusis has been recently described as "probably showing the sorrow of Demeter at the abduction of Kore and her subsequent joy at her daughter's return," and this outline fits the basic two-act structure of Shelley's *Proserpine* as well.[41] The Bacchic procession in *Midas,* described by the god himself, is among the earliest celebrations of the "Nysian impulse" in English poetry, and the first in a form that evokes the associations of Bacchus with the origins of Greek drama.[42] (That Bacchus utters this speech in soliloquy, a mode associated in the play with male fantasies of domination, may reflect the ambivalent status of this figure, a male deity leading a troop of subversive Maenads and Bacchantes, for women writers.)

Placing an emphasis on the plays' "cultic" aspects, however, with their connotations of the primitive and the irrational, brings out a problem latent within the earlier discussion of "relationality" as well. Shelley's resistance to patriarchal myth and monological literary modes might seem, at least as presented here, to ultimately confirm, rather than subvert, the conventional configurations of the feminine valorized and even appropriated by male Romantic poets: emotionality, sympathy, intuition, the nurturing mother.[43] Her mythological dramas' critical relation to Ovid might seem undercut by their subtler adherence to a tradition of representations of the female that tends to alienate women from subjectivity and the poetic voice: Homans warns that "Mother Nature is hardly powerless, but, enormous as her powers are, they are not the ones that her daughters want if they are to become poets."[44] It is important before concluding, then, to stress that for Shelley the mother goddess is not silent but rather herself a framer of myths. *Proserpine* opens with a request as significant for its emphasis on female narrative as for its foreshadowing of the play's crisis in the forced rupturing of female bonds: "Dear Mother, leave me not! I love to rest / Under the shadow of that hanging cave / And listen to your tales" (5). Throughout the play's first act Ceres, the two nymphs, and Proserpine herself are all presented as figures of capable imagination, weavers of "tales and songs" (9), of "poesy" (15), of "verses sweet" (8).

In the first act of *Proserpine* Shelley mends the conventional rift between goddess and bard, (female) muse and (male) poet, to imagine a community of mythmaking women, precursors for her own revisionist project. As otherwise unprecedented works of feminist mythic revisionism, Shelley's mythological poems demand the critical attention usually reserved for the more extended (and more fully realized) attempts of her male contemporaries in works like *Prometheus Unbound* and *Hyperion*. We should not forget in approaching her mythological dramas that it was Mary Shelley who, in *Frankenstein*, created the most popular and enduring of modern myths.[45] Not that the plays are nearly as interesting as the novel; *The Modern Prometheus* is far more complex both in itself and in its critical relation to earlier mythic codes (that of Milton as well as that of Aeschylus) than either of Shelley's revisionist versions of Ovid. But to acknowledge that *Proserpine* and *Midas* are not of the same caliber as *Frankenstein* or *Hyperion* is quite different from dismissing them as "little classical fancies"; it should no longer be possible to patronize Shelley for adding, as Norman puts it, her "small tinkle to the sonorous note" of Percy's lyrics.[46] As revisionist responses to Ovid and to the tradition he represents, as generic experiments related in a complex, critical manner to the "visionary" lyrics framed within them, and as early, if oblique, attempts to explore the cultic roots of Greek tragedy and myth, *Proserpine* and *Midas* are considerable works which add both to our sense of Shelley's achievement and to our conception of the mythological revival in the Romantic period.

Notes

1. Douglas Bush, *Mythology and the Romantic Tradition in English Poetry* (1927; New York: Norton, 1963), 172. Cf. A. Koszul's remark that "Shelley's encouragement, probably his guidance and supervision, have raised his wife's inspiration to a place considerably higher than that of *Frankenstein* or *Valperga*" in his introduction to *Proserpine & Midas: Two Unpublished Mythological Dramas by Mary Shelley* (London: Humphrey Milford, 1922), xxxi. All quotations from *Proserpine* and *Midas* cited in the text follow Koszul's edition.

2. Elizabeth Nitchie, *Mary Shelley: Author of "Frankenstein"* (New Brunswick: Rutgers University Press, 1953), 157; Sylva Norman, "Mary Shelley: Novelist and Dramatist," *On Shelley* (London: Oxford University Press, 1938), 98.

3. Margaret Homans, *Women Writers and Poetic Identity: Dorothy Wordsworth, Emily Brontë, and Emily Dickinson* (Princeton: Princeton University Press, 1980), 12–13.

4. Stuart Curran, "Romantic Poetry: The 'I' Altered," *Romanticism and Feminism,* ed. Anne K. Mellor (Bloomington: Indiana University Press, 1988), 189–90.

5. Tilottama Rajan, "Romanticism and the Death of Lyric Consciousness," *Lyric Poetry: Beyond New Criticism,* ed. Chaviva Hôseck and Patricia Parker (Ithaca: Cornell University Press, 1985), 206. See also Alan Richardson, *A Mental Theater: Poetic Drama and Consciousness in the Romantic Age* (University Park: Pennsylvania State University Press 1988), 1–19, 175–78.

6. Susan Gubar, "Mother, Maiden and the Marriage of Death: Woman Writers and an Ancient Myth," *Women's Studies* 6 (1979): 303.

7. Mitzi Myers, "The Dilemmas of Gender as Double-Voiced Narrative; Or, Maria Edgeworth Mothers the Bildungsroman," *The Idea of the Novel in the Eighteenth Century,* ed. Robert W. Uphaus (East Lansing, Mich.: Colleagues Press, 1988).

8. William A. Walling, *Mary Shelley* (Boston: Twayne, 1972), 115.

9. Koszul, xxx. Cf. Bush, *Mythology,* 171; Walling, *Mary Shelley,* 115.

10. For Mary Shelley's lack of a formal education, see Anne K. Mellor, *Mary Shelley: Her Life, Her Fiction, Her Monsters* (New York: Methuen, 1988), 8–12. Homans suggests that Keats, as the canonical Romantic poet with the "humblest origins," might be considered as sharing his female contemporaries' experience as "outsiders relative to the major literary tradition" (*Women Writers,* 240).

11. Koszul, xiii.

12. Eva C. Keuls, *The Reign of the Phallus: Sexual Politics in Ancient Athens* (New York: Harper and Row, 1985), 1.

13. Alicia Ostriker, "The Thieves of Language: Women Poets and Revisionist Mythmaking," *The New Feminist Criticism: Essays on Women, Literature, and Theory,* ed. Elaine Showalter (New York: Pantheon, 1985), 317. See also Burton Feldman and Robert D. Richardson, *The Rise of Modern Mythology 1680–1860* (Bloomington: Indiana University Press, 1972).

14. Gubar, "Mother, Maiden and the Marriage of Death," 301. Gubar here is summarizing the view of Simone de Beauvoir as developed in *The Second Sex,* trans. H. M. Parshley (1952; New York: Vintage, 1974), 157–223.

15. *Shelley's Prose, Or The Trumpet of a Prophecy,* ed. David Lee Clark (Albuquerque: University of New Mexico Press 1954), 216, 220–21.

16. "The necessity of a Belief in the Heathen Mythology / to a Christian," given in whole by Koszul, xxiv–xxvi.

17. Walling, *Mary Shelley,* 115.

18. Phyllis Chesler, *Women and Madness* (1972; New York: Avon, 1973), 18–19; Marilyn Arthur, "Politics and Pomegranates: An Interpretation of the Homeric Hymn to Demeter," *Arethusa* 10 (1977): 8; Gubar, "Mother, Maiden and the Marriage of Death," 302.

19. Keuls, *Reign of the Phallus,* 112, see also 64, 351–53, and William Blake Tyrell, *Amazons: A Study in Athenian Mythmaking* (Baltimore: Johns Hopkins University Press, 1984), 69–71.

20. Sarah B. Pomeroy, *Goddesses, Whores, Wives, and Slaves: Women in Classical Antiquity* (New York: Schocken, 1975), 216–17.

21. *Mathilda,* ed. Elizabeth Nitchie (Chapel Hill: University of North Carolina Press, 1959), 19.

22. Chesler, *Women and Madness,* 15.

23. Gubar, "Mother, Maiden and the Marriage of Death," 304.

24. Jean de Palacio, *Mary Shelley dans son oeuvre: Contribution aux études shelleyennes* (Paris: Editions Klincksieck, 1969), 447.

25. Barry Cornwall [Bryan Waller Procter], *Marcian Collonna An Italian Tale with Three Dramatic Scenes and Other Poems* (London: Warren and Ollier, 1820), 151, 156.

26. See Keuls, *Reign of the Phallus,* 47–55. The glamorization of rape on daytime television has recently become of concern even to *TV Guide:* see Gerard Waggett, "A Plea to the Soaps: Let's Stop Turning Rapists into Heroes," *TV Guide* 37 (1989): 10–11.

27. See Gubar, "Mother, Maiden and the Marriage of Death," 306.

28. Larry D. Benson, ed., *The Riverside Chaucer,* 3rd ed. (Boston: Houghton Mifflin, 1987), 118 (lines 979–80); the suggestion that the wife has learned this version from her militantly antifeminist husband Jankin was first made by Edgar Finley Shannon in *Chaucer and the Roman Poets* (Cambridge, Mass.: Harvard University Press, 1929), 319. James Kinsley, ed., *The Poems and Fables of John Dryden* (London: Oxford University Press, 1962), 782 (lines 155–56 of "The Wife of Bath Her Tale").

29. "Mother, Maiden and the Marriage of Death," 305.

30. Bush, *Mythology,* 171.

31. Froma I. Zeitlin, "Cultic Models of the Feminine: Rites of Dionysus and Demeter," *Arethusa* 15 (1982): 132.

32. Pomeroy, *Goddesses,* 217.

33. See Keuls, *Reign of the Phallus,* 352; Pomeroy, *Goddesses,* 77, 216–17.

34. For a critical account of Bachofen, see Joan Bamberger, "The Myth of Matriarchy: Why Men Rule in Primitive Society," in *Woman, Culture, and Society,* ed. Michelle Zimbalist Rosaldo and Louise Lamphere (Stanford: Stanford University Press, 1974), 263–80. While Ostriker celebrates the "attempt by women to retrieve, from the myth of the abstract father-god who creates the universe *ab nihilo,* the figure on which he was originally based, the female creatrix" ("Thieves of Language," 320), Homans rejects the myth of matriarchy as a resource for women's poetry: "Whether as a cultural or political memory, or as a personal myth transmitted into poetry, Mother Nature is not a helpful model for women aspiring to be poets. She is prolific biologically, not linguistically, and she is destructive as she is creative" (*Women Writers,* 13).

35. Jacob Bryant, *A New System; Or, an Analysis of Ancient Mythology,* 3rd ed., 6 vols. (London: J. Walker, 1807), 2:299, 304, 352–53; 3:184, 310.

36. Richard Payne Knight, *A Discourse on the Worship of Priapus and Its Connection with the Mystic Theology of the Ancients,* rpt. in *Sexual Symbolism: A History of Phallic Worship,* ed. Ashley Montagu (New York: Julian Press, 1957), 76, 91, 142–50.

37. Charles Dupuis, *Origine de Tous les cultes, ou Religion Universelle,* 3 vols. (Paris: H. Agasse, L'An III de la République [1794]), 2: Part 2, 12–15. On Persephone and Dionysus as related divinities of the afterlife, cf. Keuls, *Reign of the Phallus,* 129.

38. See Mark O. Kistler, "Dionysian Elements in Wieland," *Germanic Review* 35 (1960): 83–92; and E. M. Butler, *The Tyranny of Greece over Germany: A Study of the Influence Exercised by Greek Art and Poetry over the Great German Writers of the Eighteenth, Nineteenth and Twentieth Centuries* (Cambridge: Cambridge University Press, 1935), 294–95.

39. August Wilhelm Schlegel, *Course of Lectures on Dramatic Art and Literature,* trans. John Black (New York: AMS Press, 1973), 70, 80. Cf. the first of Coleridge's 1813 lectures on Shakespeare: "The Greek stage had its origin in the ceremonies of a sacrifice, such as the goat to Bacchus;—it was erroneous to call him only the jolly god of wine, among the ancients he was venerable; he was the symbol of that power which acts without our consciousness from the vital energies of nature, as Apollo was the symbol of our intellectual consciousness." Samuel Taylor Coleridge, *Lectures 1808–1819 On Literature* 2 vols., ed. R. A. Foakes (London: Routledge and Kegan Paul; Princeton: Princeton University Press, 1987), 1:517–18.

40. Keuls, *Reign of the Phallus,* 351.

41. Pomeroy, *Goddesses,* 77.

42. A more extended and still earlier Romantic celebration of Bacchus occurs in book IV of Keats's *Endymion* (1819).

43. For the male Romantic writer's appropriation of conventionally "feminine" characteristics, in a manner that suggests modifying Homans's notion of a "masculine" Romantic tradition without challenging her contention that women writers are effectively excluded from it, see Alan Richardson, "Romanticism and the Colonization of the Feminine," in Mellor, *Romanticism and Feminism,* 13–25.

44. Homans, *Women Writers,* 16.

45. See Chris Baldick, *In Frankenstein's Shadow: Myth, Monstrosity, and Nineteenth-Century Writing* (Oxford: Clarendon Press, 1987).

46. Koszul, vii; Norman, "Mary Shelley," 99.

Beatrice in *Valperga*: A New Cassandra

Barbara Jane O'Sullivan

> He, the damned and triumphant one, sat meditating many thousand years for the conclusion, the consummation, the final crown, the seal of all misery, which he might set on man's brain and heart to doom him to endless torment; and he created the imagination.
>
> Mary Shelley, *Valperga, or the Life and Adventures of Castruccio, Prince of Lucca,* 3:47

With these words, Beatrice of Ferrara, a heroine in Mary Shelley's second novel, utters a blasphemous condemnation of the Romantic celebration of the imagination.[1] Written in Italy between the years 1818 and 1821, *Valperga* is as much a synthesis of literary derivation and creative vitality as *Frankenstein.* In it Mary Shelley turns again to the dark side of the imagination—showing that a vivid imagination can be more a curse than a gift. The vehicle for this statement, Beatrice, is a religious prophetess who is hunted, haunted, raped, imprisoned, and deceived until she is utterly destroyed. Beatrice is an extraordinary character, whose very talents alienate her from the society in which she lives. Her isolation from normal discourse puts into question the very social strictures which discredit her. That Mary Shelley created such a complex heroine is remarkable. That she knew no way to set her heroine free is tragic.

In using this inspired yet troubled figure to represent the predicament of the creative female, Mary Shelley develops an alternative to the Promethean optimism of Romanticism. Percy Shelley heralded his triumphant poetic vision with the embodiment of a Prometheus Unbound—a hero-god at the center of a metaphysical tale of the renewal and release of creative energy. Mary Shelley, on the other hand, portrays a tragic and all-too-human heroine, who is reminiscent of the ancient prophetess Cassandra. A close study of Mary Shelley's works reveals that the Cassandra figure is a pervasive image, and that Mary Shelley felt a strong personal identification with Cassandra at certain times in her life. Indeed, such is the consistency of this trope in Mary Shelley's work that we could give the name "the Cassandra complex" to the portrayal of female imaginative power and its resulting debilitation in her writing.

I intend to explore the attributes and development of the Cassandra figure in Mary Shelley's work. After a brief introduction to Cassandra, I move on to examine the links between the Cassandra model and the main female characters in *Valperga,* focusing particularly on the prophetess, Beatrice. I follow this with a discussion of the role of the creativity and vision in the novel. The final section surveys the place of the Cassandra figure in Mary Shelley's later novels and in the work of the Victorian women writers who followed her. I intend to show that in many ways Mary Shelley was a forerunner of the Victorian women authors who adapted and strengthened the portrayal of the gifted woman, or Cassandra figure.

As I will demonstrate, the Cassandra model is fluid, embodying a variety of attributes. These attributes are grounded in the politics of self-expression and are particularly concerned with the ability to reach and influence an audience. Ironically, the audience is not always external. The Cassandra figure in Mary Shelley's work is often self-silencing, undercutting her own prophetic impulse through a variety of self-destructive strategies. This predicament highlights Mary Shelley's personal ambivalence toward Cassandrism as a radical model of female potential.

The attributes of Cassandra have special significance for the female artist. According to legend she was a priestess who was beloved by the god Apollo. Apollo, the god of poetry and prophecy, gave Cassandra the gift of prophecy as a love token. When she refused to consummate his love he cursed her, declaring that her prophecies would never be believed. She went on to foretell the destruction of her city, Troy, and she later warned the conquering king, Agamemnon, that his wife, Clytemnestra, was plotting to kill him. However, the curse was effective, and Cassandra's warnings went unheeded.[2]

In myths one finds evidence for the story of the spiritual and psychological history of a culture. In the surviving legends about Cassandra, it is clear that she represents an ancient line of female spiritual leaders which was subsumed by the rise of patriarchy in ancient Greece. The god Apollo was a latecomer to the Greek pantheon, who usurped many of the functions of the old order. In effect, Cassandra is a disenfranchised prophetess who has lost out in an oracular power struggle with the new god, Apollo. In his study of the archetype of the Great Mother, Erich Neumann examines the way in which patriarchal culture overtook matrilineal cultural images in the ancient world. Neumann writes,

> Unquestionably the patriarchal development, which began very early, effaced or at least overlaid many elements of the old matrilineal culture, so that, as in studying a palimpsest, we must first remove the upper layer before we can see the matriarchal culture beneath.[3]

The story of Cassandra can be seen as the story of the troubled history of female spiritual and imaginative power which is buried alive beneath the surface of Western culture. In modern terms, Cassandra embodies the predicament of having a special talent that goes uncelebrated and is considered socially unacceptable. Marginalized to the point of being thought mad, even by her own family, she is doomed to practice her art in isolation. Cassandra's visions and her passion make her a threat to the order and stability of society, for if she is to be believed, too many comfortable assumptions must be questioned. This is clearly illustrated in the rejection of her warnings regarding the Trojan horse. It was much easier for people to believe the horse was a peace

offering than to recognize the threat it posed. Likewise, for Agamemnon to
have believed Cassandra, he would have had to face some ugly truths about
himself and his wife.

It is ironic that Cassandra's prophecies proved to be correct. In retrospect
she is vindicated, for events have proved her right. Even the audiences of
Aeschylus, who saw her story acted in 458 B.C., would have been aware of this
awkward truth. Yet it is still challenging to come to terms with her achievement, because hers are messages of doom, not hope. This pessimism continues to make them problematic even if they are true.

As a role model for the female artist Cassandra is obviously a mixed
blessing. Yet her adoption by Mary Shelley represents a radical step in the
portrayal of gifted women by gifted women. Over one and a half centuries
later, the metaphor is still being explored. In 1982 the German writer Christa
Wolf published a personal meditation on the Cassandra story which explores
its potential as a myth of female creativity. Wolf explains, "I ask questions
about the historical reality of the Cassandra figure and conditions for the
woman writer past and present. My overall concern is the sinister effects of
alienation, in aesthetics, in art, as well as elsewhere."[4]

It is exciting to discover Mary Shelley's early adoption of Cassandra as an
archetypal figure of female creative energy, yet it is also disturbing to know
that the prophetess is a tragic character whose example is ultimately debilitating rather than liberating. While Percy Shelley successfully unbound the
Promethean urge in his poetry, the key to the unbinding of Cassandra remained elusive. The challenge for modern readers is to identify Mary Shelley's achievement in adapting the Cassandra figure to suit her artistic vision
and to understand the significance of the artistic and personal limitations this
figure represents. This is in some ways a complementary exercise to the
analysis that was first proposed in Mary Poovey's study of the works of Mary
Wollstonecraft, Jane Austen, and Mary Shelley.[5] In *The Proper Lady and the
Woman Writer,* Poovey concentrates on a thesis of accommodation, showing
how women authors learned to reconcile social expectations of the behavior of
proper ladies with the "masculine" role of authorship which they had chosen
for themselves. Poovey investigates a variety of strategies adopted by these
women, but she does not touch upon the specific image of the Cassandra
figure as a model for the female experience of an artistic vocation. We catch a
further glimpse of the Cassandra figure in Gilbert and Gubar's *The Madwoman in the Attic.*[6] Investigating the nineteenth-century female literary
imagination, Gilbert and Gubar identified the recurring figure of the madwoman as a manifestation of the woman writer's own insecure self-image. As
we shall see, this figure is a close sister of Mary Shelley's Cassandra.

As *Valperga* is not easily available to readers at present, I begin with a brief
outline of the plot. The novel is based on the life of Castruccio Castracani, a
tyrant who thrived in the political strife of the fourteenth-century Italian city
states. It describes Castruccio's career and his relationships with two remarkable women, Euthanasia and Beatrice. The prophetically named Euthanasia

is modeled on Dante's Beatrice, especially as she is represented in the *Vita Nuova,* and on the ideals of Percy Shelley and Godwin. Euthanasia is a natural leader, whose supremacy among her peers is earned through the gracious upholding of purity and high moral values. Valperga is the name of Euthanasia's castle, which lies partway between Euthanasia's political home, Florence, and Castruccio's military headquarters at Lucca. It is thus the symbolic center of the novel.[7] The love affair between Euthanasia and Castruccio is doomed by her refusal to abandon her Florentine dedication to liberty, and by Castruccio's equal determination to cling to his tyrannical and oppressive political ambitions. Castruccio's illicit liaison with the lovely but naive prophetess, Beatrice, introduces a third significant character to the plot. The resulting love triangle has some surprising consequences, for although they are potential rivals for Castruccio's affections, Euthanasia and Beatrice find themselves drawn together by "their love for one who loved only himself" (*MSV,* 3:53). Toward the end of the novel, Euthanasia is left nursing the brokenhearted Beatrice as they both struggle to overcome Castruccio's influence in their lives.

The characters of Euthanasia and Beatrice complement each other in many ways. While Beatrice is essentially disenfranchised and rootless, Euthanasia enjoys the personal autonomy which economic, political, and moral independence can bring. Like Beatrice, Euthanasia is gifted with a powerful imagination, but she recognizes that the imagination is best indulged in private. She tells Castruccio,

> Being alone, I have not feared to give the reins to my feelings; I have lived happily within the universe of my own mind, and have often given reality to that which others call a dream. . . . You have asked me to relate the events of my life; I may say that it is a blank, if you would not hear the history of many a strange idea, many an exalted feeling, and reverie of wondrous change. (*MSV,* 1:192)

Eight years later, Mary Shelley described her early life in a manner very similar to Euthanasia. In the 1831 "Author's Introduction" to *Frankenstein,* Shelley wrote,

> Still, I had a dearer pleasure than this, which was the formation of castles in the air—the indulging in waking dreams—the following up of trains of thought, which had for their subject the formation of a succession of imaginary incidents. My dreams were at once more fantastic and more agreeable than my writings. . . . I accounted for them to nobody, they were my refuge when annoyed—my dearest pleasure when free.[8]

Both Mary Shelley and Euthanasia are acutely aware that their dreams are best kept to themselves, to be treasured and enjoyed in privacy. Euthanasia recognizes that to a man of action her rich but internal life must be seen as "a blank." When she describes her beliefs and visions to Castruccio he proves incapable of comprehending.

Cherished as it is, Euthanasia's inner life contains within it the seeds of her destruction. Euthanasia deceives herself about Castruccio's true nature. In fact, she makes a god of him, attributing to this Machiavellian autocrat her own high principles and morality. The realization that he is far different from what she has imagined involves a painful awakening. However, Euthanasia's fate has been sealed before she has time to understand what is happening. In a passage leading up to the moment when Euthanasia and Castruccio fall in love, Shelley writes,

> Is there not a principle in the human mind that foresees the change about to occur to it? Is there not a feeling which would warn the soul of peril were it not at the same time a sure prophecy that peril is not to be avoided? So felt Euthanasia. (*MSV,* 1:172)

This then is Euthanasia's predicament—a predicament common to the Cassandra figure throughout Mary Shelley's work. At one level of consciousness a truth is whispered which another level of consciousness is powerless to act upon because it simply cannot recognize or adequately interpret the insight. This, in turn, is interpreted as "fate." What this seems to indicate is a fragmented psyche unable to respond to awkward questions, much as Agamemnon was unable to see and react to Clytemnestra's treachery, despite Cassandra's prognostications.

If Euthanasia becomes a victim despite all the benefits of her rank, then Beatrice seems almost born to be a victim. Her background is described in an episode in which Mary Shelley invents a cult of female messianism reminiscent of the life of Joanna Southcott. Drawing on Muratori's *Antichrista Italiane* No. 60, Mary Shelley transcribes two passages detailing the heresy of a woman named Wilhelmina of Bohemia.[9] The first passage from Muratori announces that Wilhelmina had "secretly formed a sect, founded on the absurd and damnable belief that she was the Holy Ghost incarnate upon earth," to which Mary Shelley adds the words "in favour of the female sex" (*MSV,* 2:26). The second explains "the angel Raphael announced to her mother the incarnation of the Holy Spirit," and again, Mary Shelley adds "in favour of the female sex" (ibid.). Shelley then goes on to invent a daughter for Wilhelmina. When Wilhelmina dies, the infant, Beatrice, is adopted by a priest who has participated in the Inquisition against her mother's heresy. To protect Beatrice he vows to raise her in complete ignorance of her maternal heritage (her father is unknown), but he has no qualms in telling Castruccio the whole story during the equivalent of after-dinner drinks.

Although it is not the only medieval heresy to have been put down, the story Mary Shelley tells of the dismantling of Wilhelmina's cult suggests the existence of a conspiracy which suppresses the alternative visions of women and destroys their network. Wilhelmina's memory is obliterated by the Inquisition, which silences and even kills the women entrusted with her story. The repression is further exacerbated by the genuine belief of the priest, Marsillio, and his fellow Inquisitors that the destruction of Wilhelmina's heretical network is morally right. Indeed, the patriarchal conspiracy extends beyond religion to the very fabric of society. By sharing the secret of Beatrice's origins with Castruccio,

Marsillio reduces Wilhelmina's messianism to an entertaining anecdote and gives Castruccio sensitive knowledge which Beatrice herself is denied.

Breaking the link between Wilhelmina and Beatrice is thus more than a religious imperative; it is a political maneuver, aimed at undermining the development of a female subculture that threatens the social stability of the patriarchy. There is evidence of this in the collaboration of Castruccio and Marsillio, which is designed for their mutual political gain. In *Women of Ideas and What Men Have Done to Them,* Dale Spender describes the phenomenon of repression to which the visions of women have been subjected: "It is therefore in the patriarchal interest to prevent women from sharing, establishing and asserting their equally real, valid and *different* experience."[10] To prevent women from establishing alternative networks it is therefore imperative to ensure that their strongest ties to each other are broken. It is with this goal in mind that Wilhelmina's memory is exiled from her daughter's life.

In her imaginary account of the last moments of Cassandra, Christa Wolf emphasizes the thwarted impulse to pass a message from one generation to the next. Her Cassandra cries out,

> "But I implore you: Send me a scribe, or better yet a young slave woman with a keen memory and a powerful voice. Ordain that she may repeat to her daughter what she hears from me. That the daughter in turn may pass it on to her daughter, and so on. So that alongside the river of heroic songs this tiny rivulet too, may reach those far away, perhaps happier people who will live in times to come."[11]

This tragedy of female generations that are cut off from each other is one which Mary Shelley had experienced personally in the loss of her own mother. The loss affected her deeply, although she rarely wrote openly about its impact on her life. Perhaps this was because of the ambivalence of Mary Wollstonecraft's reputation. In some ways Wollstonecraft was herself a reviled heretic, but at least Mary Shelley had the opportunity to learn what her mother stood for by reading her work. In *The Wrongs of Woman,* a novel left unfinished at her death, Mary Wollstonecraft had written:

> Addressing these memoirs to you, my child, uncertain whether I shall ever have an opportunity to instruct you, many observations will probably flow from my heart, which only a mother—a mother schooled in misery could make.[12]

In the story of Beatrice and Wilhelmina we see the traumatic separation of mother and daughter which Mary Shelley knew so intimately, while in the obliteration of Wilhelmina's life's work we have a poignant reminder of how easy it is for women's stories to become lost and devalued, as indeed much of Shelley's work has been.

One of the most intriguing aspects of the character of Beatrice is the marked ambivalence with which her story is told. When she first appears, she is portrayed as the *Ancilla Dei,* the angel of God, a saintly, respected, and vestal figure who is accepted as part of the Christian community. Gradually, the saintly vestige fades away and is replaced by the revelation that she is born under the the curse of Eve, with no apparent possibility of redemption. Her own protector, Marsillio, laments in private, "alas! the hand of god is upon thee, born in an evil day of a guilty and impious mother!" (*MSV*, 2:50). His statement is an ironic reversal of Beatrice's own understanding of herself, for she believes the hand of God which touches her is a blessing. An initial examination seems to prove that Beatrice is right. Her experience of prophetic inspiration has the hallmarks of authenticity. It is described in the following terms:

> She felt her soul, as it were, fade away, and incorporate itself with another and a diviner spirit, which whispered truth and knowledge to her mind, and then slowly receding, left her human nature agitated, joyful, and exhausted. (*MSV*, 2:80)

The scene is reminiscent of an encounter Mary Shelley had with the *improvissatore* Sgricci in 1820. After seeing his remarkable rendition of Cassandra in a prophetic trance, Mary Shelley wrote to her stepsister, Claire Clairmont.

> The madness of Cassandra was exquisitely delineated—and her prophecies wondrous and torrent like—they burst on the ear like the cry the Trojans cry—of Shakespear and music eloquence & poetry were combined in this wonderful effort of the imagination—or shall I say of the inspiration of some wondrous deity. (*MSL*, 1:182)

She went on to report a conversation she had with Sgricci:

> I was extremely pleased with him he talked with delight of the inspiration he had experienced the night before, which bore him out of himself and filled him as they describe the Pythyness to have been filled with divine & tumu[l]tuous emotion—especially in the part where Cassandra prophesies he was as overcome as she could {   } & he poured forth prophecy as if Apollo had also touched his lips with the oracular touch.

Sgricci's performance and conversation had a lasting impact on Mary Shelley, and she was clearly reminded of him when she wrote about Beatrice's prophetic experience.[13] However, while she was delighted with Sgricci and his act, she could be ambivalent when confronted with the uncontrolled overstepping of the boundaries between fact and fantasy. She remarks of Beatrice's visionary episode "these were her dreams,—alas to her they were realities!" (*MSV*, 2:80).

In making a cautionary tale of Beatrice's uncritical indulgence in fantasy Mary Shelley may have drawn on her knowledge of the hallucinations and horrors of Percy Shelley and Claire Clairmont. In her diary of their early life together there are many reported instances of Shelley and Clairmont leading each other on by giving free reign to their imaginations.[14] These sessions often ended in hysterics and nightmares which tried Mary Shelley's patience. Still, she participated to some extent in this flirtation with supernatural horrors, as we can see in the "Author's Introduction" to *Frankenstein*. There, she claims that she had wanted to think of a story "which would rival the mysterious fears of our nature and awaken thrilling horror . . . to make the reader dread to look round, to curdle the blood and quicken the beatings of the heart." Her desires were answered when, "My imagination, unbidden, possessed and guided me, gifting the successive images that arose in my mind with a vividness far beyond the usual bounds of reverie. I saw with shut eyes, but acute mental vision." Mary's account of her "possession" is similar to that experienced by Beatrice. However, even if this account is true, and not simply an authorial dramatization, the experience of imaginative synthesis is followed by the lengthy and conscious effort of composition. The idea is grappled into shape by the author. For Beatrice, however, there is no transmutation; as Mary Shelley explains, her dreams *are* her realities.

Although the nightmare episodes of Shelley and Clairmont were intrusions into the life of the household, Mary had learned that there was another danger which lurked in the untrammeled sexuality that accompanied this propensity to self-delusion. In *Valperga,* Beatrice is sheltered in her world of spiritual ecstasy until she is confronted by a real man of flesh and blood. It is then that her imaginings lead her into serious trouble. Mary Shelley explains that in believing her attraction for Castruccio to have been divinely inspired, Beatrice "had followed that as a guide, which she ought to have bound with fetters, and to have curbed and crushed by every effort of reason" (*MSV,* 2:87). These are harsh words, suggesting that in Mary Shelley's experience women with deep feelings, particularly feelings arising from strong sexual energy, must bind themselves to silence out of an instinct for self-preservation.

Mary Shelley's portrayal of Beatrice's relationship with Castruccio hearkens back to her own early romance with Percy Shelley. Both Mary Shelley and Beatrice nearly overwhelm their lovers by giving themselves openly and unashamedly.[15] Yet there are more striking parallels in the relationship between Byron and Claire Clairmont. In attempting to reenact the seduction scene between Mary and Percy Shelley, Claire Clairmont had deceived herself into believing that Byron would in some way reciprocate her feelings—much as Beatrice imagines that Castruccio shares hers simply because she wants him to. Byron's reaction to Clairmont's advances was forthright. He wrote to Douglas Kinnaird "I never loved nor pretended to love her, but a man is a man, and if a girl of eighteen comes prancing to you at all hours of the night there is but one way."[16] Likewise, Castruccio takes full advantage of what is offered to him, despite the fact that he is engaged to Euthanasia and has no inclination for a lasting relationship with Beatrice.

The similarities between romantic love and the sympathetic imagination become apparent in these intertwinings of romantic relationships and fantasies. Both love and imagination can represent a vulnerability, an entering into the subject and an opening of the self which is simultaneously an exultation and an annihilation. In the case of Beatrice and Castruccio, this delicate balance is ruptured by Castruccio's abrupt withdrawal from the relationship. The withdrawal affects not only the relationship itself, but it also brings about the collapse of Beatrice's entire imaginative perspective. When the dalliance is no longer convenient to Castruccio, he disengages from Beatrice with a ruthless sangfroid:

> But the time arrived when he was obliged to undeceive her; and the hand that tore away the ties her trusting heart had bound round itself, at the same time tore away the veil which had for her invested all nature, and shewed life as it was—naked and appalling. (*MSV,* 2:90)

The language of this passage is physical and traumatic. It describes Beatrice's painful initiation in terms of a sexually aggressive encounter. The veil of the hymen, the veil of the prophetess, the veil of self-delusion, and the veil which covers physical nakedness are concentrated in a single image which Castruccio rips to shreds. In case we miss the underlying symbolism of the moment, which occurs in a chapter entitled "Fall of Beatrice," we are told that Castruccio "fled as the dæmon might have fled from the bitter sorrows of despoiled Paradise; he left her aghast, overthrown, annihilated" (*MSV,* 2:97).

Retrospectively, what had been a voluntary giving of herself becomes an act of rape in which Beatrice has been unwittingly complicit. It recalls the negative aspect of the power struggle in the relationship between Apollo and the prophetess, which is described in Virgil's *Aeneid.* No longer is the imagination an ecstatic reverie; instead it is a torment and a violation of the self. Depicting the Cumaean Sibyl at the moment of prophetic utterance Virgil writes,

> Meanwhile the prophetess, who had not yet submitted to Apollo, ran furious riot in the cave, as if in hope of casting the God's power from her brain. Yet all the more did he torment her frantic countenance, overmastering her wild thoughts, and crushed her and shaped her to his will.[17]

Feeling, and indeed knowing, that she has lost herself, Beatrice becomes a wanderer and is soon taken captive by a sex maniac named Tripalda. Tripalda's character encompasses the negative aspects of Castruccio's ruthless thirst for power and Marsillio's religious fetishism. Kept captive for three years, Beatrice suffers unnamed horrors which serve to further break her spirit.

The realization that the beliefs she held most dear are an illusion leaves Beatrice vulnerable to the Paterin heresy, for having been undeceived about the nature of the visible world she can no longer use her imagination to find God. The Paterins, who were active in Italy, "recognized . . . in the universe two creative powers: that of the invisible world, whom they called the Good God, and that of the visible world, whom they named the Evil God."[18] Beatrice embraces this philosophy, rejecting the possibility of personal redemption within the physical universe. She asks Euthanasia rhetorically, "God created me: am I the work of a beneficent being?" (*MSV,* 3:46). It is a question that hearkens back to the epigraph of *Frankenstein,* which Shelley had borrowed from Milton's *Paradise Lost.* The recurrence of this question on the motives of a deity who forms innocent creatures and allows them to suffer suggests Shelley's preoccupation with a world in which monsters and prophetesses become outcasts through no conscious action of their own. This theme makes explicit the unwitting and unwilling complicity of the victim in a postlapsarian world.

In turning to Paterinism, Beatrice convinces herself that her imagination is inherently evil, because it has led to her downfall. Thus, with no good to hope for from herself, Beatrice's imagination becomes its own torment. Instead of being a refuge and a source of comfort it comes to symbolize her fallen condition. Her frustrated railing at God is the ineffectual rebellion of the suppressed woman artist, for whom the courage to speak the truth leads only to madness and entrapment.

To emphasize the savage misogyny of the society in which Beatrice and Euthanasia exist, Shelley created two characters who act as foils to the heroines. The first, Mandragola, is a witch whose lifelong ambition is to rival the power of Castruccio.[19] Both Mandragola and Castruccio begin their careers as disenfranchised outcasts. However, Castruccio eventually rises to the pinnacle of political and military status, while Mandragola becomes a witch inhabiting a hovel in the forest near Valperga. Her only companion is an albino dwarf named Bindo, who has been adopted by Euthanasia with the same compassion that later leads to Euthanasia's attempted rescue of Beatrice. In a coarse mimicry of Beatrice's prophetic role, Bindo is described as interpreting the dreams of the inhabitants of Valperga and predicting the best time for commencing any new enterprise. His physique, coupled with his mental deficiencies, suggest a reviled femininity;

> [He] was of brief stature, and as slender as he was short; the softness of his features and the roundness and flexibility of his limbs manifested his want of strength; his mild, but almost meaningless physiognomy betrayed the want of judgement, courage, and all the more manly virtues. His mind seemed to approach the feebler spark of animal life, had it not been redeemed by an imagination of which he hardly appeared conscious himself. (*MSV*, 1:50)

Bindo's personal defects are almost childlike, but in other ways he appears to be a monstrous reflection of what a self-critical nineteenth-century woman might see when she looked in the mirror. Although he is a somewhat farcical character, his appearance in this novel highlights the insecurity and ambivalence with which Mary Shelley viewed the female prophetic impulse.

Bindo's purpose in the story is to bridge the gap between the world outside and the world of Mandragola. To this end, he is a crucial player in the Walpurgisnacht, or Night of the Witch, to which the name Valperga alludes. In this climactic scene, Beatrice is drawn into a conspiracy with Bindo and Mandragola in an attempt to recapture Castruccio's affections. The plot fails and the prophetess's feeble grasp on reason and on life itself are finally relinquished. When Castruccio sees her for the last time she has changed almost beyond recognition: "I find her with grey hairs and a wasted form, a young fruit utterly blighted, and, worse than all her reason fallen victim of her misery. Am I the cause of this?" (*MSV*, 3:157). Although Castruccio quickly discounts the notion of his own guilt, it is clear that through his actions and through the complicity of the society he represents, he has been directly and indirectly involved in Beatrice's downfall.

The question of Castruccio's complicity in the downfall of Beatrice raises the issue of Shelley's own complicity in discrediting her heroine. Shelley deserves credit for revealing the predicament of the creative woman in a society which refuses to celebrate her gifts, but she also supports the denial and betrayal of female power which takes place. She even undermines her initial portrayal of Beatrice as a gifted and saintly character, by commenting "Poor Beatrice! She had inherited from her mother the most ardent imagination that ever animated a human soul" (*MSV*, 2:86). This is a clear indication that despite the urge to celebrate the imagination, Shelley has grave misgivings about the vulnerability of a truly prophetic character. Shelley's depiction of Beatrice's awkward and vulnerable state is in some ways a projection of deep-seated anxieties about her own status as a creative woman. Her failure to save this gifted heroine therefore rebounds on her, and shows Shelley's complicity in the very social strictures which she implicitly criticizes. Indeed, Shelley makes a point of quoting Muratori, as an authority for discrediting Beatrice's prophetic ability. In his description of the Donna Estatica phenomenon which inspired the portrayal of both Wilhelmina and Beatrice, Muratori writes,

> We may piously believe that some were distinguished by supernatural gifts, and admitted to the secrets of heaven; but we may justly suppose that the source of many of their revelations, was their ardent imagination, filled with the ideas of religion and piety. (*MSV*, 2:43)

Despite Muratori's own admission that at least some of the women were "divinely inspired," Shelley does not allow for the possibility that either Wilhelmina or Beatrice belongs to this category. Instead, she goes out of her way to discredit their experience. Because her growing influence is becoming a threat to the established church, Beatrice is arrested and subjected to a trial by fire. She welcomes the opportunity to establish that she is "inspired by the grace and favour of the blessed Virgin" (*MSV*, 2:24). However, her protector, Marsillio, has other ideas. He arranges a false trial in order to save his ward from what he believes will be her certain death. He tells Castruccio, "I do not like this, she must be protected by falsehood and perjury, a lying and blasphemous mockery of the name of God" (*MSV*, 2:53–54). Beatrice is utterly unconscious of the sin she has occasioned, nor does she realize that she is surrounded by liars and blasphemers who are denying her the one opportunity to put her claims to the test. Although in a sense her prophecy proves right, in that she does survive the trial, the manner in which this is accomplished makes a mockery of her claims of divine protection. She emerges from the fire to participate unwittingly in a world in which deception, lust, confinement, and violation reign supreme.

At least in depicting Wilhelmina and Beatrice as being misguided, Mary Shelley does not impute dishonorable motives to them. Her fiercest critique of female spiritual power is reserved for the witch Mandragola and others of her kind. She writes,

> What made these women pretend to powers they did not possess, incur the
> greatest perils for the sake of being believed to be what they were not,
> without any apparent advantage accruing to themselves from this belief? I
> believe we may find the answer in our own hearts: the love of power is
> inherent in human nature; and, in evil natures, to be feared is a kind of
> power. (*MSV*, 3:7–8)

In a novel which has as its basis the undenied political and military machina-
tions of a tyrant, it is ironic to hear such harsh words reserved for an old woman
in a thatched hut. Yet the revulsion Shelley expressed for this character is
indicative of her disgust at certain types of female self-assertion. It is "natural"
for Castruccio to be ambitious, but Mandragola's ambition and her methods
are seen as tainted and obscene. Mary Shelley's ambivalence toward female
self-assertion is evident throughout *Valperga*. Despite her triumph in creating
strong female characters, she undercuts her own achievement by her complicity in the repression and discrediting of the voices she herself has created.

The impulse to write about extraordinary women manifested itself throughout
Mary Shelley's career. Her concern for the thwarted potential of women was a
forerunner of the blossoming of Victorian feminism. At the same time her
own auctorial anxieties often impinged on her achievements, adding to the
complexity of the theme with which she was engaged on such a personal level.
In this final section I survey the development of the Cassandra figure in
Shelley's work. I also explore briefly the use of the Cassandra figure in Victorian womens' literature citing examples from Charlotte Brontë and Florence
Nightingale.

Soon after the completion of *Valperga*, Mary Shelley suffered the death of
her husband. This cataclysmic event opened the floodgates of fatalism within
her, and she came to believe that she had prophesied his death in her fiction.
Writing to her friend Jane Williams, she compared the death of Euthanasia at
the end of *Valperga* with the drowning of Percy Shelley. Mary Shelley ex-
claimed "Is not the end of mine wondrous—the fate—the shore—how miserably foretold—it is very strange" (*MSL*, 1:307). Not long afterwards she wrote
to another friend about the death of the father in her novella *Mathilda*. "Is not
the catastrophe strangely prophetic But it seems to me that in what I have
hitherto written I have done nothing but prophecy what has arrived" (*MSL*,
1:336). This sense of fatalism did not abate, and as the years went by Mary
Shelley was often overwhelmed by the feeling that the events of her life were
beyond her control. Only two years after Shelley's death she received news
that Byron had died in Greece. Once again, Mary Shelley searched her soul
for an explanation of the tragedy that surrounded her. She wrote to Byron's
mistress, Teresa Guiccioli,

> every day I am more certain that God had endowed us with the power to
> foresee our misfortunes. But we are all Cassandras; and we are so blind that
> we do not give heed to the silent voice that makes itself heard within our soul.
> We then know the truth when the prophecies are fulfilled. (*MSL*, 1:421)

The image she had chosen stayed with her. Two months later Shelley wrote to Leigh Hunt,

> What should I have said to a Cassandra who 3 years ago should have prophe-sied that Jane and I—Edward and Shelley gone, should watch the funeral procession of LB. up Highgate hill—All changes of romance or drama lag far behind this. (*MSL*, 1:440)

Mary Shelley's propensity toward fatalism was evident even in her early writ-ing. There is a dramatic moment in *Mathilda* (written in 1819) when the young heroine pauses in the pursuit of her suicidal father to prophesy that if a certain tree in her path is struck by lightning, he will die. The tree is struck, and moments later, her father's body is discovered in the hut of some people who have pulled him from the sea. Mathilda is the first of Shelley's Cassandras, although Frankenstein's monster arguably embodies a very early and horrific manifestation of the character. Mathilda's secret knowledge of incest sets her apart from human society. Despite her isolation, which is partially self-imposed, Mathilda has a strong desire to make a final and complete communi-cation with the outside world. In a long letter to her one friend she describes her situation:

> I was on earth the sole depository of my own secret. . . . I must be silent lest my faltering voice should betray unimagined horrors. Over the deep grave of my secret I must heap an impenetrable heap of false smiles and words . . . (*MSM*, 47)

The very act of writing about such pathological isolation is in itself perplexing. Yet for Mathilda this is the social and psychological reality of the world she inhabits. *Mathilda* was written during a break in the composition of *Valperga*, and at a time when Mary Shelley was herself extremely depressed. It is there-fore a book written by an isolated woman about an isolated woman who writes a book about being isolated. *Mathilda* represents an exploration of personal grief and loneliness, which was later to prove useful in the develop-ment of the character of Beatrice.

Valperga was the last novel Mary wrote during Percy Shelley's lifetime. In her first novel after his death she returned with renewed vigor to the subject of prophecy. Her introduction to *The Last Man* is an extraordinary artistic statement which places her firmly within the female prophetic tradition. By adapting Virgil's story of the Cumaean Sibyl she takes possession of an an-cient female prophetic figure and uses it to explain her own literary function. The novel itself introduces a number of women with prophetic propensities. One—Evadne—is a startling character who seems to merge with the super-natural forces that cause the plague. Her apocalyptic vision accurately pre-sages the devastation of a plague which wipes out all of humanity until only one person, the last man, is left.

Another aspect of Evadne's role is her participation in one of Shelley's recurring love triangles. This was a theme which Shelley continued to use, and in her 1830 historical romance, *Perkin Warbeck,* she once again created two visionary heroines whose lives are drawn together by their love of one man. Katherine, the wife of the eponymous hero, is pathetic in her hand-wringing ineffectuality. Like Cassandra, she appears to see into the future without being able to avert the coming disaster, and her fatalism is repeated throughout the novel like a dirge. Despite the tediousness of this character she does offer a new development in Mary Shelley's work. Up to this point, an early death was the norm for prophetic female characters. However, in *Perkin Warbeck,* Katherine outlives her husband and is faced with the challenge of finding her niche in a world from which she had relinquished her social and political ties. After accomplishing this, she is confronted with a friend from her youth who criticizes her accommodating strategies. Katherine responds frankly, explaining that she has made peace with her former enemies because she needs love and companionship:

> Remember I am a woman, with a woman's tutelage in my early years, a woman's education in the world, which is that of the heart—alas! for us—not the head. I have no school-learning, no logic—but simply the voice of my own soul which speaks within me. (*MSP,* 3:348–49)

This speech is made all the more poignant because Shelley explicitly states her affection for Katherine in the final chapter of *Perkin Warbeck.* There is little doubt that Katherine was a vehicle for Shelley's own message to those who criticized her lifestyle after Percy Shelley's death. It is a statement which indicates a newfound confidence to acknowledge her needs and her determination to come to terms with them. One of the most remarkable aspects of this development in Mary Shelley's writing is that it highlights the dilemma of the survivor. In some ways it seems easier to die young so that one's radicalism can be remembered. Those who live on have to change tactics; they have to learn accommodating strategies which their companions would never have dreamed of. It is here that we catch a glimpse of the way in which Mary Shelley and her successors could unbind the Cassandra figure. The original Cassandra died young, but what would have happened if she had lived another twenty years as a slave in the household of Agamemnon? Perhaps she too would have learned to live again as a member of a social group.

If Katherine is in some ways a reworking of the Euthanasia figure, then Monina, the ardent follower of Perkin Warbeck, is an updated version of Beatrice. Monina is a born public speaker. Her effect on one of her listeners is described in the following terms:

> The melodious voice of Monina, attuned by the divine impulses of her spirit, as the harp of the winds by celestial breezes, raised a commotion in his mind, such as a prophetess of Delphi felt, when the oracular vapour rose up to fill her mind with sacred fury. A word, a single word, was a potent northern blast to dash aside the mist and to re-apparel the world in its, to him, naked, barren, truth. (*MSP,* 2:26)

Monina's influence is not simply that of a prophetess. She is the *spirit* of prophecy, breathing inspiration into the souls of her listeners. However, once again, Shelley limits the scope of an extraordinary character. When Monina's presence in the novel becomes too much of a distraction, she conveniently drowns in a storm. It is an unfortunate end, leaving Monina's full potential unexplored, much as Beatrice's downfall in *Valperga* curbed her radical career.

A similar hesitancy caused Shelley to refrain from fully developing another unusual heroine, Fanny Derham, in *Lodore* (1835). Fanny's creed is advanced and intellectual. In some ways she is a hybrid of the three Wollstone-craft women, Mary Wollstonecraft, Fanny Imlay, and Mary Shelley.[20] Like her creator, Fanny places the highest possible value on the power of words. She tells her friend Ethel

> "Words have more power than any one can guess; it is by words that the world's great fight, now in these civilized times, is carried on; I never hesitated to use them, when I fought any battle for the miserable and oppressed. People are so afraid to speak, it would seem as if half our fellow-creatures were born with deficient organs; like parrots they can repeat a lesson, but their voice fails them, when that alone is wanting to make the tyrant quail."
> (*Lod,* 3:8)

This remarkable speech seems to herald a new confidence in Shelley's work, but once again she draws back when required to stretch beyond the socially acceptable parameters of the novel. At the end of *Lodore* Shelley hints at what she herself has left unsaid about Fanny:

> What the events are that have already diversifed her existence, cannot now be recounted; and it would require the gift of prophecy to foretell the conclusion. In after times these may be told. (3:310)

Was Shelley suggesting that she herself was hoping to write Fanny's story, or was she looking forward to a future generation of women writers who could make Fanny their own? No matter how Fanny's statement is interpreted, Mary Shelley's inability to see her way through to a radical and successful heroine continued to be problematic in terms of her own vocation as a woman writer.

Her final novel, *Falkner,* goes some way toward achieving a solution to the dilemma of female assertiveness. In *Falkner* a number of disparate elements are reconciled through the healing power of two significant women. The power exerted by the young heroine is based on love and forgiveness, and it is heartening to see her influence grow and mature as the novel progresses. Essentially, what we have here is a model Victorian heroine, emerging intact from a Gothic melodrama. *Falkner* is an exciting cross-over book, and one which deserves further attention in terms of its theme of appeasement and reconciliation. Although there are still many unresolved anxieties, this novel puts the ghost of Cassandra to rest.

By domesticating female power, Shelley finally finds an acceptable way to write about it. Many of the traits of the characters in *Lodore* and *Falkner* are present in the earlier novels, but through her concentration on the rejuvenation of the family unit Shelley achieves a new kind of healing which is first hinted at in the closing pages of *Perkin Warbeck*. In *The Proper Lady*, Mary Poovey sums up the transformation that takes place in Mary Shelley's work;

> Each of Shelley's novels embodies to a greater or lesser degree her ambivalence about female self-assertion, but what the overall development of her career reveals is the way that a certain kind of literary self-expression could accommodate a woman's unorthodox desires to the paradigm of the Proper Lady.[21]

While I concur with Poovey regarding the role of ideology and the importance of accommodating strategies for the emerging woman writer of the nineteenth century, I believe that the paradigm of Cassandra offers a more potent image of the predicament of the woman writer, because it allows for the possibility of using a single model for the expression of a range of characteristics. The predicament of Cassandra as a talented woman whose integrity is constantly and consistently undermined allows us a new perspective on the struggle of the woman writer to establish the authority of her creative vision.

Mary Shelley is often studied in terms of her early life and her connection with the predominantly male Romantic movement. When this horizon is broadened we begin to fully appreciate Shelley's contribution to the development of a female literary tradition. As early as her portrayal of Elizabeth Lavenza in *Frankenstein,* and certainly in her portrayals of Elizabeth Raby and Alithea Neville in her final novel, *Falkner,* Mary Shelley was describing the typical Victorian heroine who holds the key of salvation and domestic beatitude. Moreover, in her development of the Cassandra figure she made a groundbreaking attempt to express the creative potential of women. In doing so, Mary Shelley presaged some significant developments in women's literature.

The fury of the caged passions evident in such characters as Frankenstein's monster, Beatrice of Ferrara, and Evadne in *The Last Man* are also evident in some of the darker byways of the Brontës' fiction. For example, in her 1853 novel *Villette,* Charlotte Brontë depicted an extraordinary interlude in which the heroine, Lucy Snowe, watches an actress named Vashti, who completely mesmerizes her. Lucy is dismayed to find her companion, Dr. John, unmoved by Vashti's extraordinary powers:

> Her agony did not pain him, her wild moan—worse than a shriek—did not much move him; her fury revolted him somewhat, but not to the point of horror. Cool, young Briton! The pale cliffs of his own England do not look down on the tides of the Channel more calmly than he watched the Pythian inspiration that night.[22]

Lucy continues, "he judged [Vashti] as a woman, not an artist: it was a branding judgement. That night was already marked in my book of life, not with white, but with a deep-red cross." Lucy finds her encounter with Vashti disturbing and intense, as Charlotte Brontë had found her own encounter with the French actress Rachel. Indeed, Vashti represents a passionate aspect of Lucy's nature which has been suppressed and which remains unresolved. It is also possible to see her as a projection of Charlotte Brontë's own passionate but repressed nature.

In 1852, the year after Mary Shelley's death, a frustrated Florence Nightingale wrote a bold, angry essay on the bigoted discrepancies between women's capabilities and their role in society. She called her essay "Cassandra." Nightingale argued for an alternative to the image of the suffering Christ which is held up to women as an ideal of patient submission. She remembered Christ's anger at injustice and his active lifestyle. It was this model she wanted women to emulate:

> Why have women passion, intellect, moral activity—these three—and a place in society where no one of the three can be exercised? Men say God punishes for complaining. No, but men are angry with misery. They are irritated with women for not being happy. They take it as a personal offence. To God alone may women complain without insulting him.[23]

Nightingale's complaint echoes a comment Mary Shelley had made in her diary thirty years previously: "The most contemptible of all lives is where you live in the world and none of your passions or affections are called into action—I am convinced that I could not live thus" (*MSJ*, 2:399). When Mary Shelley wrote this she was living a full, if complicated, life with Shelley. After his death, when her life had dramatically altered and she found herself living as an isolated and impoverished widow, she might well have smiled wryly on being reminded of her youthful prediction. Florence Nightingale is not content merely to identify the problem of the restrictiveness of women's lives; in a blaze of energy she goes on to assert:

> The more complete a woman's organisation the more she will feel it, till at last there shall arise a woman who will resume, in her own soul all the suffering of her race, and that woman will be the Saviour of her race.[24]

Nightingale's Cassandra is a symbol for the suppressed power of women. Her notion of a female messiah has strong links with the emerging woman writer of her time. This vision of a female messiah, of a liberated Cassandra, is not unique. Like the Old Testament prophets who foretold the coming of Christ, we realize that many of Mary Shelley's female characters are literary precursors to Nightingale's Saviour. In *Valperga,* Beatrice of Ferrara, her mother, Wilhelmina, and Euthanasia are what Virginia Woolf might have called Judith Shakespeares of fourteenth-century Italy. It is to Shelley's credit that she shared the dream of the emergence of a New Woman with other pioneer feminists. Ironically, however, neither Mary Shelley, nor Florence Nightingale, nor even Virginia Woolf seems to exploit the implications of her own position as embodiments of the powerful women whom they describe. It is up to those of us who have come after to recognize the significance of their work in the establishment of a strong female literary tradition.

Notes

1. Mary Shelley, *Valperga, or the Life and Adventures of Castruccio, Prince of Lucca,* 3 vols. (London: G & W. B. Whittaker, 1823) 3:47. All further references to Mary Shelley's works are cited in the text as follows: *Valperga MSV; The Fortunes of Perkin Warbeck,* 3 vols. (London: Henry Colburn & Richard Bentley, 1830) *MSP; The Journals of Mary Shelley 1814–1844,* 2 vols. ed Paula R. Feldman and Diana Scott-Kilvert (Oxford: Clarendon Press, 1987), *MSJ; The Letters of Mary Wollstonecraft Shelley,* 3 vols. ed Betty T. Bennett (Baltimore: John Hopkins University Press, 1980–88), *MSL; Lodore,* 3 vols. (London: Richard Bentley, 1835), *Lod; Mathilda* (written 1819) ed. Elizabeth Nitchie (Chapel Hill: University of North Carolina Press, 1959), *MSM.*

2. References to Cassandra can be found in Homer's *Iliad,* Aeschylus's *Agamemnon,* in the Oresteia trilogy, and Virgil's *Aeneid.*

3. Erich Neumann, *The Great Mother: Analysis of an Archetype,* trans. Ralph Manheim (Princeton: Princeton University Press, 1963), 305–6.

4. Christa Wolf, *Cassandra: A Novel and Four Essays,* trans. Jan Van Heurck (London: Virago Press, 1984), 142.

5. Mary Poovey, *The Proper Lady and the Woman Writer: Ideology as Style in the Works of Mary Wollstonecraft, Mary Shelley, and Jane Austen* (Chicago: University of Chicago Press, 1984).

6. Sandra M. Gilbert and Susan Gubar, *The Madwoman in the Attic: The Woman Writer and the Nineteenth-Century Literary Imagination* (New Haven: Yale University Press, 1979).

7. Betty T. Bennett, "The Political Philosophy of Mary Shelley's Historical Novels: *Valperga* and *Perkin Warbeck,*" in *The Evidence of the Imagination* ed. Donald H. Reiman, Michael C. Jaye, and Betty T. Bennett (New York: New York University Press, 1978), 358.

8. Commenting on this passage, Poovey writes, "only the unbounded and therefore nonbinding imagination can escape censure and thus protect the dreamer against exposure and pain" (*The Proper Lady,* 140).

9. Jean de Palacio, *Mary Shelley dans son oeuvre: Contributions aux études shelleyennes* (Paris: Editions Klincksieck, 1969), 288–89.

10. Dale Spender, *Women of Ideas and What Men Have Done to Them* (London: Routledge and Kegan Paul, 1982), 4–5.

11. Wolf, *Cassandra,* 81.

12. Mary Wollstonecraft, *Mary, A Fiction and the Wrongs of Woman,* ed. Gary Kelly (1798; rpt. London: Oxford University Press, 1976), 124.

13. Sgricci's performance also affected Percy Shelley's ideas on the imagination. For a discussion of the impact of this episode, see P. M. S. Dawson, "Shelley and the *Improvissatore* Sgricci: An Unpublished Review," *Keats-Shelley Memorial Bulletin,* 1981: 19–29.

14. See also *The Journals of Claire Clairmont,* ed. Marion Kingston Stocking with David Stocking (Cambridge, Mass.: Harvard University Press, 1968).

15. See P. B. Shelley, *The Letters of Percy Bysshe Shelley,* 2 vols., ed. Frederick L. Jones (Oxford: Clarendon Press, 1964), 1:408, and also *Valperga,* 2:85.

16. Letter to Douglass Kinnaird, quoted in Leslie Marchand, *Byron: A Biography,* 2 vols. (London: John Murray, 1957), 2:681.

17. Virgil, *The Aeneid,* trans. W. F. Jackson Knight (Harmondsworth: Penguin Books, 1956), 149.

18. Sismondi, qtd. in James Reiger, "Shelley's Paterin Beatrice," *Studies in Romanticism* 4 (Summer 1965): 179, 183.

19. Machiavelli wrote a biography of Castruccio, and he also wrote a play entitled *Mandragola.* I have been unable to ascertain any connection between Machiavell's *Mandragola* and the character of the same name in *Valperga.* See Niccolò Machiavelli *The Chief Works and Others,* 3 vols., trans. Allan Gilbert (Durham, N.C.: Duke University Press, 1965), 2:553–60, 776–821.

20. Elizabeth Nitchie, *Mary Shelley, Author of "Frankenstein"* (1959; Westport Conn.: Greenwood Press, 1970), 99. See also Mary Shelley's Journal entry *MSJ* II:557.

21. Poovey, *The Proper Lady,* 116.

22. Charlotte Brontë, *Villette* (1853), *The Life and Works of Charlotte Brontë and Her Sisters,* Intro. Mrs. Humphrey Ward. (London: Smith Elder & Co., 1899), 7:308–9.

23. Florence Nightingale, "Cassandra" (1852), in *The Cause: A Short History of The Women's Movement,* ed. Ray Strachey (London: G. Bell & Sons, 1928), 396.

24. Ibid., 414.

God's Sister: History and Ideology in *Valperga*

Joseph W. Lew

> Absolute monarchy . . . is the easiest death, the true *Euthanasia* of the
> British Constitution.   David Hume, *Essays, Moral and Political,* 53

In the early 1790s, Richard Brothers began to announce—to anyone who cared to listen—that he was the "Nephew of the Almighty."[1] The implications of this claim are mindboggling. Who was God's sibling, and what happened to him or her? Within a Christian tradition, that God should have a brother is almost unimaginable. To cope with the question at all, one must posit an immortal despot who, like the Ottoman sultans, "removes" all rivals for the throne, thus providing a divine precedent for the slaying of Abel by Cain. Conversely, one might recreate a Greek-style cosmology, establishing godly spheres of influence reminiscent of the division of air, sea, and the underworld among Zeus, Poseidon, and Hades.

In light of feminist research, the other possibility (that God might have a Sister) seems more plausible. God's Sister might have been written out of history, as Catherine Morland complained had happened to human women. Or, in an analogy to Shakespeare's sister Judith (as imagined by Virginia Woolf), she might have found no room for action within a patriarchal universe. Or, as happened historically with the Near Eastern fertility goddess Astarte, she might first have been masculinized (ashtoreth),[2] then demonized— degraded, in other words, from the status of independent deity to spiritual gadfly.

That Richard Brothers never revealed his exact pedigree is less important than the fact that, a few years before Mary Shelley was born, a number of religious and intellectual movements arose which questioned many aspects of the economic and sexual hierarchies. Although students of literature are familiar with women's contributions to the intellectual movements, we know much less about women's involvement in the religious revival of the late eighteenth century. Strange as it may at first appear, the sometimes unorthodox theologies of these movements (of which Richard Brothers's announcement is only one example, albeit an extreme one) played an important role in shaping Mary Shelley's third completed novel, *Valperga*.[3]

If, as Wordsworth claimed in 1815, "every author, as far as he is great and at the same time *original,* has had the task of *creating* the taste by which he is to be enjoyed,"[4] then (ignoring Wordsworth's sexism) Shelley has significantly failed to do so with *Valperga*. Unlike its most famous sibling (and Mary Shelley's Introduction to the third edition of *Frankenstein* reveals that she did think of her novels as her "progeny"), *Valperga* was never staged; it spawned neither imitations nor sequels. And unlike *Falkner* (1837), *Mathilda* (1819–20, first published 1959), or *The Last Man* (1826—the first novel composed after Percy's death), this "Life" set in Renaissance Italy has scarcely been mined for autobiographical information.

In this essay, I would like to propose an alternative reading for this unjustly maligned novel. I do so by creating new theoretical, historic, and philosophical contexts for this work. I begin by reconsidering genre, arguing that *Valperga* is not a botched historical novel *à la* Scott, but rather belongs to the tradition of historical romances written by women and often female-centered; characteristic of this genre are the structures which Mellor calls "female Romantic ideology." Next, I look at the novel's scrutiny of female prophets and political leaders in light of its own historical milieu, concentrating upon the female cult leaders and itinerant preachers characterstic of Shelley's childhood and youth. Then I provide a reading of the novel as a lament for a time—simultaneously "lost" and "imagined"—before the differentiation of "separate spheres" of activity, a time when men and women could participate fully in both the private and public realms. Like *The Four Zoas* or *Cain*, *Valperga* functions as a Romantic and specifically feminist "myth of origins" that explains how men and women came to inhabit the worlds we live in.

As its subtitle indicates, at least part of the subject matter of *Valperga* is the "Life and Adventures of Castruccio, Prince of Lucca." I will return to the problem of the relationship of title to subtitle later; here, I wish to note the subtitle's pretensions to the status of biography. A "life" of a readily identifiable historical figure, the subtitle recalls others famous "lives," such as Boswell's *Life of Samuel Johnson* (which Shelley was reading or rereading in 1820) or William Godwin's *The Lives of the Phillips, Nephews and Pupils of Milton* (published in 1809). But "life's" accompanying term, "adventures," recalls the verisimilitude-creating formula of eighteenth-century novels, such as Robert Paltock's *Life and Adventures of Peter Wilkins* (1751; Shelley read this in 1815).

With public acceptance of the novel as a genre, this "factualizing"[5] formula (along with its quasi-synonym, "History of . . .") fell into disuse. Its pointed revival in *Valperga* suggests one of the major instabilities I view as part of the novel's "subject." The "life and adventures" formula juxtaposed with the historical figure Castruccio suggests a melting of distinctions between the "real" and the "imagined," which the title page's attribution of the work to "the Author of *Frankenstein*" could only reinforce. The brief preface (iii–iv) contributes to this confusion: after providing a translation from "the article respecting [Castruccio] in Moreri," Shelley indicates that "the dates here given are somewhat different from those adopted in the following narrative." The historical Castruccio, then, begins to disappear, to be replaced by a character who fits the ideological demands of Shelley's fiction. Lest we should find this disturbing, Shelley has already reminded us that the "accounts . . . known in England" are "generally taken" from a "romance" by Machiavelli. Castruccio's "real" adventures are available [in England] in Sismondi's *Histoire des Républiques de l'Age Moyen*—in other words, only to those who read French.

The English "accounts" of Castruccio's life, then, are already fictionalized, distorted to fulfill the requirements of romance. Shelley continues this process, revising Castruccio's "life" and creating new characters out of whole cloth. Shelley's Castruccio is exiled from Lucca "in the year 1301," when he was "eleven years of age" (1:3, 4:1; not coincidentally, Percy enrolled in Eton two days before his twelfth birthday). The "real" Castruccio, who was born in 1281, would have been about twenty at the time. The historical Castruccio married sometime between 1304 and 1309, fathering several children whose matrimonial alliances expanded Castruccio's power.[6]

Rather than criticizing Shelley's apparent disregard for historical "fact," we need to understand the goals of historical romance Shelley worked within. In order to do this, we need to look, not at the tradition of the *Waverley* novels, but at that of Shelley's older female contemporaries. As Gary Kelly has shown,[7] novelists of the 1790s almost inevitably confronted the ideology of the French Revolution, with pro-French novels such as Elizabeth Inchbald's *Nature and Art* (1796) exposing the corruption inherent in what William Godwin, in the subtitle to *Caleb Williams,* called "things as they are." Anti-Jacobin writers such as Elizabeth Hamilton tended "not only to reduce large political and public issues to their domestic, everyday, commonplace consequences. . . . but also actually to translate the political and public issues into private and domestic equivalents."[8] When, after the brief Peace of Amiens, war resumed against Napoleon in 1803, the enemy seemed to have changed from an ideology into a person. Popular prints, especially caricatures, are instructive here: satires on a personified French Revolution came to be replaced by attacks on Bonaparte.[9] In a historical romance such as *The Scottish Chiefs,* a conservative writer such as Jane Porter could criticize the Napoleonic regime and suggest strategies (some of which were later implemented) for resistance to the modern tyrant by choosing a historical figure who resembled Napoleon. In the oath- and treaty-breaking Edward III, Porter makes not a facile allegory, an improbable one-to-one correspondence between contemporary events and Edward's ruthless attempts to subjugate Scotland. Instead, what Lindenberger asserts for historical drama, that "the continuity between past and present is a central assertion in history plays of all times and styles"), holds true for early nineteenth-century historical romances as well.[10] Porter invites her readers to discover the analogies between the struggle of Scotland to maintain its independence and that of Britain and Portugal against Napoleon. Where Porter could adopt techniques traditionally associated with Jacobin novels, radical writers such as Sidney Owenson turned the anti-Jacobin tradition against itself, commenting upon the geopolitical by concentrating upon the domestic in the novel of courtship.[11] (Mary Shelley's *Journal* indicates that she read Owenson's *Wild Irish Girl, The Missionary,* as well as her directly political *France* in 1817.)[12] In *Valperga,* Shelley fuses these traditions, creating a novel of abortive courtship in which the characters are the Napoleon-like Italian princeling, Castruccio of Lucca, and the republican Countess of Valperga, Euthanasia.

Valperga is about politics, about the fate of women "in the imperialist England of [Shelley's] day."[13] At the novel's core is a republic's desperate efforts to preserve itself from what Hume calls an absolute monarchy. The two most important female characters, Euthanasia and Beatrice, together illustrate how easy it is to be "seduced" by despotism—each of them falls in love with the "hero" of the novel, Castruccio. On this level of the narrative in which sexuality and politics are fused, Shelley demonstrates the very real, yet demonic, magnetism of despotism. As Grosrichard argues for the eighteenth century, and as holds true for the Romantic period as well, Western Europe was obsessed with its Oriental and despotic Other.[14]

Hence, far from being an otherwise "remarkable" lapse of taste[15] the name of *Valperga*'s principal female encodes this political meaning. As my epigraph suggests, Shelley derived her countess's name from Hume's Essay 7, which she had read December 12, 1817 (*MSJ,* 87). In this essay, "Whether the British Government Inclines More to absolute Monarchy, or to a Republic," Hume argues that the power of the Crown, despite appearances to the contrary, is actually increasing. Even more "terrible," although less "imminent," is the threat of a truly "popular" government, one in which the House of Commons "must be the only legislature." The essay concludes:

> If the house of commons, in such a case, ever dissolve itself, which is not to be expected, we may look for a civil war every election. If it continue itself, we shall suffer all the tyranny of a faction, subdivided into new factions. And, as such a violent government cannot long subsist, we shall, at last, after many convulsions, and civil wars, find repose in absolute monarchy, which it would have been happier for us to have established peaceably from the beginning. Absolute monarchy, therefore, is the easiest death, the true *Euthanasia* of the BRITISH constitution. Thus, if we have reason to be more jealous of monarchy, because the danger is more imminent from that quarter, we have also reason to be more jealous of popular government, because that danger is more terrible. This may teach us a lesson of moderation in all our political controversies.[16]

Hume's sentiments jive perfectly with what we know of Shelley's politics, especially with her disdain for and fear of the lower classes.[17] *Valperga* is deeply marked by this: the only stable and relatively "happy" government is the pointedly mixed or moderate aristocratic one of Florence.

As I have hinted, *Valperga* is also autobiographical: a caricature of Percy Shelley appears in Castruccio, Mary Shelley distributes her own traits between Euthanasia and Beatrice,[18] and, as I will show later, provides an alternative version of her own mother in the dead Wilhelmina of Bohemia. Perhaps because of this, *Valperga* also provides a remarkably detailed exposition of what Anne Mellor calls "the female Romantic ideology." Shelley's female characters explain to us "why women didn't like romanticism," why Austen and Shelley seem to be anachronistic, preferring Enlightenment traditions to the newly dominant Romantic ideology.[19] The life and death of Beatrice, the prophetess of Ferrara, demonstrates the dangers to women of the ambition, egocentrism, emotionalism, and familial and social irresponsibility valorized by the male Romantics. Euthanasia spends her life struggling to preserve the anonymous domesticity, concern for others, rationality, and attention to duty Mellor sees as central to the female Romantic tradition.

While these seem large claims for an almost forgotten novel, readers of *Frankenstein* who are accustomed to the polyvalency of that novel will not be surprised by the richness of *Valperga*. Accompanying the political, autobiographical, and ideological layers of the novel is a historical lament for the rapid disappearance of public roles for talented women, an occurrence notable in the twenty-five years Shelley had lived before publishing *Valperga*. Most obviously, Shelley regrets the deaths or silencing of so many of the politically motivated women writers of her youth: not only her own mother, but also Helen Maria Williams, Elizabeth Hamilton, Elizabeth Inchbald, Maria Edgeworth (who seemed to have retired after her father's death in 1817), and even Anne Radcliffe.

More pertinent to *Valperga,* however, was the resurgence of religion in the latter half of the eighteenth century; scholars have only begun to document the many ways in which women dominated this resurgence. As feminist historians are rediscovering, religion became one public sphere women could enter. Maison demonstrates that, particularly among the Dissenters, "dissent from orthodoxy . . . often involved dissent from . . . sexist stances." Especially in movements such as the Moravians and the Wesleyans, women could "act" as "missionaries, musicians, choristers, and organisers of conferences and communities."[20] Women were among the most popular and prominent of poets, as Curran shows; poets such as Anne Steele, Elizabeth Scott, and Anna Letitia Barbauld were instrumental in developing the English tradition of the hymn.[21] Within the Methodist revival, D. Colin Dews argues, "female preachers played a small but not insignificant part" (68). Yet, "as early as the 1820s"—the period during which Shelley composed *Valperga*— "it was clear that Wesleyan Methodism had finally rejected the use of women as preachers."[22]

Women were even more prominent in the millenarian cults that flourished around the turn of the century. Most spectacularly successful was Joanna Southcott, a self-taught domestic servant from Devonshire who became convinced that she was the recipient of a new revelation from God. Southcott predicted a great reversal, a coming era of prosperity when, after having resisted the threat posed by the atheistical French, even the poor of England (and especially those who had received one of Joanna's Seals) would have plenty to eat. Despite the obvious appeal to the down and out, in 1815 the *Edinburgh Review* declared that "it is by no means true . . . that the sect has been confined to the lowest and most ignorant persons." The most reliable of the many contemporary estimates of Southcott's following claimed forty thousand members for the movement.[23] Blake, intrigued by the movement, wrote a poem entitled "On the Virginity of the Virgin Mary & Johanna [sic] Southcott."

In 1814, when she was sixty-five years old, Southcott announced that the Spirit had told her "this year . . . thou shalt have a son, by the power of the MOST HIGH".[24] Seventeen physicians believed Southcott was pregnant. Needless to say, this brought Southcott a great deal of attention. On October 8, 1814, the *Manchester Gazette* published an article about the Southcottians subtitled "Deplorable effects of Religious Delusion."[25] A London newspaper, the *Sunday Monitor,* declared "we had no idea that either Mrs. Southcott, or her doctrines, were of such universal consequence." Southcott had become the sole interest "in the minds of many. . . . In every street, alley, court, and house, nothing was heard but the name of Southcott."[26] On December 28, 1814, more than a year after she believed herself to have become pregnant, Southcott died. An autopsy found no evidence of a child.[27]

As I will show, the life and prophecies of Joanna Southcott lie behind not only the novel's depiction of Beatrice and her following in Ferrara, but also behind the account of Beatrice's mother, Wilhelmina of Bohemia. That I should also link Wilhelmina to Mary Wollstonecraft might seem contradictory; however, Southcott's biographer also sees resemblances between Southcott and Wollstonecraft:

> Joanna as well as Mary devoted her life to pushing against the restricted opportunities available to women. In a different but no less valid sense, Joanna, as Mary, became one of the most remarkable women of her age, relying on what she saw as the truth of her own experience to establish a vivid, original, and fully realized identity for herself, and her sex, within the traditional perspectives of popular piety.[28]

In the following section I hope to illustrate that it is necessary for us to understand each of these strands (the political, autobiographical, ideological, and historical) in order to "make sense" of *Valperga.*

Like *Caleb Williams, Frankenstein,* and other works which Alan Liu calls "novels of pain," *Valperga* follows a principle of "shell" narration.[29] Inside the "life" of Castruccio, we find other major tales about the lives of women: Euthanasia, Beatrice, Fior di Mandragola, Wilhelmina of Bohemia. Just as the biographical accounts of the first three of these women are circumscribed by the ruling narrative, so are the lives of these women affected and limited by that of Castruccio. Although they are scarcely passive, Euthanasia, Beatrice, and Fior di Mandragola cannot initiate action but may only react to plots generated by the males surrounding them, as is made clear late in the novel when Euthanasia agrees to participate in the political plot against Castruccio. While Castruccio's "life and adventures" make the novel's actions possible, the novel explores the ways in which women (and especially talented women) adapt themselves to and eventually disappear into the tapestry of male history. In other words, *Valperga* attempts to create the kind of historiography Catherine Morland would have approved: a response to histories with "hardly any women at all."[30] Hence, one might conclude that William Godwin, in changing the novel's title from *Castruccio* to *Valperga,* had actually displayed a rare and uncharacteristic insight.[31] As with *Frankenstein,* this novel derives its title not from the major character in its outer frame, but rather from one closer to its imaginative heart. *Frankenstein* has always invited confusion between the creator and his unnamed creature, enhancing the affinity between them; the later novel suggests a similar affinity between Euthanasia (the countess of Valperga) and the fortified estate she has inherited through her mother.

Valperga begins by recounting the early life of its hero. Castruccio Castracani, we learn, is victimized by the civil wars between the Guelphs (republicans or supporters of the pope) and Ghibellines (followers of the emperor). His family, along with other prominent Ghibellines, is exiled when the Guelphs come to power in his native city, Lucca. Castruccio's mother dies soon after, and Castruccio's father dies in a plague which devastates Italy—only Castruccio's "excellent constitution" enables him to recover, unaided, after a month-long illness (1:39). Partly because of his own sense of injury, Castruccio accepts the dominant ideology of Renaissance Italy, of fame achieved through military deeds:

> Imagination, ever at work, pictured his future life, brilliant with glowing love, transcendent with glory and success. Thus, in solitude, while no censoring eye could check the exuberant vanity, he would throw his arms to the north, the south, the east, and the west, crying,—"There—there—there, and there, shall my fame reach!"—and then, in gay defiance, casting his eager glance towards heaven:—and even there, if man may climb the slippery sides of the arched palace of eternal fame, there also will I be recorded. (1:42–43)

This passage provides an unexpectedly dark portrait of Imagination, that human quality so admired by the male Romantics, providing the novel's first clear indication of the links between male Romantic ideology and the growth of empire.

Soon after this Manfred-like statement,[32] Castruccio accepts the protection of Guinigi, an old warrior friend of his father's. Castruccio expects a thrilling apprenticeship in the arts of war and of diplomacy; instead, he is subjected to a year's disciplining in a "world with whose spring of action he could not sympathize" (1:48) in what Mellor calls "the female Romantic ideology." For Guinigi has grown old in warlike activity, coming to see the futility of the endless violence which has torn Italy: when recollecting his so-called glorious youth, "his heart sickened." Neither poetry nor the visual arts, neither "the banners of triumph" nor "the song of victory" can "drive from his recollection the varieties of death, and the groans of torture that occasion such exultation to the privileged murderers of the earth" (1:49). Instead, Guinigi values the picturesque productivity of peaceful Este: "when the corn waves among the trees, and the ripening grapes shade the roads; when on every side you see happy peasants leading the beautiful oxen to their light work" (1:51).

Castruccio cannot accept this supposedly unmanlike activity. He travels to England, where he becomes a favorite of Edward II, the king who would be displaced by his own son and murdered by his "discontented and turbulent" nobles (1:70).[33] Ironically, the first human blood Castruccio sheds is caused by love, although of the lawless and unnameable variety that Edward II feels for Gavaston (Shelley's spelling). Having been struck by a member of the anti-Gavaston faction, Castruccio cries, "By blood, and not by words, are blows to be avenged!" He draws out his stiletto, that most Italian of weapons, and "plunge[s] it into the bosom of his adversary" (1:83); as a result, he is forced to flee England. He consoles himself that his adversary "might not have died—and then what was he?" (1:86). Castruccio never troubles himself with that unnamed man's fate. The apparent non sequitur question, however, will ring through the novel, never satisfactorily answered: not who, but "what was [Castruccio]?"

Once in France, Castruccio offers his services to Alberto Scoto, the former tyrant of Milan now in the employ in Philip le Bel of France. He becomes a member of Scoto's "evil school," gaining "true insight into Italian politics," as well as "the use of those arts which then so much disgraced that people" (1:94). He learns to repress his innate good qualities, his "frankness," "ingenuousness," "shame," and "tenderness of nature" in order to adapt a transplanted *"Punica fides,"*[34] which he drinks from a papal "well of poison" (1:94). Indeed, he learns to pervert his good qualities. Later, he will use his "frank countenance and unembarrassed voice" in order to deceive Euthanasia about his intentions toward Florence (1:242).

After leaving his demonic tutor and returning to Florence, Castruccio begins to court Euthanasia. As long as he can remember, Euthanasia has been a part of his life; in a typically Romantic "more-than-sibling" manner, the two "had been educated together almost from the cradle"—a fact we do not learn until chapter II, when Castruccio is fourteen years old (1:26). In fact, the text seems to conspire in order to keep Euthanasia at a distance until she is about eighteen.

Like Shelley herself, Euthanasia has doted on her father; when he loses his sight, she learns Latin in order to be able to read to him. The "accident" of the count's blindness becomes the vehicle by which Euthanasia gains access to male domains of knowledge. Like Milton's daughters, Euthanasia eventually substitutes for the patriarch's lost eyesight; Euthanasia, however, can profit from her filial duties. In the Miltonic paradigm, all parties *suffer* the father's blindness.[35] Milton's direct access to the line of male poets is broken: blindness condemns him to depend upon the intermediary of a female voice. As if in compensation, he insists upon the metaphoric blindness of the intermediary by condemning his daughters to uncomprehending recitations of texts in foreign tongues. Reading out loud dehumanizes Milton's daughters: they are forced to become "parrots."

In contrast, Euthanasia, as an Italian, is "acquainted with a rude and barbarous Latin"; with the help of an old priest, she can "exchange" this degenerate tongue for "the polished language of Cicero and Virgil" (1:28). When, in a later chapter, she relates to Castruccio the "blank" of her eventless life (1:194), she explains how she came to associate "Wisdom" and "Liberty": "none but a freeman could have poured forth" the poetry to which she listens. The "mental history of the rest of the world, who are slaves," she claims, "is a blank" (1:196). Here, we must note the intentional echo, the distinction Euthanasia draws between the "true" events of the mind and meaningless activity. To a casual observer, Euthanasia's life as a kind of "hermitess" (1:192) would seem tranquil, broken in upon only by the deaths of her parents and brothers, and now by the arrival of Castruccio. In other words, Euthanasia's "freedom" and "wisdom" depend upon the accident of her father's blindness, and her subsequent introduction to the bare possibility of a "history" of the mind.

Euthanasia has been able to stand aloof from the violence of Italian politics partly because of her gender. As she does not choose to enter petty intrigues, the neighboring nobles decide that it would be cheaper to woo than to fight her. Her true test arises when she encounters a female rival for her favored suitor—when she discovers that, not long before her own scheduled wedding to him, Castruccio had been unfaithful to her with the prophetess Beatrice.

Like the story of the creature in *Frankenstein,* Beatrice's history forms the imaginative heart of *Valperga.* More so even than Euthanasia, Beatrice resembles Shelley herself. Yet unlike both the creature and Mary Shelley, Beatrice never becomes aware of her early history; instead, it is recounted to Castruccio and to the reader by her first male protector, the Bishop of Ferrara.

Castruccio first encounters Beatrice when he visits Ferrara on a secret diplomatic mission: to explore the possibility of ousting the tyranny supported by the papacy and of restoring the Ghibellines to power. His conference with the bishop is interrupted by the bishop's sister and by an almost anonymous figure, so bound up by a capuchin that "it was impossible to judge of the age, and hardly of the sex" (2:16). She asks the bishop to allow this cypher to pronounce the "fortunate day" to undertake this work and, as she speaks, throws back Beatrice's hood, so that the "almost divine beauty" of the young woman can add its wordless eloquence (2:17). Throughout this portion of the narrative, Shelley simultaneously emphasizes and undercuts Beatrice's quasi-angelic qualities, drawing attention to the manner Beatrice's eyes beam "as [if] with inspiration" (2:23).

When the two women depart, the bishop relates what he knows of Beatrice's past to Castruccio, although he "can hardly tell" why (2:44). The bishop is not alone in feeling strangely compelled to reveal secrets to Castruccio. Earlier, Benedetto Pepi feels unaccountably drawn to "confide" in Castruccio's "discretion" (1:155). The Barthes of *S/Z* would argue that we here see the logic of narrative playing itself out, prolonging itself by drawing other narratives to itself, postponing its own ending, its own death, through digression. *Sarrasine* continues itself by withholding the crucial fact that the singer is a castrato; similarly, the "life and adventures" of Castruccio endure by forcing other characters to narrate, to allow their own stories to be appropriated by Castruccio.[36] Castruccio, although not the controlling consciousness of the novel, becomes the narrational analogy of a black hole, self-consciously abusing his own appearance of frankness in order to draw stories—potentially useful bits of information—from others, rarely reciprocating. In return, he inspires narrative, whether it be merely through the repetition of "his name" and exploits when he returns to Italy in his early twenties (1:133), or the novel itself.

This apparent digression into narrative theory needs to be integrated with my main point: that *Valperga* explores the struggle between opposing romantic ideologies. In Shelley's own lifetime, narrative—and particularly historical narrative—had become an increasingly important tool in European and global politics. In his monumental six-volume *History of British India* (1819), for example, James Mill condenses two millennia of Indian history into a preparation for India's domination by Britain, yet he devotes almost a full volume to the impeachment of Warren Hastings.[37] The ideological abuse of narrative was widespread: Edward Said and Martin Bernal describe how Orientalism and Classics became battlegrounds in the early nineteenth century; what Clifford Siskin calls "the developmental narrative" of Western civilization itself was rescripted during Mary Shelley's youth.[38] During the long intellectual apprenticeship of her years with Percy, Mary immersed herself in Classic and Orientalist scholarship;[39] by 1817, she had read several of Sidney Owenson's fictionalizations of this ideological struggle.[40]

These considerations would remain only peripherally interesting were it not that Castruccio uses and abuses narrative in order to transform knowledge into power. Castruccio's political initiation occurs, not as a result of his expulsion from Lucca or his entanglement in English courtly intrigues, but in the previously mentioned "evil school" of Alberto Scoto. Experience alone, one's own "life and adventures," do not suffice to create this successful Machiavellian "prince." If Castruccio gains "true insight into Italian politics" (and note that here Shelley carefully avoids universalizing this politics, but insists upon its historical contingency), he does so after hearing the "lives and adventures" of his unsuccessful predecessors—and Scoto is remarkably forthcoming not only with the stories of others, but also with a careful analysis of the reasons for his own fall from power. Castruccio becomes a male version of DuClos's Madame Merteuil, utilizing a carefully monitored deceptive exterior to inspire confidence and to derive confidences from others while remaining noncommittally silent himself. The knowledge of Beatrice's past which Castruccio obtains from the Bishop of Ferrara enables him to seduce the prophetess.

In confiding Beatrice's story to Castruccio, the bishop's ostensible goal is to find another male protector for Beatrice. He relates that, in the year 1289, a "heretic and dangerous impostor," Wilhelmina of Bohemia, first arrived in Italy (2:26). Although outwardly professing Catholicism, she secretly promotes a dangerous heresy founded on the absurd and damnable belief, that she was the Holy Ghost incarnate upon earth for the salvation of the female sex. She gave out that she was the daughter of Constance, queen of Bohemia; that, as the angel Gabriel had descended to announce the divine conception to the blessed Virgin, so the angel Raphael announced to her mother the incarnation of the Holy Spirit in favour of the female sex; and that she was born twelve months after this heavenly annunciation. (2:26)

This new, female-centered religion would "entirely supersede" Christianity. Despite this, the new sect would maintain Christian trappings and the Catholic hierarchy; Wilhelmina's devoted follower, Magfreda, would "be papess, and . . . succeed to all the power and privileges of the Roman pontiff" (2:26–27). Thus far, the new religion resembles countless other medieval and early modern rites of inversion in that it maintains the systemic structure of its model, merely changing the human occupants of that structure's predetermined slots.[41]

Wilhelmina, in relinquishing the "papessy" to Magfreda, strangely blends Christ and Shelley's own mother, Mary Wollstonecraft. Like Christ, she leaves neither institution nor text behind, leaving it to her followers to preserve her memory and to codify her teachings. Like Wollstonecraft, she dies in "the odour of sanctity" and is lauded for "her piety, her abstinence, and modesty" (2:27). However, two years after her death—and here we cannot miss echoes of the furor caused by Godwin's publication of Wollstonecraft's literary remains—"the terror and abomination of the discovery filled the town with horror." The bishop himself, then just become a "Padre," preaches against this new heresy which appears to him "so impious, so absurd, so terrifically wicked" (2:27); he seems to stop just short of denouncing Wilhelmina as a "hyena in petticoats"—Horace Walpole's famous dismissal of Wollstonecraft.

The church's reaction forces us to confront the ideological threat posed by Wilhelmina's teachings. Whereas the French Revolution had had to be repressed because, in setting up universal "rights of man," it threatened the privileges of the existing orders, this feminist revolution needs to be stamped out and its proponents extirpated because it endangers a kind of privilege prior to that of class: male domination predicated upon the submission of women. Walpole, in calling Wollstonecraft a "hyena," had at least granted her the status of an animal; the Dominican inquisitors consider the new sect a "lurking pestilence" (2:27). Before the acceptance of the germ theory of disease, of course, "pestilence" was commonly believed to be caused by a degeneration or putrefaction of the air itself, and to be spread by people or even articles of clothing that have been contaminated by this bad air. In Defoe's *A Journal of the Plague Year* (which Shelley read in 1817; *MSJ,* 80), H. F. records the report that plague was imported to London along with luxury cloths from the Levant.[42] Londoners attempted to bring the plague under control by closing off the entrances to the city; they quarantined houses that had been visited by the infection by shutting them up—and the unhappy inhabitants along with them. They lit bonfires of sulfur and char-

coal to purify the air, and they burned the clothing of all those who had died
of the plague.

My dilation upon *A Journal of the Plague Year* might at first seem more
relevant to a discussion of Shelley's next novel, *The Last Man* (1826). But in
this brief passage from *Valperga,* Shelley demonstrates how intangible dangers, such as bad air and bad ideology, could be made to seem continuous with
each other, and hence could be *treated in the same way.* As the bishop's use of
the term "pestilence" indicates, heresy could be thought of as attacking the
spiritual body of the church in a manner precisely analogous to the plague's
assault on physical bodies. Shelley had lived through a secularized version of
this: in her childhood, the ideology of the French Revolution was often described as a plague upon the body politic.[43] The Dominican inquisitors respond to the outbreak of heresy in Milan just as the secular authorities respond
to outbreaks of bubonic plague or of leprosy. The rank-and-file heretics, like
lepers, are expelled from the community by being "commanded to perform
several pilgrimages" (2:26).[44] Magfreda and her "principal follower" are first
quarantined, separated from the ideologically healthy inhabitants of the town
by being put into the inquisitorial prison, and finally burned in an attempt to
stop the spread of heretical pestilence. Here again, we need to note the parallel with the *cordon sanitaire* Britain and her continental allies drew around
Revolutionary France.

The bishop meets his first heretic ("a monster I had never before seen";
2:28–29), Magfreda, when she is in the dungeons of the Inquisition. In her
turn, Magfreda feels compelled to tell the bishop a story—that of the existence of Beatrice. Unlike the bishop, Magfreda can account for the compulsion she feels: it is by the command of Wilhelmina that Magfreda "now
confide[s] . . . the treasure of [her] soul" (2:33). Two years before her death,
Wilhelmina bore a child. Echoing Southcott's announcement of the coming
birth of Shiloh, Magfreda believes that the conception of Wilhelmina's child
"partook of divinity"; Wilhlemina, however, refuses to comment at all, "never
confirm[ing]" or saying "aught against" this belief. Magfreda puts the child
out to nurse. Wilhelmina never sees it again, yet "would sit for hours" hearing
Magfreda's reports of its growth (2:33, 34).

Just as clearly as in *Frankenstein*'s centrally located but buried account of
the mother of Safie, we have encoded here an account of Shelley's relationship to Wollstonecraft. The differences between the two versions are equally
informative. A few years earlier, Shelley fictionally recreated Wollstonecraft
in an entirely laudable, yet human way. In *Valperga,* however, the fictional
conjoining of Wollstonecraft and Southcott makes Wilhelmina's grandiose
conception of herself seem to illustrate what the *Manchester Gazette* had
called the "Deplorable effects of Religious Delusion." The narrator, who
never allows us to forget the female romantic adaptation of enlightenment
thinking, insists again and again upon the dangers of such illusions. In *Frankenstein,* Shelley had been able to express her anger at Godwin's ill-treatment
of her by caricaturing him as the perfidious Turk; she now represses that
anger, writing him entirely out of the text. More importantly, *Valperga* is the

first of Shelley's novels to depict women (Wilhelmina and later Beatrice) actively desiring and participating in their own sexual falls in a way remarkably similar to those depicted in anti-Jacobin works such as Elizabeth Hamilton's *Memoirs of Modern Philosophers.*[45] Striking about this version is not only the self-criticism inherent in Shelley's characterization of the Beatrice–Castruccio affair (as I will soon show), but also recognition that, as a child of a bastard-bearer who went on to bear bastards herself, Shelley belonged to what Peter Laslett calls the bastardy-prone subsociety.[46] As Mary Poovey claims, we see the woman writer transforming herself into the Proper Lady.[47]

When the Dominicans discover the existence of this "monstrous" heresy, this "pestilence," Magfreda frantically searches for a safe haven for Wilhelmina's child. She decides to shelter Beatrice with a leper who lives outside of Milan "in the depths of the forest" (2:36). Magfreda fervently believes that the child's mother, *"who is above all the saints in heaven,"* will preserve both her follower and her offspring from the dreaded disease (2:36; emphasis in the original). We, however, can recognize that this stolen child, like Poe's purloined letter, has been concealed in the most obvious place: the child of spiritual pestilence is hidden in the home of physical disease. While the child remains physically healthy, corruption will dog her throughout her brief life, and the absence of any effective parenting during her first four years lays the groundwork for her future falls. The sudden transformations of abodes during these early years (from cottage nurse to leper house to the palace of the bishop's sister) foreshadow the ideological swerves of her later life.

As I just suggested, the bishop agrees to become Beatrice's protector on condition that she be raised a Catholic. Yet Beatrice cannot be molded into orthodoxy. Instead of lisping rote-learned prayers as so many model children do in novels, she becomes a Romantic poet, singing "extempore hymns with wild, sweet melody" (2:41). She seems to have inherited the taint of heresy much as one can inherit syphilis: the bishop believes "her mother's soul had descended into her," for she often "said things of God and the angels that were heretical" (2:42). As she enters puberty, she begins to prophesy, and since some of her prophecies "were interpreted as true," her fame spreads throughout Ferrara. Like Southcott's, her cult includes not merely peasants, but also nobles, including the bishop's sister. Before she turns sixteen, she believes herself to be the *"Ancilla dei,* the chosen vessel into which God has poured a portion of his spirit" (2:43). One cannot miss the sexual overtones or the unmistakable allusion to the way contemporary religious movements, especially Southcottianism, provided women with a spiritual substitute for carnality: in 1819, one of Southcott's followers, George Turner, claimed that there were no fewer than 1,556 women waiting "to *be married to the Lord."*[48]

At this stage of her life, Beatrice enters the novel—in other words, Castruccio now meets her for the first time. As I noted before, he has come to Ferrara to meet with prominent Ghibellines in hopes of expelling the papal forces. He witnesses Beatrice's preaching, her sudden arrest by the inquisitors, and the public outrage. She appeals to the bishop, insisting upon the

Judgment of God, a trial-by-ordeal in which innocence is determined by one's ability to walk barefoot across white-hot iron.

As the narrator, the reader, and even the bishop and Castruccio realize, Beatrice has no chance of surviving a legitimate ordeal. The bishop appeals to the abbot of the convent of St. Anna, who is also an ardent Ghibelline. The abbot promises that no harm shall come to Beatrice, for "he and his monks had the charge of the preparation for the Judgement. . . . [M]uch was in their power" (2:53). The bishop hesitates at protecting his charge at the expense of "falsehood and perjury, a lying and blasphemous mockery," yet he allows the abbot to have his way (2:53–54). As a result, Beatrice successfully passes "over the burning shares with a quick, light step" (2:61); as she is entirely ignorant of the fraud, this Judgment becomes an additional proof to her—and to the mob—that she truly is the *Ancilla dei*. Subsequently, she announces that, since the popes "have deserted their sacred city [and] have relinquished their lawful rule," the Visconti will be restored within four days (2:66).[49]

The reader cannot overlook the political implications of these events. The Dominicans are supported by the papacy's Gascon soldiers; those who rally behind Beatrice are all Ghibellines. Although the bishop presents himself as sincere, one cannot help suspecting that Beatrice is, in actuality, a pawn in the great game of Italian politics: but in this match, the Ghibellines win by pretending to sacrifice the pawn. By saving her life, however, the Ghibellines prepare the greater, specifically sexual falls which eventually drive Beatrice insane.

As the narrator makes clear, Beatrice now believes that her newly awakened sexual feelings toward Castruccio are "inspired by the special inspiration of heaven" (2:86). Beatrice's sexual fall occurs in a stunning periphrasis, a topographical displacement of the sexual act which foreshadows the fall of Valperga itself: "Castruccio sought the secret entrance of the viscountess' palace, and was received by the beautiful Beatrice, enshrined in an atmosphere of love and joy" (2:85).

Until this moment, the narrator has been wise and sympathetic to her characters, yet detached. Here, however, the third person gives way to the first:

> Beatrice was hardly seventeen, and she loved for the first time; and all the exquisite pleasures of the passion were consecrated to her, by a mysteriousness and delusive sanctity that gave them tenfold zest. It is said, that in love we idolize the object; and, placing him apart and selecting him from his fellows, look on him as superior in nature to all others. We do so; but, even as we idolize the object of our affections, do we idolize ourselves: if we separate him from his fellow mortals, so do we separate ourselves, and, glorying in belonging to him alone, feel lifted above all other sensations, all other joys and griefs, to one hallowed circle from which all is banished; we walk as if a mist or some more potent charm divided us from all but him; a sanctified victim which none but the priest set apart for that office could touch and not pollute, enshrined in a cloud of glory, made glorious through beauties not our own. Thus we all feel during the entrancing dream of love. (2:87–88)

Up to now, the narrator has carefully avoided gender markings. Only those sensitive to the implications of Shelley's treatment of her subject matter or aware of the true identity of "the author of *Frankenstein*" could be certain this novel was written by a woman. Hence, the move to "we" and the identification of the loved one as "him" is revealing, for this brief dropping of the mask occurs immediately after a new indication of Beatrice's age, "hardly seventeen"—the age of Shelley when she met Percy.

This rhetorical move, then, is more than just a strategy to involve the reader by universalizing a character's feelings. It is a sign of Shelley's own identification with Beatrice—the "we," in this reading, means "Beatrice and I." This passage records Shelley's own sense of betrayal and her disillusionment with her lover-husband in the tumultuous period before Percy's sudden death. Castruccio's betrayal of Euthanasia and his callous mistreatment of Beatrice do not merely replicate the replacement of Mary as "epipsychidion" by Emilia Viviani and then Jane Williams, but they also implicate Mary in the similar displacement of Harriet Westbrook. In a piling up of images similar to that characteristic of Percy's poetry, Shelley reviews her own past: her separation not merely of Percy, but also of herself from all others; the creation, by lovers, of an illusory sacred space around themselves, produced by "mist" or "charm"; finally, the identification of female self with "sanctified victim," a self-devoted (in both senses of the term) sacrifice on the altar of an indifferent god. Moreover, in linking the discourses of love and religion, Shelley also forges a link between the apparently opposed characters of Beatrice and Euthanasia.

René Girard has taught us that we can no longer mystify rituals of sacrifice. In Girard's paradigm, sacrifice regains its originary qualities of communal violence.[50] The sacrificial victim is the scapegoat, the bearer of all of the expelled guilt of the community. Because such expiation must, by its very nature, be only temporary, sacrifice must be repeated, be institutionalized. This, from Shelley's perspective during 1820–21, must have seemed the pattern of Percy's life: the idealizations and later demonizations of Elizabeth Hitchener, Harriet Westbrook, Mary Shelley, and Emilia Viviani—not to mention Percy's responsibility for the deaths of the Shelleys' children.

This brings me once again to the heart of Mellor's thesis: that women could perceive and respond to the Romanticism of the now-canonized male poets as a threat. For Shelley was an ardent student of the first-generation Romantics Wordsworth, Coleridge, and Southey. She was at the center of the younger circle which included not just Byron and Percy Shelley, but also Hogg, Peacock, Trelawny, Hunt, and, at its periphery, Keats. From this position, she could watch the effects of the male Romantics upon women: the madness which afflicted Dorothy Wordsworth (first suggested in her reaction to William's marriage), Mary Lamb, and, quite publicly and histrionically, Caroline Lamb (Byron's mistress); the trail of women abandoned by Byron and Percy Shelley, but also Coleridge, who had separated from his wife; the deaths of her own children and of Byron's daughter by Claire Clairmont. This pattern of women destroyed by men which Mellor sees characteristic of *Fran-*

kenstein[51] recurs in *Valperga* in the deaths of Euthanasia, Beatrice, Magfreda, and Fior di Mandragola.

It might be objected that, however deeply Shelley experienced the male Romantic ideology, the effects of this ideology remained purely personal and intransigently domestic. As we have learned in the late twentieth century, the personal *is* political. Moreover, as I have tried to suggest in my discussion of female historical romance as genre, early nineteenth-century women writers shared this same insight. As Shelley learned from Owenson's *The Missionary,* the Wordsworthian "egotistical sublime" could be the same mentality that explored and conquered the Orient; without such an insight, the otherwise gentle Henry Clerval's grandiose dreams of commerce and conquest seem oddly misplaced.

We can also now understand Shelley's revision of history, especially the odd nonappearance of the historical Castruccio's wife. *Valperga,* by rewriting Italian history as an aborted courtship, takes advantage of hindsight to provide Castruccio with an alternative career. As Shelley and her readers knew, the historical Castruccio failed: he died too soon. The dynasty he hoped to found crumbled, and with it, the power of Lucca. Through Euthanasia and the possibilities she and the castle of Valperga represent, Shelley suggests that history need not have progressed as it did: Castruccio could have chosen the female Romantic ideology, as did Guinigi. But of course he chose to become a tyrant, becoming enmeshed in the violence of Italian politics, exiling hundreds of Lucchese families, resorting to judicial murdering, and even attempting to assassinate Robert of Naples. Euthanasia rejoices she has had the strength to choose duty over love: that she had broken off her engagement to the enemy of her country.

Euthanasia's decision, although personally satisfying, literally devastates Valperga. Recognizing that the consolidation of Italian city-states into what Green calls "regional tyrannies"[52] means the eventual end of Valperga's independence, she plots her foreign policy in what she believes to be the best interests of her subjects. Her political "inclinations," her belief in republics, make her wish to "join [her]self to Florence"; historical accident, however, the "immediate vicinity of Lucca," show her that project's "impracticability" (1:246). We must discount neither her identification with her physical inheritance (Valperga itself) nor the language of courtship and contractual marriage. "Joining" this feminine citadel to a "more powerful" republic is precisely analogous to marriage: it will mean the "incorporation" of the one into the other, the fusing of the female parties' moral and legal identity into that of the males. Rather than passively acquiesce in and hence co-write male violence, Euthanasia hopes to turn Lucca into a greater Valperga: "when Lucca is as peaceful and happy as Valperga," she declares to Castruccio, she "will no longer arrogate a power" to which she "ought not to have a pretension" (1:247).

After Euthanasia breaks off her engagement, Castruccio continues to expand the territory under his control; soon, Valperga itself is an island in a Lucchese sea—isolated in a way militarily analogous to Lovelace's plots to drive a wedge between Clarissa and her family. Because of Euthanasia's alliance with Castruccio's enemy, Florence, Castruccio decides that this potentially hostile stronghold must be destroyed. He declares war; yet, instead of proceeding "honorably" to a siege, Castruccio plots to take Valperga by stratagem. He turns his former intimacy with the countess to advantage. He knows "the secret of the place," a path that leads from a valley near the castle's postern gate to a fountain where he and Euthanasia used to meet, a path that is "long, difficult, and almost impracticable" (2:227, 228). Castruccio and his servants "penetrate a complete wilderness" whose "undergrowth . . . ferns, and brambles" seem distinctly uterine (2:232). When, at the end of volume 2, enemy soldiers suddenly appear within the fortress of Valperga itself, the castle is truly "at [Castruccio's] mercy" (2:229).

The physical embodiment of the female Romantic ideology, the castle Valperga, henceforward disappears from the landscape and from the novel to which it gives its name, for Castruccio ensures that Valperga is utterly destroyed. Volume 3 of *Valperga* recounts the ultimate fates of Castruccio, Euthanasia, and Beatrice, the logical culmination of Castruccio's ideology of territorial and sexual conquest. After having been missing for several years, Beatrice resurfaces, only a shadow of her former self. Once again, she is a prisoner of the Inquisition, this time for being a Paterin, a member of a heretical sect which believed that the evil spirit is ascendent in this world. With Castruccio's aid, Euthanasia has her freed. Beatrice's mind, however, is so nearly unhinged that her ideological fluctuations become not merely more extreme, but more rapid. In a retrospective narrative, she tells Euthanasia how she had learned of the falsification of the Judgment of God from the bishop and, as a result, had abjured her early pretensions and become a humble pilgrim—uniting in this pilgrimage expiations for her sexual and religious heresies. On the road to Rome, however, she falls into evil hands. What she experienced in captivity is too terrible to be told: a "tale for the unhallowed ears of infidels" (3:85). Her involuntary sojourn there, possibly as a sex slave, has "changed" her: "I entered young, I came out grey, old and withered; I went in innocent; and, if innocence consist of ignorance, I am now guilty of the knowledge of crime, which it would seem that fiends alone could contrive" (3:85). On the level of the novel which recalls the French Revolution, Beatrice has experienced, to her cost, the revolution's early linkage of *liberté* and *libertinage*[53]—a conjunction which, whatever its effects upon men, was inevitably destructive to its female victims.

Beatrice becomes a willing disciple of Euthanasia and a kind priest until Bindo, Euthanasia's albino dwarf, leads her to the horrifying Fior di Mandragola, a witch who lives in a forest on the outskirts of Lucca. Fior di Mandragola is malice personified, an old and impotent woman who has been "turned to ferocity by wrongs which had been received so long ago, that the authors of them were all dead" (3:116). Having no personal grudge against Bindo, Castruccio, Euthanasia, or Beatrice, Fior di Mandragola merely thinks "that there would be a pleasure in expiring amidst the groans of the victims of her malice" (3:117). She is a character out of a fairy tale, a Hecatelike dark mother who brings death, not life, and who delights in the sufferings of others. She is the dark side of Magfreda, Beatrice's surrogate mother, the obverse image of the saintly Wilhelmina. Appropriately, she brings about Beatrice's madness and ultimate death, destroying her body and mind. Fior di Mandragola is burned as a witch and her small helpmate, Bindo, dies a prisoner of the Inquisition (3:167).

Her remaining tie to Lucca severed by the death of Beatrice, Euthanasia returns to Florence, where she joins a conspiracy against Castruccio hoping at least to save his life. The chief conspirator, her old friend Bondelmonti, plays upon her well-known beliefs: she comes to believe that she can actually restore the "old" Castruccio by reducing him to a childlike dependence upon her—a fantasy foreshadowing the blinding of Rochester in *Jane Eyre*. A sudden plunge into political impotence, followed by exile on the island of Ischia and tutelage in philosophy, would cause him eventually to "love obscurity." He would, Euthanasia believes, be even better for his past crimes: "he would then have become . . . an extinguished volcano; and the soil would prove more fertile, more rich in beauty and excellence, than those cold natures which has never felt the vivifying heat of might and subdued passions" (3:206). The conspiracy is betrayed, however, by Tripalda, who has also been involved in Beatrice's awful captivity. Castruccio condemns the other conspirators to death but exiles Euthanasia to Sicily, a place that is "far away, so that [Castruccio] never more may hear her name." Castruccio succeeds better than even he had wished, for the ship upon which Euthanasia sails is lost, and "even her name" perishes. Euthanasia falls prey at last to another Fior di Mandragola, the sea itself, a strangely un-Wordsworthian image; this scene oddly seems to predict Percy Shelley's subsequent death: "She slept in the oozy cavern of the ocean; the sea-weed was tangled with her shining hair; and the spirits of the deep wondered that the earth had trusted so lovely a creature to the barren bosom of the sea, which, as an evil step-mother, deceives and betrays all committed to her care" (3:261–62). The novel proper ends with this and another paragraph which describes how no humans "wept" for Euthanasia's death (3:262). A brief conclusion recounts Castruccio's continued meteoric rise and sudden death, which undoes the dreams but not the evils of his life.

It remains for us to ask why Euthanasia could not succeed, and why Shelley herself found it impossible to imagine Valperga's success. Facilely, one might respond that Shelley was only describing the reality she knew: the unsettled times which had thrown up not only Mary Wollstonecraft and Johanna Southcott, but also the vast movement of female preachers in the Evangelical and Methodist movements. However, one must also recognize the fact that the female Romantic ideology was itself implicated in destruction, that its ideological bases (at least in Euthanasia's enunciation of them) might themselves be tainted.

In order to explore this, I must return to Euthanasia's narrative of her childhood and education. Euthanasia is unable, or at least unwilling, to see how gender and class control access to liberty and knowledge. In fact, until she meets Beatrice, she seems to move among males: her father, priests, "distinguished youths," unspecified but male "nobles," and, eventually, the conspirators against Castruccio (1:168, 170).

This failure accompanies an even greater contradiction: the dependence of Euthanasia's version of "liberty" upon colonial expansion. Despite her hard-won appreciation of history, Euthanasia decontextualizes literature with the ruthless rigor of a New Critic. She conveniently forgets that her favorite Latin poet, Virgil, was court poet to the first emperor, Augustus. She lauds the Scipios among the "heros of Rome" (1:202, 201). Surnamed "Africanus," this famous grandfather and grandson participated in the long colonial struggle between Rome and Carthage: the elder defeated Hannibal (202 B.C.), the younger destroyed Carthage (146 B.C.).[54] She regrets the decline of the "dead empire," asking "Why did not Cato live?" (1:202), ignoring Cato the Elder's lifelong crusade for a "final solution" to the problem of Carthage. Euthanasia wishes to view political liberty in strictly existential terms. Yet the liberty of her Roman heroes was enabled by Rome's military expansion; it was maintained, and eventually undermined, by an extensive system of increasingly large slave-estates. Her world, Valperga itself, literally crumbles when the economic, military, and ideological contradictions upon which it is based are finally exposed.

In describing Euthanasia as a kind of New Critic, however, I risk falling into the same error I seem to be accusing Euthanasia of committing. It is not enough merely to note Euthanasia's decontextualization of literature or even to point out what has been suppressed from her "reading." Instead, her segregation of literature and history (or, to put it more accurately, literature and politics) must itself be historicized: What does Euthanasia gain by her act of repression?

Most obviously, Euthanasia creates transhistorical concepts of "wisdom" and of "liberty" that logically transcend class and gender boundaries, becoming universally available rights: like Guinigi, she can see that to view a peasant's life as "incompatible with intellectual improvement" is "a strange mistake" (1:33). Her management of her own estate helps to establish the material preconditions necessary to an almost Godwinian perfectibility.

Second, and perhaps more important, Euthanasia's ideology enables her at first to stand aloof from, and later to escape from, the cycle of violence Italy was then prey to. As I noted earlier, Castruccio serves a kind of military apprenticeship to Alberto Scoto, who had driven the Visconti from Milan only to become a tyrant himself and to be driven awain in his turn. This pattern is repeated over and over again, most notably by Uguccione of Pisa. Euthanasia's psychological development hinges upon her forced witnessing of the means by which Castruccio supplants Uguccione. Of the males in the novel, only Benedetto Pepi, the miser of Cremona, can imagine the cycle's end. He imagines a world despotism supported by a plutocracy, one universal monarch supported by men of wealth: "If the rich would only know their own interests, we might chain the monster, and again bury Liberty" (1:126). Euthanasia, however, envisages a confederation of small republics similar to the "townships" described by Hannah Arendt in *On Revolution*.[55] In Euthanasia's vision of the new world, once peace produces material plenty, humans will no longer desire material objects but intellectual accomplishments: violence will be sublimated into human perfectibility.

Fior di Mangragola, strange though it may seem, suggests another, supplementary explanation for the failure of the female Romantic ideology. Earlier called Fior di Ligi (flower of the lily), she has in old age exchanged that name for the sinister one meaning "flower of the mandrake." This switch, the substitution of mandrake for lily, provides a paradigm for Beatrice's sudden ideological swerves (from belief in her own prophetic powers to humble Christian, to Paterin, to Christian again, to even more extreme self-belief, and finally to madness), as well as for the general curve of Castruccio's life. On the one hand, we see here another Romantic myth of innocence destroyed by the fall into experience. Shelley's myth, however, differs from Blake's because in *Valperga,* these extremes are gendered: Shelley's "innocence" is identical with female Romantic ideology, her "experience" with the male form (although being biologically female does not automatically associate one with the former, or being biologically male with the latter, as my discussions of Fior di Mandragola and Guinigi illustrate). Salvation, in Shelley's system, can be achieved only through a renunciation of experience akin to Prometheus's recall of his curse in Percy Bysshe Shelley's *Prometheus Unbound:* Euthanasia is impotent to transform Lucca into a greater Valperga; Guinigi, however, can help to bring prosperity to his small estate.

Here, finally, we can find the ground common to both versions of "Romantic ideology." As in Wordsworth's *The Prelude,* Shelley's solution comes to rest not upon a general political solution, but upon personal reform. Yet the drawbacks of this solution are glaringly obvious: the tenets of the female Romantic ideology cannot be enforced; adherents to male Romantic ideology will always, it seems, emerge victorious. Guinigi may become a thoroughly admirable character, but neither his example nor his lectures can "convert" Castruccio. Even romantic love, the novel shows, fails, for Castruccio can never move beyond viewing Euthanasia as a possession, something he can call "mine" (1:267). In his view, a woman's love should succeed in overriding all objections based upon mere principle; he cannot view Euthanasia's rejection of him as anything other than a sign of her fickleness, of her inability to love deeply. Of course, he does not apply this philosophy reciprocally to himself.

If, as Spark claims, *Valperga* fails, it fails for the same reasons that Euthanasia fails and that Valperga falls: because the game is fixed.[56] For Castruccio accepts violence and, as Girard argues, it is difficult to combat violence without entering the mimetic crisis. Euthanasia comes close to defeating Castruccio only when she becomes Castruccio-like: when she agrees to become a conspirator. As her other fiction shows and as Mellor demonstrates, Shelley seems to have embraced the tenets of the female Romantic ideology for herself. *Valperga,* however, suggests that a final solution lies not in the ultimate victory of one or the other side, but in a new ideology that will simultaneously synthesize yet transcend its "parents."

If the novel cannot imagine this solution, we cannot accuse Shelley of a failure of vision without implicating ourselves. We also have not yet succeeded in imagining.

Notes

1. James K. Hopkins, *A Woman to Deliver Her People* (Austin: University of Texas Press, 1982), 170.

2. Merlin Stone writes: "the writers of the Judeo-Christian Bible, as we know it, seem to have purposely glossed over the sexual identity of the female deity." *When God Was a Woman* (New York: Dial Press, 1976), xi.

3. Mary Shelley, *Valperga* (London: G. and W. B. Whittaker, 1823). All citations are from this edition.

4. William Wordsworth, "Essay, Supplementary to the Preface of 1815," *Prose Works of William Wordsworth,* ed. W. J. B. Owen and Jane Worthington Smyser (Oxford: Clarendon Press, 1974), iii, 80.

5. For a discussion of this technique, see Lennard Davis, *Factual Fictions* (New York: Columbia University Press, 1983). The classic account of "formal realism" can be found in Ian Watt, *Rise of the Novel* (University of California Press, 1964).

6. Louis Green, *Castruccio Castracani* (Oxford: The Clarendon Press, 1986), 50n.

7. Gary Kelly, *The English Jacobin Novel* (Oxford: Clarendon Press, 1976).

8. Gary Kelly, "Jane Austen and the English Novel of the 1790s," in *Fetter'd or Free? British Women Novelists, 1670–1815,* ed. Mary Anne Schofield and Cecelia Macheski (Athens: Ohio University Press, 1986), 285–306.

9. See Peter Dale Scott, "The Psychopolitical Integrity of *Frankenstein,*" *The Endurance of Frankenstein,* ed. George Levine and U.C. Knoepflmacher (Berkeley: University of California Press, 1979); and Anne K. Mellor, *Mary Shelley: Her Life, Her Fiction, Her Monsters* (New York: Methuen, 1988).

10. Herbert Lindenberger, *Historical Drama* (Chicago: University of Chicago Press, 1975), 6.

11. See my "Sidney Owenson and the Fate of Empire," *Keats-Shelley Journal* 39 (1990): 39–65.

12. Mary Shelley, *Journal.* Ed. Frederick L. Jones (Norman: University of Oklahoma Press, 1947), pp. 89–90. Cited in the text as *MSJ.*

13. Mellor, *Mary Shelley,* op. cit., 210.

14. Alain Grosrichard, *Structure du Serail* (Paris: Seuil, 1979).

15. Christopher Small, *Ariel Like a Harpy* (London: Victor Gollancz, Ltd., 1972), 199.

16. David Hume, "Whether the British Government Inclines More to an Absolute Monarchy, or to a Republic," *Essays, Moral and Political* (Indianapolis: Liberty Classics, 1985), 52–53.

17. See especially the *Journal* accounts of Shelley's jouney through France in 1814 (*MSJ* 4–10).

18. Here, I disagree with Dunn, who only sees Byron in Castruccio, and Small, who believes Euthanasia to be a "curious blend of Shelley and Mary"; Jane Dunn, *Moon in Eclipse* (New York: St. Martin's Press, 1978), 199.

19. Anne K. Mellor, "Why Women Didn't Like Romanticism: The Views of Jane

Austen and Mary Shelley." *The Romantics and Us,* ed. Gene W. Ruoff. (New Brunswick: Rutgers University Press), 1990. Mellor responds, in part, to the sexism she sees inherent in Jerome J. McGann's description of what he calls "the" romantic ideology. McGann's account, Mellor argues, excludes an entire counter-tradition of writing by women. Not surprisingly, in *The Romantic Ideology* (Chicago: University of Chicago Press, 1983), McGann does not discuss Mary Shelley.

20. Margaret Maison, " 'Thine, Only Thine!' Women Hymn Writers in Britain, 1760–1835," *Religion in the Lives of English Women, 1760–1930,* ed. Gail Malmgreen (London: Croom Helm, 1986), 11–40.

21. Stuart Curran, "Romantic Poetry: The 'I' Altered." In *Romanticism and Feminism,* ed. Anne K. Mellor (Bloomington: Indiana University Press, 1988).

22. D. Colin Dews, "Ann Carr and the Female Revivalists of Leeds." *Religion in the Lives of English Women, 1760–1930,* ed. Gail Malmgreen (London: Croom Helm, 1986), 68–87.

23. Hopkins, op. cit., 82, 84.

24. Ibid., 199, original emphasis.

25. Ibid., 202.

26. Ibid., 206.

27. Ibid., 210.

28. Ibid., 216.

29. Allan Liu, *Wordsworth: The Sense of History* (Stanford: Stanford University Press, 1989), 189.

30. Jane Austen, *Northanger Abbey* (London: J. M. Dent and Sons, 1906), 85.

31. Emily Sunstein, *Mary Shelley* (Boston: Little, Brown, and Company, 1989), 162.

32. I allude, of course, to Byron's drama. But the historical setting of *Valperga* requires us to seek other resonances of this name. Shelley informs us that, in early fourteenth-century Italy, memories of the historical Manfred, Holy Roman Emperor, were still strong; cf. especially i, 249.

33. Shelley read Hume's eight-volume *History of England* in 1818; she doubtless also knew Marlowe's play on the subject, *Edward II.*

34. Here we cannot avoid hearing the accusations against "perfidious Albion" which the nations of Europe, and particularly France, were beginning to make against Great Britain.

35. For a discussion not only of Milton's relationship with his daughters, but also of the resonance of this relationship in nineteenth-century literature by women (including Shelley), see Sandra M. Gilbert and Susan Gubar, *The Madwoman in the Attic* (New Haven: Yale University Press), 1979.

36. Roland Barthes, *S/Z* (New York: Hill and Wang), 1974. It is difficult to avoid noting the aural resemblence of "Castruccio" and "castrato." Obviously, one of the results of Shelley's suppression of the prince's wife is the metaphorical castration of the hero.

37. James Mill, *A History of British India* (London: James Madden), 1848.

38. See Martin Bernal, *Black Athena* (New Brunswick: Rutgers University Press), 1987; Edward Said, *Orientalism* (New York: Pantheon), 1978; and Clifford Siskin, *The Historicity of Roman Discourse* (New York: Oxford University Press), 1988.

39. According to *MSJ,* Shelley read not only Orientalist fiction such as Beckford's *Vathek,* Southey's *Thalaba* and *The Curse of Kehama,* and Lawrence's *Empire of the Nairs,* but also 'serious' works such as Lord Macartney's *Journal,* Clarke's *Travels*

in . . . Asia and Africa, Elphinstone's *An Account of the Kingdom of Caubul . . . ,* and Ockley's *History of the Saracens.*

40. For a fuller discussion of how Owenson's *The Wild Irish Girl* (1806) explores the political ramifactions of this supposedly esoteric infighting among scholars and antiquaries, see my "Sidney Owenson and the Fate of Empire," op. cit.

41. For a fuller discussion of representations of rites of inversion in early modern Europe, see J. Lafond, et al., "The Image of the World Upside-Down and its Literary and Para-literary Representations from the End of the 16th Century to the Middle of the 17th-Century," *Renaissance Quarterly* (1981): 443–445.

42. Daniel Defoe, *Journal of the Plague Year* (New York: Signet, 1960).

43. See "Colonization and Sexual Dis-Ease," in my Ph.D. Dissertation, "The Deceptive Other: English Writing and the Orient 1717–1820," Stanford, 1990.

44. Interestingly, this expulsion of 'minor' heretics provides a fascinating analog for the treatment of adultresses in eighteenth- and early nineteenth-century novels. Novelists commonly send adultresses to the peripheries of the kingdom (as with Miss Milner/Lady Elmwood in Inchbald's *A Simple Story*), or out of the country altogether (as with Maria Bertram in *Mansfield Park* or Mrs. Gerrarde in Frances Sheridan's *Memoirs of Sidney Bidulph*).

45. Elizabeth Hamilton, *Memoirs of Modern Philosophers* (New York: Garland Publishers) 1794. In this novel, Hamilton had mercilessly satirized both William Godwin and Mary Wollstonecraft. Shelley read this in 1816 (*MSJ* 71).

46. Peter Laslett, "The Bastardy prone sub-society." *Bastardy and Its Comparative History,* ed. Peter Laslett (Cambridge, Mass: Harvard University Press), 1980.

47. Mary Poovey, *The Proper Lady and the Woman Writer* (Chicago: University of Chicago Press) 1984.

48. Hopkins, op. cit., 87, emphasis in original.

49. The Popes resided in Avignon from 1309–1377. During this period, they were more or less tools of the French kings, rivals of the German emperors.

50. See especially Rene Girard, *Job, The Victim of His People* (Stanford: Stanford University Press, 1987), and *Violence and the Sacred* (Baltimore: Johns Hopkins University Press), 1977.

51. Anne K. Mellor, "The Female in *Frankenstein*," In *Romanticism and Feminism,* ed. Anne K. Mellor (Bloomington: Indiana University Press), 1988.

52. Green, op. cit, 9.

53. Liu, op. cit.

54. One should note the parallel between Rome's struggle against Carthage (264–146 B.C.) and the only slightly shorter colonial wars between England and France (1702–1815).

55. Hannah Arendt, *On Revolution* (New York: Viking Press), 1963.

56. Muriel Spark, *Mary Shelley* (New York: E. P. Dutton), 1987.

II

CULTURE AND CRITICISM

Swayed by Contraries:
Mary Shelley and the Everyday

Laurie Langbauer

Writing in the first issue of *Cultural Studies,* the Australian critic Jennifer Craik cites Stuart Hall and Tony Bennett to argue that "the development of cultural studies has seen an uneasy alliance . . . which overlooks the intrinsic incommensurability of structuralist (or, strictly speaking, idealist) and materialist positions."[1] The antimaterialism that Craik calls "idealist" we might call instead skeptical (and poststructuralist). In casting that skepticism as idealist and pitting it against materialism, Craik gestures to a larger institutional struggle; what interests me is the way that struggle has been transferred onto the site of cultural studies. The fundamental differences of irreconcilable theories troubling recent literary debate have been recast as a problem in the definition of cultural studies (an institutional dynamic we have also seen played out on the site of that other loosely defined field, feminism). Because cultural studies (and feminism) have been set up as test cases, these fields have had to ask themselves troubling questions: What is the status within them, for instance, of the contradictions Craik outlines? Does the diversity of approaches within them—especially the uneasy contiguity of materialism and skepticism—mean that these fields are only in some sense repeating a kind of discursive pluralism (as materialism has often charged poststructuralism), thereby blunting their political effect?[2]

In cultural studies (and in feminism too), such questions often form themselves around the topic of "the everyday." Variously defined, the everyday has also been the focus of debate in critical theory in general recently (one might think of the influx of the social sciences into literary criticism, of Jean Baudrillard's emphasis on the banal, Michel Foucault's on the normative, Henri Lefebvre's and Michel de Certeau's on the everyday); as another contributor to *Cultural Studies* notes, these days "high academic theories . . . scour the terrain of popular culture, searching for truths in the domains of the profane, the commonplace, the demotic."[3] Attention to the everyday in "high academic theory" has, in a sense, helped establish the very field of cultural studies. Defined in part as the arena that attends to discursive formations of the everyday—such formations as fashion systems or rubbish theory—cultural studies seems to develop logically out of the theoretical discussions, such as Foucault's, that have come before.

At the same time, however, the everyday has been used to point directly to problems within cultural studies; critics like Craik claim that the everyday both marks the site of, and covers over, that field's contradictions. She sees the category of the everyday brandished speciously to mask divisions: it is claimed as a broadly populist, somehow politically progressive, point of connection, a rallying cry meant to "overcome" the fundamental incompatibility within the field. In criticizing the "crude Marxism," that results when—through such concepts as " 'the everyday,' 'people,' 'popular,' and 'nation' "—class politics are oversimplified into a "coherent entity," Craik implies that the synthesizing of disparate approaches within cultural studies is so forced that the seams cannot help but show.[4]

This figure of a monstrous entity patched together of mismatched parts, of parts that are roughly sutured, and those sutures made up of the thread of the everyday, ought to be familiar. It repeats a complex of concerns in the work of a writer who in past critical discourse has particularly lent herself to cultural critique. Mary Shelley's writing seems to follow just this pattern: for such disparate critics as Harold Bloom and Anne Mellor, for instance, Shelley's novel *Frankenstein* has been seen as a kind of monstrous cultural patchwork, important because it connects the most important, and widely disparate, discourses of Shelley's culture.[5] For other recent critics, the importance of Shelley's work goes beyond what it tells us about the daily life of Percy Shelley to engage instead with such crucial issues as the discontinuities of (eighteenth-century notions of) the idealist and materialist.[6] Such interest suggests that *Frankenstein* may have become one of our most powerful modern cultural icons not just because it comprises so much within its scope, but also because it bears directly on the problem of incompatibility and complexity within any given subject. We keep turning to *Frankenstein* in our cultural critiques because the idea of a riven, complex entity is crucial to the study of culture itself—may, in fact, describe that very construction we call culture.[7]

That such cultural divisions in Shelley's work are sutured by the everyday is perhaps not so familiar to us. In this essay I consider the overlooked topic of the everyday in Shelley's writing and ask what it tells us about that writing's contradictions. After considering the meaning of the everyday as Shelley inherits it from the Romantics and redefines it in her letters and well-known works (such as *Frankenstein*), I focus on a story Shelley wrote for a more popular market, the English literary annual *The Keepsake*. Shelley's 1830 story "The Swiss Peasant" looks at the construction of a monstrous entity particularly in terms of class and materialism. In it, the first-person narrator uses the ordinary occasion of having nothing to engage his imagination on a rainy day to record a debate about the status of the ordinary in the imagination; Shelley uses the commonplace exercise of an English annual story to debate the role of the ordinary in telling tales. Its tale of the commonplace becomes the tale of the common (wo)man, and the story of revolution in which Shelley places her is one in which she just can't win: she is forced to mediate between incompatible allegiances, and her steadfastness to both ultimately resolves the story. What interests me is why the everyday becomes the site for the negotiation of incompatibilities, and why Shelley uses it precisely to insist on incompatibility, to refuse to resolve contradiction. Shelley's meditation on the role of the everyday also tells us something about our interest in it as critics, the ways we conjure the everyday to settle issues, cover over fissures, insist on coherence. The point not just of *Frankenstein* but also of all of Shelley's generically mixed work (is it science fiction, gothic, domestic realism?) is the impossibility of coherence, as well as the price we pay striving for it.

What especially intrigues me in this struggle is the way it relies on the conflation of the everyday and woman—and the way this conflation falls into prevailing assumptions about gender and culture. In her deconstructive essay about *Frankenstein,* Barbara Johnson argues that the contradictions in Shelley's works express precisely the irreconcilableness that marks woman's position in culture, especially in writing.[8] The everyday becomes for Shelley the site of this division much as it has become such a contested ground in current critical debate: the everyday—as the term for the very ground of our activities or articulations, a ground we ignore or cannot see, the ground of culture itself—is precisely what Shelley wishes to unsettle. What seems crucial to me about Shelley's writing, however, is the way it leaves open the political status of such unsettling; rather than insisting that a turn to the everyday is for women either a subversive or a reappropriating narrative strategy, Shelley's writing, in making the issue impossible to decide, reveals and puts into question the impulse to simplify that lies behind such political claims. The insurgent forces that Shelley describes in a story of class conflict such as "The Swiss Peasant" are ultimately managed by conservative impulses, but those conservative impulses are still called into question by such insurgence, and a woman—Shelley's heroine, but also Shelley—finds herself in the middle of this struggle. Shelley may indeed be trying to have it both ways, but that also seems to me to be her point: that women are caught in double binds, that the shifting bedrock on which we try to ground woman's daily life reveals how our political options are more complex than convenient—shifting, uncertain, ultimately contradictory.

The familiar debate about Shelley's politics—Was she a radical or conservative?—becomes like the current debate over the everyday—Is it what undoes or carries power? Shelley's reluctance to decide suggests that such an insoluble contradiction is actually what defines fields of study like feminism and cultural studies and makes easy answers impossible. By showing that division *produces* discourse, Shelley's work asks us to do more, politically, than just choose sides (no matter how important those sides may be). In a sense, her fiction demonstrates the pertinence of Foucault's later discursive analysis, in which specious opposition *creates* the speaking subject unwittingly testifying to power. But Shelley's fiction also supplies a critique of that analysis: in its impossible attempt to hold open incompatibility, to keep from resolving complexity into one position or another (an attempt written into the contradictions and breakdowns of its form), Shelley's fiction tries to imagine a (political) alternative to a cultural analysis that itself collapses everything into a monolith.

Mary Shelley may seem at first an odd writer to use to discuss the everyday. Her best known work, *Frankenstein,* appears a prime example of a Romantic preoccupation with the extraordinary. In her other fiction and her letters, Shelley similarly tends to deplore the monotony of the ordinary, to revile the everyday as the commonplace, anathematizing it as "the vile every day life that clings to one" and "that tedious routine which makes up the daily round of most men's lives."[9] Shelley work seems so unconcerned with the everyday that her shorter fiction, in particular, may even have been neglected because of that. The editor of the first collection of this work, at any rate, argues that it seems unsuccessful and unrealistic because it ignores the everyday: "her heroes and heroines . . . [are] generally above the ordinary plane of humanity. . . . Her fault . . . arises from a positive incapacity for painting the ugly and the commonplace."[10] Although the celebration of the ideal (both in the sense of the perfect and that which transcends the material) might be applauded in a poet such as Percy Shelley, traditional critics have often seen Mary Shelley's emphasis on it as simply bad writing.

In turning from the everyday, Shelley is in fact mimicking the male Romantics, despite Wordsworth's preface to the second edition of the *Lyrical Ballads,* which seems to align Romanticism with the common man and the commonplace. There (in part responding to what he sees as a cultural crisis figured by men's diseased "craving for extraordinary incident"), Wordsworth tells his readers that he wishes to present "incidents and situations from common life" because they give us direct access to our most important thoughts and feelings.[11] Yet, regardless of such claims, Wordsworth himself remains divided about everyday. In the midst of directing our attention to common experience, he worries about "the vulgarity and meanness of ordinary life" and decrees that "ordinary things should be presented to the mind in an unusual aspect."[12] Unless transformed by the poet (himself more than common men) into something unusual, colored by his imagination, the usual and routine are not in themselves interesting—and may even be harmful.[13]

In her introduction to *Frankenstein,* Shelley seems to agree with the Romantic doctrine that the untransfigured commonplace can be a bar to narrative. She tells us that, as a child

> I wrote then—but in a most commonplace style. . . . I did not make myself the heroine of my tales. Life appeared to me too common-place an affair as regarded myself. I could not figure to myself that romantic woes or wonderful events would ever be my lot; but I was not confined to my own identity, and I could people the hours with creations far more interesting to me.[14]

In suggesting that her commonplace life is not the stuff of stories, Shelley is repeating the words put into her mouth in the original preface to *Frankenstein,* which Percy Shelley wrote in her name; there, he asserts that the story of *Frankenstein* "however impossible as a physical fact, affords a point of view to the imagination for the delineating of human passions more comprehensive and commanding than any which the ordinary relations of existing events can yield."[15] This statement repeats the Romantic commonplace Percy Shelley takes directly from Wordsworth: the extraordinary is important because it is able to interest our imagination; it becomes the source of narration.

Yet, like Wordsworth, Mary Shelley too seems to be at odds about the everyday: she is divided about the status of the exceptional as the impetus for stories. Early on in *Frankenstein,* we learn that "The Ancient Mariner" is more responsible than anything else for prompting Walton to seek the pole, for it helped instill or foster in him a habit of mind at odds with the ordinary: "there is a love for the marvellous, a belief in the marvellous, intertwined in all my projects, which hurries me out of the common pathways of men."[16] This exceptional poem seems on the face of it to be inspiration for Shelley too: critics have long recognized that in its marvels (its hero's spectacular over-reaching, its journey to the mysterious pole, its reanimated dead) there are sources enough for *Frankenstein.*[17] In one of her short stories, Shelley has a character repeat the Ancient Mariner's lesson: the extraordinary is the impulse for narrative because it is precisely what *must* be told.[18] Yet in her allusion to this poem, Shelley also comments ironically on past Romantics: in her novel, Walton's desire to reach the pole is questionable. He never gets there, but, with the monitory image of Frankenstein before him, he gives up his ambition and, rather than endanger the life of his crew, turns back. Anne Mellor argues that Shelley's novel is a critique of the "Promethean politics" of past writers such as Coleridge; in Mellor's reading, Shelley exposes how an emphasis on the exceptional can actually be a cover for a dangerous (male) self-aggrandizement, a strategy wielded by those who believe that their lives and their needs are special.[19] In believing themselves somehow above the common man (for whom nonetheless they intend their poetry), the Romantic poets themselves repeat this strategy and the system of power that goes with it—what the revolutionary in "The Swiss Peasant" calls the system that makes "the few, the tyrants of the many."[20]

By questioning the Promethean politics of "The Ancient Mariner," Shelley may hope to break the cycle that keeps narrators repeating the same old story of the exceptional. As with the dead bodies of the Mariner's crew, who mutely go through the motions until spirits allow them to sing a sweet song, Shelley may wish to transform the body of the dead tradition in which she works with a new inspiration for its stories. But the problems of such reanimation are made clear in a work like *Frankenstein,* which makes monstrous the attempt to do so. Shelley herself works out of a tradition in which it is impossible to dispense with the exceptional altogether, but her writing at least exposes the rough seams holding that tradition together.

This distinction from the Romantics seems crucial to Shelley's writing. In criticizing the tradition from which she draws her own forms and stories—and criticizing it particularly for failing to maintain a division that her own stories share—Shelley is working through her own divided relation to that tradition: such forms and stories give her the power to write and yet constrain her within them. Writing to one old friend of another, she says: "He belongs to my past life to days of bliss—of Paradise before the fall—common place as I am become now only to see him will remind me vividly that once Shelley . . . [was] my [companion]."[21] Locating Percy Shelley in a garden of Eden that associates him with Milton and the overreaching of *Paradise Lost,* Shelley seems to find herself outside this imaginative sphere. And yet later letters suggest that this fallen world, this untransfigured, commonplace world, is just a different version (a workaday, everyday version) of what Shelley figures as the Romantics' paradise of imagination: the image Shelley most consistently associates in her letters with the everyday world is precisely that of a garden. Worrying about a friend, she tells one correspondent "she [does not] take interest in the common affairs of life—None of its littlenesses approach her— That is a virtue but even none of its every day interests—none of those slighter ties & occupations (a garden &c) without which life is dull."[22] The philosophy of her later life, the life which she often berated as monotonous and routine, but in which she also wrote most of her fiction, becomes, as she tells her friend, a determination to "cultivate my garden—& wish it were finer weather—& be as happy as I can."[23]

The garden she cultivates becomes more than (although it draws on) the commonsense alternative to insoluble dilemmas offered by Voltaire (himself a master at having it both ways): the allusion to *Candide* here suggests that in her very disclaimers Shelley is aligning herself with a past tradition. She continues to share the garden that was the Romantics' paradise, but she experiences it very differently. That her imaginative realm is still a garden blunts the force of Milton's bogey, of the feeling of disinheritance and exclusion, the female "anxiety of authorship" that Gilbert and Gubar have argued informs Shelley's relations to the male tradition in which she writes.[24] But what's even more important to my argument is the difference she feels in this realm; for Shelley, this is also a material, rather than a simply ideal, realm. Unlike the Romantics, she has to *work* in her garden: one of the things she works at is maintaining an alternative to the view of paradise and writing offered by the male poets who have gone before her, by trying (perhaps futilely) to maintain the incompatible alternatives they ultimately collapse.

In its treatment of Shelley, feminist criticism seems to repeat the division about the everyday. On the one hand, feminist critics accept the devaluation of the everyday in order to try to make Shelley's work fit into some category, to resolve into some coherent unity. In trying to make sense of Shelley's stories, which seem mixed to her in their aims and quality, Joanna Russ finds one connection: in them, Shelley "shun[s] the here-and-now" in favor of the gothic, the romantic, the supernatural. To Russ, Shelley is a "refugee" from the everyday because, given her biography, "the here-and-now of un-idealized human relations [was] intolerable."[25] Yet, Russ writes, such a repugnance was actually lucky for Shelley as a writer: while it made her a bad storyteller, it also made her a good mythmaker, it allowed her to establish a mode of popular fiction, to "move into the speculative and the future, into what we now call science fiction."[26] Ellen Moers also makes Shelley's work over into one kind of popular writing, although a different kind altogether; Moers's classic piece on "The Female Gothic" uses *Frankenstein* to define that mode. According to Moers, that mode too depends on an evasion of the everyday;

an important part of the female gothic, Moers argues, is that "the strange [predominates] over the commonplace."[27]

Yet women's association with the everyday has also become a critical commonplace, and an important issue in feminist revision of past critical views and feminist rediscovery of neglected texts.[28] The connection between women and the everyday also informs feminist readings of Shelley. Feminist reaction to Shelley's work—even to a work like *Frankenstein*—has actually focused on what Moers herself recognizes as the "mundane side to this fantastic tale."[29] Feminists have read past the gothic horrors of *Frankenstein* to see it as what Anne Mellor calls "a trope of everyday life"[30]—especially as an allegory of the horrors of women's ordinary lives, filled in variously. For Moers, it is "a horror story of maternity" and the emotions it records "fear and guilt, depression and anxiety[,] are commonplace reactions to the birth of a baby."[31] For Barbara Johnson, what is monstrous in the story *Frankenstein* tells is the suturing women are forced to do as they live without everyday models of identity. For a woman to write herself into existence or to write a book is like creating a monster, and *Frankenstein* shows us how this struggle is continually enacted at the micro level, through what seem the most unremarkable and trifling details. Johnson remarks that "the impulse to write the book and the desire to search for the secret of animation both arise under the same seemingly trivial circumstances: the necessity of finding something to read on a rainy day."[32]

Frankenstein, as you remember, arises from this necessity: Mary Shelley's party—Percy Shelley, Byron, Polidori—rained in in Switzerland, decide to tell each other ghost stories; in similar weather, Victor Frankenstein decides to read alchemy, and ultimately creates a monster. More than a decade later, Mary Shelley's story "The Swiss Peasant" returns to this problem of how to occupy a rainy day, but this story does not simply record such a trifling commonplace; it is an explicit meditation on the category of the commonplace itself.

As the story opens, its narrator, finding himself rainbound in Switzerland, is reminded of Byron, who wrote *The Prisoner of Chillon* under similar circumstances. This, the narrator's only book in his mountain solitude, is also a book he has exhausted ("I have read it through three times within an hour" ["Swiss," 136]). Unlike Byron, however, this narrator can come up with nothing himself to occupy his time, for, he tells us, he is so incapable of invention that he could never lie, even when he was a child:

> [*The Prisoner of Chillon*'s] noble author composed it to beguile weary hours like these when he remained rain-bound for three days in a little inn on the shores of the Lake of Geneva; and cannot I, following with unequal steps, so cheat the minutes in this dim spot? I never, by the by, could invent the commonest incident. As a man of honour, of course I never lie; but, as a nursery child and schoolboy, I never did; simply, as I remember, because I never could concoct one. ("Swiss," 136)

To while away the time, rather than telling tales, the narrator tells us of an ongoing debate he has had with his friend Ashburn (a suspiciously Percy

Shelley-like painter), a debate precisely about such boredom. To pass the time on another occasion when traveling with Ashburn:

> I continued to speak in support of an argument we had entered upon before. I had been complaining of the commonplace and ennui of life. Ashburn insisted that our existence was only too full of variety and change—tragic variety and wondrous incredible change.—"Even," said the painter, "as sky, and earth, and water seem for ever the same to the vulgar eye, and yet to the gifted one assume a thousand various guises and hues . . . so do our mortal lives change and vary. No living being among us but could tell a tale of soul-subduing joys and heart-consuming woes, worthy, had they their poet, of the imagination of Shakspeare or Goethe. The veriest weather-worn cabin is a study for colouring, and the meanest peasant will offer all the acts of a drama in the apparently dull routine of his humble life." ("Swiss," 137)

At this point, a beautiful peasant woman conveniently appears on the scene, and Ashburn "wager[s] a louis that hers has been no common fate" ("Swiss," 137). Rain descending, the friends retire with her to her mountain cottage where they hear such a story that the narrator tells us "it lost me my louis, but proved Fanny at once to be a fitting heroine for romance" ("Swiss," 138).

Fanny's story—the tale within the frame—in its extraordinary events seems ordinary enough for a romantic *Keepsake* story. As a young maiden, the beautiful and virtuous orphan Fanny falls in love with the handsome, but oppressed, peasant Louis. Fanny is the pet of the wife of the governor of the chateau, whose son, Henry, ill-advisedly falls in love with her. At Henry's prompting, the governor banishes Louis, the appropriate lover, from the district. It is the age of the French Revolution, however, and Louis returns at the head of an army of peasants to overthrow the tyrannous governor. Just as the peasantry are about to harm the governor's family, Fanny, out of gratitude to the governor's wife, lies to Louis (for whom she has actually been waiting faithfully) and tells him that she has married the governor's son. Out of love for Fanny, Louis spares the family and, in hopes of forgetting his broken heart, rushes off to fight in France. There, he is dangerously wounded but, through a lucky coincidence, later reunited with Fanny, and they live happily ever after.

This brief summary of frame and tale doesn't do justice to the shifting involutions within them. Class position and natural worth become both equivalent and contradictory, for instance—Fanny is paradoxically worthy to be raised by the governor's wife (if only temporarily) above her "natural position in society" ("Swiss," 140) precisely because she unconsciously remains so true to her station. Such paradoxes in the tale reflect the paradoxes in the frame: as Ashburn suggests, the common woman's story becomes interesting precisely because it is so exceptional.

But rather than acceding to the teachings of this Percy Shelley figure on the role of the exceptional in tale-telling, Shelley may once again be suggesting something else. Charles Robinson, the modern editor of her short stories, finds "The Swiss Peasant" an extended and ironic comment on the Romantic tradition and "the restrictions of [Shelley's] medium"—the *Keepsake* annual.[33] What is particularly at stake in her critique is the status of the ordinary within Romanticism. Robinson writes:

> The first-person narrator ostensibly concedes [the Wordsworthian] point [that the "veriest weather-worn cabin is a study for colouring, and the meanest peasant will offer all the acts of a drama in the apparently dull routine of his humble life"] and retells Fanny's "true tale," but the narrator, like the Solitary in Wordsworth's *Excursion,* is afflicted by ennui and boredom. He benefits neither from Ashburn's aesthetic nor from the [theme] that opposites can be fruitfully reconciled. . . . By having the narrator disparagingly compare himself to Byron and his tale to *The Prisoner of Chillon* . . . Mary Shelley makes evident her theme: that the genial spirits of the narrator's imagination have failed him. Like Wordsworth's Solitary and Byron's Bonnivard, the narrator finds no meaning in Nature.[34]

We might wish to push a little futher Robinson's reading that "the genial spirits of the narrator's imagination have failed him": it is not really Shelley's narrator who has failed, but Wordsworth and Byron. The flashback about Fanny seems to validate the position of the Percy Shelley figure—he wins the bet—and therefore to uphold the Romantic tradition. But the narrator's continuing ennui and boredom (in the frame) suggest that winning is not enough; Ashburn might be right, but the tradition Shelley, Byron, and Wordsworth represent is still tired, if not bankrupt. The narrator is himself at a loss to continue it; he can't read Byron anymore; he can't write like him, and when he does finally come up with a tale to imitate his, we might argue that actually he can only eke out what tradition would find the most commonplace story, one fitted for a *Keepsake* annual.[35]

Faced with writing in the tradition of Byron, the narrator cannot "concoct" a tale. If he implies a reason for this failure (besides that he simply "never . . . could invent the commonest incident"), it might be simply that such stories don't do justice to the paradoxical situation in which he finds himself. In his story's opening sentence, he asks "Why is the mind of man so apt to be swayed by contraries?" ("Swiss," 136). Although he doesn't explicitly draw this comparison, like Byron's narrator in *The Prisoner of Chillon,* this narrator wants at once things which can only cancel each other out: seeking solitude, he finds himself surfeited with it, just as Byron's prisoner finds, once he has freedom, that he misses the monotony of his chains. But rather than simply repeat Byron in order to represent these contraries, the narrator turns to another source.[36] His imagination simply cannot sustain a story from *his* own life, another story from the same old background, but his memory is haunted by a tale somehow more "true" ("Swiss," 137): the tale the narrator finally does tell is a woman's story instead. It is as if the commonplace story of her own life as a woman that Shelley was hesitant to relate in the introduction to *Frankenstein* is finally given its importance here.

The importance of the woman's story has to do with the way she is swayed by contraries. Robinson notes in this story a (failed) attempt at a Wordsworthian moral ("that opposites can be fruitfully reconciled"). The narrator tells us that when he meets Fanny and Louis, her husband,

> There was something incongruous in the pair, and more strangely matched they seemed when we heard their story. . . . [It] was a lesson, moreover, to teach the strange pranks love can play with us, mingling fire and water, blending in one harmonious concord. ("Swiss," 138)

Yet, rather than blending disparities into harmony, Fanny's story emphasizes a different moral. It is nothing if not a record to the tensions and conflicts that structure women's lives, impossibly asserting as a commonplace tale of everyday life a story of extraordinary incident, a tale of the woman torn between family and lover, the state and the revolution. Although the "incongruous" Fanny and Louis are ultimately united, the story Fanny tells is not of that union but of the loss and sacrifice that lead to it. Her tale emphasizes the irreconcilable double binds within which women operate and which they represent.

This may be why, in directing our attention to the everyday, Shelley's story does not really achieve the subversive political status that some strains of recent criticism have claimed for the marginal. Certainly when it comes to a materialist analysis, "The Swiss Peasant" seems to be dodging the very structural analysis it offers, deliberately trying to have it both ways.[37] Although Fanny and Louis are the heroes of the story because capable of greater feeling and nobility than the spoiled aristocrats, Shelley seems nonetheless to share the governor's wife's belief in "natural position[s] in society": Fanny's satisfaction with her station seems to underwrite this belief, and Louis's discontent comes as much because he has been unnaturally raised out of his station (his mother was "accustomed to a bourgeois' life" ["Swiss," 141]) as because his family is later "oppressed, reduced to poverty, [and] driven from their homes by some feudal tyrant" ("Swiss," 141). And although, before their revolt, Lousi and his family "traced all to the social system, which made the few, the tyrants of the many" ("Swiss," 141), that structural analysis gets lost during the revolt itself: class antagonisms get eclipsed by personalities, displaced onto a love triangle. Louis attacks the governor of the district and his son because of unfounded jealousy about Fanny. The closest Shelley comes to maintaining a critique of the social system is a nervous and nostalgic indictment of a precapitalist mode; the peasants resent "feudal" tyranny ("Swiss," 141, 144) and the "inheritance" of private property it involves ("Swiss," 151). The pun within the story—the narrator may lose his louis, but Fanny gains hers—moves its readers closer to recognizing the kind of ungrounded speculation involved in capital, but remains on the edges of the text.

Such moments do suggest that the story's ultimate conservatism is troubled within. Shelley's characterization of Louis as a kind of criminal—his revolt is depicted as "guilty and sanguinary" ("Swiss," 144)—and the peasantry as "savage Indians" ("Swiss," 148) certainly seems to suggest a conservative politics. Yet that she also compares Louis to what the governor and his wife call "the monsters who then reigned in France" ("Swiss," 144) complicates those politics however slightly: the status of monsters is not one-sided for Shelley. "The Swiss Peasant" would seem a proper subject for such complication, for, in her fiction, Shelley appears to cast the Swiss, and especially a heroine such as Fanny, as the very types of republicanism. When introducing a similar character, Justine, in *Frankenstein,* she has Elizabeth tell Victor:

> The republican institutions of our country have produced simpler and hap-
> pier manners than those which prevail in the great monarchies that surround
> it. Hence there is less distinction between the several classes of its inhabit-
> ants. . . . A servant in Geneva does not mean the same thing as a servant in
> France and England.[38]

Yet it is actually Percy, not Mary, Shelley who, when referring to Justine, sings the praises of the common (wo)man: this passage is one of his editorial additions to *Frankenstein.* That Mary Shelley has Justine executed gives us another way to read what seems a conservative reestablishment of the status quo in the face of contradiction. For Justine's death suggests Shelley's estimate of the relevance of such public politics to women's lives.

It may be hard to read what Shelley feels about the possibilities for revolution and change because she also associates such causes with another oppressive regime: in "The Swiss Peasant," Louis learns from his father to trace all problems back to the inequitable social system ("his father, a man of violent passions, nourished in his own and in his son's heart, sentiments of hatred and revenge against the 'proud oppressors of the land' " ["Swiss," 141]); Louis's revolutionary politics are a patriarchal inheritance. Translating class allegiances into a lovers' triangle, rather than into circumscribing politics, may also show the ways in which women become pawns in what are struggles and systems set up between men. The contradictions and antagonisms traceable to the social system get played out on the site of the woman; she gets torn apart by them. Fanny finds her role as a mediator between Henry and Louis the "worst possible" ("Swiss," 142), and neither does very much to help. Throughout the story, she remains true to both; her choice between them, in fact, may be figured as a lie precisely because Shelley wants to emphasize that there is no real choice. In Shelley's fiction, neither side in the public struggle provides very different options for women. Although we tend to displace what we see as Shelley's wavering class allegiances onto personalities ourselves—awaiting a title for her own son, we argue, Shelley was reluctant to critique an entrenched social system with which she identified—the reasons for that wavering may be more complex. Shelley may not maintain a programmatic analysis of the economic system, even as she recounts its ills, partly because she sees how such programs can feed back into traditional gender politics.

Although all the characters remain in their original—and therefore seemingly proper—class positions at the end of "The Swiss Peasant," Shelley has Fanny and Louis retreat from the public scene. In doing so, she may be shifting her attention to the sphere of the everyday as itself a political arena—an important feminist move. But that move is not in itself a solution; that the everyday has always inhered in male Romanticism makes it difficult to celebrate a turn to the everyday as necessarily different and revolutionary. The political status of a woman's story such as Fanny's, in her simultaneous identification with the everyday and the extraordinary, is actually left up in the air. These difficulties do not mean that Shelley is renouncing politics; the story yoyos between possibilities that seem similarly bleak for her heroine, that ultimately seem to resolve into the same political valence for her, suggesting even more emphatically the necessity of maintaining differences that give women some political choice.

What the shift of attention does seem to allow, if nothing else, is a way for woman to tell her story. Inserting the everyday into the realm of the exceptional opens a narrative space: rain, the symbol for the monotony of the everyday, exhausts the narrator's powers but gives Fanny the opportunity to speak. In *Frankenstein,* rain similarly accompanies the creation of the monster; it also forces him into the De Lacey's hut, where he is introduced to language and culture, and it later drives him and Frankenstein to shelter together in a mountainside cabin, allowing the creature to tell his story. It also seems to be what allows Shelley to write, or to write this story at least; despite her desires elsewhere in her letters for better weather, the dreary rain she complains of while writing "The Swiss Peasant" seems also to permit its composition.[39]

Moreover, this ability to turn the monotonous into an occasion for a specifically female narrative suggest another relation to the literary annual. Rather than critiquing the *Keepsake* for its pedestrianism and formal restrictions, Shelley might be making use of its precisely because it was directed toward women—designed for a female audience, it was later under the direction of that woman writer the Countess of Blessington, as well as of Shelley's friend, that important woman activist Caroline Norton.

But the possibilities for women's stories are fragile and tenuous. Other parallels between frame and tale put into question the extent to which those stories are yet possible. At the same time that they are repetitions that foster one harmonious concord, tying the story together through careful patterning, these parallels can also be read as pointing to contraries between which the story oscillates, or limits defining a potential for change. Fanny tells a tale because she can literally do just that, do the thing the narrator, a "man of honour," cannot—lie. Because she is able to lie to Louis, she is able to prevent a precipitous end to her tale; her lie is the climax of the action and, in a sense, determines the plot, determines that she *has* a story to tell at all. Although Shelley may be critiquing a past male tradition, may be charting her differences from it, she is also not completely comfortable with those distinctions. That a woman's tale has to be associated with deceit, that it is still contained within a male frame, that it seems on the surface to validate the position of the male romantics (Percy Shelley especially), that the indirect discourse in which it is conducted keeps it far from clear who really tells this story to the narrator (maybe it is Louis, rather than Fanny)—all these continue the anxiety about female authorship that other critics have found in Shelley's earlier works; all suggest that writing is not yet so everyday an activity that a woman can take it for granted. And that the story is patterned through such contraries, such polar oppsitions between the narrator and Fanny, suggests something more about the role of the everyday.

For the question remains, Who wins in this story? In the debate about the everyday, the narrator may lose his bet, but is this only, as Robinson argues, an ironic victory? Does Mary Shelley actually privilege the everyday and common-place as a source of critique, if not of change? In a sense, no matter how one reads the story, the commonplace life of which the narrator complains remains unchanged, a source of discontent. Nor is Fanny's story, whatever it means, a story of "the dull routine of humble life." Although Ashburn insists that we can find something of interest in the everyday, it only becomes interesting when it is no longer the everyday but the exceptional and uncommon: "no common fate." These gaps in the story's seeming valorization of the everyday suggest that the narrator must be right: most of life has to be commonplace enough in order for singular incidents to stand out at all. The commonplace may provide a locus of woman's stories, but they become narratable only when they become extraordinary. They must be part of the tradition in order to critique it. Mary Shelley's stories remain swayed by this contrary. Critical division in the reception of her work, if nothing else, demonstrates that it is the *tension* between the ordinary and extraordinary that informs her works.

Yet this tension, while it may have its salutary aspects, remains a creation of a system of power that can also profit from managing energies in such a fashion: the revolt in Shelley's story doesn't change much, but it does keep the system going—it does give its characters something to talk about. Looked at in this way, Shelley's story tells us something about the current impasse in critical dis-cussions of politics. In part, Shelley provides us with a response to the Foucault-inspired critique not just of Marxism's emphasis on taking sides, but also of deconstruction's emphasis on contradiction. This critique sees the collapse of binaries not as subversion of a hierarchy, but one more strategy in a dynamics of power. In this argument, opposition is a ploy, a feint of power, that provides the illusion of dissent and autonomy while just recycling us back into power. The vis-ible rough suturing in Frankenstein's monster or the generically fissured *Keep-sake* stories, however, record Shelley's efforts to maintain contradictions, to keep oppositions open. In a sense, her stories suggest that recent criticism's de-scription of the collapse of oppositions within power is also prescriptive, itself a function of power; to emphasize similitude in dissimilitude is an old strategy, and one that has the simple effect of closing off options. The attempt to resolve incompatibility becomes another way of choosing sides, and the horrific poten-tial of paring down to a single vision may be the message encoded in *The Last Man*. The confusion of Fanny's story, of the position of Shelley's stories in literary culture, if nothing more, maintains alternatives, maintains choices. The clumsiness with which they do so, like the clumsiness of Frankenstein's crea-ture, calls attention to Shelley's attempt, and underscores its difficulty.

As Barbara Johnson has argued, this tension of multiple positions is what allows politics itself.[40] Shelley's work keeps from advocating pluralism—the competition of positions in a supposedly "free" economy that has already (invisibly) established the terms for debate, and thereby invalidates alternatives while seeming to give them voice—because it not only makes (sometimes shockingly) visible the structures in which we operate, but it records the painful and destructive impact of the very opposition it supports. Yet the way these issues are tied up with the question of women's stories suggests that smoothing over such destruction may be even more risky to women than to men. The clumsy maintenance of incompatibilities may be the only way to give women voice; we seem still to need to struggle for an arena that allows for contestation, for contradiction, and the complicated but important arguments with which we define it—with which we attempt to separate diversity from pluralism, for example—might be what keeps politics alive in the fields of feminism and cultural studies.

Collapsing incommensurable positions, or settling for one side or another, could mean silence: this might explain why Shelley's characters argue about the ordinary—and might explain too why we critics turn to it when we are faced with what seems a theoretical impasse. On the face of it, the everyday seems itself to be aligned with one side of the dichotomy Craik brought up in the passage I quoted at the beginning of this essay, the side of the material. In Shelley's story, it is what is presented as true: the narrator cannot make up anything, himself, but he can give us a "true tale" told by an ordinary woman. As a supposedly unconstructed category, as what as critics we might be tempted to call the real somehow outside of ideology, the everyday seems to provide a foundation upon which to build, upon which to ground our arguments. But I think that we turn to the everyday for another reason altogether—not because it naturally supports one position or another but because it resists such essentializing. What Shelley's story also shows is that the ordinary woman's story is not so ordinary after all; we can only attend to the everyday when, swayed by contraries, it becomes its own opposite. Rather than providing a stable ground, the everyday is a category that sends us shuttling back and forth between two positions. Although hazardous because it seems to divide allies (materialist feminists, skeptical feminists), it is also useful because it is something we can never be sure of, something we can only be divided about. No one wins the argument in Shelley's story, and her characters turn to the category of the ordinary precisely because it gives them something to argue about. The incompatibilities between them, rather than being some mistake that must be exorcised from their discussion, is precisely what defines it, creates their field of discourse. Cultural studies—and culture itself—are built on such a divide; Shelley's stories ask us to attend to the way such divisions produce discourse; they go beyond Foucault's analysis of this dynamic, by striving, at the cost of their own coherence, to maintain such oppositions.

Notes

1. Jennifer Craik, "The Road to Cultural Studies," *Cultural Studies* 1, 1 (Jan. 1987): 122. Even though her essay is, in part, a defense of Roland Barthes's *Mytholo-*

gies, Craik's construction of what is not materialist as "idealist" overlooks the poststruc-turalist critique of metaphysics, which, with its skepticism about traditional definitions of the marginal, has had much to do with the formation of cultural studies as a discursive field (that is, overlooks the poststructural, rather than structural, aspect of Barthes's thought operating even in an early text such as *Mythologies*). Craik's essay claims to substitute complexity for the one-sidedness of most cultural analysis, but her complaint about "the eternal ambiguity of most of the work in cultural studies—namely, an inability to locate the determinants of cultural fields or the forces that shape their tendencies" (123) makes it difficult to separate complexity from ambiguity in her argument. As this essay argues, the need to work through such differences in order to get beyond one-sidedness seems the impulse prompting Mary Shelley's poli-tics, and what may make them seem ambiguous themselves.

2. For a discussion of the danger of pluralism within feminism, see Annette Kolodny, "Dancing Through the Minefield: Some Observations on the Theory, Prac-tice and Politics of a Feminist Literary Criticism," *Feminist Studies* 6, 1 (Spring 1980): 1–25; Judith Kegan Gardiner, Elly Bulkin, Rena Grasso Patterson, and Annette Kolodny, "An Interchange on Feminist Criticism: On 'Dancing Through the Mine-field,' " *Feminist Studies* 8, 3 (Fall 1982): 629–75.

3. John Hartley, "Regimes of Truth and the Politics of Reading: A *Blivit*," *Cul-tural Studies* 1, 1 (Jan. 1987): 39.

4. Craik, 123, 122.

5. Their reading of what this cultural document means is of course radically different. Bloom's afterword to the Signet Classics edition of *Frankenstein* makes available to a more general readership the traditional patriarchal view of Shelley's work: she is only important as the passive receptor of male ideas, predominantly Percy Shelley's and Godwin's; see Harold Bloom, afterword, *Frankenstein,* by Mary Shelley (New York: Signet, 1965), 212–23. Mellor articulates the feminist revision of Shelley's work: her works, like of those of any important writer, directly comment on and critique her cultural discourse; see Anne K. Mellor, *Mary Shelley: Her Life, Her Fiction, Her Monsters* (New York: Methuen, 1988).

6. For a discussion of idealism, see Maurice Hindle, introduction, *Frankenstein,* by Mary Shelley (New York: Penguin, 1985), 7–42; for more of the kind of claim that ranks Shelley's importance in terms of her husband and father, see Frederick L. Jones's assertion that her *Journal* is "the richest mine of information about [Percy] Shelley's daily life," in Jones's preface, *Mary Shelley's Journal* (Norman: University of Oklahoma Press, 1947), viii.

7. Recent critics have used Shelley's work precisely to consider such questions. *Frankenstein* has been seen as telling about culture in the way that it repeats and negotiates particular divisions: using *Frankenstein* in her critique of the representations of patriarchal culture, for instance, Mary Jacobus exposes the familiar oedipal struggles that actually underlie high academic theory; see Mary Jacobus, "Is There a Woman in This Text?" in *Reading Woman: Essays in Feminist Criticism?* (New York: Columbia University Press, 1986), 83–109. For Mary Poovey, Shelley's fiction in general is a record of the double binds in which patriarchal culture places women, *Frankenstein*'s mon-strousness in particular one symbol of the struggle between the proper lady and the woman writer; see Mary Poovey, *The Proper Lady and the Woman Writer: Ideology as Style in the Works of Mary Wollstonecraft, Mary Shelley, and Jane Austen* (Chicago: University of Chicago Press, 1984), 114–42. Gayatri Spivak in particular emphasizes that *Frankenstein* is about the very constitution of culture; it deconstructs the division between cultural other and imperializer, exposing the need for their division in the

production of cultural representation; see Gayatri Chakravorty Spivak, "Three Women's Texts and a Critique of Imperialism," in *"Race," Writing, and Difference,* ed. Henry Louis Gates, Jr. (Chicago: University of Chicago Press, 1985), 262–80.

8. Johnson, "My Monster/My Self," in her *A World of Difference* (Baltimore: Johns Hopkins University Press, 1987), 144–54.

9. The first passage quoted in Shelley's letter "To Leigh Hunt. [14 Speldhurst Street. Brunswick Square] October 20th (Nov. 3rd) [1823]," in *The Letters of Mary Wollstonecraft Shelley,* 3 vols., ed. Betty T. Bennett (Baltimore: Johns Hopkins University Press, 1980–88), 1:398; the second is from Shelley's story "Recollections of Italy," in *Mary Shelley: Collected Tales and Stories,* ed. Charles E. Robinson (Baltimore: Johns Hopkins University Press, 1976), 27.

10. Richard Garnett, introduction, *Tales and Stories,* by Mary Wollstonecraft Shelley (Philadelphia: Lippincott, 1891; Boston: Gregg Press, 1975), xi.

11. William Wordsworth, "Preface to the Second Edition of Several of the Foregoing Poems, Published, with an Additional Volume, under the Title of 'Lyrical Ballads,' " in *The Poetical Works of William Wordsworth,* 5 vols. ed. E. de Selincourt (Oxford: Clarendon Press, 1952), 2:389, 386.

12. Wordsworth, "Preface," 2:392, 386.

13. Wordsworth writes: "What is a Poet? To whom does he address himself? And what language is to be expected from him?—He is a man speaking to men: a man, it is true, endowed with more lively sensibility, more enthusiasm and tenderness, who has a greater knowledge of human nature, and a more comprehensive soul, than are supposed to be common among mankind" ("Preface," 2:393).

14. Mary Shelley, "Author's Introduction to the Standard Novel's Edition [1831]," *Frankenstein,* 52. Mary Shelley's claim that she wrote in a "commonplace style" might be more than just authorial humility; the phrase connects this work to her later periodical and annual pieces. As she writes of a friend attempting himself to place things with the periodicals, "it was anxious work at first—for he wrote & wrote but did not catch the proper tone of common place—& his articles were thrown into the fire" ("To Claire Clairmont. Saturday [20 December 1845] Putney," in *Letters,* 3:269). That commonplace style might be connected to writing about the commonplace is suggested by the hero of an early periodical tale of Shelley's; apologizing for his disjointed recollections, he explains in part his story's fragmented and episodic form: "these are nothings, you will say; but such nothings have conduced more to my pleasure than other events usually accounted of more moment" ("Pecollections of Italy," 29).

15. [Percy Shelley,] "Preface [1818]," *Frankenstein,* 57.

16. Mary Shelley, *Frankenstein,* 66.

17. Biographical legend has it that the poem attracted Mary Shelley so much as a girl that she hid behind a sofa to hear Coleridge recite it at her father's house; for this story, see Hindle, Introduction, *Frankenstein,* 12.

18. The lines from "The Ancient Mariner" are:

> Forthwith this frame of mine was wrenched
> With a woful agony,
> Which forced me to begin my tale;
> And then it left me free.

> Since then, at an uncertain hour,
> That agony returns:
> And till my ghastly tale is told,
> This heart within me burns.

("The Rime of the Ancient Mariner," lines 578–85.) These lines provide the epigraph to Shelley's short story "Transformation," the opening line of which reads: "I have heard it said, that, when any strange, supernatural, and necromantic adventure has occurred to a human being, that being, however desirous he may be to conceal the same, feels at certain periods torn up as it were by an intellectual earthquake, and is forced to bare the inner depths of his spirit to another." ("Transformation," in *Mary Shelley: Collected Tales and Stories,* 121.) Yet "The Ancient Mariner" may actually itself be divided about the ordinary; it does present as its moral the banality "He prayeth best, who loveth best/ All things both great and small" (lines 614–15). The tension between the great and small is also articulated in Coleridge's epigraph to the poem: "Meanwhile it is desirable, I grant, to contemplate in thought, as if in a picture, an image of a greater and better world; lest the mind, accustoming itself to the minutiae of daily life, should become too narrow, and lapse into mean thoughts. But at the same time we must be vigilant for truth, and set a limit, lest we fail to distinguish certain from uncertain, day from night." Whether the tension between the "greater and better world" of the imagination and "the minutiae of daily life" can be maintained is raised as the issue which prompts this poem. The epigraph goes on to chart the breakdown of oppositions, confounding certain and uncertain, day and night. Yet, despite this poem's recognition of such breakdowns as a danger, it seems to circle back to emphasize great things nonetheless. It may be their continued repetition of the very danger they recognize, their ultimate collapse of the distinctions between the "great and small," the exceptional and everyday, that characterizes the male Romantics for Shelley.

19. Mellor, 71. Mellor argues: "No revolutionary herself, Mary Shelley clearly perceived the inherent danger in a Promethean, revolutionary ideology: commitment to an abstract good can justify an emotional detachment from present human relationships and family obligations, a willingness to sacrifice the living to a cause whose final consequences cannot be fully controlled, and an obsession with realizing a dream that too often masks an egotistical wish for personal power" (86).

20. Shelley, "The Swiss Peasant," in *Mary Shelley: Collected Tales and Stories,* 141; all other references to this story appear in the text.

21. "To John Howard Payne. Kentish Town. 11 June 1826," *Letters,* 1:521.

22. "To Marianna Hammond. Casa Quadri. Firenzi. 23 Jan [1843]," *Letters,* 3:56.

23. "To Marianna Hammond [Sorrento. 20 June 1843]," *Letters,* 3:78.

24. Sandra M. Gilbert and Susan Gubar, *The Madwoman in the Attic: The Woman Writer and the Nineteenth-Century Literary Imagination* (New Haven: Yale University Press, 1979); they discuss the anxiety of authorship on page 49 and Shelley's particular anxiety on pages 213–47. Partly in response to Gilbert's and Gubar's claims, Anne Mellor questions Shelley's anxiety of authorship; she argues that such anxiety is blunted because Shelley did have "female role models to emulate" (52). In this light we might also remember Mary Poovey's reading of Shelley's sacrifice to propriety. In a letter to Maria Gisborne, Shelley uses the image of a garden to suggests loneliness, constriction, and imprisonment: "[I] live in a solitude, such as since the days of Hermits in the desert, no one was ever before condemned to! . . . I never walk out beyond my garden—because I *cannot* walk alone:—you will say I ought to force myself—so I thought once, & tried—but it would not do—The sense of desolation was too oppressive—I only find relief from the sadness of my position by living a dreamy existence from which realities are excluded—but going out disturbed this—I wept— my heart beat with a sense of injury & wrong—I was better shut up." ("To Maria Gisborne. Harrow. October 30. Nov. 17 [1834]," *Letters,* 2:214.) Yet Poovey suggests

this image allows Shelley to have several different things at once. Declaring that she is shut up in her garden, the image of propriety, "enabled her to win social approval, to channel her impermissible aggressions into acceptable expression, to retreat from public view, and yet to display her sense of her own sef-importance in an indirect but effective form . . . that permitted her to take refuge in—while taking full advantage of—the resources of her culture's ideology" (Poovey, 170). I would add that her garden might also represent a sphere that could provide some alternative to that ideology—an alternative Shelley recognizes as imaginary ("a dreamy existence from which realities are excluded"), and a realm of pain and separation, not the wishful utopia we tend to associate with the attempt to will away our immersion in culture and ideology.

25. Joanna Russ, introduction, to *Tales and Stories,* ix.

26. Russ, x.

27. Ellen Moers, *Literary Women* (New York: Doubleday, 1976; New York: Oxford University Press, 1985), 90.

28. Margaret Homans, for instance, in her book *Bearing the Word: Language and Female Experience in Nineteenth-Century Women's Writing* (Chicago: University of Chicago Press, 1986), implies that an attention to the association of women with such categories as the everyday allows us to make sense of male writers' use of woman as a figure buttressing their representational structures, and women writers' relations to those male structures. She argues that the literalization of woman, her alignment with the lost and absent real that we can never recover, is necessary for the workings of language and of culture; we might elaborate Homans's argument to claim that one effect of women's association with the (absent) real is to align her with images of the mundane and pedestrian, which have become in many ways our cultural symbols for the real itself.

Other feminists move beyond description of the workings of the cultural association of women and the everyday, to actually embrace that association and to privilege the everyday as a woman's category. They argue that those details and activities we characterize as mundane or everyday (ordinary, rather than important) seem so because they are women's sphere, associated with, or left to the care of, that gender which is itself seen as unimportant and marginal. The feminist critic Bettina Aptheker, in her book *Tapestries of Life: Women's Work, Women's Consciousness, and the Meaning of Daily Experience* (Amherst: University of Massachusetts Press, 1989), and the sociologist Dorothy E. Smith, in her book *Everyday Life as Problematic: A Feminist Sociology* (Boston: Northeastern University Press, 1987), for example, argue for a woman-centered revalorization of the meaning of daily experience as one way to circumvent the male structures of thought and representation that otherwise organize meaning. (In doing so, unlike Homans, they accept the everyday as a ground of the real to which we somehow have unmediated access, an arena somehow outside of ideology, and they come close to essentializing woman by connecting her with a particular system of values.) Whatever the differences of their conclusions, however, both approaches agree that an attention to women's relation to representation—to what woman herself represents—involves an attention to what our culture tends to define as the everyday.

29. Moers, 98.

30. Mellor, 38.

31. Moers, 95, 93.

32. Johnson, 150.

33. Robinson, notes, *Mary Shelley: Collected Tales and Stories,* 382.

34. Robinson, 382.

35. And a book like *Frankenstein* too repeats this undecidability of form. That *Frankenstein* itself has no firm place within this culture, no fixed cultural position—critics typify it alternately as both high and low fiction, for instance—shows how questions of defining a field of culture are endlessly split and endlessly sutured.

36. Byron may be unsatisfactory because he works too closely in the tradition of Wordsworth and Coleridge, which, despite disclaimers, ultimately associates the everyday and gender with the *breakdown* of contraries. In discussing meter in the preface to the Lyrical Ballads, Wordsworth, for instance, associates meter with both the everyday and gender. For Wordsworth, meter in a sense represents the everyday as a kind of formal process; it is what is regular, routine, and recurring, what keeps the "unusual and irregular" excitement of poetry within its proper bounds. Meter, which imparts "an intertexture of ordinary feeling" to poetry ("Preface," 399), is also important because it also imparts "the pleasure which the mind derives from the perception of similitude in dissimilitude. This principle is the great spring of the activity of our minds, and their chief feeder. From this principle the direction of the sexual appetite, and all the passions connected with it, take their origin: it is the life of our ordinary conversation" (400). What connects gender and the everyday here is the way both unsettle opposition, point to the pleasure of similitude in dissimilitude. Yet Wordsworth's pleasure here also seems to fit into the narcissism Mellor critiques in the Romantics: what attracts sexual appetite is the way the sexes are like each other, and—given the sexual hierarchy that Wordsworth's writing also upholds—this traditionally means the way women are like men, are defined in terms of men. This narcissism is both grounded and concealed in the everyday; the everyday becomes the mechanism that asserts the masculine as standard, so naturally that it becomes a commonplace to which we need not even attend. To find similitude in dissimilitude, to resolve contradiction in this way, results simply in collapsing everything under the privileged term in the hierarchy.

37. For materialist analyses of other of Shelley's works, see Franco Moretti, *Signs Taken for Wonders: Essays in Sociology of Literary Forms,* trans. S. Fischer, D. Forgacs, and D. Miller (New York: Verso, 1988); Kate Ellis, "Monsters in the Garden: Mary Shelley and the Bourgeois Family," *The Endurance of Frankenstein: Essays on Mary Shelley's Novel,* ed. George Levine and U. C. Knoepflmacher (Berkeley: University of California Press, 1979), 123–42; and Elsie Michie, "*Frankenstein* and Marx's Theories of Alienated Labor," *Approaches to Teaching Shelley's Frankenstein,* ed. Stephen C. Behrendt (New York: Modern Language Association of America, 1990), 93–98.

38. Shelley, *Frankenstein,* 109.

39. See "To Frederic Mansel Reynolds. Grosvenor Place—Southend. Essex. Monday—[5 July 1830]," and "To Frederic Mansel Reynolds. [Grosvenor Place. Southend. Essex. 9 July 1830]," in *Letters,* 3:414. This may be part of Shelley's heritage from, as well as critique of, the Romantics, since it is the reanimating rain that allows speech in "The Ancient Mariner."

40. Johnson, "Apostrophe, Animation, and Aboriton," in her *A World of Difference,* 193–94.

Disfiguring Economies:
Mary Shelley's Short Stories

Sonia Hofkosh

I, fearful of annoying by silence, by speaking, by my very looks (so it was
all last winter) am anything but myself— . . . now I cannot talk of myself
to you; the being so long disfigured, so long depreciated in your [eye]
cannot pour out her heart—.
                              Mary Shelley to Jane Williams, 5 June 1828

Besides that I, your partial friend, strongly object to coarseness, now
wholly out of date & beg you for my sake to make the omissions necessary
for your obtaining feminine readers—Amidst so much that is beautiful,
imaginative & exalting, why leave spots which believe me are blemishes?
                              Mary Shelley to Edward Trelawny, 27 Dec. 1830

These extracts from Mary Shelley's letters[1] articulate the constellation of
issues I want to explore in Shelley's writing for annual gift-book anthologies in
the 1820s and 1830s. Shelley's cosmetic concern to edit out the "spots" and
"blemishes" that disfigure Trelawny's "beautiful" autobiographical narrative
and render it unreadable for a female audience echoes her concern about self-
representation, about the way she and her language look to Jane Williams.
While she edits Trelawny's text to make it acceptable to female eyes, Shelley
feels herself censored in the sight of her feminine reader. Throughout the late
1820s and 1830s, she records a particular consciousness of how she appears to
others. Ontologically conceived in the letter to Jane Williams, such consciousness has specific reference to bodily and to textual representation: her sensitivity about her complexion after smallpox in April 1828, for example ("I continue sufficiently marked to make me wish to hide myself altogether"; 16 May
1828), reverberates in her anxiety about the publication of her private life ("it
would destroy me to be brought forward in print"; 15 Dec. 1829). Increasingly
active as a literary professional in her own and in others' behalf, Shelley
comprehends that representation entails some kind of marking or omission.
For Shelley, to appear as an author, or, more broadly and significantly, to
appear as herself, is to be disfigured.[2]

By focusing on the recurring images of disfigurement in Shelley's letters, I
do mean to invoke Paul de Man's argument on Percy Shelley in "Shelley
Disfigured."[3] But with a crucial difference: I do so to elaborate not just the
rhetorical implications of what de Man calls the "erasure" inherent in figuration, in the "face" of language, but also the historical situation of a woman

writing to make a living, trying to shape a life and a self in the face of circumstances that appear in and through linguistic form, but on her own form as well. For the woman writer might experience the effacements of representation in a particularly emphatic, embodied fashion. De Man's allegorical "erasure" is accomplished on the bodies of women in a culture that inscribes difference *as* disfigurement and then tries to cover it up, smooth it out, naturalize it.[4] Shelley's short stories enact this process, revealing as they do so the disfiguring permutations that constitute at once the "very looks" and "the being" of the author.

By the time she writes the letters I quote to Williams and Trelawny, Mary Shelley is a proficient cosmetologist, practiced as a writer of abbreviated tales that appeal especially to the "feminine readers" of the literary annuals and gift books, volumes famous for their lavish formats and expensive, original engravings. Between the death of Percy Bysshe in 1822 and the death of Sir Timothy in 1844, Shelley supplements the subsistence income her father-in-law begrudgingly lends her out of her son's future estate by writing short stories, many for such annual gift books as *The Keepsake* and *Heath's Book of Beauty*. These narratives explicate in their various frames Shelley's negotiations between two economies of value—of authority, authorship, self—in which the body, especially the female body, is inseparably implicated. Shelley's stories respond on the one hand to an aristocratic economy of patrilinear inheritance, emblematized by Sir Timothy's loans which seek (by regulating Shelley's production and consumption) to enforce the father's authority and to ensure the continuity of his line, unblemished; on the other hand, she recognizes an economics of the marketplace, wherein production and consumption are compelled and constrained by publishers, editors, and readers. The two hands, each both dependent and resistant, meet in one body: writing at the juncture of these disfiguring economies, Shelley describes in her short fiction a figure of the author who is, by definition, "anything but [her]self."

Beauty Is Truth

The annual gift books in particular, presenting literature as they do—elaborately made up—play into Shelley's concerns at once with her appearance as an author and with the authority of appearances. Functioning as commodities in an evolving market economy, yet modeled largely on aristocratic assumptions and priorities, the gift books themselves materially enact the very negotiations that Shelley performs in her writing. These anthologies of verse and prose were specifically designed "to adorn my lady's boudoir, or grace her drawing room table."[5] They were thus issued in various fancy formats. Bound in "plush, velvet, stain, ornately decorated silk, heavily gilt cloth and morocco" or embossed leather, with presentation plates and original engravings, sometimes enclosed in an ornamental slip case, the gift books were produced precisely "for display."[6] They appealed to a readership of women, primarily ladies of the emergent middle class—in the words of one historian, "ambitious housewives"—eager to attain an "atmosphere of culture and refinement" by acquiring these literary *objets*.[7] Advertised as "tokens of remembrance, friendship, or affection,"[8] the gift books functioned metonymically not only for individuals in the personal realm of feeling or relationship, but also publicly as recognized signs of education, taste, luxury; they functioned as signs, in other words, of that excess which delineates the very sphere of the private. Purchasing a piece of that excess, the middle-class reader bought the privileges of ownership, a bourgeoise semblance of aristocratic (self-) possession. Descended from the pocket-book album, a combination of almanac and scrapbook in vogue in the early 1820s, in which, Leigh Hunt remarks, "people read the names of dukes and marquises, till they fancy coronets on their own heads,"[9] the annuals simulate elite wealth and status.

In the case of the annuals, you can thus apparently tell a book by its cover. Their formal features manifest what has been called the aristocratic "intention" of the gift books,[10] also instantiated by the appointment of titled editors, such as Lady Emmeline Stuart Wortley, who edited *The Keepsake,* and the Countess of Blessington, who edited *Heath's Book of Beauty,* and by editorial efforts to secure blueblood contributions. Robert Southey bitterly observes that social station rather than literary merit is the standard of value in the annuals: "young men of rank and fashion" are paid "dearly for the use of their names" in the anthologies' table of contents. Acknowledging its "ostentatious trumpery," Charles Lamb sends some of his own poems to *The Bijou* and entreats one from Lucy Barton in a letter to her father: "it is actually to have in it schoolboy exercises by his present Majesty, and the late Duke of York, so Lucy will come to Court." With a measure of characteristic irony, Lamb nonetheless participates in "the barefaced sort of emulation" displayed in what he calls the annuals' "frippery"—"the paper, the type, the gloss, the dandy plates, the names of contributors poked up into your eyes . . ."— which allows writers and readers alike to *appear* aristocratic, as if at Court.[11] What you see is what you get. In their own rich materials, the gift books represent materiality per se. In the tradition of domestic objects that exhibit aristocratic wealth and perpetuate its authority, they operate on the logic of a cultural fetish.[12] The gift annuals reproduce a system of value styled on the appearance of aristocracy for an emulous, upwardly mobile reading public.

As a fashion, the gift annuals' success is premised on the reproduction of exclusive style, on the reproducibility of that most private of properties. Bradford Booth asserts in his collection of stories from the English annuals, "there was no more significant literary phenomenon in the second quarter of the nineteenth century than the spectacular rise of annual gift books."[13] Though perhaps hyperbolic, Booth's claim is suggestive. Increasing in number from the entrepreneurial, first English annual, *The Forget Me Not,* in 1823 to nine competing gift book volumes two years later, to sixty-three by 1832, these "elegant bijouteries"[14] do indicate a significant transition in the development of the literary marketplace and in the phenomena of culture promulgated there: in the gift annuals, what we might call, following Hazlitt, "the aristocracy of letters"[15] intersects with capitalist strategies of reproduction and dissemination.

Most striking in illustration of this intersection and of the gendered and class-coded site of its accomplishment is the function of the engravings, which constituted such a prominent feature of the gift annual's attraction. Publishers advertised the volumes on the claims of the "beauty and elegance of art" decorating their pages. It is on the appeal of its "embellishments" that the initial volume of *The Keepsake* (1828), for example, is willing "unhesitatingly to challenge a comparison" with rival gift books. While the dedicatory verse that opens this volume of *The Keepsake* suggests that form and content are mutually enhancing, it is precisely in its dedication to "the beautiful" that *The Keepsake* underscores what it calls the "sovereignty" of appearance:

> Unto the beautiful is beauty due;
> For thee the graver's art has multiplied
> The forms the painter's touch reveals to view,
> Array'd in warm imagination's pride
> Of loveliness (in this to thee allied).
> And well with these accord poetic lays
> (Two several streams from the same urn supplied);
> Each to the other lends a winning grace,
> As features speak the soul—the soul informs the face.

This "union" of literary content—"soul"—and visual forms—"face"—here betrays another crucial alliance: the embodiment of beauty in the "graver's art" and the beautiful bodies of the gift book's readers jointly define both the origin and end of the enterprise. *Heath's Book of Beauty* will, in 1833, take this conjunction to its logical extreme, highlighting its "beautifully finished engravings" specifically and exclusively "of beautiful and fashionable ladies."[16] The literary "soul"—"poetic lays"—merely serves to complement/ compliment these lovely forms.

Heath's Book of Beauty renders "finished engravings" synonymous to "fashionable ladies," underscoring the link between appearances and privilege implicit in the gift annuals' emulative logic. As the verse from *The Keepsake* suggests—"Unto the beautiful is beauty due"—beauty is the standard that rules this economy and the currency that sustains it. The gift annuals present a model of beauty that associates the integrity or purity of women's bodies ("finished": complete, unblemished) with the preservation of patrilinear order (the fashioning of the aristocratic self).[17] But at the same time the engravings also function to reveal an incipient commodity culture, a culture which posits women as the object of the male gaze, multiplying and marketing that view of them so insistently and persuasively that even they can look at themselves through no other eyes.[18] The engravings in the gift books thus trace the emergence of a commercial ideology which at once replaces and reconstitutes assumptions about value—about the relationship between form and content, appearance and reality—inherited from an aristocratic model.

In fact, it is the introduction of steel engraving—"the graver's art"—in 1823 that makes the gift book commercially possible as well as popular. This new technology had the capacity at once to signify the privileges of art and art ownership and to "multiply" and circulate these privileges more widely than ever before; such was the interest generated by this dual capacity that the engravings commissioned for the annuals often constrained the writers who contributed poetry or prose by preemptively setting a scene or depicting a character for them. "There are suspicions," a bibliographer delicately suggests, "that oftentimes the story was written up to the pictures."[19] Appearances dictate content. Indeed, in his introduction and notes to Shelley's *Collected Tales and Stories,* Charles Robinson identifies a number of significant instances in which Shelley's own narratives for the gift volumes serve to "embellish" the engravings, rather than the other way around.[20] The visual in this way might be seen to engender the "soul" or meaning of Shelley's stories.

Operative as a marketing strategy, the sovereignty of the "very looks" of the gift annuals *is* what many of Shelley's narratives are about. What I want to focus on in these stories is the way Shelley turns such expropriation of her authorial rule (the "pride" of her own "warm imagination") to her own creative account. For she may fashion her narratives to accord with someone else's "view," someone else's "eye"—the painter's, the engraver's, the editor's, the reader's—but she enacts her apparent compliance—to the market, as to Sir Timothy—by incorporating the disfiguring efficacies of both economies into the thematic and formal composition of her writing. In other words, she deploys disfigurement, conceiving her project in terms of its risks and its rewards. Shelley addresses the primacy of form over content in her stories: she thereby "reveals to view" the dynamics which support such hegemony.

As the category of the visual that seems to incarnate an ideal standard of value—integrity and privilege—beauty is, for Shelley, only skin deep. But she also shows how deep and how constitutive that skin can be. Shelley's stories manipulate the visual—face and form—and its relation to meaning to uncover the blemishes not only on the surface but also in the very foundation of beautiful appearances. While for some Romantics, "Beauty is truth" and "truth, beauty," Mary Shelley's stories tell us all we need to know about the way beauty is always getting packaged to sell. The truth her work uncovers is cosmetics, the inevitably contorted constructions of truth itself.[21] If prose narrative is, as Percy Shelley would claim in his "Defense of Poetry," "as a mirror which obscures and distorts that which should be made beautiful," Mary Shelley's stories reflect the process whereby making beauty and its attendant truth always itself implies distortion. In the stories, Shelley reveals that the creation and celebration of beauty may keep the lines of patriarchal dominance smooth or put a pretty face on capitalist exploitation, but that in doing either it also exacts a certain and a substantial price.[22]

One Picture Is Worth a Thousand Words

The line engraving that illustrates Shelley's tale "The False Rhyme," written for *The Keepsake* in 1829, shows a man, Francis I, king of France, sitting with pen in hand, dagger, sheathed, across his lap, a woman leaning over him as she pulls aside a curtain and looks, with him, out the window. But appearances can be misleading. In Shelley's story, created in response to the plate supplied by the editor, the gaze we follow does not lead through the window to some object or event situated transparently outside it, beyond the frame, as the picture might suggest; rather, the gaze stops at the window, at its surface, regarding this surface as the opaque site of representation. The dynamics of looking, of attributing meaning to the seen/scene, itself becomes the subject of observation in Shelley's narrative.

As Shelley describes it, the king has written, or, more precisely, inscribed a couplet about female inconstancy on the window with a diamond. Francis uses neither the masculinized pen nor the dagger on his lap that the engraving depicts. In the story, his tool is instead a jewel, the first in a series of jewels that figure female beauty and truth—that figure the ideal of femininity itself—in the tale. As such, the diamond points to Shelley's interest in the way beauty and truth, taken to be at issue in the very essence of women—their integrity, value, their "very being"—get etched on surfaces, like women's bodies, as the sign of their dispossession. This authorial shift in the instrument of inscription from engraving to tale allows Shelley to contest the authority of appearance even as she demonstrates its tyrannical, transformative powers.

Objecting to the couplet that she calls high treason ("lèse majesté"), the king's sister Margaret proposes a bet. She will prove the integrity of Emilie de Lagny, "the most beautiful and the most virtuous of her maids of honour," who reputedly disappeared from France with her "pretty" page, "bearing her jewels with her," and leaving her husband, the Sire de Lagny, languishing in prison as a traitor. If she loses, says the Queen of Navarre, "I will bear this vile rhyme of thine as a motto to my shame to my grave." If she wins, the king her brother will break the window and grant her any boon.

On the eve of losing her wager ("Margaret would have given many bright jewels to redeem her word"), the imprisoned de Lagny appears to offer proof of Emilie's fidelity and attain his pardon as Margaret's boon. When he kneels at the king's feet, "his frame attenuated by privation," "the sunken cheeks and pallid brow" of Emilie are revealed in his place. The king cries "treason," but the faithful Emilie explains that "wiser men than [the jailor] have been deceived by woman" and that she has assumed the chains of her husband, he her "attire," so that the Sire de Lagny could join the king's army and gather "testimonials of his innocence." Francis breaks "the false-speaking window" and at the celebration of "this 'Triumph of Ladies' " that follows, "there was more loveliness in Emilie's faded cheek—more grace in her emaciated form" than in "the most brilliant beauty."

But appearances can be misleading, as the tale truly tells. Mary Shelley's story turns on the potential of appearances at once to mask and to manufacture the truth. Deception, falsehood, inconstancy are treason, but they are also the means by which the integrity and authority of the sire—father, husband, brother, king—can be redeemed. The story also reveals that the tools of such redemption perpetuate its fiction, and that the stakes in such a transaction are high. With his diamond, Francis cuts the false rhyme that his sister, losing her bet, will have to "bear" as "a motto to [her] shame"; Emilie, "bearing her jewels with her," effects the exchange that restores her husband to honor and reward while it attenuates her own frame. In both cases, the body, particularly the woman's body, bears the mark, the "blemish" of trangression and of the truth it ultimately authorizes. The king smashes the rhyme that has been proven false by the fidelity of a deceptive woman, but it is really Emilie who is wrecked by representation that chains truth together with falsehood and makes her body the site of such productive, destructive coupling. In the triumph of Emilie's "faded cheek" and "emaciated form," Shelley inscribes her own motto: this "one true tale of woman's fidelity," "this lady's truth," tells of her own diminishment.

"I am worried to death to make my things shorter & shorter—till I fancy people think ideas can be conveyed by intuition—and that it is a superstition to consider words necessary for their expression" (11 June 1835). As a writer of attenuated stories, Shelley explains her own authorial project as an economical one: "Never was poor body so worried as I have been . . . money of course is the Alpha and Omega of my tale" (16 Jan. 1833). And if her authorship—being a worried body—reproduces the "mutilated lives" of women in patriarchal culture generally, as Anne Mellor argues,[23] her gift annual stories also unsuperstitiously express that profit and loss are both risks of the market, and that for women, especially, that investment is often at great cost. Shelley's worries, then, are those of the working woman struggling to earn her living in an economy that wrecks as it rewards. Working within the limitations imposed on her—by the conditions of Sir Timothy's loans (no biography of Percy; no edition of his works) and by the generic constraints of the gift annuals ("make my things shorter & shorter")—her struggle as a writer is a struggle to survive and to prosper by telling tales of her own disempowerment. It is thus a struggle to tell her own tale, which is not simply a tale of submission or compromise; it is a tale that in its telling, from beginning to end, bespeaks the truth of her intuition, of her insight into what she gives up and what she gains through the fictions these economies share.

Shelley depicts in "The False Rhyme" how one woman's loss may be another's (a man's) gain, and how the losses women sustain uphold ideals of (intrinsic) beauty and truth, of authority, even as they imply the precarious foundation of those ideals. As an index of value, beauty fluctuates with the market. "The Mortal Immortal" (*The Keepsake,* 1833) also traces the revaluation of the ideal through the disintegration of the female body. In that tale, the narrator, Winzy, inadvertently becomes immortal by drinking the alchemist's potion ("admirable beauty, more bright than . . . the diamond") he thinks will cure him of love and thus render him independent, invulnerable; consequently, he also gains another "inestimable treasure" in finally winning the beautiful Bertha, whom he has loved since childhood. Bertha with her beauty personifies Winzy's transcendent achievement of complete self-sufficiency. She also naturalizes it: she is his rightful "inheritance," leaving her aristocratic partroness to enrich Winzy in his "natal cottage," under his "paternal roof." But this redemptive "good fortune"—in which, through Bertha, Winzy drinks

Painted by Henry P. Briggs   Engraved by Frederick Bacon

BERTHA

his value and has it too—is precisely the treasured ideal that the story is designed to interrogate. Such an interrogation takes place in Shelley's implicit dialogue with the engraving that "embellishes" her tale.

The engraving depicts the moment Bertha crosses her imperious patroness to marry her humble lover, renouncing the "detested luxuries" of aristocracy for the real "happiness" of an alternative economy—as Winzy puts it, "I am honest, if I am poor!" Here, aristocracy stands revealed as an artificial paradise in the person of the elaborately draped, shaded figure of "the old highborn hag" whose walking stick, held in front of her as a sign of her masculinized authority, foregrounds the picture. Centering the opposition between this bloated, enshadowed figure and the clear, light form of the beautiful Bertha, the walking stick both blocks Bertha's path and, visually, reinforces the true contours of her body, outlined through the folds of her dress as she gracefully moves down the stair. The engraving highlights this opposition in order to reveal Bertha's beauty in its true feminine form and, indeed, as the feminine form of the "honest" truth itself.

But rather than simply adhere to the contrast at the center of the engraving, Shelley's narrative takes its cue from it and departs, following Bertha out of the picture to see her turn into a "hag" herself and belie the truth of the vision immortalized in the engraving. Shelley's story says that we, watching Bertha, must also change the way we look: look at the way the engraving employs tricks of light and shade to make up the truth we would accept at face value; look at the way faces and bodies create truths they appear merely to discover. Writing beyond the frame of the engraving, Shelley redraws the lines of the contrast in order to illustrate what is at stake in the form of truth Bertha embodies.

Like the "old crone" she trades for "nature and liberty," Bertha inevitably grows old and ugly too, "antiquated" as a piece of dysfunctional machinery; the mechanism of inherent ("honest") value incarnate in her "very look" does not work in the world she must inhabit. Apparently transcending this world, the immortal Winzy in comparison retains his "good looks":

> I was laughed at for my vanity in consulting the mirror so often, but I consulted it in vain—my brow was untrenched—my cheeks—my eyes—my whole person continued as untarnished as in my twentieth year.

The tarnish that is thus invisible on the man is rendered in exaggerated form on Bertha's female body. He loses nothing, while she becomes a "mincing, simpering, jealous old woman" who recognizes her own loss in his perfect person. The story indeed turns on this disjunction in their appearances. Winzy's immortality, his wholeness, *counts* (as "good" or bad "fortune," for him or for her) exactly insofar as it is measured against Bertha's disintegrating body. Opposites, they reflect (on) one another. Winzy may be laughed at for his self-love, but Bertha looks all the more pathetic as she vainly tries to mask the signs of her inevitable vulnerability. "Her beauty sadly diminished,"

> she sought to decrease the apparent disparity of our ages by a thousand feminine arts—rouge, youthful dress, and assumed juvenility of manner . . . I should have revered her gray locks and withered cheeks; but thus!

Her vanity is a grotesque and painful deflection of his.

Winzy's ideal is thus both realized and ruined in Bertha; he sees in her "feminine arts"—makeup, clothes, affectation—the measure at once of his ultimate success and his ultimate failure. Initially a mirror for his achievement, Bertha discloses in the vulnerabilities of her body and her anxious efforts to hide them both the power and the tenuousness of the ideal (beauty, truth, wholeness) he has apparently accomplished, risk-free. She manifests what cannot be seen on Winzy; the price of his self-regenerating economy is displaced onto her. "Did not I myself wear a mask? Why quarrel with hers, because it was less successful?" But being "less successful," Bertha and her wrinkles (those "tell-tale chroniclers") expose the limitations to which, in his very transcendence, Winzy is nonetheless subject; her wrinkles tell the tale of the distortions and inequalities upon which his seemingly immutable power depends.

These limitations are finally represented, for Winzy as for Bertha, as bodily constraints:

> I yield this body, too tenacious a cage for a soul which thirsts for freedom, to the destructive elements of air and water—or, if I survive, my name shall be recorded as one of the most famous among the sons of men.

The disappearance of his body may yield a kind of freedom, but here it is survival within the limits of and on the body that constitutes individual presence. Understood as mutually exclusive, "soul" and "name" alternate as the content of identity. The body forms the site of these trade-offs. Bertha escapes from the "gilt cage" of aristocratic design—silk dresses and marble mansions—into "nature and liberty," but her liberation is purchased at the cost of a heightened sense of what she has got to lose. Similarly, Winzy has to die to be free, survive, caged, to be recognized; either way, his story records the exchanges—the losses and gains—necessitated and masked "among the sons of men" by the logic of a patrilinear economy.

Shelley evolves her own strategies for survival in writing her stories for the gift annuals, exploring at once the liberating and destructive elements of the exchanges that mark her labor. In "Transformation," also written for *The Keepsake* (1830), the hero exchanges his body for a "mine of wealth," a chest of treasure, and the figure of "a misshapen dwarf, with squinting eyes, distorted features, and body deformed." Guido starts out with a "well proportioned body and handsome face"; the narrative repeatedly remarks his "comely face and well made limbs." But Guido cannot *be* himself until he becomes "anything but" himself, a "being so long disfigured" like the dwarf. While in his own body—beautiful as it is—Guido squanders his inheritance and by his criminal behavior forfeits his character as well as his claim to Juliet, his beloved from childhood. He is restored to himself, to his paternal property, that is, and his paternally sanctioned love, when the "monstrous dwarf" in Guido's body, but "penitent" and "reformed"—reformed indeed—humbles himself as Guido could not have done to regain his own squandered position. Stabbing himself and the dwarf simultaneously, Guido gets his body back, though with his "cheek . . . paler" and his "person a little bent":

> Juliet sometimes ventures to allude bitterly to the malice that caused this change, but I kiss her on the moment, and tell her all is for the best. I am a fonder and more faithful husband—and true is this—but for that wound never had I called her mine.

The "mine of wealth" Guido trades for a wounded body changes into Juliet—"I called her mine"—who embodies his place and his possessions in the line of the fathers. Guido thus gets both less and more than he bargained for, and as in the earlier *Keepsake* stories, transgression purchases the truth, "a little bent."

Pictured in the plate accompanying "Transformation," Juliet, "an irradiation of beauty spread over her face," illuminates the selling point of this kind of story; she is the visible locus of interest and value in the tale, for Guido certainly, but also for the reader of gift annuals like *The Keepsake*. Though the central action of the story takes place in and on Guido's body, Juliet's is

Painted by Miss Sharpe   Engraved by J. C. Edwards

JULIET

foregrounded in the illustration as the final, angelic redemption of the fiend-ish contortions his has suffered. As in "The False Rhyme" and "The Mortal Immortal," Shelley here plays on the subtle interchanges between story and picture, the tensions between content and form; her narrative shifts the inter-est determined by the engraving just enough to dramatize the way interest, in and like bodies, is always being mis- or displaced. Engaging dialectically with the engraving in its generically privileged position, Shelley's narrative points to the discrepancies involved in assuming that position, discrepancies that the engraving, in its focus on the beautiful Juliet, would itself gloss over, smooth out. Looking at Juliet's bare shoulders at the center of the engraving, Shel-ley's tale remarks that exposure, like telling tales, is always by design.

The transformation that takes place in "Transformation" indeed occurs *through* the monstrous dwarf—that "shape of horror"—but significantly *into* the pleasing, soothing form of the feminine. Such an evolution exposes the distortion that is a necessary step in the progress toward beauty, truth, self-possession. Guido aspires at the start of his narration, as he says, "to be a man, free, independent," that is, "a man accustomed to make his will, law." But the possession of such an ultimate and unified subjectivity, Shelley shows, depends upon a prior displacement. No prodigal son, Guido returns to Genoa, to "the last relic of [his] inheritance," with his foreign companions: "we showed our dainty persons in the streets, scoffing at the sober citizens, casting insolent glances on the shrinking women." As the term "dainty" antici- pates, it is Guido, in the place of the woman, who shrinks in "Transforma- tion." Later, exiled "with nor sword at my side, nor ducat in my purse," Guido experiences the absence of those signs of male potency even before he confronts his monstrous dispossession in the form of the dwarf. After getting his own body back—possessing himself, his "mine"—Guildo looks "wan and ghastly"; his body bears the irrevocable marks—the wounds—of his diminish- ment. In the end, Guido confesses the "weakness" conventionally associated with this diminishment: "[I] have more mirrors in my house, and consult them oftener than any beauty in Venice." A parody of female vanity that rivals Winzy's in "The Mortal Immortal," Guido registers the particularly feminized diminishment integral to masculine ideals of subjectivity, of "will" and "law."

Envisioning her own changes and her own truths in the contested space between "persons" and "glances," the body and its appearances, content and form, Shelley represents the transformations—the wounds—inflicted by the assumptions of a patrilinear economy; crucially, her portrayal of these disfigur- ing necessities to which she herself is subject involves an empowering gesture. Like Guido, who must throw himself on his own sword in order simulta- neously "to make and to mar" his true self, Shelley exposes the wounds that signify woman's disempowered body in order to manipulate, to reproduce, that body according to other laws, another economy. Subject to change her- self, Shelley can yet wield the weapons (charges of infidelity; fantasies of eternal youth; monstrous appropriations of identity) that are used against her in order to accomplish (ex)changes that could work to her own advantage.

"The Elder Son," published in *Heath's Book of Beauty* (1835), addresses this simultaneous making and marring by elaborating the interrelation of what I have been calling a patrilinear economy and the vagaries of the market, both disfiguring, each sustained by images of ideal female beauty. The logic of exchange—of getting and spending, of producing and selling, of reading and writing—supplants the laws of inheritance in this story, revealing that the merely circumstantial nature of those laws render its truth, and hence its authority, its "will," as changeable as the market. Clinton, the "elder son" upon whom the whole of his grandfather's estate is entailed, turns out to have been born before his parents were married. As a bastard, he cannot be the legal heir, and his "dark mysterious brother" Vernon, long resentful of his status as second son, succeeds to the estate. In another version of the "Trans- formation" story, the real identities of Clinton and Vernon are distorted fabri- cations of one another: the brothers are revealed as themselves by being revealed as other than themselves, as self-transgressive. As Vernon proclaims to his older brother, who is nonetheless *not* the legal "elder son": "Your station is a fiction, your very existence a disgrace!"

But what this story truly tells is that the law of primogeniture itself entails such fiction; such law is, as Ellen, the narrator of the story, experiences it, "a monument of falsehood." This law leaves its distorted trace on and as the lying Vernon, so long resentful of his status as second son, whose "violent passions convulsed his countenance" and whose "disagreeable ironical smile . . . deteriorated greatly from his good looks." Moreover, the transgression of his parents that Clinton embodies as the offspring of their unsanctioned love is precisely what buys Ellen's emancipation from the "falsehood" of her coerced, regretted vow to the scheming Vernon. The disgrace that disfigures the father's name and line is the very mark of a successful romance. And in this tale, it is significantly the father who most suffers the bodily consequences of his economy:

> While carrying on a system of dissimulation, he had appeared gay; he was extravagant; giving up to pleasure, and spending even beyond his large income. . . . As soon as the discovery was made, Sir Richard . . . set his heart on saving a fortune for his beloved boy . . . he saved every farthing that he could.

The consequence of such economizing is that Sir Richard becomes "emaciated and ill," his "penurious style of life" motivated by and mirroring the "error" and "injury" he feels he has done to his bastard child.

In the form of Sir Richard, then, Mary Shelley subverts the authority of the aristocratic model, discovering that there is dissimulation built into its unblemished appearance. Sir Richard has "designed" Ellen—"naturally frank"—as the consolation prize for the dispossessed Clinton, "to repair [the father's] faults towards [the son]." But redemption always has its price. The engraving—as we might expect, a portrait of Ellen—exhibits the way the father's truth countenances or contains its own displacement, its fault. Robinson observes, "as in so many of the stories in the Annuals, the engraved plate for 'The Elder Son' is artificially linked to the narrative."[24] But the engraving is also incorporated *into* the narrative, pointing explicitly to its own artificiality. Ellen self-consciously describes Clinton making "the sketch copied in the portrait accompanying this tale"—a "hasty sketch, which genius and love united to render a perfect likeness." Ellen's account of the portrait's genesis suggests that this "perfect likeness"—this truthful embodiment of the embodiment of truth ("I was without disguise")—is composed on an artificial, an imperfect, pretext. Ellen, upset, "recover[s] an appearance of serenity" when she "[takes] up a book," but instead of reading it, falls asleep thinking about Clinton. Like Clinton's birth before the law or even like Shelley's writing in response to the prior engraving, Ellen's composure—or rather the "appearance" of her composure—that the portrait reproduces, is that fiction, that pose, which at once reveals and re-covers its own imposture.

If Mary Shelley's efforts at composing shorter and shorter stories for the gift annuals are directed at both underscoring and underwriting the faults of aristocracy until her son can reconstitute it "whole" in his own person, those efforts involve submitting to the pragmatics of the marketplace, as Clinton

Painted by Henry Wyatt; engraved by J. Henry Robinson

ELLEN

does when, declared a bastard, he "enters at once on active service . . . to follow up his profession with energy." Following up her own profession with energy, though reading and writing have by the late 1830s "so violent an effect on [her] health" (20 July 1839), Shelley learns to trade on her own disfigurement. She may be like the invisible girl in her story of that name—a "slender, wasted form"—dismissed by her aristocratic patron, Sir Peter or Sir Timothy, to fend for herself in an isolated, ruined tower, but her stories and tales, such as "The Invisible Girl," for example, a "slender narrative," "but a slight sketch," nonetheless reveal the clear outlines of Mary Shelley's true complexion. As a professional writer, Shelley masters appearing other than herself; like the fashionable woman elaborately and luxuriously depicted in the painting of "The Invisible Girl," Shelley even masters appearing invisible: "for I could not make up my mind to be exhibited among the portraits, I have such a dislike of display" (10 Feb. 1835). Disliking display, she deploys the privileged position of the engravings in the gift books' emulative logic to exhibit the faults, the blemishes, the *dis*appearances that embody and empower her authorship.

Notes

I want to thank Betty Bennett, Paula Feldman, and Emily Sunstein for their remarks on an early version of this work, presented at the MLA Convention, Chicago 1990. I am also grateful to Sarah Webster Goodwin, William Keach, Alan Richardson, Willard Spiegelman, Lynn Wardley, and the editors of this book for their responses to the essay in progress.

1. *The Letters of Mary Wollstonecraft Shelley,* 3 vols., ed. Betty T. Bennett (Baltimore: Johns Hopkins University Press, 1980–88), 2:42, 120. Shelley's letters are cited by date in the text.

2. Tracing Shelley's "pronomial play," in "Bringing the Author Forward: *Frankenstein* Through Mary Shelley's Letters" (*Criticism* 30, 4 [Fall 1988]: 431–53), James P. Carson observes "the gender divisions which mark the first-person singular as other than self-identical" (445). Drawing on Carson's characterization of Shelley's alternative account of the Romantic self, I emphasize the empowering potential of such an alternative that is nonetheless born out of a consciousness of the constraints of fashion. The kind of struggle between identity and its social constructions that Mary Poovey outlines in *The Proper Lady and the Woman Writer* (Chicago: University of Chicago Press, 1984) becomes in my argument a struggle to enact an identity through the very dynamics of social construction.

3. In *The Rhetoric of Romanticism* (New York: Columbia University Press, 1984), 93–123.

4. See Steven Goldsmith's comments on de Man's argument as it pertains to Mary Shelley and gender in "Of Gender, Plague and Apocalypse: Mary Shelley's *Last Man,*" *Yale Journal of Criticism* 4, 1 (1990): 129–73.

5. F. W. Faxon, *Literary Annuals and Gift Books: A Bibliography* (Boston: Boston Book Co., 1912), xii.

6. Anne Renier, *Friendship's Offering* (London: Private Libraries Association, 1964), 12; Eleanore Jamieson, *English Embossed Bindings 1825–1850* (Cambridge: Cambridge University Press, 1972), 3.

7. Bradford Allen Booth, ed., *A Cabinet of Gems: Short Stories From the English Annuals* (Berkeley: University of California Press, 1938), 13. Also see Remy Saisselin, *The Bourgeois and the Bibelot* (New Brunswick: Rutgers University Press, 1984) on the way feminized *objets* function in the bourgeois market for nobility (esp. chapter 4).

8. Renier, *Friendship's Offering,* 5.

9. "Pocket Books and Keepsakes," in *The Keepsake for 1828* (London, 1827), 1–18.

10. Jamieson, *English Embossed Bindings,* 2.

11. Quoted in Renier, *Friendship's Offering,* 14, 9–10.

12. See Nancy Armstrong, *Desire and Domestic Fiction* (New York: Oxford University Press, 1987), 59–95, on the tradition that associates aristocracy's "ornamental body," women's bodies, and object fetishism. Leigh Hunt also suggests these links in "Pocket Books and Keepsakes," quoted above, when he imagines the most "costly" keepsakes, concluding his elaborate, bejeweled description: "it is easy to combine with a literary keepsake the most precious of all keepsakes—hair. A braid of it may be used instead of a ribbon to mark the page with, and attached to the book in the usual way of a register" (*The Keepsake for 1828,* 18).

13. *A Cabinet of Gems* (Berkeley: University of California Press, 1938), 1.

14. C. H. Timpeley, *Dictionary of Printers and Printing,* 1839, qtd. in Jamieson, *English Embossed Bindings,* 4.

15. "On the Aristocracy of Letters," *The Complete Works of William Hazlitt,* 21 vols. ed. P. P. Howe (London: J. M. Dent and Sons, 1931), 8: 205–14.

16. Andrew Boyle, *An Index to the Annuals 1820–1850* (Worcester: Andrew Boyle, 1967).

17. The juxtaposition of two passages from Edmund Burke's writing suggests the association of a certain model of feminine beauty with the idealized reification of aristocratic privilege that the gift books exploit decades after Burke. On beauty: "I do not now recollect anything beautiful that is not smooth. In trees and flowers, smooth leaves are beautiful; smooth slopes of earth in gardens; smooth streams in the landscape . . . in fine women, smooth skins; and in several sorts of ornamental furniture, smooth and polished surfaces" (*A Philosophical Enquiry into the Origin of Our Ideas of the Sublime and the Beautiful,* ed. J. T. Boulton [Notre Dame: University of Notre Dame Press, 1958], 114). On Marie Antoinette: ". . . surely never lighted on this orb, which she hardly seemed to touch, a more delightful vision. I saw her just above the horizon, decorating and cheering the elevated sphere she just began to move in. . ." (*Reflections on the Revolution in France,* ed. Conor Cruise O'Brien [New York: Penguin Books, 1969], 169).

Explicitly engaged in the project of designing the middle-class estate in the early decades of the nineteenth century, John Claudius Loudon exemplifies the persistence of Burke's implicit associations in a treatise on suburban residences in which, according to Leonore Davidoff and Catherine Hall, he is interested in everything "from the planting of garden seeds to the appropriate authors to display on a dining room shelf." Aligning decorative women with ornamental furniture in his scheme for the gentrification of the commercial class, "he saw beauty as associated with love of possession and considered those qualities as most beautiful 'which approach nearest to that of woman; thus gentle undulations, insensible transitions, smooth and soft surfaces' " (Leonore Davidoff and Catherine Hall, *Family Fortunes: Men and Women of the English Middle Class, 1780–1850* [Chicago: University of Chicago Press, 1987], 189, 191).

18. Shelley registers her self-consciousness that to be seen is to be seen through masculine eyes: "to be in print—the subject of *men's* observations—of the bitter hard world's commentaries, to be attacked or defended!" (April 1[829]; Shelley's emphasis).

19. Faxon, *Literary Annuals and Gift Books,* xiv.

20. *Collected Tales and Stories,* ed. Charles E. Robinson (Baltimore: Johns Hopkins University Press, 1976), xvi. All the stories quoted in the essay are from Robinson's edition.

21. Barbara Freeman argues that in *Frankenstein,* "moments of pure vision indeed illuminate 'the truth,' but its shape is as monstrous as it is sublime." See "*Frankenstein* with Kant: A Theory of Monstrosity, or the Monstrosity of Theory," *SubStance* 52 (1987): 21–31, 25. In her gift-book stories, Shelley looks at the way the visual is an inadequate index to truth that nonetheless prescribes how truth appears and is perceived; in other words, her stories acknowledge that it is the packaging that determines what we buy as truth.

22. A number of recent studies detail the high price women pay for ideals of beauty. Among them see Diane Barthel, *Putting on Appearances: Gender and Advertising* (Philadelphia: Temple University Press, 1988); Rita Jackaway Freedman, *Beauty Bound* (Lexington, Mass.: Lexington Books, 1986); Robin Tolmach Lakoff and Raquel L. Scherr, *Face Value: The Politics of Beauty* (Boston: Routledge and Kegan Paul, 1984); Naomi Wolf, *The Beauty Myth: How Images of Beauty Are Used Against Women* (New York: William Morrow, 1991).

23. *Mary Shelley: Her Life, Her Fiction, Her Monsters* (New York: Methuen, 1988).

24. Robinson, *Collected Tales,* 392.

Subversive Surfaces:
The Limits of Domestic Affection
in Mary Shelley's Later Fiction

Kate Ferguson Ellis

> I am by no means indifferent to the manner in which whatever moral tendencies exist in the sentiments or characters it contains shall affect the reader. Yet my chief concern in this respect has been limited to the avoiding [of] the enervating effects of the novels of the present day and to the exhibition of the amiableness of domestic affection and the excellence of universal virtue.
>
> 1818 Preface to Frankenstein

> Shelley's conviction that it was "unwomanly to print," that it was "an offence against the conventionalities of society," was a learned response, the result of a head-on collision between the aggressive desire epitomized by her mother and reinforced by Percy Shelley's Romantic ideals and, on the other hand, the conservative, conventional wisdom that delimited the woman's proper sphere. . . . For a woman writer in the early nineteenth century, some version of this conflict was almost inevitable. While few writers allowed their monstrosity as resonant a voice as Mary Shelley did, many other women followed her into the side streets where propriety permitted women to express desire, resentment, and even rage.
>
> Mary Poovey, The Proper Lady and the Woman Writer

As the fortunes of *Frankenstein* have risen in the last two decades, propelled by the work of feminist scholars, Mary Shelley's other novels have remained on "the side streets," far from the bustle of scholarly traffic. Their exclusion can no longer be attributed to the presence of "desire, resentment, and even rage" in their pages, since feminist scholars such as Poovey have succeeded in calling into question, at least, Virginia Woolf's pronouncement that a woman writer "will never get her genius expressed whole and entire" when she writes "in a rage where she should write calmly."[1] *Frankenstein* has been admired as a controlled but passionate protest against the horrors of birth and maternal bonding, the crippling restraints of the domestic sphere, the overreaching arrogance of men, and the excesses of imperialism and scientific rationalism.[2] In its concern with justice and injustice, and with the institutions that promote one and retard the other, art and politics converge in *Frankenstein*.

Yet the feminist attention that has been directed to Shelley's later novels has found in them too little, rather than too much rage. Mary Poovey sees in Shelley's later fiction an accommodation to the constraints on women summed up in the figure of "the proper lady" who suppresses, perhaps even annihilates, the radical impulses that animated the author's younger self. More recently, Anne Mellor has continued and developed Poovey's narrative, exploring what she sees as Shelley's ambivalent idealization of the bourgeois family, the constitutive institution of the proper lady. For Mellor, "Mary Shelley's continuing commitment to the bourgeois family energizes some of her most powerful writing." Indeed, what makes her later novels worth reading "is just the tension they reveal between Mary Shelley's psychic need to idealize the bourgeois family and her painful recognition of how much participation in such a family can hurt a woman."[3]

I want to question Mellor's assertion that Mary Shelley had a "continuing commitment" to the bourgeois family, a commitment that her "painful recognition" of its limits as a supportive structure for women does not dislodge. If we see the bourgeois family as an institution grounded in an ideology of separate spheres that engenders ambitious male protectors as well as docile female dependents, the "flaws" in Shelley's celebration of family life cease to be problematic. They do not undercut her agenda but rather inform her, and her readers, of another agenda being brought forth in dialogue with the assumptions of her cultural milieu, an argument against an accepted view of domestic life which, in her experience, did not hold up.

There is, of course, evidence to support a conservative Mary Shelley, along with a now common assumption that radical parents produce conservative children. Thus many critics and biographers, as well as some of her contemporaries, have condemned the daughter of two famous radicals for personal pettiness and intellectual narrowness.[4] This Mary Shelley is supported by comments in her letters and journal in which she rejects the role of a public political person, describing herself rather as one who is unwilling to plead causes, to take sides, or even to have opinions. In one of her more frequently quoted journal entries on the subject of political participation, Shelley asserts: "When I feel that I can say what will benefit my fellow creatures, I will speak: not before."[5] Yet do we ask of male writers that they participate in the world of public politics in order to be taken seriously as social critics?

Nevertheless, I would like to extend the claim I have made elsewhere about *Frankenstein,* and to put forward a Mary Shelley who was, throughout her career as a novelist, very much the daughter of her radical parents. Each generation of critics looks back and creates its own literary history, and my appreciation of Shelley's opus comes from my own experience as an activist in the sixties now facing an increasingly conservative future. It is true that Shelley was not old enough to be a participant in the iconoclastic ferment in which her parents were so central. Nevertheless, in her formative years she invoked, through reading, the intellectual passions of her mother, and she struggled until his death with a father who refused to let go of a belief that he was right and the rest of the world was wrong.

In the following pages I make several points about the continuity of Shelley's political concerns throughout her career as a novelist. First of all, her thinking did not follow a line of development we see in the so-called postfeminist generation—those born, as Shelley was, into a time of radical activism who have become suspicious or scornful of the militancy of their mothers' generation. It is true that, when urged to be outspoken in the political arena, Shelley refused. Rather, she did what her mother did: she wrote. I believe that, in a period where radical ideas were not only vilified but censored, her writing was a vehicle for a radical vision that may even go beyond her mother's veneration of bourgeois domesticity as the highest expression of woman's God-given rationality.

Second, I want to suggest that Shelley's radicalism is not necessarily, or even particularly, feminine. The work of Carol Gilligan has proposed thoroughgoing rethinking of our commonly held ideas of ethics and morality in which women's focus on issues of relationship would be placed at the center, rather than erased and marginalized as they now are.[6] Shelley's critique of male Romantic egotism can certainly be discussed in these terms, and such a discussion would be accurate as far as it goes. Yet it leaves unquestioned the context in which "relationship" occurs. I am arguing that Shelley's radicalism resides precisely in questioning that context even when her heroines manage to marry happily.

The paradigmatic "happy ending" to the marriage plot of the bourgeois novel leaves the heroine and her chosen spouse in a place apart from "the world" that has created so many obstacles to their union. That place may not always be as glamorous as Pemberley, but the bourgeois family as an ideal is a family detached from what Ruskin called the "rough work" of the male domain and becomes, as Christopher Lasch put it over a hundred years later, "a haven from a heartless world." It is not simply the institutional expression of companionate marriage or romantic love, though each of these concepts fits inside the others like a series of Chinese boxes. Rather, it is a political institution, constituted as much by political forms of ownership and control as by the feelings among its members for one another.

It is this institution that Shelley regarded warily and depicted critically in her work. Elsewhere I have offered a reading of *Frankenstein* in which that novel indicts not affection per se but "domestic affection," the kind that flourishes only within the confines of the home as haven. As her marriage became increasingly a site of conflict, Shelley depicted with increasing vehemence the damaging effects of domestic isolation on the natural affections engendered by family ties. Mathilda, Euthanasia, and Beatrice, the three women in the novel Shelley wrote between *Frankenstein* and the death of her husband, are all casualties, in different ways, of the separation of domestic affection from its surrounding milieu of "rough work" and unrelated people.

Finally, I am proposing to look at Shelley as a writer who dealt with a loss of radical idealism, both in her own emotional life and in the political climate of the early nineteenth century. The English victory against Napoleon released a nationalistic celebration of English military invincibility, coupled with a suspicion of radical ideas from abroad and of feminist ideas from anywhere, that a reader today can recognize all too easily. Shelley might have followed this tide, but my reading of her later work represents a claim that she did not.

Confronted with political reaction and personal disappointment she explored the pitfalls of revolutionary idealism by looking to its institutional sources in a set of relations that are supposed to stand apart from politics.

This claim depends, however, not simply on an empathetic reading of Shelley's biography, but also on a way of reading novels *as* ideological formations in the making. In the realistic novel this "making" is concealed beneath a surface of believable characters and plots whose constructedness is intentionally negated. In modernism this surface is intentionally broken, and "meaning" is found in the gaps and fissures created thereby. Feminist hermeneutics, following Gilbert and Gubar, has read texts as "palimpsestic, works whose surface designs conceal or obscure deeper, less accessible (and less socially acceptable) levels of meaning."[7] *Frankenstein,* being a "tale" told by several narrators, has been inviting readers to look beneath its surface designs since its publication.

Yet Shelley's later work does not seem to be a palimpsest at all. Forbidden emotions are right on the surface, where Virginia Woolf declared they did not belong. But Woolf was herself expressing an entirely canonical view of great writing whose surface is free of the awkward breaks she finds, for instance, in *Jane Eyre.* Yet it is through these breaks, according to more current feminist literary theory, that we can glimpse the deeper truths that have been obscured, suppressed, violated, or dismembered by patriarchal culture. In "good" feminist texts these truths are discoverable by good feminist readers, while in deservedly obscure works there are no subversive "layers" because the surface overlay is all there is. Thus neither our high art theory of unbroken surfaces nor our feminist theory of gaps and fissures allows us to locate subversion in Shelley's later novels. To find it we need to read for ideology without the disguises we have learned to call art.

Both William Godwin and Mary Wollstonecraft were ambivalently critical of the gender system that conferred upon women the power of "forming and improving the general manners, disposition, and conduct of the opposite sex, by society and example."[8] In the heroine of *Maria, or the Wrongs of Women,* Mary Wollstonecraft embodies the appeal of this power for women, as Maria, receiving her fellow prisoner, Darnford, "as her husband . . . imagining that she had found a being of celestial mould—was happy,—nor was she deceived.—He was then plastic in her impassioned hand, and reflected all the sentiments which animated and warmed her."[9] But she also indicated, in the "scattered heads for the continuation of the story" that Godwin transcribed, that this happiness was to be temporary, that Darnford would lose his "plasticity" once out in "the world."

Godwin's novel *St. Leon* also presents true love and perfect union as a paradise which is doomed to fall. Its protagonist has in Marguerite everything a man could want in a wife. Yet on a visit to Paris he succumbs to the lure of gambling. Though he tries, on returning home, to "revel in the luxury of domestic affections," he himself expresses the male side of the ideology of separate spheres, and is not willing to be "satisfied in obscurity and a low estate."[10] Like Victor Frankenstein, he cannot confess his obsession to the wife and children whose very subsistence he is endangering. Instead, he receives from a stranger the power to recreate unlimited wealth on condition that he keep this secret, too, from the inhabitants of his domestic circle. His perfect wife is thus doubly disempowered. Indeed, her disempowerment is a condition of her perfection.

In her fiction Mary Shelley continued to explore the damaging effects, on men and women both, of a gendered division of labor built upon a separation of "home" and "world." Victor Frankenstein's idyllic family life does not allow for the expression of anger or ambition, and his inability to control the monster he so furtively creates arises, I have suggested, from the way in which the monster embodies "the repressed," that which has no place in bourgeois family life. In one sense, Shelley falls short of late twentieth-century feminism inasmuch as she treats anger and ambition only in men. Yet part of her critique of the structure of bourgeois family life is directed at its deformation on account of this very monopoly.

In *Frankenstein* three of the women are formed on the model of the sentimental heroine of the period: suffering cheerfully is the only expression of their virtue available to Caroline Beaufort, Victor's mother, Elizabeth Lavenza, his fiancee and childhood sweetheart, and Justine Moritz, their unjustly accused servant. Against these, Safie stands out by reason of a mother who taught her daughter to "aspire to higher powers of intellect, and an independence of spirit forbidden to the female followers of Mahomet."[11] We assume that Safie survives, but in *Valperga,* the heiress of the castle that gives the novel its name, having been educated by both parents to a life that goes far beyond "forming and improving the manners, disposition, and conduct of the opposite sex," is not so fortunate.

It was her father, Euthanasia explains, who taught her "to fathom my sensations and discipline my mind," and told her that "either my judgement or passions must rule me, and that my future happiness and usefulness depended on the choice I made between these two laws." Unorthodox as these Godwinian precepts may have been for a daughter, her mother was an even more powerful force in Euthanasia's development:

> She was a Guelph, a violent partizan, and, heart and soul, was taken up with treaties of peace, acquisitions of war, the conduct of allies, and the fortune of her enemies. . . . She was acquainted with all the magistrates of Florence, the probabilities of elections, the state of the troops, the receipt of imposts, and every circumstance of the republic.[12]

It is her mother's example that will not allow Euthanasia to follow her heart into marriage to Castruccio, whom she had known since childhood but whose early influences have directed him toward the cause of the Ghibellines.

But even the love of a woman of Euthanasia's caliber cannot redirect what the novel's reviewer in *Blackwood's* magazine called "the slow and gradual formation of a crafty and bloody Italian tyrant of the middle ages, out of an innocent, open-hearted, and deeply feeling youth."[13] Shelley has the two grow up together, as do Elizabeth and Victor, to make the point that the seclusion of the bourgeois family fosters on the part of the girls a devotion that cannot, in face, succeed in "forming" the ambition of their male companions, given that its direct expression is denied them. Seclusion is also the undoing of Beatrice, the other woman in the novel who loves Castruccio. Raised in a convent, her response to him begins, like Euthanasia's, with deification (1:189, 2:87–88), and ends, after he abandons her, with suicide.

But the failure and deaths of these two women (the novel ends with Euthanasia drowning at sea) is not individual but institutional. In *Of Woman Born,* Adrienne Rich observes: "Few women growing up in patriarchal society can feel mothered enough; the power of our mothers, whatever their love for us and their struggles on our behalf, is too restricted."[14] Thus Safie's independent mother paves the way for a destiny for her daughter no higher than, as Anne Mellor comments, "the future wife of Felix De Lacey" (209), though in Shelley's world a happy marriage, for a woman of Safie's initiative, is not a small achievement. Nor is it the fate of Shelley's other independent heroines.[15] Euthanasia, who became a potent political force in Italy and who is the only major woman character in Shelley's fiction who enters the public sphere, is finally defeated by the institutional forces that impelled her lover toward military glory.

Yet for as long as she lives, Valperga castle remains a symbol of political freedom in a world ruled by Castruccio. The castle in this novel performs the opposite function from the role it plays in the popular genre of Shelley's day, the gothic romance. In the world of Walpole, Radcliffe, and their fellow gothicists, the castle was a place cut off from the public world, a place where violence against women could be performed outside of the network of "voluntary spies" in which Henry Tilney has such a faith.[16] In *Valperga,* the castle where Euthanasia has presided alone since the death of her parents, virtue in the public realm is upheld while in the "sphere" governed by men we see the tyranny that gothic villains were able to exercise, unimpeded, over gothic heroines and other helpless individuals. Woman's power in this novel is not determinative, but it is not destructive either. It supports liberty not only on the political front but in the area of private life as well.

The determinative power in *The Last Man* belongs to the Plague, which is indifferent not only to gender but to national boundaries and castle walls, to distinctions between rich and poor, virtuous and vicious. It has begun in the non-European world and is encountered first by Shelley's protagonists in the liminal city of Constantinople. Yet the Plague has spread, the novel suggests, because Europe in general and its heroes in particular, have become "soft"— their ideological immune systems unable to protect them, as Audrey Fisch suggests. Consequently, on the political level, Constantinople and Greece, the cradle of civilization as the characters in the novel understand it, is now "infected" with Turkish infidels while the domain of personal life has been equally "infected" by the extramarital liaisons of Raymond, England's Lord Protector.

The Last Man, as Audrey Fisch demonstrates in her essay in this book, is thematically driven by a concern with boundaries. For the purpose of this paper, I focus on the boundary created by the ideology of separate spheres between the "fallen" world of work under capitalism and the "unfallen" home. "Home" is Windsor, ancestral seat of Adrian, the son of the last (and now deceased) king of England. In the early part of the novel, it is the site of harmonious "domestic affection," untroubled by work or politics, for its five major characters: two couples plus Adrian.

> Years passed thus,—even years. Each month brought forth its successor, each year one like to that gone by; truly, our lives were a living comment on that beautiful sentiment of Plutarch, that "our souls have a natural inclina- tion to love, being born as much to love, as to feel, to reason, to understand and remember." We talked of change and active pursuits, but still remained at Windsor, incapable of violating the charm that attached us to our secluded life.[17]

But ambition must and does enter this Paradise, since the world of the novel is only temporarily reorganized, as Jane Tompkins puts it, "from the woman's point of view," that is, centered in the domestic sphere.[18]

Raymond is the agent of this "fall," not only because he is drawn back into politics to assume the Lord Protectorate of his country, but because, in the course of his duties, he meets Evadne, a childhood friend and (unrequited) love object of Adrian's whose passion for Raymond is secretly consummated. When Perdita finds this secret out, she is distraught, and Raymond responds by rushing off into the battlefield, where he can lose his sense of "infection" by engaging in a larger struggle against a political disease that demands its solution on the battlefield. But the Plague is more powerful than national or personal imperatives: Constantinople is blown up, Raymond is killed in the explosion, and Perdita commits suicide.

This leaves Lionel, the narrator and "last man" of the novel, along with Adrian, Adrian's sister Idris, who is also Lionel's wife, and Clara, the daugh- ter of Raymond and Perdita, to struggle to keep the Plague out of England, then out of Windsor, and finally out of their own bodies. On his way to visit Evadne, who is living in extreme poverty in London, Raymond, newly be- come Lord Protector, comments: "I have much to do before England be- comes a Paradise" (78). Later Windsor, presided over by Idris, becomes

> a colony of the unhappy, deserted by their relatives, and in themselves helpless, sufficient to occupy her time and attention, while ceaseless anxiety for my welfare and the health of her children, however she strove to curb or conceal it, absorbed all her thoughts, and undermined the vital principle. After watching over and providing for their safety, her second care was to hide from me her anguish and tears. Each night I returned to the Castle, and found there repose and love awaiting me. (199)

Idris embodies here another aspect of the ideal of womanhood in its separate sphere, "contributing daily and hourly to the comfort of [everyone who enters it] under every vicissitude of sickness and health, of joy and affliction."[19]

Needless to say, her efforts preserve neither her charges nor herself. Women cannot even "rule" in their proper sphere, Shelley is saying, because the evil that supposedly originates outside its walls has no respect for those man-made boundaries.

Moreover, evil may not originate outside the domestic enclave after all. We have been speaking thus far about Shelley's depiction of women's power-lessness to perform the tasks assigned to them as "rulers" of the sphere of home: ministering to the needs of dependent people and "reforming" the manners of men. This essentially maternal role, for which the role of the daughter is a training, is fraught, in Shelley's fictional world, with opportunities for emotional victimization. In *Mathilda, Lodore,* and *Falkner,* and to a lesser extent in *Frankenstein,* we have older men "rescuing" a daughter, or much younger woman or child, from poverty and desertion. They are rewarded with absolute, unqualified devotion, and the effect of this compelling emotion upon the daughter, and the dependency it entails, is a concern that Shelley develops in these later novels.

Mathilda is the earliest written of the three, and the most unequivocally critical of the ties hallowed by the name of "family." Its heroine begins her narrative in a state of eager anticipation of her own death, and she proceeds to recount for the reader the events that have led her to this state. In telling her story, Mathilda immediately focuses on her father, his education conducted by "a weak mother with all the indulgence she thought due to a nobleman of wealth," and his marriage to the woman with whom he had been "playmates from infancy."[20] Like Elizabeth in *Frankenstein,* Diana is well read, with an emphasis on the past rather than on the present:

> Thus although she appeared to be less initiated in the mysteries of life and
> society than he, her knowledge was of a deeper kind and laid on firmer
> foundations; and even if her beauty and sweetness had not fascinated him
> her understanding would ever have held his in thrall. He looked to her as his
> guide, and such was his adoration that he delighted to augment to his own
> mind the sense of inferiority with which she sometimes impressed him. (5)

The ambiguity of the final sentence expresses the ambiguity of the idealized wife in the bourgeois family, impressing on a husband a "sense of inferiority" not firmly anchored by its syntax.

Death is the most serious assault on any social grouping, but the barrenness of the human landscape in which Mathilda's parents have established their relationship intensifies the effects of losing anyone in it. Diana "had lost her mother when very young," and although "her father had devoted himself to the care of her education," there are no other siblings or friends of any age on the scene except for the man she eventually marries. "She had lived from birth a retired life," and when she marries that retired life is extended to both parties, as it was for Caroline Beaufort and the elder Frankenstein as well as for Perdita and Raymond in *The Last Man.* The kind of harmony celebrated in the bourgeois family as an ideal can be obtained only by keeping "the world" at a distance.

Once the "forming and improving" influence of Diana is removed by her death, her husband cannot remain inside the domestic circle. " 'I must break all ties that at present exist,' he exclaims. 'I shall become a wanderer, a miserable outcast—alone! alone!' " (7). Abandoning his daughter for sixteen years to a home bereft of warmth and people, to an aunt and, for a while, a servant, he apparently imposes upon himself the same lack of human contact that stunts his daughter's development. Neither one can strengthen, through mutually supportive contact, their ability to express loving feelings. The sphere of "the world" is inhospitable to such expression because the home is its proper sphere. Diana could regulate her husband's sexuality because, as a childhood playmate, she had known him before he could fully express it.

The central problem with the bourgeois family as an institution is that tasks of regulating the sexuality of "the opposite sex," as well as "contributing daily and hourly to the comfort of husbands" and other family members, is placed into too few hands. A daughter can take them on from her mother once she is old enough, but the death of a mother when her child is an infant does irreparable damage, Shelley insists, to an institution that could not perform the functions for which it existed without her "forming and improving" influence. In all of her novels that touch upon the issue of "domestic affection," Shelley shows that this female power that is one of the constitutive premises of the bourgeois family is simply illusory.

In *Mathilda,* moreover, we are directed to look within the domestic circle itself for the source of those beliefs and practices that inhibit its exercise. Mathilda's father reappears when she is sixteen, after an interval in which both have been paralyzed by the absence of the one person who, in the only model of "domestic affection" they have known, can make everything all better. Neither one can control the excessive dependency they unleash upon one another. Engendered in an isolation as deep as that of Victor Frankenstein's laboratory, their "family" feelings have become monsters in whose presence they cannot be. Consequently no other human being, no matter how loving, can enter this dyad: Woodville in *Mathilda* is a case in point. It cannot be "formed and improved" except by the ultimate isolation of death, which is why Mathilda's father rushes off and commits suicide as soon as he discovers the real nature of his feelings for his daughter, and why Mathilda awaits the embrace of death so eagerly.

Given the isolation of the home, and the nuclear family that enacts the roles by which it is constituted, its members are subject to feelings uninhibited by any constraints except those embodied in the mother. No "world" is there to offer other outlets to its members, other experiences of success and failure, other sources of comfort or insight when the ideal does not match the lived experience of domestic life "under every vicissitude of sickness and health, of joy and affliction." It has been pointed out by many Shelley scholars that Mary herself did not manage to transcend the scars of her own early life. But I think we can read beyond a suffering child's wish for a perfect family, and even beyond the revenge that U. C. Knoepflmacher sees in Shelley's behavior after Godwin's death,[21] to a fictional critique of an institutional context in which these feelings are all too easily fostered.

The events of 1818 and 1819 offer an almost excessive list of provocations for Shelley's anger and grief. The deaths of Clara and William, her father's impatience with her mourning for her children, and the rift that these feelings brought into her relationship with her husband plunged the twenty-two-year-old Mary into depths of despair that are hard for a twentieth-century reader to imagine. In addition to personal struggles, her crisis may also be seen as playing out changing atitudes toward children that were a constituent part of the more isolated, "affective" bourgeois family. In their study *Children in English Society,* Hewitt and Pinchbeck note that

> even though toward the end of the [eighteenth] century, the old formality was beginning to break down in some families, children no longer kneeling to ask their parents' blessing or standing in their presence, in many households the old, more formal usage remained.[22]

Godwin's early upbringing of Mary, alternating concern and affection with distance and formality, can be seen as an expression of changing ideas about children and childhood. His complaint that she, who still has "the husband of [her] choice," can look upon this blessing as "nothing, because a child of three years old is dead," cannot but call to mind the fact that he faced the reverse situation in 1797.[23]

Godwin refused to give Mary back the manuscript of *Mathilda,* objecting not only to its morbidity but to his belief that, without a preface, a reader would find Mathilda guilty of incest.[24] Nevertheless, she returned, ten years later, to the subject of parent–child bonds whose very intensity kills one, and then the other, of the parties. The orphaned heroine of "The Mourner" has two names, one known to each of her two would-be lovers: Horace Neville, who narrates the story, and Lewis Elmore, to whom she was engaged while her father was alive. Horace's Ellen enacts Mathilda's role as a young woman dying of an unexplained sorrow. Lewis's Clarice Eversham was, with her father, "a matchless example of happiness in the dearest connexion in life, as resulting from the exercise of their reciprocal duties and affections."[25]

Ellen/Clarice assumes that she is responsible for her father's death at sea as they are traveling home from Barbados. In his note to the story, Charles Robinson refers to her as "a parricide," while Emily Sunstein describes her as "a girl whose willfulness led to the drowning of her adored father."[26] But the text tells otherwise:

> The fire on board the St. Mary had raged long and fearfully before the Bellerophon, and boats came off for the rescue of the crew. The women were the first to be embarked; but Clarice clung to her father, and refused to go till he should accompany her. Some fearful presentiment that, if she were saved, he would remain and die, gave such energy to her resolve, that not the entreaties of her father, nor the angry expostulations of the captain, could shake it.

This captain, it is true, "transported with anger by her woman's obstinacy," said to her: "You will cause your father's death—and be as much a parricide as if you put poison into his cut—you are not the first girl who has murdered her father in her wilful mood."

Yet this accusation may be more a reaction to her "woman's obstinacy" in not doing what he tells her to do (that is, leave her father and get on the rescue boat) than in any action she might be construed to have taken. Indeed, she does not act at all:

> The boats returned with difficulty, and only one could contrive to approach; it was nearly full: Lord Eversham and his daughter advanced to the deck's edge to get in. "We can only take one of you," vociferated the sailors: "keep back on your life! throw the girl to us—we will come back for you if we can." Lord Eversham cast with a strong arm his daughter, who had now entirely lost her self-possession, into the boat; she was alive again in a minute, she called to her father, held out her arms to him, and would have thrown herself into the sea, but was held back by the sailors.

Lord Eversham then "contrived to heave a spar overboard, and threw himself into the sea, clinging to it. . . . Clarice saw her father struggling with his fate—battling with the death that at last became the victor." For the rest of the voyage home the other passengers blamed Clarice for this death, and when the ship landed, she disappeared, turning herself into "Ellen."

It is a convoluted logic that would make a daughter responsible for actions her father took, first against her will and then of his own accord. It is, in fact, precisely this logic, which makes children feel responsible for actions of their parents in no way instigated by them, that Shelley is putting under a spotlight in *Mathilda* and "The Mourner." Twentieth-century studies abound of children who feel responsible for parental death, abandonment, and abuse, who interpret avoidable and unavoidable lacunae in attention and care as responses to some inadequacy on the part of the child. What could Clarice have done that would have saved her father and allowed him to save her too? Yet in her own eyes, as well as in the eyes of Shelley's other characters and readers, she is not the perfect daughter, and therefore at fault. Perhaps what is at fault is the ideal of perfect daughterhood against which she is measured, an ideal that prefigures one of perfect wife-and-motherhood in which no self-effacement can be enough.

Shelley returned a third time to the bond between a father and daughter who live apart from "the world" in *Lodore,* the novel she published a year before the death of her father. It is a novel of reconciliation in which Ethel, the heroine, not only survives the intensity of her early devotion to her father but wins over the mother who neglected her in her crucial early years. But the novel also takes up again the thematic concerns of *Frankenstein:* it could be called *Frankenstein* without the science. When we first meet Lord Lodore, he has taken his three-year-old daughter to the wilds of America, where, like Walton, "he could find no friend, tempered like him, like him nursed in the delicacies and fastidiousness of the societies of the old world."[27] He has a sister whose "affections, her future prospects, her ambition, were all centered on him" (42). And he marries, like Victor's father, a woman half his age.

But Lodore has not found, in rural Wales, a compliant Caroline Beaufort. Cornelia Santerre is flirtatious and carelessly provokes a situation where her husband feels compelled to leave England for America to save his honor. Forced to choose between her mother and her husband, Cornelia stays with her mother while Ethel, her daughter, loses a mother when Lodore takes her with him. Ethel suffers, in other words, as much from her father's poor judgment of women, itself a component of the code of masculinity that emphasizes abstract honor over concrete relationships. In case the reader misses the point, Shelley has Lord Lodore killed in a duel with the man he fled England to avoid twelve years earlier. He dies just as he and Ethel are on their way back to England, he having decided that she would be safer in England from "uncultivated" men who want to marry her for the wrong reasons.

Living alone (except for a black woman and her child) in America with her father has given Ethel an opportunity to be the perfect daughter to a man who "drew his chief ideas" about women "from Milton's Eve":

> She had no fears, no deceit, no untold thought within her. Her matchless sweetness of temper prevented any cloud from ever dimming her pure loveliness. . . . Nothing with her was centered in self; she was always ready to give her soul away: to please her father was the unsleeping law of all her actions, while his approbation imparted a sense of such pure but entire happiness, that every other feeling faded into insignificance in comparison. (19–20)

That Ethel goes on to marry the man who was her father's second in this duel, and to bring her stubborn mother around to a delayed experience of the joys of motherhood, cannot simply be read as evidence of Shelley's "psychic need to idealize the bourgeois family," and of the triumph of the "proper lady" over Mary Wollstonecraft's critique of this emerging female ideal. Rather, what Shelley makes clear in *Lodore* is that Ethel's happiness, as a daughter and wife, is predicated on her ability to forgive both her parents, an act that calls into question the very discursive practices that have produced proper ladies and their male protectors.

Forgiveness is the precondition of resolution in *Falkner,* and there is much to forgive in the behavior of its eponymous protagonist. Mathilda's father has sinned in thought, but never in deed, against his daughter, and Lodore is motivated by a concern for his daughter's future, however misguided his practice. But Falkner actually abducts the woman he loves and he compounds this injury by "accidentally" leaving her son behind on the road when he carries her off in a carriage. In his written account of the abduction, he tells of an unsuccessful attempt to get the driver of the coach to stop, but after that he has no further thought of the abandoned boy. Had Shelley aimed to idealize the central actor in the bourgeois family, would she have heaped upon him such gratuitous indifference to its strongest bond?

Falkner, like *Lodore,* concludes on an ostensibly happy note, the same one we find in *Lodore* where two lovers and the erring parent of one of them are drawn back into the circle of "domestic affection." Technically Falkner is not the heroine's father. He adopted Elizabeth Raby after she unwittingly intervened as he was about to commit suicide at the site of her mother's grave. He is thus one of Shelley's middle-aged males who rescue a woman, either as a child or as a much younger but marriageable woman, from a life of "unmerited" poverty. Nevertheless, he is responsible for, if not legally guilty of, the death of Alithea Neville, the mother of Elizabeth's lover, who slipped and drowned trying to get back to her abandoned son. Yet Falkner indeed did abduct her, and subsequently made no attempt to support her efforts to recover her child.

Mary Poovey, in *The Proper Lady,* cautions that Falkner's purely mental "punishment" represents an accommodation to a conservative sexual politics that would not allow women to express either anger or desire directly. "The expression of these unconscionable wishes," she notes, "requires the illusion—though not the reality—of self-effacement. Thus in *Falkner* the punishment of the father is exacted on behalf of the wronged mother, not on behalf of the self" (169). Yet the "self" of the daughter in this novel is not a unitary one. The wish to possess *and* to punish may well be a more inclusive representation of her feelings than either one of these wishes represented alone. Shelley divides these conflicting desires, to idealize and to avenge, between Elizabeth, the beloved daughter, and Gerard, the wronged son.

A jury exonerates Falkner in the novel, but Shelley does not convince her readers of his innocence. Nor, I would argue, is it a failure of the novel that she perceives the contradictions he represents in the ideology of the bourgeois family and does not reconcile its imaginary ideal with the domestic triad in whom she posits closure. It is Elizabeth's equally compelling love for her adopted father and her lover that requires the son to forgive the man who caused his mother's death. It is because Gerard Neville can rise "to her requirement" that even the possibility of happiness can be raised for all three. It is a gesture that undermines, rather than idealizes, the opposition between male and female behavior on which the bourgeois family is built.

I am arguing that these "sentimental" novels of Shelley's are not about idealization at all. Forgiveness is the opposite of punishment, an alternative resolution that depends not upon force but upon language, and upon a full recognition of harm done. Idealization ignores the harm while revenge turns it upon its perpetrator. Both strategies, of course, perpetuate the damage "unto the third and fourth generation." Writing to an audience that is facing, as she did, a period of conservative ascendancy after a burst of radical hope, an audience that sees domestic violence as a cultural, not simply a personal problem, Shelley carried forward the vision of her mother in ways that we are only now in a position to discover.

What she would not do was provide her readers with fictional alternatives to the institution she found so problematic. I think she was too much her father's daughter for that. In *Political Justice,* Godwin argued:

> As long as parents and teachers in general shall fall under the established
> rule, it is clear that politics and modes of government will educate and infect

us all. They poison our minds, before we can resist, or so much as suspect their malignity. Like the barbarous directors of the Eastern seraglios, they will deprive us of our virility and fit us for their despicable employment from the cradle. So false is the opinion that has too generally prevailed, that politics is an affair with which ordinary men have little concern.[28]

The radical reading of Shelley that I am proposing depends on the now-widespread feminist perception of the family as a "mode of government" whose operations affect us all. Political justice in this area will not be possible as long as no one stands apart from "the established rule" and criticizes it as a cultural system rather than a natural phenomenon. Shelley may be the first of our foremothers to do so, and for this we are much in her debt.

Notes

1. Virginia Woolf, *A Room of One's Own* (New York: Harcourt, Brace and World, 1957), 72–73.
2. For a summary of thematic approaches to the novel, see George Levine, "The Ambiguous Heritage of *Frankenstein*," *The Endurance of Frankenstein: Essays on Mary Shelley's Novel,* ed. George Levine and U. C. Knoepflmacher (Berkeley: University of California Press, 1979), 8–17.
3. Anne K. Mellor, *Mary Shelley: Her Life, Her Fiction, Her Monsters* (New York: Methuen, 1988), 178.
4. For a revisionary summary of Shelley's reputation, in her lifetime and subsequently, see Emily W. Sunstein, *Mary Shelley: Romance and Reality* (Boston: Little, Brown, 1988), 387–403.
5. *Mary Shelley's Journal,* ed. Frederick L. Jones (Norman: University of Oklahoma Press, 1947), 204. See also journal entry for October 21, 1838, quoted in Mellor, 179, for a further elaboration of Shelley's political stance.
6. Carol Gilligan, *In a Different Voice: Psychological Theory and Women's Development* (Cambridge, Mass.: Harvard University Press, 1982).
7. Sandra M. Gilbert and Susan Gubar, *The Madwoman in the Attic: The Woman Writer and the Nineteenth-Century Literary Imagination* (New Haven: Yale University Press, 1979), 73.
8. Thomas Gisborne, *An Inquiry into the Duties of the Female Sex* (London, 1797), 12.
9. Mary Wollstonecraft, *Maria or the Wrongs of Woman* (1798; New York: Norton, 1975), 138–39.
10. William Godwin, *St. Leon; A Tale of the Sixteenth Century* (1799; London: Colburn and Bentley, 1835), 101.
11. Mary Shelley, *Frankenstein, or The Modern Prometheus* (London: Oxford University Press, 1971), 124.
12. Mary Shelley, *Valperga: or, the Life and Adventures of Castruccio, Prince of Lucca,* 3 vols. (London: G. and W. B. Whittaker, 1823), 1:194, 198, 199–200.
13. Quoted in William Walling, *Mary Shelley* (New York: Twayne, 1972), 59.
14. Adrienne Rich, *Of Woman Born* (New York: Norton, 1976), 243.
15. Fannie Derham, a minor but important character in *Lodore,* expresses perfectly Shelley's reservations about combining heterosexuality with female indepen-

dence. But she uses this character to criticize the education of daughters within (and for) the bourgeois nuclear family, with its emphasis on female dependence and helplessness. Raised to be independent and self-sufficing rather than the lover and companion of a man, Fanny experiences an "autonomous selfhood" which Ethel, given a "sexual education" by her father, can only admire and which Shelley, educated by Godwin and Mary Jane Clairmont, could not imagine for herself.

16. Jane Austen, *Northanger Abbey,* ed. Anne Ehrenpreis (Harmondsworth: Penguin, 1972), 199.

17. Mary Shelley, *The Last Man,* ed. Hugh Luke, Jr. (Lincoln: University of Nebraska Press, 1965), 66.

18. See Jane Tompkins, *Sensational Designs: The Cultural Work of American Fiction, 1790–1860* (Oxford: Oxford University Press, 1985), 124.

19. Gisborne, *Duties,* 12.

20. Mary Shelley, *Mathilda,* ed. Elizabeth Nitchie (Chapel Hill: University of North Carolina Press, 1959), 2, 4.

21. U. C. Knoepflmacher, "Thoughts on the Aggression of Daughters," in *The Endurance of Frankenstein,* 119.

22. Ivy Pinchbeck and Margaret Hewett, *The Child in English Society, Volume I: From Tudor Times to the Eighteenth Century* (London: Routledge and Kegan Paul, 1969), 305.

23. William Godwin to Mary Wollstonecraft Shelley, 9 Sept. 1819, qtd. in Sunstein, 174.

24. See *Maria Gisborne and Edward E. Williams: Shelley's Friends, Their Letters and Journals,* ed. Frederick L. Jones (Norman: University of Oklahoma Press, 1951), 44; Sunstein, 178; Elizabeth Nitchie, introduction to *Mathilda,* xi.

25. Mary Shelley, *Collected Tales and Stories,* ed. Charles E. Robinson (Baltimore: Johns Hopkins University Press, 1976), 92–93.

26. Shelley, *Tales and Stories,* 379; Sunstein, 299.

27. Mary Shelley, *Lodore* (Brussels, 1835), 14.

28. William Godwin, *Enquiry concerning political justice and its influence on general virtue and happiness,* 2 vols. (London, 1793), 1:50–51.

Mary Shelley in Transit

Esther H. Schor

> The essential purpose of diligent and brave observation of the Other is to clarify the nature and limits of the self. . . .   —Russell Banks

> Everybody always thinks that my career [as a travel writer] has been one long search for self, but I never found it so. . . . Certainly in my case I have been an observer above all.   —Jan Morris

Transit and Transition

In a recent symposium, two contemporary writers give us opposing views that, taken together, suggest an ambiguity at the heart of travel writing.[1] According to Banks, travel writing is a search for the self; "observation of the Other," merely an occasion for exploring and mapping out the inner life. In this autobiographical mode, the voyage out, in the end, is a voyage in. For Morris, however, travel writing is a type of accurate, disinterested reportage; beneath the artfulness of accomplished journalism lurks the guidebook's commercial usefulness.[2] Not surprisingly, travel writing commands a dual readership, linking ever-increasing numbers of travelers with chairbound readers seeking reassurance that in our shrinking world there are yet places difficult of access. Perhaps travel writing endures because its generic ambiguity—one part self-portrait, one part portrait of the other—allows us to be two readers at once: active tourist and contemplative philosopher.

In this essay on Mary Shelley's *Rambles in Germany and Italy, in 1840, 1842, and 1843* (1844), I propose to historicize the generic ambiguity of travel writing, translating from the parochial terms of genre into the broader terms of the history of ideas. I seek not to fix the literary-historical origins of contemporary travel writing—not to send travel writing "home"—but to associate post-Enlightenment writing "in transit" with a particular moment of ideological transition: the turbulent decade of the 1790s. Literary critics have generally thought this decade to have witnessed a transition between so-called Enlightenment values and Romantic ones. Inaugurated by the storming of the Bastille in 1789, issuing in the debacle of the Terror in 1793–94, and culminating in the publication of *Lyrical Ballads* in 1798, the 1790s are often said to trace an arc from revolutionary vision through reactionary disillusionment to Romantic displacement. But by placing Shelley's 1844 *Rambles* in the context of two transitional writings from the 1790s—Wollstonecraft's *Vindication of the Rights of Woman* (1792) and her *Letters from Norway* (1796)—I hope to complicate the notion of ideological transition as a culture's tour among ideas. In both works, Wollstonecraft brings together two complementary discourses of the self—the philosophic and literary discourse of sentimentalism and the discourse of Enlightenment anthropology—that conceptualize the relationship between self and other as dialectical, rather than dualistic. I call these discourses complementary because the former begins with the world of the self, while the latter begins with the world of the other. The generic ambiguity of *Rambles*—and perhaps that of post-Enlightenment travel writing more generally—can be traced directly to Wollstonecraft's dialectical construction of selfhood.

I argue here that Shelley derives from Wollstonecraft's dialectic of selfhood the intellectual framework for an egotism markedly different from that of William Wordsworth and Percy Shelley. By so arguing, I hope to illuminate—and perhaps move beyond—the perennial problem of Mary Shelley's relationship to British Romanticism.[3] Having ceased to be read as a mere satellite to such Romantic luminaries as Percy Shelley and Byron, Mary Shelley has entered the canon and the classroom with *Frankenstein,* as a preeminent critic of Romantic egotism. Shelley's *Rambles,* like many of her post-*Frankenstein* works, demonstrates that this formula oversimplifies both Romantic egotism and Shelley's works. Shelley's lyricism, her aesthetics of the sublime, her nationalism, even her diction and her choice of allusions render any attempt to distance her from Romanticism strained. On the other hand, Shelley and Romanticism alike were conceived during the 1790s; both are children of the Enlightenment. If Shelley is to move beyond her frequent characterization as a critic of Romantic egotism, then we must acknowledge that Romantic egotism is exhausted neither by its idealist manifestations in the work of Percy Shelley nor by Wordsworth's poetic ambition to espouse the whole world in the philosophical *Recluse.* I argue here that Shelley participates in a dialectical strain of Romantic egotism anticipated by Wollstonecraft, in whose works two Enlightenment discourses meet *in transit.*

My insistence on tracing Shelley's *Rambles,* published two years after Queen Victoria's first train ride,[4] to Enlightenment sources may imply a certain nostalgic revivalism on Shelley's part. I would be the last to deny Shelley her nostalgia, but I understand her discursive mode to signal not her resurrection of Enlightenment ideals, but rather her sense of their continuous vitality and availability. That *Rambles* is written during a transitional decade in the history of European social analysis only renders Shelley's ideological eclecticism more emphatic. Shelley, impatient with the developmentalist methods of Enlightenment anthropology, outstrips her Enlightenment paradigms to anticipate the analytic methods of twentieth-century social anthropology. In her ideological eclecticism—and, indeed, her visionary reach—Shelley reminds us that intellectual history is best described not as a tour among ideas, but rather as the sojourning of ideas among us.

Self: "this sensitive, imaginative, native, suffering, enthusiastic pronoun"

In an 1823 essay on the fourteenth-century Florentine historian Giovanni Villani, Shelley comments:

This habit of self-analysation and display has also caused many men of genius to undertake works where the individual feeling of the author embues the whole subject with a peculiar hue. . . . Such persons turn to the human heart as the undiscovered country. They visit and revisit their own; endeavour to understand its workings, to fathom its depths, and to leave no lurking thought or disguised feeling in the hiding places where so many thoughts and feelings, for fear of shocking the tender consciences of those inexpert in the task of self-examination, delight to seclude themselves. As a help to the science of self-knowledge, and also as a continuance of it, they wish to study the minds of others, and particularly of those of the greatest merit. The sight of land was not more welcome to Columbus, than are these traces of individual feeling, chequering their more formal works of art, to the voyagers in the noblest of terrae incognitae, the soul of man. . . . Half the beauty of Lady Mary Montagu's Letters consists in the *I* that adorns them; and this *I,* this sensitive, imaginative, native, suffering, enthusiastic pronoun, spreads an inexpressible charm over Mary Wollstonecraft's Letters from Norway.[5]

In an essay written only a few months after Percy Shelley's death, it is striking that Shelley declines to model her egotist on the Shelleyan figure of the lyric poet. Nor does she select the Wordsworthian poet returning to the banks of the Wye, nor even the Byronic figure of the melancholic wanderer. Instead, she chooses Columbus, linking the Renaissance voyage of discovery with the Enlightenment study of humanity. To speak of the heart as "the undiscovered country" and the soul as "terra incognita" is to understand the ego as alien to itself. Egotism, for Shelley, is a remedy for self-alienation; not a stance so much as a process; not a positive position so much as a condition of capable negativity whose telos is "self-knowledge." While the sight of land may have delighted Columbus, it did not satisfy him; similarly, after sighting the foreign places within, the egotistical voyager "visits and revisits" them. A process of writerly sounding and fathoming, egotism entails dangers, for enlightenment may be had only by probing the dark and secluded places where fugitive thoughts and feelings abide. While Shelley's essay sounds at such moments like a eulogy for her late husband, it stands firmly to one side of the radical idealism with which his egotism is interwoven, preferring literary modes in which the self's journeys entail encounters with the other. Perhaps for this reason, Shelley's egotistical bibliography in this essay consists largely of sentimental sources, in which the self is most keenly gauged in terms of its responsiveness.[6] This "science of self-knowledge," according to Shelley, is both aided and continued by the study of others, whether they are the "best and wisest" or simply those who "artlessly and truly [portray]" human feelings. From Shelley's figure of egotism as a sentimental journey emerges a recognition of travel writing as an exploration of the self through an encounter with the other. Not surprisingly, the final works she cites are travel books by two eighteenth-century travelers: Lady Mary Wortley Montagu and Mary Wollstonecraft.

This allusion to Wollstonecraft's *Letters* is one of several in Mary Shelley's writings. As Mary Wollstonecraft Godwin, she took the book on her elopement journey; her *History of a Six Weeks' Tour* (1817) finds her reading it aloud with Percy Shelley on the eve of her seventeenth birthday.[7] And what could be more appropriate than a birthday reading of Wollstonecraft's *Letters,* a crucial pretext not only for Shelley's travel writing, but also, if Godwin's *Memoirs of the Author of "The Rights of Woman"* are to be trusted, for Shelley herself:

> The narrative of this voyage is before the world, and perhaps a book of travels that so irresistably seizes on the heart, never, in any other instance, found its way from the press. . . . If ever there was a book calculated to make a man in love with its author, this appears to me to be the book. She speaks of her sorrows, in a way that fills us with melancholy, and dissolves us in tenderness, at the same time that she displays a genius which commands all our admiration. Affliction had tempered her heart to a softness almost more than human; and the gentleness of her spirit seems precisely to accord with all the romance of unbounded attachment.[8]

Godwin's own effusive reading identifies Wollstonecraft as a prototypical heroine of sensibility: his responsive sympathies—the filled, dissolving, even ravished heart—testify to the intensity of her own. Though he focuses on her responsiveness, Godwin virtually ignores Wollstonecraft's detailed, informed, and sympathetic responses to the places and people she visits; he simply nods to "a genius which commands all our admiration."

And yet even the ravished Godwin cannot ignore the "calculated" quality of Wollstonecraft's persona. Indeed, Wollstonecraft's advertisement notes that her sentimental persona has a professional calculus; it is intended to gain an attentive audience for a female writer's opinions and reflections:[9]

> In writing these desultory letters, I found I could not avoid being continually the first person—the "little hero of each tale." I tried to correct this fault, if it be one, for they were designed for publication; but in proportion as I arranged my thoughts, my letter, I found, became stiff and affected: I, therefore, determined to let my remarks and reflections flow unrestrained. . . .
>
> A person has a right, I have sometimes thought, when amused by a witty or interesting egotist, to talk of himself when he can win on our attention by acquiring our affection.[10]

Just as Wollstonecraft fetishizes her rationalism in the *Vindication* in order to gain a hearing for her impassioned polemic, she here represents her social, political, and economic observations as the effusions of sensibility in order to "win on" her audience's attention. In order to gain sympathy for her analytic reportage and reasoned opinions, Wollstonecraft adopts a diminutive ("little hero"), feminine persona derived from sentimental fiction. Shaping her journey into discrete "tales," she installs herself as heroine to provide her audience with a focus, apologizing for the lubricity of her "impressions." Accordingly, Wollstonecraft calls on her reader to be a more receptive addressee than the fickle and acquisitive Imlay, her lover and dispatcher. Hence, to connect her reader with the world of the other, Wollstonecraft adopts not one, but two personae: one modeled on the rationalist rhetoric of the *Vindication,* and another modeled on such heroines of sensibility as her own Maria.

Like Wollstonecraft *Letters,* Shelley's *Rambles* triangulates the relations between the self and its two counterparts: the reader, and world of the other. Unlike Wollstonecraft, however, Shelley's persona accommodates both rationalism and sensibility by balancing two senses of the term "sympathy": the sympathy of emotional accord, and the sympathy of political inclination.[11] From the start, Shelley cultivates the reader as an intimate, preferring that her book be a companion, rather than a guide:

> I have found it a pleasant thing while travelling to have in the carriage the works of those who have passed through the same country. Sometimes they inform, sometimes they excite curiosity. If alone, they serve as society; if with others, they suggest matter for conversation.[12]

For Shelley, sympathy is a promoter of civil society but, more importantly, of enlightenment: "knowledge, to enlighten and free the mind from clinging, deadening prejudices—a wider circle of sympathy with our fellow-creatures;— these are the uses of travel" (1:158). While Shelley claims that the knowledge gained in travel enlightens the traveler, the enlightening "uses" of travel are available only to those who have "broken the chain" of confinement *intellectually* as well as physically; the physical act of traveling allegorizes a mental journey. Satirizing a snobbish, philistine young Englishman at a Swiss inn, Shelley focuses both on the tourist's superficiality and on his imperviousness:

> He was *doing* his Saxon Switzerland; he had *done* his Italy, his Sicily; he had *done* his sunrise on Mt. Etna; and when he should have *done* his Germany, he would return to England to show how destitute a traveller may be of all impression and knowledge, when they are unable to knit themselves in soul to nature, nor are capacitated by talents or acquirements to gain knowledge from what they see. We must become part of the scenes around us, and they must mingle and become a portion of us. (1:265)

Shelley's ethic of travel maintains that only when travel is an affair of the body *and* the mind does it become a matter for the heart; the failure to sympathize indicates a homebound mind. Through the companionable and sympathetic Shelley, the reader is asked to sympathize not only with the abused and maligned Italian populace, but also with an explicit politics of Italian emancipation from foreign powers and native despots.[13]

Because the fate of her polemic lies with her ability to arouse her readers' sympathies, Shelley's descriptions of landscape are expressly designed to exercise her reader's sympathetic imagination. Instead of exploiting description to portray her own sensibility, Shelley assimilates description to the discourse of companionship.[14] She seeks, in her own words, a type of descriptive language that eschews

> a vagueness and a sameness that conveys no distinct ideas. . . . [U]nless you can be placed beside us in our rough-hewn boat, and glide down between the vine-covered hills, with bare, craggy heights towering above; now catching with glad curiosity the first glimpse of a more beautiful bend of the river, a higher mountain peak, a more romantic ruin; now looking back to gaze as long as possible on some picturesque point of view, of which, as the boat

floated down but slightly assisted by the rowers, we lost sight forever—
unless you can imagine and sympathise in the cheerful elasticity of the
setting out at morning sharpened into hunger at noon, and the pleasure that
attended the rustic fare we could command . . . ; then, the quiet enjoyment
of golden evening, succeeded by still and gray twilight; and last, the lassi-
tude, the fatigue, which made us look eagerly out for the place where we
were to stop and repose:—there is a zest in all this . . . and a great sense of
novelty, which is lost in mere words:—you must do your part, and feel and
imagine, or all description proves tame and useless. (1:23–24)

Shelley's meandering, periodic sentence, shaped by anaphora and punctuated
by brief, participial phrases, conveys the rhythm, pace, and mood of this
journey down the Rhine. Calling on all five senses—sight, hearing, touch,
taste, and smell—this lingering description attempts to break through the
pictorialism of the picturesque,[15] evoking neither words nor pictures, so much
as the physical sensations of the journey and an ineffable sense of leisure. In
the first of these long clauses (beginning "Unless you can be placed beside
us") the perceiving subject commands one vista ahead and another behind,
while at the same time responding to a rapid succession of random impressions. The second clause (beginning "unless you can imagine") restructures
the journey chronologically, tracing a temporal progression from morning to
noon to evening.

Shelley would return to this descriptive strategy in her expansive description of the mountains near Cadenabbia:

When I rise in the morning and look out, our own side is bathed in sunshine,
and we see the opposite mountains raising their black masses in sharp relief
against the eastern sky, while dark shadows are flung by the abrupt preci-
pices on the fair lake beneath. This very scene glows in sunshine later in the
day, till at evening the shadows climb up, first darkening the banks, and
slowly ascending till they leave exposed the naked summits alone, which are
long gladdened by the golden radiance of the sinking sun, till the bright rays
disappear, and, cold and gray, the granite peaks stand pointing to the stars,
which one by one gather above. (1:67–68)

Instead of arranging her description spatially and pictorially, Shelley renders
the scene temporally, lyrically. With the arc of the sun, the reader's emotions
rise and sink; the penultimate "gladdening" of the mountaintops finishes
"cold and gray." By the end of the passage, the obscured peaks have become
mere indicators of the remote, yet surpassing, radiance of the stars. Thus, the
most lyrical passages of *Rambles* display the self in the service of a particular
political agenda: the reader's sympathies, trained in the textual landscape by
the example of Shelley's sympathies, can be trained as well toward the social
landscape of Italy.

Just as social and generic pressures together inform Shelley's lyrical poetics of landscape, they mutually inform the shape of her narrative. Wollstonecraft, identifying herself as the "little hero of every tale," emphasizes the
episodic, picaresque quality of her journey, aligning it with such sentimental

journeys as Sterne's and Smollett's. Shelley, on the other hand, emphasizes the questlike trajectory of her journeys, both of which, taking Germany as a way station and Italy as a destination, retrace the familiar itinerary of the grand tour.[16] But Shelley, favoring contemporary Italy and its timeless landscape over the neoclassical values of grand-tourism, does not quest after the sources of a now-decadent civilization; hers is a Romantic quest, internal and spiritual:

> All Italian travellers know what it is, after toiling up the bleak, bare, northern Swiss side of an Alp, to descend towards ever-vernal Italy. The rhododendrons, in thick bushes, in full bloom, first adorned the mountain sides; then, pine forests; then, chestnut groves; the mountain was cleft into woody ravines; the waterfalls scattered their spray and their gracious melody; flowery and green and clothed in radiance, and gifted with plenty, Italy opened upon us. Thus . . . after dreary old age and the sickening pass of death, does the saint open his eyes on Paradise. (1:60)

Like the saint crossing through "the sickening pass of death," Shelley quests after the transcendence of her personal martyrdom in Italy. What her quest ultimately achieves, however, is neither the pastoral transcendence of an earthly paradise, nor a "paradise within," but a transcendence entailed in a discovery of the self within the other. In Shelley's travels, the internalized Romantic quest is wedded to the ethos of sentimental response; the questing self first endures a negative phase of deflection and disappointment that prepares it to discern sympathetically its own image anew in another. Hence, the psychological trajectory of *Rambles* traces not a quest so much as an antiquest. Shelley's first journey (1840) implicates her in a dark parody of a deliverance from the burdens of selfhood, while her second (1842–43) circuitously arrives at redemption by way of the romance motif of the false cure.

Returning to Italy in 1840 for the first time since her departure in 1823, Shelley is initially buoyed with anticipation. After "years of desolate solitude, and hard struggle with the world" (1:2) she celebrates the breaking of "a chain that had long held me" (1:3); on leaving Paris, she declares, "I feel a good deal of the gipsy coming upon me" (1:9). Travel, Shelley observes, affords the self an unprecedented autonomy, a loss of "all sense of caste":

> In society you are weighed with others according to your extrinsic possessions; your income, your connexions, your position make all the weight— you yourself are a mere feather in the scale. But what are these to me now? My home is the readiest means of conveyance I can command, or the inn at which I shall remain at night—my only acquaintance the companions of my wanderings—the single business of my life to enjoy the passing scene. (1:10)

Shortly, however, freedom, classlessness, and leisure evoke an array of anxieties. Though maintaining a lively pace, she muses on the "restless agony" (1:31) of medieval women, whose feudal occupations were "to hope, to fear, to pray, and to embroider" (1:30). Smitten with a desire to remain at Baden-Baden, she reflects on her perversity:

> How seldom do human wishes flow smoothly towards their object. . . .
> [W]hen all is smooth and free for their accomplishment, then they shrink
> and are frightened. . . . We fear treachery on the part of fate. . . . With
> regard to the feelings that hold my wishes in check when I think of Italy—,
> these are all founded on fear. Those I loved had died there—would it again
> prove fatal, and do I only please my fancy to destroy my last hope? (1:37)

For Shelley, returning to the place where her two children, husband, and even her own youth had died, Italy is more urgently a place of fatal treachery than of redemption. In part, her anxieties are focused on her son Percy's determination to go boating on Lake Como; for her, water is "the antipathetic" (1:157), even "fatal" element. But her anxieties express themselves more subtly in a sense of her own inauthenticity, and a corollary fascination with the talismanic power of objects.

At the first sight of Italian curtains and "wash-hand stands":

> Strange and indescribable emotions invaded me, recollections long forgot-
> ten, arose fresh and strong by mere force of association, produced by those
> objects being presented to my eye, inspiring a mixture of pleasure and pain,
> almost amounting to agony. (1:61)

"Invaded" by emotions and recollections prompted by these objects, Shelley submits to their haunting influence. A more elaborate version of this phenomenon occurs as Shelley returns to Villa Diodati, where she, Percy Shelley, and Byron sojourned during the fateful summer of 1816:

> There were the terraces, the vineyards, the upward path threading them, the
> little port where our boat lay moored; I could mark and recognise a thou-
> sand slight peculiarities, familiar objects then—forgotten since—now re-
> plete with recollections and associations. Was I the same person who had
> lived there, the companion of the dead? For all were gone: even my young
> child, whom I had looked upon as the joy of future years, had died in
> infancy—not one hope, then in fair bud, had opened into maturity; storm,
> and blight, and death, had passed over, and destroyed all. While yet very
> young, I had reached the position of an aged person, driven back on mem-
> ory for companionship with the beloved; and now I looked on the inanimate
> objects that had surrounded me, which survived, the same in aspect as then,
> to feel that all my life since was but an unreal phantasmagoria—the shades
> that gathered round that scene were the realities—the substance and truth.
> (1:140–41)

Once again, Shelley's inventory of familiar objects evokes an agonizing train of recollections. Crucially, she counts her youthful self among fate's casualties; while memory renders her a "companion of the dead," a former self also lies among them. Her own existence becomes solipsistic, inauthentic, "an unreal phantasmagoria," her own reality wholly absorbed in the objects she perceives.

On returning to Venice, the site of her infant daughter's death, during her 1842–43 journey, Shelley theorizes this phenomenon as follows:

> Holcroft . . . alludes to the notice the soul takes of the objects presented to the eye in its hour of agony, as a relief afforded by nature to permit the nerves to endure pain. . . . I have experienced it; and the particular shape of a room—the progress of shadows on a wall—the peculiar flickering of trees—the exact succession of objects on a journey—have been indelibly engraved in my memory, as marked in, and associated with, hours and minutes when the nerves were strung to their utmost tension by the endurance of pain, or the far severer infliction of mental anguish. Thus the banks of the Brenta presented to me a moving scene; not a palace, not a tree of which I did not recognise, as marked and recorded, at a moment when life and death hung upon our speedy arrival at Venice. (2:78–79)

Shelley theorizes this "marking" or "recording," following Holcroft, as a saving diversion of the mind from severe physical or psychological trauma—what Freud called a "screen memory." But her theory of "marking" or "recording" fails to account for the traumatic repetition of the losses which these objects have become charged with suppressing. Nor does it account for the propensity for objects at Cadenabbia and Diodati—objects unconnected with the soul's "hour of agony"—to induce a similarly traumatic disorientation. In these scenes of return, Shelley spontaneously repeats the traumatic loss of self which she associates with her extended sojourn in Italy.[17]

At Cadenabbia, her radical disorientation is signaled parabolically in a confrontation with a madman, an incident she narrates in exquisite and unaccustomed detail. A young Englishman in the throes of paranoid delusions arrives at Cadenabbia, brandishing a pistol; asked to reason with him, Shelley fears yet sympathizes with "the miserable wanderings of his mind" (1:72). Bilingual, like Shelley herself, he ingratiates himself with the English; turning to the Italian innkeeper, he disparages his compatriots in Italian. For fear of being poisoned, he has not eaten in days. Finally the man is taken captive, allowing Shelley to reduce the incident to a comic vignette, but she seems haunted by the specter of an emaciated, prematurely old expatriate Englishman with a ruined mind. As he departs by boat, she fixes him with her eye: "he was a spare man, with an adust, withered face and unquiet eye" (1:73). Like the other "marked" objects in which she loses herself—Italian washstands, the terraces of Diodati, the palaces along the Brenta—the madman's face haunts Shelley with a vision (afterimage or premonition?) of her own demise. In short, Shelley's first return to Italy demands indeed that she traverse "the sickening pass of death," delivering her not to paradise, but to a haunting, posthumous existence.

If Shelley's first journey demonically parodies the quest-romance, her second journey redeems the romance motif of the false cure:

> I suffer in my health, and can no longer apply to my ordinary employments. Travelling is occupation as well as amusement, and I firmly believe that renewed health will be the result of frequent change of place. (1:158)

Suffering from fatigue and headaches—the first symptoms of what would prove a fatal brain tumor—Shelley seeks out the curative waters of Kissingen, Brukenau, and Toplitz. Soon after arriving in Kissingen, Shelley voices an anxious reluctance to count herself among the ill:

> The morning walk I find pleasant: I leave the gardens after each glass, and stroll beyond into the meadows bordering the Saale, away from the garish spectacle of the smart toilettes, and the saddening sight of the sick. (1:185)

As for her youthful companions, "it is rather an infliction . . . to live, as they say, surrounded by *lepers*" (1:188) in this "dim limbo" (1:195). On entering the baths, Shelley is unnerved to find them "mere wooden coffins" (1:188). Among the curative waters of Bavaria, the face of death seems to float before her: in a convent, she pauses before a series of paintings representing death "as coming upon men and women at all moments, during every occupation . . . the Mother fostering her first-born—the Bride, proud in her husband" (1:209).

By and large, however, Shelley displaces her fear of death onto the arbitrary and repressive medicinal regime of the *"cur."* As the *"cur"* progresses, her anger and resentment mount. According to Shelley, red meat, pork, fruit, salad, butter, tea, coffee, and milk, as well as excitement, dancing, gambling, parties, and even intellectual exercise are all proscribed. At times, frustration modulates into sparkling social satire; Shelley shrewdly intuits that this medicinal regime is instituted and maintained by the king of Bavaria, who fears a loss of tourism should his enfeebled visitors expire from overexertion. "Kissingen will not be perfect," she comments ironically, "until the post is put under medical surveillance."

Surveillance, regime, tyranny; for all its wryness, Shelley's politics of the false cure of Kissingen launches the central concerns of her second journey: the tyranny of Austrian and French imperialism, and the abuses of papal and priestly authority. Like the cowed, enfeebled patients of Kissingen, the Bohemians "bear the marks of a conquered people. . . . They remember that they were once free" (2:16–17). The journey through the Tyrol evokes a detailed narrative of Hofer's "glorious struggle" against the French forces in 1809; arriving in Italian-speaking Trent, she revels in being "restored to the privilege of speech" which returns her to human contact. Even the extraordinary beauty of Styria fails to tempt her away from her newfound focus on society and politics: "What a summer might here be spent!—what a life, I would say . . . were it not a dream that we can be happy only in the contemplation of nature, removed from all intercourse with our equals" (2:33).

In Venice, Shelley finds "the little roots, generated by sympathy and enjoyment, begin to strike out" (2:123). This reaching for depths would be played out not in the heart, but in the heartland, as Shelley makes her way south: "We left the abrupt, gloomy, sublime north, and gently dropped down to truly Italian scenes" (2:72). For Shelley, once a dweller in Pisa and Livorno and, more recently, a sojourner at Lake Como, the essential Italy has become the Italy of the south: arriving in Naples, she dismisses Tuscany and Lombardy as "an improved France, an abundant, sunshiny England" (2:262). Just as Wollstonecraft had yearned to travel north beyond Christiania (Oslo), Shelley voices "a great desire to penetrate into the south of Italy" (2:280), beyond Naples and Sorrento to Calabria. Only south of Naples do the "undiscovered country" of the heart and of Italy become one and the same. From Amalfi, she travels in from the coast, to encounter "a torrent whose 'inland murmur' . . . was grateful to our ears, long accustomed only to the roaring of the surges of the sea." Coming upon the " 'inland murmur' " of her own heart, Shelley discovers near Amalfi the curative waters that had eluded her in Germany.

Other: "the state of Italy and the Italians"

Let us consider two metaphors, one from Wollstonecraft's *Vindication,* one from Shelley's *Rambles.* Wollstonecraft's argument against the existence of what she calls a "sexual character"—the identification of a specific set of traits with women's biologically determined sex—is driven by an insistence on the formative power of environment. In one of several provocative analogies, Wollstonecraft likens the situation of women to that of the aristocracy:

> For if, excepting warriors, no great men of any denomination have ever appeared amongst the nobility, may it not be fairly inferred that their local situation swallowed up the man, and produced a character similar to that of women, who are *localized*—if I may be allowed the word—by the rank they are placed in by courtesy?[18]

"Localization" isolates women from intellectual argument and controversy, yet at the same time prevents them from enjoying the "solitude and reflection" on which "great resolves are built" (*VRW,* 149). Calling for a "revolution in female manners," Wollstonecraft declares that "It is time to separate unchanging morals from local manners" (*VRW,* 132).

To speak of an oppressive and degrading culture as the "localiztion" of women is to imagine the reformation of culture as the relocation of women from one political "place" to another. Relocation—or, in other words, locomotion: "[T]he unfortunate victims to [hereditary property]—if I may so express myself—swathed from their birth, seldom exert the locomotive faculty [of] body [or] mind" (*VRW,* 253). Localization, it would seem, is not simply a metaphor, for the swaddling clothes of culture—the "drapery of situation"— binds both body and mind. In the latter chapters of the *Vindication,* Wollstonecraft urges physical training for girls, and the widening of women's (even mothers' and wives') options for useful employments outside the home. It is not difficult to see in Wollstonecraft's *Vindication* a license for the vigorous relocations and locomotions—in other words, *travels*—of women in the coming century.

A second metaphor. In the preface to *Rambles,* Shelley remarks:

> Time was, when travels in Italy were filled with contemptuous censures of the effeminacy of the Italians—diatribes against the vice and cowardice of

the nobles—sneers at the courtly verses of the poets, who were content to celebrate a marriage or a birth among the great . . . [C]ontempt was the general tone. (1:ix–x)

In the heyday of grand tourism, the Italians undoubtedly appeared to British eyes as lamentable blots on the landscape of ruins; at its best, Italian poverty could be counted on to enhance the aesthetic of the picturesque. The British habitually associated the Italians' political weakness with a variety of negative traits—"superstition, luxury, servility, indolence, violence, vice" (1:x)—which, as Shelley notes in using the term "effeminacy," subtly eroticizes power relations between the imperial British and the subject Italians. Shelley offers not to debate these characteristics of the Italians so much as to provide an alternative account of them, to *represent* them differently:

[Italy] is struggling with~its fetters,—not only with the material ones that weigh on it so heavily, and which they endure with a keen sense of shame, but with those that have entered into and bind the soul. (1:x)

These mental fetters parallel those which Wollstonecraft finds women wearing even (or, if we follow her argument closely, especially) at the highest social echelons. When Shelley urges the English to "sympathise" with, not pity, the Italians, she is urging a new and unaccustomed regard for them as peers. Just as Wollstonecraft urges "a civil existence in the State" (*VRW*, 262) for women, Shelley's discussion of the "state of Italy and the Italians" expresses a utopian belief in the necessity of a civil existence for an Italian state in Europe. If Wollstonecraft's *Vindication* licenses the "rambles of woman," Shelley's *Rambles* offers a "vindication of the rights of Italians."

Despite the generic difference between Wollstonecraft's political treatise and Shelley's travel book, these complementary figures of "localization" and "effeminacy" suggest a striking confluence of currents. Both writers attribute a situation of oppressive and degrading power relations to the influence of culture. Both analyze culture (in Shelley's case, contemporary *and* historical) in order to polemicize against the so-called naturalness of a certain cluster of unproductive or immoral traits; both maintain that a reformation of culture is necessary to reform oppressive and degrading power relations. Finally, while eschewing violence, both writers envision reformation in revolutionary terms, foreseeing an "other" culture in which the most basic social and political institutions are radically transformed.

Before pursuing Shelley's debt to Wollstonecraft in her discourse of the "other"—as well as her striking departures from Wollstonecraft—it will be helpful to place both analyses in the general context of eighteenth- and nineteenth-century social inquiry. In several important ways, Wollstonecraft's *Vindication* is rooted in the assumption of what is often referred to as "Enlightenment anthropology."[19] First, as Alan Bewell notes, Enlightenment study of so-called primitive cultures occurs under the aegis of moral philosophy; such inquiry offers, among other things, speculative developmental accounts of social institutions and concludes by postulating ethical principles derived from these accounts.[20] Second, according to historian of ethnology Fred Voget, Enlightenment developmentalism is teleological in orientation:

> The [Enlightenment] idea of progress provided the intellectual stimulus for the view that human society began with a stage of savagery, advanced to barbarism, and then achieved the final threshold of civilized development. Through the exercise of reason in accordance with laws governing mental processes, human beings gradually accumulated a greater store of knowledge and utilized this organized experience to advance their social life and to realize the true human potential.[21]

As Bewell puts it, the "other" is examined as a "monument" of human history; the study of "savage" and "barbaric" cultures, conducted largely over travel narratives or by observing natives brought to Europe by commercial travelers, is intended to produce an archaeology of civilization. Thus inquiry about ancient or barbaric institutions assists inquiry about civilized ones; where civilization is defined as the self, inquiry about the other is inquiry about the self.

Wollstonecraft's relationship to the discourse of Enlightenment anthropology is complex. On the one hand, she endorses its central values: rationalist progressivism, and the use of social inquiry to promote and inculcate moral virtue. She frames her argument as an attempt "to prove that the prevailing notion regarding a sexual character was subversive of morality" (*VRW,* 87); she intends to illuminate both the rights *and* duties of women. Civilization is, for Wollstonecraft, a desirable, perhaps perfectible, state; attacking Rousseau, she writes, "to assert that a state of nature is preferable to civilization, in all its possible perfection is, in other words, to arraign supreme wisdom" (*VRW,* 93). Through much of the *Vindication,* Wollstonecraft holds up the male-dominated state as a perfectible, if imperfect, model of civilization in which women, too, "must have a civil existence." (To judge from her dedication to Talleyrand, France in 1791 enjoys a more advanced state of civilization than Britain.) With additional and deserved rights and a change in "the prevailing notion of a sexual character," women would be enabled to enjoy the ripest fruits of civilization—provided they exercise their reason, will, and imagination, and fulfill their moral obligations.

On the other hand, Wollstonecraft lays the blame for female degradation with time-honored practices, mores, and values of this same civilization; moreover, the perpetuation of such practices endangers the health of the body politic:

> I think the female world oppressed; yet the gangrene, which the vices engendered by oppression have produced, is not confined to the morbid part, but pervades society at large. (*VRW,* 299)

Under this description, society itself is moribund, decadent, dysfunctional—in a word, *uncivilized.* When the limbs on the body politic are gangrenous, that body can hardly be deemed the telos of development. Only by framing the problem in this way does Wollstonecraft manage her most signal departure from Enlightenment anthropology—examining critically a society that is not only contemporary and European, but *her own:* "I shall not go back to the remote annals of antiquity to trace the history of woman; it is sufficient to allow that she has always been either a slave or a despot, and to remark that each of these situations equally retards the progress of reason" (*VRW,* 144). More specifically, Wollstonecraft examines the position—and the positioning—of women in her society, a group of which she herself is a member. In choosing as her subject *the other who is already the self,* Wollstonecraft introduces a radical self-criticism into the agenda of Enlightenment anthropology.

Following on from this consideration of Wollstonecraft's *Vindication,* I propose to triage Shelley's discourse of the other, considering, first, Enlightenment values she inherits through Wollstonecraft and others; second, values— and methods—that emerge from Wollstonecraft's critique of Enlightenment social inquiry; and third, methods that anticipate nineteenth- and twentieth-century developments in the social sciences.

Shelley is most truly a daughter of the Enlightenment in her equation of moral virtue with Enlightenment itself. Here is Shelley on Luther: "[Luther's] name is rendered sacred by his struggle the most fearful human life presents, with antique misbeliefs and errors upheld by authority" (1:208–9). Once Luther can be called a *philosophe,* the project of Enlightenment has become synonymous with the inculcation of moral virtue. It is this sort of equation that prompts Shelley's observation that "the root of the evil rests in the absence of education and civilisation" (1:100). Visiting a primary school in Venice, Shelley advocates the education of "the multitude":[22]

> [T]he most extensive advantages must result to the cause of civilisation from the enlightenment, however partial and slight, of the multitude. Knowledge must, from its nature, grow, and rooting it out alone can prevent its tendency to spread. (1:121)

Education, by instilling knowledge as well as inculcating rationalism and discipline, promises to advance the material condition of Italian life. Just as Wollstonecraft advocates raising degraded women to the level of civilized men, Shelley's developmentalism entails a political gradualism that will raise "the low to the level of the high":

> The blessing which the world now needs is the steady progress of civilisation: freedom, by degrees, it will have, I believe. Meanwhile, as the fruits of liberty, we wish to perceive the tendency of the low to rise to the level of the high—not the high to be dragged down to the low. This, we are told by many, is the inevitable tendency of equality of means and privileges. I will hope not; for on that hope is built every endeavour to banish ignorance, and hard labour and penury, from political society. (1:143–44)

In several important ways, however, Shelley follows Wollstonecraft's departures from Enlightenment anthropology. Like Wollstonecraft, Shelley focuses on a contemporary European culture. Just as Wollstonecraft insists that the degradation of women extends to all classes,[23] Shelley insists that the aristocratic Venetians and Lombards, the bourgeois Tuscans, and the impoverished Sorrentines alike are degraded; where literal hunger is not felt, a "hunger of the mind" (2:185) gnaws. Furthermore, Shelley follows Wollstonecraft's example in arguing that the faults and vices of the Italians are not natural but are rather (to borrow Wollstonecraft's words) "the natural consequence of their education and station in society" (*VRW,* 319):

> The more I see of the inhabitants of this country, the more I feel convinced that they are highly gifted with intellectual powers, and possess all the elements of greatness. They are made to be a free, active inquiring people. But they must cast away their *dolce far niente.* They must learn to practise the severer virtues; their youth must be brought up in more hardy and manly habits; they must tread to earth the vices that cling to them as the ivy around their ruins. They must do this to be free; yet without freedom how can they? . . . Their faults are many—the faults of the oppressed—love of pleasure, disregard of truth, indolence, and violence of temper. But their falsehood is on the surface—it is not deceit. Under free institutions, and where the acquirement of knowledge is not as now a mark inviting oppression and wrong, their love of pleasure were readily ennobled into intellectual activity. (1:86–87)

Under the rubric of the Italians' putative "effeminacy," Shelley names many of the same vices that Wollstonecraft attributes to women—indolence, secretiveness, mendacity, superstition, unreason, lack of discipline.[24] Just as Wollstonecraft exposes a societal scheme of dominance and degradation that describes itself as a natural (sexual) difference, Shelley reveals the ethnic bias implicit in British stereotypes of the Italians. Taken together, British and Austrian disdain for the Italians bespeaks an ethos of northern superiority triumphing over southern inferiority; Shelley unmasks this disdain as part of an entrenched, tyrannical system of political and economic exploitation.

Finally, like Wollstonecraft, Shelley whets her gradualism with an anxious revolutionary vision. While the preface censures the apocalyptic violence of the Carbonari—"Cannot it be that peaceful mediation and a strong universal sense of justice may interpose, instead of the cannon and bayonet?" (1:xiii)—Shelley frequently voices a revolutionary impatience:

> For the present governments of Italy know that there is a spirit abroad in that country, which forces every Italian that thinks and feels, to hate [the Austrians] and rebel in his heart. (1:123)

> It cannot be expected that Italy should be able to liberate itself in a time of lethargic peace like the present. (2:260)

> The present affords no glimmering light by which we may perceive how the regeneration of Italy will be effected. . . . Yet the hour must and will come. (2:261)

> At present the spirit of revolt is checked, but not quelled in the pontifical states. A volcanic fire smoulders near the surface, ready at every moment to

burst forth in a flame. The whole of the country before disturbed, the
Marches, Romagna, the four legations, together with the population of the
mountains, are bound together by secret associations, and wait impatiently
for the favourable moment when to break their chains. (2:258)

[O]ut of Rome the cry has been loud, and will be repeated again and again.
(2:247)

In part, Shelley contains this impulse by representing Italian nationalism not
as a violent, revolutionary movement, but as a movement toward enlightened, peaceful restoration: "[The Italians'] habits, fostered by the governments, alone are degraded and degrading; alter these, and the country of
Dante and Michel Angelo and Raphael still exists" (1:87). Where the grand
tourist had viewed contemporary Italy as the ruin of ancient Rome, Shelley
emphasizes the genealogical link between the Italians and their illustrious
Renaissance forebears. For Shelley, the dream of an Italian state is nothing
less than the dream of restoring "man's lost state in this country" (1:97). In
this dream of restoration—of a renaissance of the Renaissance—Shelley
builds on and exceeds Wollstonecraft's bold critique of the Enlightenment.
Whereas Enlightenment anthropology aims to colonize the other for the imperial self, Wollstonecraft critically addresses an other that is also the self. And
through Wollstonecraft, Shelley is empowered to envision the selfhood of the
other—to envision the liberating transformation of the other *into an autonomous self.*

Columbus in Sorrento

Written during the mid-1840s, *Rambles* coincides with the emergence of
Comtean sociology and its emphasis on developmentalist study of contemporary Western culture. Comte's *Positive Philosophy* (1830–42) systematizes
developmentalism, calling for the discovery of "laws which regulat[e] societal
continuity and the course of human advancement."[25] Following the turbulent
events of 1848, the urgency of Comte's positivism came to rest in a scientistic
politics of progressive reform. The mid-1840s, however, find Shelley chafing
against the methodological tautologies of developmentalism. Writing on the
eve of the emergence of evolutionary social theory, Shelley appears to glimpse
two major developments that would ensue on the demise of Social Darwin-
ism: historical interactionism, which arises with the ascendancy of Franz Boas
during the final decade of the nineteenth century; and holistic structural-
functionalism, the brainchild of Radcliffe-Brown and Malinowski, which
came into influence in the 1920s, 1930s, and 1940s.

Historical interactionism, supplanting what Voget calls "the psychogenic
'history' of the evolutionists" with "a verified [and verifiable] 'scientific history' " focuses "on specific cultures and their mutual interconnections and
unique environmental adaptations in place of the philosophic study of culture-
in-general."[26] While Shelley's developmentalism may at times suggest a "psy-

chogenic historicism," her methodology, on the contrary, bespeaks a scientific historicism: "Must we not seek in [the Italians'] political history for the causes wherefore superstition and vice have replaced ardour for science and the virtues of industrious and brave citizens?" (2:282). Part II of *Rambles* is interwoven with historical accounts of the Bavarian occupation of the Tyrol, the Battle of Wagram, the revolt of Hofer, the conversion of the Bohemians to Catholicism, the Neapolitan revolt of 1820, and the French occupation of Ancona. Shelley avails herself of a variety of documentary sources in both English and Italian, in addition to live informants;[27] she reveals her familiarity with and esteem for Italian historiography by including the Italian historian Colleta in her review of the state of Italian letters. "Interactionist" in orientation, Shelley's historicism focuses variously on Anglo-Italian relations; on the Italian experience of Napoleonic reform; on the impact of Austria on the Venetian and Tuscan aristocracy; on the Austrian cultivation of higher learning in Italy; on collusion between the papacy and France and between local priests and Austria. Perhaps most striking is Shelley's appreciation for the differences and political interactions among the various regions of Italy; *Rambles* includes discrete treatments of the Lombards, Piedmontese, Venetians, Tuscans, Romans, Neapolitans, and Sorrentines as well as discussions of shifting alliances among them during periods of Spanish, Napoleonic, Austrian, and papal hegemony.

At the same time, Shelley's appreciation of these regional differences bespeaks a relativism that is the hallmark of post-Boasian cultural anthropology. Raising the study of culture "to a special and distinct reality operating according to laws of its own being," structural-functionalism emphasized the systemic quality of culture[28] and approached cultural institutions holistically. While Shelley commonly isolates one or two institutions for examination in each region—be it marriage, infant education, the aristocracy, inheritance practices, financial institutions, nutrition and food preparation, agricultural methods, leisure and entertainment, or medicine—*Rambles* is unified by Shelley's holistic, functionalist treatment of religion. As early as her 1817 *History of a Six Weeks' Tour,* Shelley had pondered the cultural meaning of religious difference:

> The Swiss cottages are much cleaner and neater [than the French cottages], and the inhabitants exhibit the same contrast. . . . This superior cleanliness is chiefly produced by the difference of religion. (40)

By 1843, Shelley variously interprets Roman Catholicism in Italy as a tyrannical empire, a means of social control, a system of Austrian surveillance, a form of social welfare, a source of feminine community, a type of theater, an incipient humanism, and a fully achieved aesthetic of the sublime.

Shelley emphatically denounces the temporal rule of the papacy as corrupt and tyrannical. She cites "the farrago of laws" in the papal States, and accuses the pope of desiring only "to pension the clergy, and to support in splendour the state luxury of the Cardinals" (2:248). In support of her claims, Shelley describes the disastrous cholera epidemic of 1837: while the Papacy lavished money on "lamps and candles" to propitiate heaven and the priests hid in fear, 15,000 people died of cholera, typhus, and starvation. The pope, intent on infantilizing his subjects, opposes the building of railroads, "that, as he says, his revolutionary subjects of the East may not corrupt his obedient children of the West" (2:243). Outside the Papal States, Shelley describes how the institution of priestly confession serves as an instrument of Austrian surveillance:

> [A] secret society is spread throughout the country, the friend of existing institutions;—the confessional is an engine of mighty power, diffused through every portion of the city, the most populous; entering every hut, the most retired; acting on the fears of the timid and the credulity of the superstitious. . . . Every priest bids his penitents confess, not only their participation in any act of thought inimical to the church or to the government—not only to denounce father, husband, or child, who might trust to them the secret of their lives—but to reveal every little circumstance that may tend to discover the lovers of liberty. (2:175)

In view of the imperial policing of Italy through the priesthood, Shelley deems the secrecy of the Carbonari a necessary strategy; she credits Capobianco with inventing Carbonarism as a "political religion":

> Capo Bianco understood the disposition of his countrymen, and gave a religious and mystic colouring to his society. Striking rites were established; the initiation was terrible; the lessons taught often apparently abstruse; the end was single—to overturn monarchy in all its forms, and erect republics on the ruin of thrones. To attain this among a people pious to superstition, it was necessary to mingle mystic tenets with political opinions; in short, to erect and disseminate a *political religion*. (2:168)

But in Shelley's holistic analysis, Roman Catholicism has its beneficent face as well. She praises the institutions of conventual charity, the licensing of beggars, papally supported workhouses, and the good works of Catholic confraternities. She is awed by a charitable "sisterhood" devoted to serving the needs of female pilgrims: "In my life I never saw so much female beauty . . . their faces so perfect in contour; so lovely in expression, so noble, and so soft, that the recollection will haunt my memory for ever" (2:232). At Rome, she is amused by the theatricality of Holy Week observances:

> The ceremonies of the Church strike me as less majestic than when I was last here; perhaps this is to be attributed to the chief part being filled by another actor. Pius VII was a venerable and dignified old man. Pope Gregory, shutting his eyes as he is carried round St. Peter's because the motion of the Chair makes him sea-sick, by no means excites respect. (2:230)

Commenting on three Titians seen in Venice, Shelley declares the social function of Christian art to reside not in the mysticism they project, but in their dramatism: "These [three Titians] are, what surely pictures ought to be allowed to be, dramatic in the highest sense; they tell a story; they represent scenes with unsurpassed truth and vigour" (2:95).

Shelley's detailed, discriminating comments on other paintings, however, suggest a rather different insight into the function of Christian art. Commending what she calls "the age of Christian idealism," she focuses on how such type-scenes as the Nativity, the Descent from the Cross, and the Deposition serve the Romantic ideal of the "human face divine":

> [Of Raphael's *Descent from the Cross:*] The expression of agony proper to the beloved disciple, struggles with the exertion of strength necessitated by the act in which he is employed; the resolution to perform the rites due to the dead, is mingled with yearning veneration for the corpse of him whom he passionately adored. (2:222–23)

> [Of Titian's *Mary Visiting the Tomb of Jesus:*] There was something impressive in the mingled awe and terror in Mary's face, when she found the body of Jesus gone. (2:90)

> [Of Corregio's *Notte:*] When by the drawing down of the blinds, we were left nearly in darkness, the effect of this on the pictures was miraculous. The child lay in living beams, which seemed to emanate from a focus and spread rays of light around. (1:244)

Deeply moved by such paintings, Shelley discerns in both Christian art and music (particularly the Easter miserere and lamentations) an implicit aesthetic of the sublime:

> [T]he soul is rapt—carried away into another state of being. . . . It is one of the mysteries of our nature, that the feelings which most torture and subdue, yet, if idealized—elevated by the imagination—married harmoniously to sound or colour—turn those pains to happiness; inspiring adoration; and a tremulous but ardent aspiration for immortality. (2:231)

In the saints and martyrs of Christian art, the Italians find an image of their own sublimity, "the sentient link between our heavenly and terrestrial nature" (2:231); among the rapt throngs of Holy Week, Shelley finds an image of her own best self.

Within Shelley's holistic and historicizing analyses of Italian culture, we perceive afresh the dialectic of self and other: if her historicism leaves room for the other beyond the other, her holism makes room for the self within the other. In these prescient analyses, as much as in her revival of Enlightenment social inquiry, Shelley resists a brittle hypostatization of the terms "self" and "other." Selfhood, finally, is a process of Enlightenment, a discovery of the other; otherness makes possible the conceptualization of selfhood. The closing pages of *Rambles* leave Shelley at her villa near the Bay of Naples, contemplating the moon:

> If there be a moon, we see it floating in mid-air. We perceive at once that it is not a shining shape, plastered as it were, against the sky; but a ball which, all bright, or partly dusky, hangs pendant. (2:276)

A Columbus in Sorrento, where "the moon hangs luminous, a pendant sphere of silver fire," Shelley had learned that not only the earth, but the moon, too, is round.

Notes

An earlier version of this essay was presented at the 1990 MLA Convention in Chicago; I have benefited from Betty Bennett's comments on that paper. I gratefully acknowledge the editorial suggestions of Audrey Fisch and the research assistance of Sarah Zimmerman and Richard Kaye.

1. "Itchy Feet and Pencils: A Symposium," *New York Times Book Review,* 18 Aug. 1991: 1, 23.
2. For a history of the guidebook, consult John Vaughan, *The English Guide Book c. 1780–1870* (Newton-Abbot: David & Charles, 1974), 62–81. The contemporary guidebook's genealogy lies in that early nineteenth-century traveler's crib, the road book; the earliest guidebooks are little more than extensively glossed road books. Comprised of schematic, chartlike route maps, road books cite points of interest for travelers at specified distances from a given point of departure. In the early nineteenth century, guidebooks came to include maps and information about hotels, transport, and other services; still later, brief accounts of "local antiquities, customs, and lists of flora and fauna . . . and, where necessary, notes of local dialect words commonly in use" (64).
3. Several essays in this book take up Mary Shelley's relation to Romanticism with respect to constructions of selfhood; see Favret, Wolfson, Corbett.
4. "Prince Albert used the railways from the early days of his marriage but Queen Victoria did not take a train until the summer of 1842"; see Vaughan, *The English Guide Book,* 30.
5. Mary Shelley, "Giovanni Villani," in *The Mary Shelley Reader,* ed. Betty T. Bennett and Charles E. Robinson (New York: Oxford University Press, 1990), 331–32.
6. Other writers cited include Burton, Sterne, Montaigne, Rousseau, Boswell, and Spence.
7. "S. read aloud to us Mary Wollstonecraft's Letters from Norway"; see Mary Shelley, *History of a Six Weeks' Tour* (London, 1817), 62. In 1821 Shelley requested Maria Gisborne to send her the volume in Pisa; see letter of November 30, 1821 in *Letters of Mary Wollstonecraft Shelley,* 3 vols., ed. Betty T. Bennett (Baltimore: Johns Hopkins University Press, 1980–88), 1:211.
8. William Godwin, *Memoirs of the Author of "The Rights of Woman,"* ed. Richard Holmes (published with Wollstonecraft's *A Short Residence in Sweden*) (Harmondsworth: Penguin, 1987), 249.
9. See Mitzi Myers, "Mary Wollstonecraft's *Letters Written . . . in Sweden:* Toward Romantic Autobiography," *Studies in Eighteenth Century Culture* ed. Roseann Runte (Madison: University of Wisconsin Press, 1979), 8:165–85. Myers argues that "To grant primacy to either social criticism or personal revelation—or to see the two as disjunct—does a disservice to the organic integrity of the *Letters*" (166). While I agree that Wollstonecraft's *Letters* reveal the simultaneous valuing of objective fact and subjective reflection, I am unable to grant the "organic integrity" of the *Letters* regarding what Myers calls "the public/private dichtomy." Apparently, neither Wollstonecraft nor Godwin was able to theorize an integral relation between these two discourses in the context of the *Letters.*
10. Mary Wollstonecraft, *A Short Residence in Sweden,* ed. Richard Holmes (published with Godwin's *Memoirs of the Author of "The Rights of Woman"*) (Harmondsworth: Penguin, 1987), 62. Following Shelley and Godwin, I refer to this work as *Letters from Norway,* or simply as *Letters.* All excerpts from Wollstonecraft's *Letters from Norway* are drawn from this edition and cited in the text.

11. The Revolutionary–Napoleonic period soldered the rhetoric of political favor to the discourse of morals in the term "political sympathy"; the OED cites Southey's *History of the Peninsular War* (1823) as the first reference in English to a political "sympathy."

12. Mary Shelley, *Rambles in Germany and Italy, in 1840, 1842 and 1843* (London, 1844), 1:vii. Betty T. Bennett has reprinted the preface to *Rambles* in *The Mary Shelley Reader* (382–86); otherwise, no modern edition or reprint exists. All subsequent references to *Rambles* are drawn from this edition and appear in the text. Typical of Shelley's reluctance to write a compendium of tourist information: "but I will not make a list of names, to be found in a guide-book" (1:171). In a gallery, Shelley promises "not to guide you (for I cannot), in your search after pictorial excellence; nor will I long detain you in the more beaten road of the public galleries" (2:151). Wollstonecraft makes a similar disclaimer: "There are some good pictures in the royal museum—Do not start—I am not going to trouble you with a dull catalogue, or stupid criticisms on masters" (*Letters,* 176).

13. For a useful summary of Italian–English relations from the Napoleonic period until about 1840, see C. P. Brand, "English Reaction to Political Events in Italy," *Italy and the English Romantics* (Cambridge: Cambridge University Press, 1957), 196–214. For the Italian context, see H. Hearder and D. P. Waley, *A Short History of Italy* (Cambridge: Cambridge University Press, 1963), 94–140, and Denis Mack Smith, *The Making of Italy 1796–1870* (New York: Walker, 1968), passim. Shelley's keen interest in Italian politics, of course, dates back more than two decades to her days in Italy with Percy Shelley. Writing to Maria Gisborne on July 19, 1820, shortly after the failed revolution in Naples, she writes: "Thirty years ago was the era for Republics, and they all fell—This is the era for *constitutions,* I only hope that these latter may in the end remove the [?mothes] of the former. What a glorious thing it will be if Lombardy regains its freedom—and Tuscany—all is so mild there that it will be the last, and yet in the end I hope the people here will raise their fallen souls and bodies, and become something better than they are" (*Letters of MWS,* 1:156). In a letter of April 17, 1821, after the Piedmontese rising, she informs Leigh Hunt that "Naples has shamefully fallen & Piedmont is but a step behind her—however the seed may be now sown the fruit of which we may reap some years hence—" (*Letters of MWS,* 1:189).

14. Consideration of the shift toward the subject in the representation of nature in eighteenth-century travel writing appears in George B. Parks, "The Turn to the Romantic in the Travel Literature of the Eighteenth Century," *Modern Language Quarterly* 25 (1964): 22–33. Parks cites Wollstonecraft's *Letters* as an example of a Romantic handling of landscape. Wollstonecraft differs from Shelley in linking her sublime passages uneasily to the task of interlocution. After a passage in which she "bow[s] before the awful throne of my Creator, whilst I rested on its footstool" (*Letters,* 111), Wollstonecraft assures her reader that "Having turned over in this solitude a new page in the history of my own heart" has only made her more resolute in "my respect for your judgement, and esteem for your character" (*Letters,* 122). Humbling subjection follows closely upon sublime sovereignty.

15. On the picturesque and its discontents among women travelers, see Shirley Foster, *Across New Worlds: Nineteenth-Century Women Travellers and Their Writings* (New York: Simon and Schuster, 1990), 56–58.

16. Louis Turner and John Ash define the grand tour as a particular *structure* of travel that defines "the relationship of *parvenu* to aristocrat. Its development follows a shift in the focus of culture and of economic and political power. The wealthy and educated, of states whose position of dominance in the world is comparatively new,

visit countries that have passed their peak of prestige and creativity but are still venerated for historical and cultural reasons. . . . The new world pays its respects to the old"; see *The Golden Hordes: International Tourism and the Pleasure Periphery* (New York: St. Martin's Press, 1976), 29. For a discussion of grand-tourism in Italy, see Paul Franklin Kirby, *The Grand Tour in Italy* (New York: Vanni, 1952). A provocative semiotics of tourism may be found in Dean MacCannell, *The Tourist: A New Theory of the Leisure Class* (New York: Shocken, 1989).

17. Freud narrates his discovery of the repetition compulsion in *Beyond the Pleasure Principle,* trans. James Strachey (New York: Norton, 1961), 6–11.

18. Mary Wollstonecraft, *Vindication of the Rights of Woman,* ed. Miriam Brody (Harmondsworth: Penguin, 1986), 148: emphasis in original. All subsequent excerpts from the *Vindication* are drawn from this edition and cited in the text as *VRW.*

19. While the word "anthropology" was used by Kant and other Enlightenment thinkers, the modern social science of anthropology is thought to originate in the second half of the nineteenth century. By midcentury, advances in geology, paleontology, philology, and prehistory, working in concert with an emerging evolutionist perspective, had made possible the differentiation of anthropology from sociology as the ethnological study of preindustrial human life; see Fred W. Voget, *A History of Ethnology* (New York: Holt, 1975), 114–64.

20. In *Wordsworth and the Enlightenment* (New Haven: Yale University Press, 1989), Alan Bewell summarizes these materials as follows: "[T]he formal structure of these texts is interesting. They present a loose architecture of concerns, comprehensive, heterogeneous, often redundant, and yet also fluid, to the point of eclecticism. Usually they are divided into three major categories: first, synchronic analyses of the mind and passions; second, historical accounts of the mind and passions; second, historical accounts of the origins and development of mankind and social institutions; and third, the postulation of ethical principles derived from these studies. A contemporary reader, looking into a text in moral philosophy, would expect to find, in varying degrees, analytic descriptions of the different faculties of the mind and the passions; discussion of primitive customs, economic processes, social forces, law and jurisprudence, aesthetics, education, and ethics; accounts of the origin and progress of civil governments and of human institutions, such as language, the family, religion, property, justice, and affluence; and, of course, the articulation of principles of conduct" (14).

21. Voget, *A History of Ethnology,* 42.

22. In 1861, the year of Italian unification, the illiteracy rate was 78%; about 70% of the population worked the land. See "Italy," *Encyclopedia Brittanica,* 1987, 22:230.

23. "Exalted by their inferiority (this sounds like a contradiction), they constantly demand homage as women, though experience should teach them that the men who pride themselves upon paying this arbitrary insolent respect to the sex, with the most scrupulous exactness, are most inclined to tyrannize over, and despise the very weakness they cherish" (*VRW,* 145).

24. I have emphasized here the import of Shelley's metaphor of "effeminacy" for her representation of Italian degradation. Within this context, however, Shelley often takes pains to differentiate between the situation of Italian women and Italian men— even between girls and boys. Of a primary school, she remarks, "There were some thirty or forty girls; and I am sorry to say they did not show so well [at arithmetic] as the boys; the cause, *I trust,* being that the head teacher, a priest, attended only to the latter" (2:117). Also in Venice, "It is not etiquette for a lady to enter a *caffé,* and they are shocked at the English women, who do not perceive the difference between eating

their ice, or sipping their coffee, in the open Piazza, and entering the shop itself"
(2:104–5). She idealizes the extended Italian family as a "little republic," observing
that "Unmarried women all over the Continent have so much the worst of it, that few
remain single" (2:109). On the subject of Sorrentine poverty, her informant is a desti-
tute Sorrentine woman, quoted at length. Shelley repeatedly credits her femininity
with giving her access and insights into Italian domesticity; among those topics neglected in travel writing by men, Foster lists "the appearance, costume and manners of
women; details of domestic life such as household management and culinary habits;
behaviour towards children; marriage customs and female status; the importance of
'space' in the physical environment" (24)—all topics treated by Shelley. Just as women
tourists in the Middle East visited the harem (Foster, *Across New Worlds,* 16), Shelley
visits a charitable sisterhood in Rome. Quoting a Frenchwoman startled by the vigor-
ousness of English women travelers, Shelley prides herself on having been an adventur-
ous traveler for some twenty-five years. On the other hand, she regrets being unable to
travel freely south of Naples because she is a woman. Upon arriving in Paris after her
1840 journey, she writes, "The think [*thing*] I like best in the world I find is travelling—
were I a man I would set out directly to travel all over the world—so I would as I am,
had I enough money" (*Letters of MWS,* 3:5). After the mid-1840s, Shelley's health
prevented further travel.

   25. Voget, *A History of Ethnology,* 110.

   26. Voget, "Man and Culture: An Essay in Changing Anthropological Interpretation," in Regna Darnell, ed., *Readings in the History of Anthropology* (New York:
Harper and Row, 1974), 347.

   27. Among these informants was Ferdinando Luigi Gatteschi, a young Italian
exile who had fought with Young Italy in the 1830–31 rising against Austria. In 1843,
Shelley undertook to help support him with the proceeds from *Rambles,* entreating
him to write an account of the French occupation of Ancona. In 1845, the erratic,
abusive Gatteschi would attempt—unsuccessfully—to blackmail her. For an account
of the Gatteschi episode, consult Emily W. Sunstein, *Mary Shelley: Romance and
Reality* (Boston: Little, Brown, 1989), 360–71.

   28. Voget, "Man and Culture," 350–51.

"The Last Man"[1]

Barbara Johnson

When considering a subject as broad as "the ends of man," one can only ask oneself: *Where to start?* Where to start speaking of the end? But on the other hand, isn't it always from the end that one starts? Isn't every narrative in fact constructed beginning with the denouement, as every project is constructed beginning with its goal? Isn't the end precisely that which never ceases to be repeated, which one is never done with? If man is truly, as Derrida says, "that which relates to its end," he is also that which is never finished with ending. Thus the question would not be to know how to *begin* speaking of the end, but how to *finish* speaking of it, how to narrate something other than the interminable death of the penultimate, how to be finished with the end?

This is perhaps the question that Nietzsche poses in *Human, All-Too-Human* when he writes, under the heading of "First and Last Things," "We look at everything through the human head and cannot cut this head off; while the question remains, What would be left of the world if it had been cut off?"[2] The end of man would seem then to be that which cannot be *lived* by any man. But what exactly is "human" in Nietzsche's statement, "*we* look at everything through the *human* head"? The human, here, is apparently something that says "we." And what if men were reduced only to "I"? Would the word "man" still have the same meaning if there were only one left? Would the end of man take place *before* or *after* the death of the last man? Would the final cut take place only after the death of the last man, or would it consist of his testimony, his unprecedented experience of survival? In other words, what would be the relation between the last representative of the human race and the end of man?

It is the limit-narrative of decapitation, of the cutting off of the human head with which we look at all things, that Mary Shelley attempted in a novel entitled *The Last Man*. This very long narrative, written by a woman whose birth coincides with the bloodiest moments of the French Revolution, is one of the first versions of the idea—which has become so commonplace in our atomic age—of the total extinction of the human species. Postrevolutionary but preatomic, this prophetic novel could perhaps tell us something about the strange temporality of the end of man.

In fact, in the current context Mary Shelley merits our interest in more than one respect. If she risks appearing somewhat marginal today, it's precisely her marginality that has always earned her a certain celebrity. That marginality was of two kinds: one, she lived surrounded by writers whose works strongly marked the thought and literature of the epoch: her father, William Godwin, liberal philosopher and author of *Political Justice;* her mother, Mary Wollstonecraft, author of *A Vindication of the Rights of Woman;* her husband, Percy Bysshe Shelley, Romantic poet and disciple of Godwin; and the many friends of Shelley, in particular the poet Byron. Aside from this marginality in the very center of the Romantic circle, Mary Shelley knew a second sort of famous nonexistence as the anonymous author of *Frankenstein,* a novel that she wrote at the age of nineteen and whose mythic power has only increased since, independently of the name and even the notion of the author. In the shadow of her parents, her husband, and her own work, Mary Shelley thus lived the Romantic period through its folds and margins. If I put the accent in this way on her marginality, it's not in order to discover for her a new centrality, but in order to analyze the new manner in which the question of marginality is inscribed in and agitates her work.

To speak of Mary Shelley's *Frankenstein* is immediately to approach the question of *man* indirectly through what has always been at once excluded and comprehended by its definition, namely, the *woman* and the *monster.* It's undoubtedly not an accident if the conjunction of these two categories of beings has traversed history under the reassuring form of fables of the "beauty and the beast" genre—which always end by confirming the superior glory of man, since the beast is transformed into a man with whom the woman falls in love. In *Frankenstein,* the end of the story is far from reassuring, but it is precisely because the monster is not monstrous enough.

Frankenstein, as everyone knows, is the story of a scientist who, trying to create a man in his laboratory, succeeds in manufacturing a monstrous being who ends up turning against his creator. It's the creator who is called "Frankenstein" and not the monster, who has no name, but the universal tendency to call the monster by the name of its creator is far from insignificant. Contrary to what the cinematic versions of *Frankenstein* have led us to believe, Mary Shelley's monster is not manufactured with a criminal's brain, and its creator is not crazy. Aside from a certain physical ugliness, Shelley's monster is the exact realization of the dream of its creator, to whom the project of discovering the secrets of life and of making use of them to manufacture a man had seemed the consummation of science and an inestimable benefit for humanity. But there is one detail which the creator had not foreseen: his own reaction to his creature. When he sees the yellowish eye of the one he had constructed and animated with so much effort open, Frankenstein is seized with horror and flees from the laboratory, abandoning the giant newborn to his fate. This creature whose features are roughly sutured but whose heart is good tries to find a place among men, but men always reject him with horror. Choosing to reside in the shadow of a country cottage, unknown to its inhabitants, the monster acquires a full humanist education by listening to the French lessons given by the country folk to an Arab woman. The monster, who has developed a tender sympathy for these country people, finally tries to win recognition from them, but like all humn beings, they are incapable of enduring his monstrous appearance. Made furious by loneliness, the monster leaves in search of his creator, whose youngest brother he strangles when he unluckily turns up along the way. When the monster finds Frankenstein, in the shadow of Mont Blanc, he tells him his story and begs his creator to make him a wife of the same species as himself. Touched in spite of himself, Frankenstein the creator agrees to the monster's request and sets about gathering the necessary materials for this new piece of work. But suddenly the image of a new, monstrous Eve forces itself upon him and, frightened by his vision, Frankenstein ends up destroying the rough draft of the female monster. The monster, who has watched this entire process, will never forgive him for the destruction of his mate. Instead of attacking his creator directly, he murders, one after another, all those who are dear to Frankenstein, until the creator is reduced to the same isolation as his creature.

If Mary Shelley thus elaborates a work of science fiction which seems to caution us against the fictions of science, it is not, however, only in order to suggest that there are limits which man has no right to overstep. For far from marking the *limits* of the human, Shelley's monster is nothing but the perfect realization of the humanist project par excellence: mastery of the knowledge of man. The chemical details of Frankenstein's experiment are only the *literalization* of the desire to give oneself a total representation of man, to master the origins of man to the point of being able to create one. The monster is thus not what remains *exterior* to the humanist conception of man; it is the figure of that conception itself to the extent that "man" is precisely a creation of man. This perfectly reasonable monster, whose wickedness is entirely explained by the injustices that are inflicted on him, is a perfect example of man such as he was created by the Enlightenment philosophes, for whom the human being par excellence was Western, rational, and masculine. It's no accident if the humanist-creator can't or doesn't want to create a woman equal to her man, or if the monster's education is presented as a *Westernization*. (The lessons he overhears are those given by Europeans to an Arab woman. It is also interesting to note that, in order to recover from the shock of the catastrophic creation, Frankenstein begins to study, precisely, Oriental languages.) Thus if Mary Shelley's novel constitutes a critique of humanism, that critique is directed not against the hubris of the humanist who takes himself for God, but against the blindness of the humanist who can't see himself. In gathering and sewing materials with the design of creating a human, Frankenstein never doubts for an instant that he knows what a human is. But the creature only has to open his eyes, the object only has to become subject for Frankenstein not to recognize him anymore and for him literally to lose consciousness (or knowledge—"connaissance"—Tr.). The *unknown* is not located in the object of humanism, but in the desiring humanist subject. That which the humanist remains blind to in his efforts to know man is the nature of his own desire to know man. That blindness is moreover represented within the novel by the total lack of explanation concerning the motives which led the creator to reject his creature so violently. This explanatory ellipsis has always been considered a grave defect in the novel by readers who were looking to follow the psychological logic. But it is precisely by this sort of logical flaw, this blind spot in the explanation of human desire, that something like psychology can be elaborated.

The humanist's blindness in relation to his own desire to know is illustrated in an exemplary way by Rousseau in the preface to his *Discourse on the Origin and Causes of Inequality Among Men,* by the way in which he understands the meaning of the inscription of Delphi, "The most useful and the least advanced of all human knowledge seems to me to be that of man; and I dare say that the inscription of the temple of Delphi alone contained a precept more important and more difficult than all the thick volumes of the moralists."[3] As opposed to Rousseau's project, the story of Frankenstein seems to affirm that if one translates in this way the command to know oneself as a command to know *man,* one risks losing contact monstrously with what one doesn't know.

Curiously, in the article by Jacques Derrida on "The Ends of Man," one finds in an unexpected way this idea of monstrosity linked to the critique of a tradition deformed by a humanist view:

> After the war, under the name of . . . existentialism . . . , the thought that dominated France presented itself essentially as humanist. . . . [T]he major concept, the theme of the last analysis, the irreducible horizon and origin is what was then called "human reality." As is well-known, this is a translation of Heideggerian *Dasein.* A *monstrous translation* in many respects, but so much the more significant.[4]

Would this Derridean monster be the modern reincarnation of Shelley's monster? Would monstrosity always exist as a function of humanist translation? Are there nonhumanist monsters? nonmonstrous translations?

In our day the myth of Frankenstein is ceaselessly invoked by the newspapers apropos of babies conceived in a test tube and, more recently, apropos of the creation of new forms of bacteria by the recombination of their genetic codes. In the context of debates over the commercial and juridical status of these new forms of life, the question of man finds itself curiously reopened. Having to decide whether the law governing the distribution of patents applied or not to the invention of living beings, the Supreme Court of the United States decreed that life was indeed susceptible to be patented since, in the words of former Chief Justice Berger (quoted in *Time*), " '[t]he issue is not between living and inanimate things, but between the products of nature—whether living or not—the human-made inventions.' "[5] In other words, it's the opposition between man and nature which here takes over from the worn-out opposition between life and death. All the more so in that, in our day, the legal status of death is itself submitted to the opposition between natural means and technological means of maintaining life. Thus if man is indeed that which is determined beginning with his end, his end is, more and more, that which can be determined only beginning with man.

This question of man suspended between life and death returns us finally to that second untimely meditation of Mary Shelley—untimely for her time but ardently timely for our own—namely, her other novel entitled precisely *The Last Man.* While Frankenstein was the story of the one who was superfluous in the world of men, *The Last Man* is the story of the one who is superfluous in a world without men. It's the story of the one who remains. Now, what does this remainder of humanity signify in relation to the question of the ends of man?

But first of all, a question is indispensable: Why couldn't such a story be entitled *The Last Woman?* Or rather, why is it that a novel entitled *The Last Woman* would be automatically interpreted—as one sees in the film of that title by Marco Ferreri—as the story of the last love of a man or else as a narrative of castration? Would the idea that humanity could not end with a woman have something to do with the ends of *man?*

In reality, although the narrator of this book speaks in the first person masculine singular, he belongs, like the monster, to a sort of third sex. He resembles neither the men nor the women of the novel. He serves the function of witness, of survivor, and of scribe. As we will see, it is the same role that Mary Shelley plays at the moment when she writes her novel.

The story of *The Last Man* takes place in Europe near the end of the twenty-first century. The main characters are few: aside from the narrator Lionel Verney and his sister Perdita, we count Adrian and Idris, children of the last king of England; Lord Raymond, hero of the Greek wars; and Evadne Zaimi, a Greek princess who lives in England. In the year 2073, the king of England, father of Adrian and Idris, abdicates to permit the creation of an English republic. The royal family withdraws to Windsor. After many sentimental and political vicissitudes, the narrator Verney marries Idris, the former king's daughter; the hero Raymond marries Perdita, sister of the narrator; Adrian, who had been in love with the princess Evadne, remains alone; and Evadne, in love with Raymond, disappears. Raymond, for whom the tranquil life at Windsor begins to be a burden, gets elected Lord Protector of England and throws himself immediately into innumerable projects for the good of humanity. By a series of accidents, Raymond rediscovers the Greek princess Evadne, reduced to a life of misery and still in love with him. Raymond, who tries to remedy her misery, doesn't speak of the princess to his wife Perdita, but she nevertheless begins to suspect something. As the misunderstanding between the spouses becomes irreparable, Raymond resigns his post and leaves England to join the Greek army once again. The Greeks are about to achieve victory over the Turks; the Greek army needs only to take Constantinople. The Greeks besiege the city. But the besieged city becomes more and more silent. Constantinople has fallen under the sway of the Plague. The armies separate without combat, making way for a plague-ridden peace.

England once again becomes the scene of the action. For several years, the English believe themselves sheltered from the Plague that devastates the entire Orient. But little by little this scourge takes over Europe and England until the last English survivors decide to leave their island to wait for death in a gentler climate. At every step, the circle of the survivors is circumscribed, but nothing stops the progress of the Plague, which is always fatal. Verney, the narrator, is the only one among all human beings to recover from it. He is thus more than a survivor; he is a ghost. When humanity is reduced to three beings—Raymond, Adrian, and the daughter of Raymond and Perdita—

these three survivors decide to embark on a sailing ship for Greece. The boat is shipwrecked; Verney remains alone. Searching for a fellow creature, he goes to Rome, where he spends a year writing and waiting. Finally convinced that no one will come meet him in Rome, he climbs to the top of St. Peter's to carve in stone the following inscription: "the aera 2100, last year of the world." Then, accompanied only by his dog, he embarks for unknown shores.

The life of Mary Shelley was also a series of survivals. Beginning with her birth, which cost her mother her life. At the moment when Mary Shelley wrote *The Last Man,* three of her four children had died, her husband Percy Shelley had drowned in a shipwreck, and Byron had just died in Greece. At the age of twenty-six, she considered herself the last relic of an extinct race.

One could thus affirm that in writing *The Last Man* Mary Shelley only painted her mourning on a universal scale. But that universal scale, that universal perspective on human affairs was just the one which ordinarily characterized the writings of the Romantic poets, especially those of Shelley and Byron. Thus Mary Shelley takes over a typically Romantic style in order to say what she sees as the end of Romanticism. In other words, in this novel, Mary Shelley does more than give a universal vision of her mourning; she mourns for a certain type of universal vision.

For that vision is precisely that of Verney and his companions. In going to seek other survivors in Rome, birthplace of *homo humanus,* Mary Shelley's last man performs the humanist gesture par excellence: he seeks to live the death of all of humanity. On his way, he leaves two kinds of messages, two sorts of "please forward": first, in three languages, he writes, "Verney, last of the race of Englishmen, had taken up his abode in Rome"; second, in Italian, "Friend, come! I wait for thee." To speak of oneself in the third person of the past tense is to take oneself for a historical character, that is, a dead man. To make an invitation in the second person, in the other's language, is still to expect to live. But after a year of vain waiting in Rome, Verney realizes that he doesn't know how to speak the other's language anymore, for he doesn't know any longer who the other might be. It becomes clear that all roads lead to Rome only for a certain Western culture which can no longer take itself for the voice of humanity in its entirety. In leaving Rome to seek an unknown otherness, Verney also stops writing. In designating the year of his departure the last year of the world, the last man thus marks the survival of humanist discourse, that is, of the possibility of making history. And yet, in setting off to wander in search of an unknown destiny, smitten with a culture that he knows to be obsolete, but incapable of forging for himself a postplague discourse, Verney could not symbolize better the very condition of modern Western man. How indeed can one survive humanism? How can one create a language that is postplague, that is, postuniversal?

But what does the Plague signify in this book? In *The Plague,* Albert Camus writes, "In this respect our townsfolk were like everybody else, wrapped up in themselves; in other words they were humanists: they disbelieved in pestilences. A pestilence isn't a thing made to man's measure."[6] It is evident that, for Mary Shelley as well, the Plague is that which man's measures can neither foresee nor master. All systems for the amelioration of man's lot pass in review in this novel, only to end in a blind alley in front of the Plague. The Plague is at once that which stops all systems of meaning from functioning and that against which those systems are necessarily erected.

But just before having them swallowed up by the scourge, Mary Shelley outlines a critique of each of the projects of reform dear to her father William Godwin and her husband Percy Shelley. In other words, each time we are about to draw a lesson from the narrative of political events, the Plague arrives to erase the question. The book does indeed contain a series of critiques, but *there is no relation* between these critiques and the train of events. The Plague itself seems neither entirely unavoidable nor entirely avoidable. Where the poet Percy Shelley, apropos of the French Revolution, spoke of an inadequacy, a "defect of correspondence between the knowledge existing in society and the improvement or gradual abolition of political institutions,"[7] Mary Shelley sees not a defect of correspondence but a *lack of relation* between acquired knowledge and the scene of action.

But the Plague is not only that which stops us from drawing lessons from human events. For it enters the plot at a very precise and significant moment of the novel. The Western world is about to fend off definitively the threat of the East. The Greeks need only to take Constantinople for victory to be complete. But the capture of Constantinople will never happen. Where Western man expects to encounter and to master his other, he finds himself faced with the absolute Other. The novel never tells us the political consequences of this suspension of the final confrontation between East and West. The question of the relation or of the nonrelation between East and West remains open, precisely by the way in which it is badly posed. The Plague, which extends out over the entire world from the point of encounter between East and West, is thus in a sense that which replaces the victory of the West over the East. Its lethal universality is a nightmarish version of the desire to establish a universal discourse, to spread equality and fraternity throughout the world. Thus the universal empire of the Plague would not be only, as Camus suggests, what is *excluded* from Western humanism; it would also be its *inverted image*.

It is not an accident if *The Last Man* begins with praise of England, that England which was mistress of the world's most powerful empire:

> I am the native of a sea-surrounded nook, a cloud-enshadowed land, which, when the surface of the globe, with its shoreless ocean and trackless continents, presents itself to my mind, appears only as an inconsiderable speck in the immense whole; and yet, when balanced in the scale of mental power, far outweighed countries of larger extent and more numerous population. So true it is, that man's mind alone was the creator of all that was good or great to man, and that Nature herself was only his first minister. England, seated far north in the turbid sea, now visits my dreams in the semblance of a vast and well-manned ship, which mastered the winds and rode proudly over the waves. In my boyish days she was the universe to me. When I stood on my native hills . . . the earth's very centre was fixed for me in that spot, and

the rest of her orb was as a fable, to have forgotten which would have cost neither my imagination nor understanding an effort.[8]

This image of England as mental mastery, inviolable insularity, self-sufficient centrality, is in fact the image of a certain conception of *man* which will be progressively demystified throughout the novel that follows. But this pitiless demystification is narrated as a series of privations and unendurable sorrows. At each step, one loses again a fatherland which never existed. The story of *The Last Man* is in the last analysis the story of modern Western man torn between mourning and deconstruction.

In a certain sense, one can say that modern literature begins with this end of man, at the moment when the last man leaves Rome without knowing what language to speak to it. It is interesting to note that in the novel by Maurice Blanchot also entitled *The Last Man,* one no longer finds any traditional narrative landmarks. Even the certainty that this is indeed a *narrative* is acquired only in the form of a strange joy, on the last page of the book, "Later, he asked himself how he had entered the calm. He couldn't talk about it with himself. Only joy at feeling he was in harmony with the words: 'Later, he. . . .' "[9] In this end of the book, it's thus a certain relation to language which ends by at once confirming and denying the end, solitude, the possibility of speaking.

Before this last page, Blanchot's book presents itself as a monologue cut into two unequal parts. In the first part, there is an "I," a "he," and a "she" who find themselves in a sort of asylum. After the break between the two parts, the word "event" appears, but the reader no longer knows who is speaking, nor to whom, nor of whom, nor of what event. In other words, in Blanchot's *Last Man* all that remains of traditional "lastmanism" is the questions which the theme obliges us automatically to ask. For a book entitled *The Last Man* is manifestly an impossible book. If the last man is a "he," who is writing the book? If the last man is an "I," who is reading it? Unless the reader is dead. . .

But the reader is inscribed in Mary Shelley's book precisely as dead. At the moment when Verney decides to write the story of the end of man, he begins with the following dedication:

> TO THE ILLUSTRIOUS DEAD.
> SHADOWS, ARISE, AND READ YOUR FALL!
> BEHOLD THE HISTORY OF THE
> LAST MAN.

If man is the one to whom the end is important, it is evident that Verney possesses the most important story that has ever been told. But those to whom that story is important are all necessarily dead. In a certain sense, the story of the end interests only the dead. For to the living, what matters isn't the end, but the future perfect.

Indeed, from the title on, *The Last Man* presents itself as a particularly striking example of the functioning of the future perfect. While normally the future perfect is the tense itself where the meaning of a story is tied up, *The*

Last Man promises the reader only a future in which he will not be able to have read the novel. By his reading, the reader only approaches retrospectively his own elimination, while the last man continues beyond his end. But the temporality of this narrative is further complicated by a supplementary fold, an author's introduction which tells us that this story of the last man that we have under our eyes is in reality only the imperfect and doubtless deformed translation of certain inscriptions found in 1818 on scattered leaves in the cavern of the Sybil of Cumae. What is at issue is thus a translation made in the nineteenth century of a prophecy uttered in Antiquity which takes the form of a narrative written by a man of the twenty-first century on the subject of the end of man. The end of man, in other words, will have always already coincided with the moment of predicting, the moment of translating, and the moment of writing. Unless, however, this is an error of translation.

Notes

This essay is a translation of a paper written in French, delivered during a colloquium entitled *Les Fins de l'homme* which took place in Cérisy (France) in the summer of 1980. The colloquium was organized as a response to the work of Jacques Derrida, particularly to his essay entitled "Les Fins de l'homme" (translated by Alan Bass as "The Ends of Man" in *Margins of Philosophy* [Chicago: University of Chicago Press, 1982]). It is amazing to realize that in the summer of 1980 there was not yet any medical or public discussion of AIDS. The plague had already begun, but it had not yet begun as discourse. If I were to write an essay on Shelley's *Last Man* today, it would be impossible not to think about it in conjunction with the AIDS epidemic. I am happy that Audrey Fisch has written so ably on the subject in this book. My unrevised essay stands with a kind of dramatic irony as an example of the historicity of thought.

1. Translated by Bruce Robbins, originally published as "Le dernier homme" in *Les Fins de l'homme à partir du travail de jacques derrida. 23 juillet–2 août 1980,* ed. Phillippe Lacoue-Labarthe and Jean-Luc Nancy (Paris: Editions Galilée, 1980).

2. Friedrich Nietzsche, *Human, All-Too-Human: A Book for Free Spirits,* part I, trans. Helen Zimmern (New York: Russell and Russell, 1964), 20.

3. Jean-Jacques Rousseau, *The First and Second Discourses,* trans. Roger D. and Judith R. Masters (New York: St. Martin's Press, 1964), 91.

4. Jacques Derrida, "The Ends of Man" in *Margins of Philosophy,* trans. Alan Bass (Chicago: University of Chicago Press, 1982), 115.

5. *Time,* June 30, 1980, 52.

6. Albert Camus, *The Plague,* trans. Stuart Gilbert (New York: Knopf, 1977), 35.

7. Percy Bysshe Shelley, preface, "The Revolt of Islam," *Poetical Works* (London: Oxford University Press, 1970), 33.

8. Mary Shelley, *The Last Man,* ed. Hugh J. Luke (Lincoln: University of Nebraska Press, 1965), 5.

9. Maurice Blanchot, *The Last Man,* trans. Lydia Davis (New York: Columbia University Press, 1987), 89.

Plaguing Politics: AIDS, Deconstruction, and *The Last Man*

Audrey A. Fisch

I am the native of a sea-surrounded nook, a cloud-enshadowed land, which, when the surface of the globe, with its shoreless ocean and track-less continents, presents itself to my mind, appears only as an inconsider-able speck in the immense whole; and yet, when balanced in the scale of mental power, far outweighed countries of larger extent and more numer-ous population. So true it is, that man's mind alone was creator of all that was good or great to man, and that Nature herself was only his first minister. England, seated far north in the turbid sea, now visits my dreams in the semblance of a vast and well-manned ship, which mastered the winds and rode proudly over the waves. In my boyish days she was the universe to me. When I stood on my native hills . . . the earth's very centre was fixed for me in that spot, and the rest of her orb was as a fable, to have forgotten which would have cost neither my imagination nor understanding an effort.[1]   Mary Shelley, *The Last Man*, 5

The Last Man begins with Lionel Verney's tribute to the superiority of England, and of the Englishman, over the world and over nature. It is a striking begin-ning for a story[2] that will tell not of England's unique greatness but of its collapse. Nature, personified as and exemplified by the Plague, kills all but three human beings. Of these last three only one, the narrator Lionel Verney, survives a final shipwreck. Clearly England and the Englishman, in this narra-tive, have not ridden proudly over the vicissitudes of nature; England has sunk.

The question of the novel is: If England is "the semblance of a vast and well-manned ship," then why did it sink? The answer is contained in Mary Shelley's exhaustive critique of the novel's variety of political leaders and systems, a critique that pinpoints some of the blind spots of masculine Roman-ticism.[3] It is a bold project for a novel and perhaps a bolder project for a nineteenth-century woman novelist. The book was condemned, in Mary Shel-ley's lifetime, as "the product of a diseased imagination and a polluted taste".[4] Today, it has been reclaimed by feminist critics for its critique of the bourgeois family and for its negotiations of the difficulties of female authorship in the nineteenth century.[5] But its political acumen has yet to be fully appreciated.

Those who have focused on its political critique have found the novel apoliti-cal or nihilistic. But because Mary Shelley's grounds of critique have a special relevance today, we're better prepared to understand the different politics of the novel. First, our own "plague," AIDS, has devastated and promises to continue devastating the United States because we can't seem to see our way out of a dark alley—the myth that AIDS is a disease of some Other. Reading Mary Shelley's novel within the context of the discourse of AIDS[6] underlines the political lessons of the novel. Second, the increasing (counter-) institutional voices of groups such as women's studies and Afro-American studies force literary theory, and deconstruction in particular, to face searching political scrutiny. Reading the slight frame narrative of *The Last Man* as Mary Shelley's attempt at a regenerative politics helps shift the "politics of deconstruction" debate to a more nuanced, if less completely satisfying, framework.

A Tight Ship

At the end of the novel, Lionel Verney, sole survivor of the Plague and a shipwreck, together with a dog and some books, sets sail. He says, "I seek—a companion. . . . [L]eaving behind the verdant land of native Europe, adown the tawny shore of Africa, having weathered the fierce seas of the Cape, I may moor my worn skiff in a creek, shaded by spicy groves of the odorous islands of the far Indian ocean" (341–42). Finally, Lionel seems to be enlarging his vision of the world by looking beyond Europe to the lands of the Other, India and Africa, for new companions. Finally, he seems to have rethought his earlier vision of England as the "universe," "the earth's very centre" (the epigraph to this essay), and his vision of "the rest of her orb" as "a fable."

Unfortunately, his travels to the shores of Africa and India, like those of thousands of colonialists and missionaries before him, are destined to produce only the reflection of himself projected onto those foreign shores. As he says, "I have chosen my boat" (342), thus indicating that his faith in the vision of the Englishman mastering the sea is unshaken by his own shipwreck experience. Likewise, he weighs down his ship with the same ideological baggage: "I have . . . laid in my scant stores. I have selected a few books; the principal are Homer and Shakespeare—But the libraries of the world are thrown open to me—and in any port I can renew my stock" (342). It's not clear whether Africa and India promise Lionel primarily a renewed stock of Homer and Shakespeare or access to different books. In any case, Lionel's literary choices indicate that he is still invested in traditional literature and that he may not realize Africa and India offer new "texts" to study.

Only after everyone else has died does Lionel question the accuracy of his perceptions of the world:

> I would not believe that all was as it seemed—The world was not dead, but I was mad; I was deprived of sight, hearing, and sense of touch; I was labouring under the force of a spell, which permitted me to behold all sights of earth, except its human inhabitants; they were pursuing their ordinary labours. Every house had its inmate; but I could not perceive them. If I could have deluded myself into a belief of this kind, I should have been far more satisfied. But my brain, tenacious of its reason, refused to lend itself to such imaginations. (327)

Lionel's imagination was capable, previously, of deluding itself into the belief that England was the "earth's very centre" and the rest of the world was a "fable." Is Lionel then "The Last Man" only because his politics, and thus his imagination, are self-deceived? Does Lionel's myopic focus on the imperial ship of state, England, and all its cultural accoutrements such as Homer and Shakespeare, his focus on what he admits is "an inconsiderable speck in the immense whole," blind him to all of the literal world beyond that speck?

The important issue here is whether Lionel's testimonial narrative is necessarily compromised by the fact that Lionel himself remains enmeshed in the myth of England as a great and unconquerable ship of state. Writing about his work, Lionel says that his narrative is directed toward the "re-peopled" world, toward a new race, who "wandering to these prodigious relics of the ante-pestilential race," will seek to know why and "how beings so wondrous in their achievements, with imaginations infinite, and powers godlike, had departed from their home to an unknown country?" (339). Of course, the new race will seek and Lionel's narrative relic promises to help them find an understanding not just of the wondrous imaginations of Lionel's civilization but, more importantly, of the flaws that led to their destruction.

Lionel's unwillingness to admit his civilization's flaws is, however, somewhat distinct from his account of those flaws. In the first sentences of the novel, for example, where Lionel continues to reconstruct his "boyish fancy" of the English "tight ship," he also grapples with England's fragility and eventual fall. He explores and exposes the series of exclusions necessary to construct that mythic "tight ship": fixing England as the "earth's very centre" requires relegating the rest of the world to "fable." But in the process, he shows that myth to be just a myth. In other words, he both takes apart the myth of imperial England and retains the image of it differently, thus making room for a new understanding of England as a lone ship, unable to master everything, unable to see past itself or to see itself as part of the rest of the world.

Lionel continues to see England as simultaneously omnipotent and flawed. His voice never manages to move beyond hesitant and tentative criticism to the realm of final and definitive critique. The claim might be made, furthermore, that Mary Shelley's novel as a whole never achieves a cohesive critique or satisfying closure. Rather than relegate such issues to discussions of the (lack of) quality of the novel, as critics have tended to do,[7] I will integrate them into our understanding of the novel's proposal for a different kind of politics (at which point we will arrive at a new appreciation of the novel's quality).

AIDS

Much of the initial reaction to AIDS consisted of attempts to understand the disease by constructing it as a plague emanating from some place *other* than the safe ship of America. Paula Treichler in "AIDS, Homophobia, and Biomedical Discourse: An Epidemic of Signification" and Susan Sontag in *AIDS and Its Metaphors* are among the intellectuals to study the popular, medical, and political obsession with discovering the place of origin of AIDS, Africa and Haiti among the more visible candidates.[8] Noteworthy about the focus on origins in the AIDS discourse is the way two kinds of "foreignness" inform each other. There is slippage between an emphasis on the "foreignness" of the disease, in terms of nationality but often coded racially, and an emphasis on the "foreignness" within our society, often denoted as "unnatural" sexuality, that allows the foreign disease access to us. The ideology of a foreignness within, as Sontag explains, underlies the image of the " 'soft' West" made permeable to invasion because of "its hedonism, its vulgar, sexy music, its indulgence in drugs, its disabled family life" (63). Our own unnatural sexuality—and here homosexuality becomes metonymic not merely with unnatural sexual practices but with aberrant taste, morals, and ethics—has made our society "soft" to an invasion of the "African virus." Thus AIDS exposes the fact that America is no longer a "tight ship."[9]

The threat to the tight ship of America can be averted, however, through a reformulation in which the "safe ship" of the American Empire is defined as non–drug using and heterosexual, hence not in danger. This reasoning excludes the individual who engages in "high-risk" sexual behavior or intravenous drug use from the tight ship of the "general population" or, more insidiously, places him or her in the category of non-American.[10] Issues of safety, then, become issues about the proper designations and exclusions necessary for constructing the category of the "general population."[11]

I don't want to trivialize the importance of understanding the path of a disease or of recognizing who is more or less at risk of infection. But what has been trivialized in the case of AIDS are the various social and political factors that raise a disease to the status of plague. "Plagues" are not diseases that come from some exotic and mysterious elsewhere. With hindsight, it's obvious that the cholera plague Mary Shelley was perhaps thinking of when she wrote her novel, which reportedly began in India, spreading to Russia and eventually to Europe, and which by 1831 was killing as many as 30,000 people each day, was a "plague" not because of its origin in India but because the nineteenth-century medical and sociopolitical communities could not control the spread of the disease.[12] Granted, they didn't understand the biological workings of the disease; nor do we completely understand the workings of the HIV virus. But we do understand that universal use of condoms, oral dams,[13] and clean needles would virtually stop the spread of the disease (and here again the gay community's response to AIDS is exemplary).[14] That we cannot effect this "solution" since we persist in our current and continuous queasiness about open discussions of sexual practices and in our unwillingness to distribute clean needles to "law-breaking" drug users must be understood to be part of what makes AIDS a "plague."[15] In other words, "plagues" don't come merely from germs or viruses, they come from a society's inability to handle those germs, because of a lack of both medical knowledge and, more importantly, sociopolitical capability.

Mary Shelley's Plague

At this point, we need to return to Lionel's mythology of the safe ship of England and to examine how, as with AIDS, the Eurocentrism of men such as Lionel actually contributes to the Plague's devastation of England. Of this plague very little sense can be made, especially as it enters the novel both abruptly and inconspicuously as

> PLAGUE. This enemy to the human race had begun early in June to raise its serpent-head on the shores of the Nile; parts of Asia, not usually subject to this evil, were infected. It was in Constantinople; but as each year that city experienced a like visitation, small attention was paid to those accounts which declared more people to have died there already, than usually made up the accustomed prey of the whole of the hotter months. (127)

Looking beyond these noted but "insignificant" (to the narrative) deaths to the Plague's first major action, we can begin to make sense out of the Plague: in Barbara Johnson's words, the "suspension of the final confrontation between East and West."[16] The Greek army (West), with the British leader Raymond leading it, has attacked the Turkish army (East) in Constantinople. Neither army wins and the battle is stalemated. Instead of either army, it is the Plague that "takes" the city: "the city was the prey of pestilence; already had a mighty power subjugated the inhabitants; Death had become lord of Constantinople" (139).

Before we can draw any conclusion about the "meaning" of the Plague, it passes from the attention of the major actors of the story. Lionel describes how, with "rapturous delight," he "turned from . . . the physical evils of distant countries [the Plague], to my own dear home, to the selected abode of goodness and love; to peace, and the interchange of every sacred sympathy" (163); Lionel turns from Plague and war to his family, metaphor for the safely separate and separately safe ship of England.

That England should be a safe ship while Asia Minor's ship sinks has an analogue in the myth of the safety of the "general population" from AIDS. In a world of nations or ships or "populations," the Plague, and not the West or England, is the ultimate imperial power. Thus the Plague, like AIDS, by its "suspension of the final confrontation between East and West" (Johnson, 264), points to the inappropriateness of the East–West division of the world.

It is fascinating, in the discussions of the political circles of Lionel's England, not just how but precisely on what terms the Plague's dismantling of the myth of the ship of state is resisted:

> We talked of the ravages made last year by pestilence in every quarter of the world. . . . We discussed the best means of preventing infection, and of preserving health and activity in a large city thus afflicted—London, for instance. . . . Our party at length broke up; "We are all dreaming this morning," said Ryland, "it is as wise to discuss the probability of a visitation of the plague on our well-governed metropolis, as to calculate the centuries which must escape before we can grow pine-apples here in the open air."

> But, though it seemed absurd to calculate upon the arrival of the plague
> in London, I could not reflect without extreme pain on the desolation this
> evil would cause in Greece. The English for the most part talked of Thrace
> and Macedonia, as they would of a lunar territory, which, unknown to them,
> presented no distinct idea or interest to the minds. (160)

Here, the conservative response of Ryland and the liberal response of Lionel
coincide in an identification of the problem as Greece's, not a problem for the
"well-governed" ship of England. For Ryland, Greece and Greece's problem
are as remote as the future; this insular view suggests the parallel "invisibility"
of many of the communities (blacks and Hispanics) hardest hit by AIDS and
of the remoteness of "their" problem. The liberal view, which may be more
dangerously blind because it can see the myopia of the conservatives (who see
Greece as clearly as the moon), produces only pity, not action.

The Plague, however, refuses to respect the distinctions between England
and Greece so firm in the minds of Lionel and his compatriots. In its "lethal
universality" (264), as Johnson puts it, the Plague, like AIDS, "deconstructs"
the boundary lines that constrain both Lionel's and Ryland's thinking, allowing the connections between the two countries to emerge—but only by elimi-
nating both countries' human populations. Likewise, the Plague is a social
leveler among the novel's different classes, exposing the displaced connection
of common humanity between rich and poor:

> the rules of order and pressure of laws were lost, some began with hesitation
> and wonder to transgress the accustomed uses of society. Palaces were de-
> serted, and the poor man dared at length, unreproved, intrude into the
> splendid apartments. . . . We were all equal now . . . there was nothing to
> prevent each from assuming possession of his share. We were all equal now;
> but near at hand was an equality still more levelling. . . . The grave. (230–31)

The novel tells many stories of social leveling, for example, Juliet, "a high-
born girl" brought together with the "meaner" youth to whom she had given
her heart. Though "the father of the fair Juliet separated them," the Plague
renders "every impediment removed" by "the death of relatives" and the
lovers enjoy "the spirit of love, of rapturous sympathy, which once had been
the life of the world" until they too die (206–7).

Thus, the Plague is, as Johnson says, "a nightmarish version of the desire . . . to spread equality and fraternity throughout the world" (264). In the
face of terrific attempts to shore up the distinctions between imperial England
and the rest of the world, which should remind us of the attempts, on the part
of the United States, to shore up the distinction between the "general population" and the rest of the world, the Plague ruthlessly insists on the equal
humanity of all and on the spuriousness of categories used to make distinctions. But, of course, all this is done at tremendous cost.

I am suggesting that the Plague practices a kind of deconstruction which,
because it undercuts the possibility of human agency, is of little value for
progressive politics. In order to expose the inappropriateness of the East–
West division of the world, to expose both the constructed binary between

East and West and the power hierarchy involved in that binary, it literally erases Constantinople. In order to expose the repressed common humanity of all people, deconstruction erases not only all differences among people but the people themselves. In the process of deconstructing the myth of imperial England and in order to make room for some understanding of England as a ship not all-masterful but one among many in an international fleet, the Plague sinks all ships. Deconstruction, in this case, becomes simple destruction. Is this universal destruction the only potential political outcome of deconstruction? Can we conclude that the only way social and national differences can be deconstructed is by universal destruction?

It may seem that Mary Shelley is offering us only the nihilism of a politically harmful deconstruction instead of a roadmap for political change. Her treatment of the various political systems in the novel (democracy, republicanism, hereditary monarchy, and theocracy), all of which "end in a blind alley in front of the Plague [and are] swallowed up by the scourge" (Johnson, 264), would seem to suggest that Mary Shelley is treating all political programs as if they were both indistinguishable and hopeless. Anne K. Mellor suggests that *"The Last Man* first undercuts the dominant systems of government of the early nineteenth century and then shows that all cultural ideologies are but meaningless fictions."[17] Thus Mellor concludes that "Shelley's novel is on the deepest level anti-political" (164). Lee Sterrenburg is led to conclude similarly that although *"The Last Man* deals with politics . . . ultimately it is an antipolitical novel."[18] He concludes that "Mary Shelley could find no formula for rebirth, either on a personal or a collective level" (343). I will argue, however, that there is a politically progressive lesson to be learned from this universally destructive treatment of people, nations, and political systems.

Plaguing Politics

Each political system is represented in the novel by a single leader: republicanism by Raymond; hereditary monarchy by Adrian; democracy by Ryland; theocracy by the "imposter prophet." All the representatives are men. But what looks like either a conservative platitude—all these political leaders are really not different—or a nihilistic and reductive argument about the impossibility for change—none of these political systems can really make any difference—must instead be seen as an argument about how to change the *conditions* of politics in order to bring about political change. Mary Shelley's concerns are not merely, as Sterrenburg puts it, "the failure of lofty ambitions" (338), a critique of political egotism, or merely, as Mellor suggests, the feminist critique of male Romantic egotism in respect to personal politics.[19] Rather, Mary Shelley's innovative critique lies in her insistence that these political leaders, and their systems, are flawed in their emphasis on the idealization of the male leader and their glorification of imperial England, separate and safe. Mary Shelley's insight into these unreconstructed men who want to reconstruct the world adds to the purely feminist critique a less common critique of Empire and thus reformulates that critique.

Raymond's election as Lord Protector apparently succeeds in allowing England to cohere under the aegis of the perfect male leader.[20] His opponent, Ryland, resigns at the last minute, "the idea of contest was dismissed" and "Each felt that England had never seen a Protector so capable of fulfilling the arduous duties of that high office. One voice made of many voices, resounded through the chamber; it syllabled the name of Raymond" (73). We have hints of the fallacy of this unanimous support for Raymond. Lionel describes a law in the election procedure in which "a bribe" (73) is offered to one of the candidates to cause him to resign, thereby avoiding struggle between the two final candidates. When Lionel says that "the law had become obsolete, nor had been referred to by any of us in our discussions" (73), he is scorning the very possibility of struggle or dissension in Raymond's election. But Perdita, Raymond's wife, happily imagines his defeat in the election. She is disappointed by his victory, thus her voice is an immediate break in the supposed unity of celebratory voices. Significantly, it is a female voice that first fractures the myth of (male) unity under Raymond.

Later, it is another woman who will topple Raymond's leadership (and his person). Raymond becomes involved with Evadne in the process of "render[ing] England one scene of fertility and magnificence" (76). Projecting himself as "the benefactor of his country," Raymond decides to erect a great national gallery which will hold pictures and statues that he will "present to the Republic" (76). The "edifice was to be the great ornament of his Protectorship" (76), the ornament both of himself and of his imperial England. The best drawing Raymond receives for the building comes from a disguised Evadne; "The design was new and elegant, but faulty . . . evidently the work of one who was not an architect" (77). When Raymond persists in his quest for perfection with the drawing and with the plan for his gallery, he discovers Evadne and becomes mysteriously embroiled with her. He and Perdita part less because of his "affair" than because of his inability to communicate with Perdita. Whether or not someone who cannot communicate with his wife can really "represent" the people doesn't become the issue; Raymond, destroyed by "disappointment and remorse" (106), neglects and finally abandons his work.

We can read Raymond and Evadne's relations allegorically. Evadne is the flaw in the ideal union of Perdita and Raymond. Her flawed building, as well a metaphor for herself, reveals the flaw in Raymond's perfect public representation of himself and in the national unity that he embodies. Adrian suggests that Raymond should resume his work, saying—and note here the precise terms—"There does not exist *the man* in England . . . whom the world will pronounce to be [Raymond's] superior" (109; emphasis added). But Raymond retorts: "I undertook a task to which I am unequal [the Protectorship]. I cannot rule myself. My passions are my masters; my smallest impulse my tyrant" (109). The Evadne "scandal" is not a banal demonstration of Raymond's personal private foibles, which have remained and ought to remain behind his public mask. The more subtle point here is that Raymond himself is unwilling to be less than the perfect symbol of a perfect England (in the tradition of kings). His decision to go to Greece instead and enter the fight between Greece and Turkey, between, as he says, "civilization and barbarism" (110), is an attempt to reinstate coherent male selfhood; for him, this cause at least will be "simple" and "the ideal of war" (116).

Adrian, unlike Raymond, is able to see beyond the myth of imperial England to the humanity of other peoples: "The Turks are men; each fibre, each limb is as feeling as our own, and every spasm . . . as in a Greek's" (116). The "natural" monarch of England by blood, Adrian will accept a position as leader only when the plague-depressed world and England have sufficiently decimated all the world's people. He says,

> "I am now going to undertake an office fitted for me. . . . O, I shall be something now! From my birth I have aspired like the eagle—but, unlike the eagle, my wings have failed. . . . A shepherd-boy that tends a silly flock on the mountains, was more in the scale of society tha[n] I. Congratulate me then that I have found fitting scope for my powers." (179)

With the people of the world enfeebled by the Plague, Adrian's courage makes him a kind of unique center, a perfect man, and a perfect king. But his refusal to take on any leadership role until this point in the novel, until he can be the "perfect" leader, suggests that the cost of his quest for perfection in leadership is illness and death for the people. In other words, "perfect leadership," in the guise of a strong manly conqueror, is predicated upon the vulnerability and victimization of others.

This perfect man, however, survives with Lionel and Raymond's daughter Clara. When Lionel worries that "The vast universe, its myriad worlds, and the plains of boundless earth which we had left—the extent of shoreless sea around . . . shrunk up to one point, even to our tossing bark, freighted with glorious humanity . . . must perish," Adrian murmurs, "Yet they shall be saved" (321). Clara, the only possible propagator left for the survival of humanity, "visited by an human pang, pale and trembling, crept near [Adrian]—he looked on her with an encouraging smile—'Do you fear, sweet girl? O, do not fear, we shall soon be on shore!' " (321). She seems to fear not shipwreck but her role in Adrian's vision as mere human vessel for the future of glorious humanity. So great is her apparent dread of Adrian, that personification of the perfect bark of England, that Clara seems to prefer and nearly to will the shipwreck which immediately follows. She says, "Why should I fear? neither sea nor storm can harm us, if mighty destiny . . . does not permit . . . one death will clasp us undivided" (321). Mocking Adrian's embrace, Clara prefers the undividing and unsexual clasp of death, a clasp that allows her to maintain her distance from Adrian's "fearful" touch. Like Evadne with Raymond, Clara reveals the flaw in Adrian's idealization of himself as the perfect representative for "glorious humanity." For without Clara, even that perfect representative could produce no "glorious humanity." Thus Mary Shelley, through her women characters, suggests a critique of the perfect ship of state and the thematization of that body politic as self-sufficient and complete through its projection onto the body of the male leader.

The third political figure, Ryland, combines the political radicalism of democracy with conservative chauvinism, perhaps Mary Shelley's telling commentary on the balance in the early labor reform movement between concern for fellow English laborers and chauvinistic dismissal of the problems of the "foreigner."[21] "Ryland began by praising the present state of the British empire," Lionel tells us, recounting one of Ryland's political speeches,

> He compared the royal and republican spirit; shewed [*sic*] how the one tended to enslave the minds of men; while the institutions of the other served to raise even the meanest among us to something great and good. He shewed how England had become powerful and its inhabitants valiant and wise, by means of the freedom they enjoyed. As he spoke, every heart swelled with pride, and every cheek glowed with delight to remember that each one there was English. (41–42)

When the Plague does indeed come to the "well-governed metropolis" (159) of London, however, the English people lose their natural and national superiority for Ryland. At once England is flooded with foreigners seeking an escape from the unhealthy climates, and England's economy is wrecked when trade is stopped between America, India, Egypt, Greece, and England. The illusion of the separate and safe island is thus destroyed.

Not having foreseen this advance of the Plague, Ryland is politically unprepared and is forced to abandon his plans for the removal of hereditary privileges in order to expedite the more pressing issues of hunger, crime, and poverty. Finally, Ryland, advocate for the people and for equality, abandons his post saying, " 'Death and disease level all men. I neither pretend to protect nor govern an hospital—such as England will become. . . . Every man for himself! the devil take the protectorship, say I, if it expose me to danger!' " (176–77). Danger, here, is not merely the Plague, which Ryland cannot and does not flee, but the masses of people, leveled, as Ryland seems initially to have wanted, and wandering the streets en masse. The Plague thus exposes the chauvinistic limits of Ryland's democracy: a democracy which refused to forestall the disasters experienced by other countries, a democracy not intended to work in an England "corrupted" by foreigners, and a democracy which could neither foresee nor forestall the disasters brought upon England by its place in the world and the world economy.

Finally, we come to the "imposter-prophet," the last political figure. Described as having been corrupted by the "pernicious doctrines of election and special grace [of Methodism which] combined to destroy all conscientious feeling" (273–74), the "imposter-prophet" forms a small "brotherhood" (273), called "the elect" (277), out of the hundred people who remain. A literal reading of the term "brotherhood" suggests that this theocracy is the most straightforwardly patriarchal political system in the novel. That they self-congratulatingly call themselves "the elect," ironically meaning both the superior and merely those selected for office, recalls the slippery connection between an assertion of the perfection of the leaders of state and of the ship of state. That, as Lionel tells, "their purpose was . . . one, their obedience to their leader more entire, their fortitude and courage more unyielding and active" (273) reminds us both of the false unity of opinion surrounding Raymond's election and of the troubled thematics of unity as the glorification of self-completion that we've seen in each of the figures thus far.

The "imposter-prophet" 's doctrine bears quoting at length:

> His grand hold upon the minds of men, took its rise from the doctrine inculcated by him, that those who believed in, and followed him, were the remnant to be saved, while all the rest of mankind were marked out for death. Now, at the time of the Flood, the omnipotent repented him that he had created man, and as then with water, now with the arrows of pestilence, was about to annihilate all, except those who obeyed his decrees, promulgated by the *ipse dixit* prophet. It is impossible to say on what foundations this man built his hopes of being able to carry on such an imposture. It is likely that he was fully aware of the lie which murderous nature might give to his assertions, and believed it to be the cast of a die, whether he should in future ages be reverenced as an inspired delegate from heaven, or be recognized as an imposter by the present dying generation. . . . When, on the first approach of summer, the fatal disease again made its ravages among the followers of Adrian, the imposter exultingly proclaimed the exemption of his own congregation from the universal calamity. He was believed; his followers . . . reviled [Adrian] and asserted their own superiority and exemption. (295–96)

We recognize in this figure of the "imposter-prophet" a near parody of the political leadership of Raymond, Adrian, and Ryland. More than each of them, the "imposter-prophet" glorifies his own unique perfection as leader, here as God's chosen voice. He emphasizes the causal connection between the safety of his band, his little nation, and their "natural," and here God-given, superiority. The figure of the "imposter-prophet," then, seems created to drive Mary Shelley's points home: the splendid isolation of the "imposter-prophet," like the splendid isolation of each of imperial England's previous leaders, is a specious assertion of safety and a dangerously false and chauvinistic attempt to displace danger and responsibility onto an external and hence "different" group.

Furthermore, since the "imposter-prophet" segment literalizes the ideological work of the myth of imperial England as the murder of its own disruptive kind, this section also drives home the point that the creation and preservation of this myth of England comes at the expense of England herself. As Lionel tells us, when the Plague invades "the congregation of the elect" (296), the "imposter-prophet"

> endeavored to conceal this event; he had a few followers, who, admitted into the arcana of his wickedness, could help him in the execution of his nefarious designs. Those who sickened were immediately and quietly withdrawn, the cord and the midnight-grave disposed of them for ever; while some plausible excuse was given for their absence. (296)

A Politics of Imperfection

At the end of *The Last Man,* everyone is dead save Lionel. Even if we assume that Lionel has, in the end, achieved an understanding of his compatriots' blindness to issues of gender and nationality, this understanding comes at the ultimate cost: the death of the human race. Within the economy of the novel, there can be no point to the achievement of such an understanding; thus the novel seems to provide a subversion of *all* politics.

The question of the politics of the novel might be read also as a parable of deconstruction. Like *The Last Man,* deconstruction dismantles the many myths by which we structure our world. And like the novel, deconstruction seems to leave us with only the ruins of our old world. Furthermore, deconstruction, as in Barbara Johnson's dismantling of the humanist subject—"man"—reveals that the subject, like imperial England, is merely a mythical construct. Thus deconstruction, like the novel, seems to leave us without any subject—any "man"—capable of cleaning up the mess and rebuilding, without any subject capable of being an agent of change. As with *The Last Man,* deconstruction seems antipolitical.

This is the view of deconstruction offered, for example, by Barbara Christian's "The Race for Theory," a black feminist's impassioned words of political distrust for what one might call the "politics of deconstruction."[22] It is striking that Barbara Christian indiscriminately lumps all theory together and levels it all as equally politically irresponsible. But, like Mary Shelley, Christian is pointing to the ways in which even extremely different theoretical communities, like the various political leaders of the novel, share certain political blind spots.[23] Like Shelley, Christian levels her critique of theory on grounds of sexism and ethnocentrism.[24]

Furthermore, Christian's critique reminds us of the way the deconstructive Plague in *The Last Man* obviates the issue of the West's supremacy over the East only by, in its turn, subjugating Constantinople. That the Plague still works by subjugation, by becoming "lord" of the city, indicates that the Plague as deconstruction, here in its totalizing and self-aggrandizing form as universal leveler, resembles the universal conqueror—the West. Or, as Christian suggests, "the new emphasis on literary critical theory is as hegemonic as the world it attacks" (71). Neither *The Last Man* nor deconstruction empowers the men and women of Constantinople; or, rather, neither creates a form of power different from that of the hegemonic world—the "people," Christian might say, remain subjugated to literary critical theory just as they were subjugated in and by the hegemonic world and thus eradicated.

Christian's hostility to certain kinds of theory (including certain kinds of deconstruction) results, more generally, from her desire to retain a subject capable of political agency. Isn't reconstruction, Christian might ask, and the concomitant empowering of men and women as agents capable of change more politically urgent than deconstruction, which destroys existing culture? For Christian deconstruction fails because it cannot produce political agents and thus it can't empower the dispossessed or change society; it fails, that is, because every possible agent, every possible subject, is dead.

But everyone is not dead at the end of the novel. The frame narrator of the "Author's Introduction" in 1818, before the events of Lionel's narrative, finds, translates, and gives shape to a manuscript—Lionel's narrative—which begins in 2073. Lionel's narrative we now realize is really a prophecy, found inscribed on scattered Sybilline leaves and bark in the cave of the Cumaean Sybil. The "Author's Introduction" is thus positioned as a prophecy of the ends of man, intended to warn "man" so that the end of "mankind" can be averted. No one, then, is dead yet.

Critics of *The Last Man* have paid little attention to the "Author's Introduction." The attention these strange pages have received has been focused solely on how their sentiments reflect "Mary Shelley," either a sorrowful Mary Shelley after Percy Shelley's death, or a Mary Shelley as woman writer anxious either to cover over her authorial identity or to celebrate the female creativity of the Sybil.[25] The false identification of Mary Shelley with the narrator of the "Author's Introduction" obscures the profound way in which the "Author's Introduction" stands as a necessary supplement to the major predicament of the novel: the issue of politics and agency.[26] Specifically, exclusive attention to the frame narrator as a figure for an old-fashioned unitary subject—the author—obscures the frame narrator's presence as a figuration of a new kind of agent and a new kind of subject.

Mary Shelley's frame narrator mirrors not the elimination but rather the transformation of the subject by deconstruction. As Mary Poovey and Catherine Gallagher, both participants in and critics of the new historicism, have managed to show, deconstruction and reconstruction need not be mutually exclusive. We can complicate the question of individual power, or agency, and retain deconstruction without abandoning the possibility for change and thus without deleting all progressive politics. Agency, as Poovey and Gallagher insist, is more contingent, less the self-independent action of an individual against society than the circumstances under which an individual is able to mobilize both within and against that society. As Poovey puts it, "the complexity of causation" necessitates the attempt to rethink the conditions for change but it need not imply the impossibility for change.[27] Likewise, by rethinking the conditions of personal agency, we do not need to relinquish entirely the notion of individual power.[28] It is this particular agency, what I call "a politics of imperfection," that Mary Shelley takes up in the "Author's Introduction" to the novel.

In the "Author's Introduction," although the frame narrator believes in the "genuineness" of the Sybilline leaves, the narrator seems strangely unaware of any public and political function for the prophetic narrative. In classical Rome, the Sybilline leaves were kept and consulted by the Senate on political and social actions. But if the Roman senators put their leaves to use in deciding on the events that we now call history, and if Lionel's proclamations make clear that his tale is intended to teach "men" to change their political ways, the narrator says only "I have often wondered at the subject of [the Sybil's] verses" and "My only excuse for thus transforming them, is that they were unintelligible in their pristine condition" (4). Strangely, the frame narrator speaks of Lionel Verney's tale only as "wondrous and eloquent" as "poetic rhapsodies" (3–4). And the frame narrator asks, "Will my readers ask how I could find solace from the narration of misery and woeful change? This is one of the mysteries of our nature, which holds full sway over me, and from whose influence I cannot escape" (4). To the frame narrator, the manuscript, instead of offering lessons about politics and survival, instead of functioning as prophecy, has offered "solace."

Furthermore, it is with exceeding personal modesty that the frame narrator at all promulgates Lionel's fragmented tale. For example, the narrator is self-disparaging over the translation and editing: "Doubtless the leaves of the Cumaean Sybil have suffered distortion and diminution of interest and excellence in my hands" (4).

Finally, in the mysterious nonidentity of the frame narrator, we see the very opposite of what we saw in the political figures of the novel. The frame narrator, together with the companion, are enigmatic in gender, referred to only as "we" or "I" or "my companion"; there are no references to either as "he" or "she" or "his" or "him." We know nothing of the persona of the narrator: occupation, age, appearance. The narrator's former companion, in contrast, is described as "selected and matchless," embodying a perfection harkening back to the novel's thematization of totality and perfection. The absence of that perfect companion ("lost to me" [3]), confirms the narrator's own lack of personal, social, and political substance, all of which are mirrored in the imperfection of the "slight Sibylline pages" (3).

With this narrator, we are presented with a person who, whether by learning the lessons of Lionel's narrative or not, has eschewed a politics of perfection and totality. For example, the narrator's withdrawal into a cave and away from the world to "[bestow] my time and imperfect powers, in giving form and substance to the frail and attenuated Leaves of the Sibyl" (4), as she or he modestly puts it, starkly contrasts with the grandiose politics of Raymond, Adrian, even of Lionel Verney, who ceremoniously inscribes his book with "DEDICATION TO THE ILLUSTRIOUS DEAD. SHADOWS, ARISE, AND READ YOUR FALL! BEHOLD THE HISTORY OF THE LAST MAN" (339). The narrator's simplistic rendition of his or her task compares favorably with *The Last Man*'s cast of characters, whose hubris promoted self-aggrandizement but not self-reflection or examination of "imperfect powers." Likewise, the frame narrator strikes a nice balance, in reconstructing the leaves, between the assertion of agency— "Scattered and unconnected as they were, I have been obliged to add links and model the work into a consistent form" (3–4)—and the contextualization, demarcation, and questioning (the deconstruction) of that agency. It is important to notice as well that while the narrator's project does remove "him/her" from society, solitude is not "his/her" condition of life. The narrator explains that "he/she" can work "whenever the world's circumstance has not imperiously called me away" (3). In all, the narrator seems a model for the deconstructive critic, necessarily both a part of and apart from "society," shaping but also being shaped by the "materials" of his or her work, and distrusting any political agenda which, for the sake of "urgency," might preclude modest personal projects.[29] Equally a model for feminist critics, the narrator represents a gender flux or indeterminacy which is not an erasure of gender politics.

I am suggesting that the persona of the narrator represents Mary Shelley's answer to the faulty politics of Raymond, Adrian, Ryland, and the "imposter-prophet." As a figure for the deconstructive critic, and as distinct from the totalizing and costly deconstruction represented by the Plague, the narrator can also offer a model for our own politics. (A modest proposal for condom education and distribution in advance of any "solution" or "cure" for AIDS comes to mind here.) But lest we hasten to a happy ending too soon, we need to return to the issue of the narrator's nonidentity.

Reading beyond the equation of biographical frame narrator and Mary Shelley, it is important to distinguish the modesty of the frame narrator from the nineteenth century's politically and socially modest female—the Proper Lady.[30] At the same time, it is important to note that as a genderless individual, capable of learning the lessons of the narrative, the narrator is virtually nonhuman.

How does "he/she" escape the blind spots of "man"? Is it merely because this frame narrator is "The Last Woman"? Or does the nonhumanness of the frame narrator register Mary Shelley's pessimistic belief that the nineteenth-century human, like Lionel, will inevitably return to the paths of error?[31] Whether "man" can actually reconceive "himself" remains a dubious question in the face of Lionel's insistence, postplague and postplague deconstruction, on his identity as an Englishman and on the superiority of England with which I began this essay. As such, the nonhumanness of the frame narrator stands as a pessimistic rebuttal[32] to projects hopeful of political change, an insistence that deconstruction without supplementary politics is not enough, and a radical call for the very essence of "man" to be reconceived as the first step toward change.

Notes

While working on this essay I have had the help of a great number of generous readers and thinkers. I want to thank Barbara Johnson and William Galperin for their encouragement while this essay was in the early stages of its germination. And for critical comments and wonderful support, in some cases over and over again, I'm grateful to Esther H. Schor, Anne K. Mellor, Bruce Robbins, Kate Ellis, Elise Lemire, Gwen Bergner, George Levine, and Mark Flynn.

1. This and all following references to *The Last Man* are from Brian Aldiss, ed., *The Last Man* (London: Hogarth Press, 1985).

2. The reader is referred to Barbara Johnson's essay "The Last Man," pages 258–

266 in this volume, for a plot summary of the novel. Building on Johnson's essay, to which I am indebted, I attempt to distinguish and evaluate politically a kind of deconstruction which I term "a politics of imperfection."

3. Anne K. Mellor, "Why Women Didn't Like Romanticism: The Views of Jane Austen and Mary Shelley," in *The Romantics and Us: Essays on Literature and Culture,* ed. Gene W. Ruoff (New Brunswick: Rutgers University Press, 1990) describes masculine and feminine romanticism as two sorts of paradigmatic romanticisms within a multiplicity of romanticisms. "The male writers promoted an ideology that celebrated revolutionary change, the divinity of the poetic creative process, the development of the man of feeling, and the 'acquisition of the philosophic mind.' " In opposition to these men, the women writers, of whom Mellor takes Mary Shelley as exemplary, "heralded an equally revolutionary ideology, what Mary Wollstonecraft called 'a REVOLUTION in female manners' " (285). Mellor's formulations here are extremely useful, although we might want to question the validity of this clear-cut division between the genders and the social, political, and historical reasons behind any such division.

4. Hugh J. Luke, Jr., introduction to *The Last Man* by Mary Shelley (Lincoln: University of Nebraska Press, 1965), viii.

5. See respectively Anne K. Mellor, *Mary Shelley: Her Life, Her Fiction, and Her Monsters* (New York: Methuen, 1988), especially pp. 148–57; Mary Poovey, *The Proper Lady and the Woman Writer: Ideology as Style in the Works of Mary Wollstonecraft, Mary Shelley, and Jane Austen* (Chicago: University of Chicago Press, 1984), especially pp. x–xv and pp. 146–58; and Sandra M. Gilbert and Susan Gubar, *The Madwoman in the Attic: The Woman Writer and the Nineteenth-Century Literary Imagination* (New Haven: Yale University Press, 1979), 93–104.

6. My ahistorical yoking of this early nineteenth-century narrative with a discussion of the current discourses surrounding AIDS forgoes historical specificity in exchange for a theoretical acumen about "plagues" that our own AIDS discourse has enabled. In forgoing the benefits of a certain kind of historical discussion (of, for example, *The Last Man* and the medical and sociopolitical discourses of disease at the time), I'm relying on the idea that such a discussion would still be determined by current attention to AIDS—as all our historical work is determined by a nexus of contemporary problems and debates. While my historical "short-circuit" is in some ways more expedient, doubtless the urgency I feel to move from Mary Shelley directly to AIDS (bypassing a range of more obvious historical routes) entails sacrifices. This, sacrifice, however, coincides with the political agenda I've called "a politics of imperfection."

7. See, for example, William Veeder, *Mary Shelley and Frankenstein: The Fate of Androgyny* (Chicago: University of Chicago, 1986), 3–5.

8. See Paula A. Treichler, "AIDS, Homophobia, and Biomedical Discourse: An Epidemic of Signification," *October* (special issue "AIDS: Cultural Analysis/Cultural Activism" ed. by Douglas Crimp) 43 (Winter 1987): 36–37; and Susan Sontag, *AIDS and Its Metaphors* (New York: Farrar, Straus, and Giroux, 1989), 44–54.

9. Of course, America never was a "tight ship." Here we might want to connect the construction of the myth of the American "tight ship" with heterosexual America's determination to maintain a kind of tight anus—that is, to police an exclusion of anal intercourse from heterosexual sex practices.

10. See Jan Zita Grover, "AIDS: Keywords," *October* 43 (Winter 1987): 23–24, for an excellent discussion of the terms "general population," "gay/homosexual community," and "heterosexual community."

11. Linda Villarosa, in a letter to the editor, *New York Times Book Review* 18 (February 1990): 37, responding to a statement that "there will be no AIDS epidemic in the general heterosexual community," writes "I have interviewed a number of women who are now infected with the AIDS virus . . . Each woman had sex (vaginal, not anal) with a man who unbeknown to her, had engaged in high-risk behavior." Villarosa's insistence that AIDS may become epidemic in the "general heterosexual community" comes at the expense of an implicit and subtle scapegoating of the closet bisexual and the closet intravenous drug user and at the expense of "blaming the victim"—the woman. Clearly in this instance the HIV virus, like the bisexual and the closet drug user, has managed to transgress the boundary lines between homosexual and heterosexual, between promiscuous and nonpromiscuous, between homosexual sex ("anal intercourse") and heterosexual sex ("vaginal intercourse"), between high-risk group and low-risk group, exposing the artificiality of these boundary lines and categories. And yet the public, like Villarosa, has responded not by questioning the value and function of the categories but by trying to find another "right way" of defining the high-risk group and low-risk group; hence the scapegoating of the bisexual and closet drug user and the move to blame the woman who foolishly engages in sexual intercourse without sufficiently scrutinizing her partner. What Villarosa unconsciously puts her finger on is the inadequacy of any definition of the "general heterosexual community" given actual sexual practices. Villarosa exemplifies the "general" public's (here, notably not the gay communities') solution to the AIDS crisis: the attempt to shore up the categories of high-risk group and low-risk group—the bisexual and the closet drug user should be vilified. A concentration on categories diverts attention from explicit discussion of or education about sexual behavior, and distribution of condoms and needles.

12. See Brian Aldiss, Introduction to *The Last Man,* by Mary Shelley (London: Hogarth Press, 1985), 1.

13. Anyone who has ever tried to purchase an "oral dam," the preventive device necessary for oral-anal or oral-vaginal intercourse, realizes exactly how ineffectively the United States is handling the AIDS plague! It may be theorized, however, that the unavailability of the oral dam (as opposed to the present great availability of condoms) results from the fact that the oral dam is necessary for sexual practices pleasuring particular marginal groups, that is, women and gay men.

14. Among the "general population," AIDS does not seem to have effected any universal adoption of safe sex practices. This does not imply, of course, that AIDS has not effected any great changes in the discourse about sexuality. But while attitudes about the importance of the nuclear family, monogamy, and virginity may be changing, statistics on venereal disease, sexual activity, and condom use do not indicate that safe sex has become the norm. It is beyond the scope of this study to consider the variations of responses to AIDS in terms of sexual practices within different communities. Is it really accurate to say that all the gay communities have managed to respond effectively to AIDS? How does a community like San Francisco differ from New York in terms of AIDS awareness? Do we even have statistical information on smaller, less visible communities in small cities? Because of the long incubation period for the disease and because of the unevenness of testing and early disease treatment, it is difficult to determine whether AIDS has actually (or will actually) become only (and certainly not merely) a disease of the uneducated and poor (i.e., city-dwelling blacks and Hispanics, and intravenous drug users).

15. I'm thankful to Kate Ellis for pointing out to me that I make it sound as if society's unwillingness to take responsibility for distribution of condoms and clean

needles fully constitutes the problem. Rather, sufficient information and access to appropriate materials have proven insufficient for producing safe behavior in many cases. This points to the complicated and related issue of condom or clean needle use or, more generally, the issue of why safe behavior is or is not adopted.

16. Barbara Johnson, "The Last Man" p. 264 in this volume. All subsequent page references are to this volume.

17. Mellor, *Mary Shelley,* 144.

18. Lee Sterrenburg, *"The Last Man:* Anatomy of Failed Revolutions," *Nineteenth Century Fiction* 33 (1978/79): 328. See also pp. 324–47 for a fine contextualization of Mary Shelley's responses in the novel to the particular historical and literary models of revolutionary politics.

19. See Mellor, *Mary Shelley,* where she argues that "the novel tests Mary Shelley's ideology of the family against the realities of human egotism" (148). I agree with Mellor's suggestions that "military and civic glory is too often won at the expense of family relationships and the suffering of the innocent" (152), but I'm suggesting that this feminist critique needs also to be contextualized with a reading of the politics of Empire.

20. Raymond's election occurs before the Plague's emergence in the narrative.

21. Catherine Gallagher, in *The Industrial Reformation of English Fiction: Social Discourse and Narrative Form 1832–1867* (Chicago: University of Chicago Press, 1985), discusses the worker–slave metaphor and describes the ways in which William Cobett made important contributions to nineteenth-century social criticism by aligning himself with proslavery writers. Cobbett, charging the middle class with hypocrisy for exerting itself to end black slavery in the colonies without taking care of its own, wrote in 1806 "so often as they agitate this question, [slavery] with all its cant, for the relief of 500,000 blacks; so often will I remind them of the 1,200,000 white paupers of England and Wales" (qtd. in Gallagher, 8). Clearly, Cobbett's rhetoric functions to underline the urgency of the problem of white paupers not merely by calling attention to their numerical superiority to blacks but also by identifying these paupers as more properly a "British" problem since these men and women were British in a way that colonial blacks "obviously" were not.

22. Barbara Christian, "The Race for Theory," *FS: Feminist Studies* 14.1 (Spring 1988): 67–79. See my "Political Differences," *Critical Texts* 5.3 (1988): 44–48 for a more complete discussion of the complications of sacrificing complexity in the name of political urgency.

23. As a political strategy and a self-sufficient tool, perfect for all uses, deconstruction can clearly be as flawed (and flawed in much the same way) as the democracy of Ryland or the republicanism of Raymond. Deconstruction, as Christian points out, is not necessarily any different from the political strategies of *The Last Man;* it does not necessarily avoid the pitfalls of sexism, racism, and nationalism that the strategies of the novel fall into. But in analyzing and indicting the politics of deconstruction, we cannot assume that deconstruction already contains all its politics. Christian's criticism calls into question not the *inherent* politics of deconstruction, but merely the politics that have been *associated* with deconstruction but need not constitute it. Beyond the scope of this essay is the very interesting question of what kind of politics might be constitutive of deconstruction. Of course, that very question is to an extent misleading in that it accords deconstruction with a coherence that seems less than appropriate. Is deconstruction even a useful term when it can apply to the work of such diverse scholars as J. Hillis Miller, Gayatri Spivak, Barbara Johnson, Shoshana Felman, Paul de Man, and Jacques Derrida? And how can the term deconstruction accommodate

the diversity within, for example, Barbara Johnson's career—the difference between such essays as "The Frame of Reference: Poe, Lacan, Derrida" and "Apostrophe, Animation, and Abortion," both in *A World of Difference* (Baltimore: Johns Hopkins University Press, 1987)?

24. Christian writes that she is "tired of being asked to produce a black feminist theory as if I were a mechanical man" (69). Here, Christian echoes not merely the monster of *Frankenstein* but the suspicion voiced in both *Frankenstein* and *The Last Man* that Romanticism may be for men only. See Christian also for her attack on feminist theory as ethnocentric when she asks why, given their concentration on the body and female language, French feminists haven't considered the way "Some native American languages . . . use female pronouns" (75–76). Christian also asks if French feminist theory is only *white* theory. Thus she suggests a topic parallel to the question of a Romanticism for men only: Is French feminist theory for white women only?

25. Here, see respectively, Brian Aldiss, Introduction to *The Last Man*, by Mary Shelley (London: Hogarth Press, 1985), 1–10; Poovey, *The Proper Lady and the Woman Writer;* and Gilbert and Gubar, *The Madwoman in the Attic*. Brian Aldiss writes, "To find one's way through the first volume, it should be remembered that portraits of those Mary knew and loved best—almost all of them dead—are presented in thin disguise in the text" (2). Poovey, on the other hand, writes, "Shelley places her most elaborate strategy of indirection in the 'Author's Introduction' to the text. . . . The result of this elaborate narrative and temporal mediation is an ostentatious disengagement of Mary Shelley from a story that is patently autobiographical. . . . This extensive distancing of the emotion and the events of the story of *The Last Man* is Shelley's most complex strategy for simultaneously sanctioning and disavowing the publication of her most private grief" (157). With reference to this same "Author's Introduction," Gilbert and Gubar write, "This last parable is the story of the woman artist who enters the cavern of her own mind and finds there the scattered leaves not only of her own power. The body of her precursor's art, and thus the body of her own art, lies in pieces around her, dismembered, disremembered, disintegrated. How can she remember it and become a member of it, join it and rejoin it, integrate it and in doing so achieve her own integrity, her own selfhood" (98). Note that Poovey and Gilbert and Gubar all take up the question of female agency in their arguments; it is interesting how the "Author's Introduction" gets treated when the concept of agency is not reconceptualized.

26. That the deconstructive imperative of *The Last Man* concerns the personal and political limits of "man," should come as no surprise to readers of *Frankenstein*. It is interesting, in this context, to note that *Frankenstein* also undertakes the question of the possibility for change and regeneration after the "lesson," *Frankenstein*'s critique, has been unfolded. Framed as it is by a chain of listeners (Walton, Walton's sister), *Frankenstein* asks whether Walton can learn from Victor's mistakes; that is, more generally—Who is in a position to draw lessons from a testimonial narrative? Thus *Frankenstein* mirrors the question of deconstruction's regenerative powers and of its political potential, in other words—for whom it would make any difference to undergo the deconstruction of "man's" myths. *Frankenstein* seems vaguely pessimistic about the purpose of all this critique; Walton, for example, only gives up his "scientific" mission faced with mutiny. Mrs. Saville, the absent recipient of the manuscript and thus of the critique, in some way resembles the frame narrator of the "Author's Introduction." Yet *Frankenstein* does not engage the question of what difference all this makes to her. In contrast, *The Last Man* is frankly, if obscurely, optimistic.

27. "The complexity of causation," according to Poovey in *Uneven Developments: The Ideological Work of Gender in Mid-Victorian England* (Chicago: University of Chicago Press, 1988), teaches us "how difficult it is to access women's participation [or to evaluate] the extent to which we have participated in our own oppression" (21).

28. In our criticism of the "Englishman" and his mistaken attempt to master alone the waves and the winds, Poovey might remind us that his hubris is not merely chauvinistic (in terms of nation and gender) but reflective of a liberal humanism that can trap not just "man" but feminists and politically committed critics (like Barbara Christian) with whose desire for individual agency and change we may be sympathetic.

29. This is not to make our negotiation between seemingly "large" political projects and seemingly "small" personal projects seem easy. It will remain difficult to determine what kind of political agendas we might withdraw our support from and which personal projects we will take up. In *A World of Difference,* Barbara Johnson writes, "The profound political intervention of feminism has indeed been not simply to enact a radical politics but to redefine the very nature of what is deemed political—to take politics down from its male incarnation as a change-seeking interest in what is *not* nearest to hand, and to bring it into the daily historical texture of the relations between the sexes" (31). But the point here is not merely to revivify personal projects as political but to unravel the idea of a therapeutic teleology for political criticism and thus to avoid the search for a political "antidote." For a further discussion of these issues, see my "Political Differences."

30. See Poovey, *The Proper Lady and the Woman Writer,* x–xv.

31. Think here of the monster's modest desire to retire from society in the company of a mate. Victor gives no credence to this desire, insisting that the monster wants to re-populate the world with little monsters like himself. Victor's human and altogether worldly projection onto the monster's desires erases the possibility that in his non-humanness the monster might desire something entirely different.

32. It is in this pessimistic political sense that *The Last Man,* as Mellor writes in *Mary Shelley,* opens "the way to twentieth-century existentialism and nihilism" (169). But again, this pessimism is based less on the fact, as Mellor puts it, that "all conceptions of human history, all ideologies are grounded on metaphors or tropes which have no referent or authority outside of language" (164) than on a more straightforward critique of humanism.

Contributors

Paul A. Cantor is professor of English at the University of Virginia and a member of the National Council on the Humanities. He is the author of numerous books and articles on Shakespeare and Romanticism, including *Creature and Creator: Myth-making and English Romanticism* and the *Hamlet* volume in Cambridge's Landmarks of World Literature series.

Mary Jean Corbett, assistant professor of English and Affiliate of the Women's Studies Program at Miami University in Oxford, Ohio, is the author of *Representing Femininity: Middle-Class Subjectivity in Victorian and Edwardian Women's Biographies* (Oxford, 1992). Her current research concerns English-Irish literary relations in the nineteenth century.

Kate Ferguson Ellis is Associate Professor of English at Rutgers University. She is the author of *The Contested Castle: Gothic Novels and the Subversion of Domestic Ideology* (1989) and co-editor of *Caught Looking: Feminism, Pornography, and Censorship* (1986).

Mary A. Favret is an assistant professor of English and Women's Studies at Indiana University, Bloomington. She is the author of *Romantic Correspondence: Women, Politics, and the Fiction of Letters* (Cambridge, 1992) and is co-editing *At the Limits of Romanticism* (Indiana, 1993).

Audrey A. Fisch is a graduate student in English at Rutgers University. She is completing a dissertation in Victorian studies entitled, "Uncle Tom in England: The Black American Abolitionist Campaign, 1852–1861." Her article on the British reception of *Uncle Tom's Cabin* is forthcoming in *Nineteenth-Century Contexts*.

Sonia Hofkosh is assistant professor of English at Tufts University. She is completing a book on the social construction of Romantic authorship.

Barbara Johnson is professor of English and Comparative Literature and Chair of Women's Studies at Harvard University. She is the author of *The Critical Difference* and *A World of Difference*, editor of *The Pedagogical Imperative, Consequences of Theory* (with Jonathan Arac), and *Freedom and Interpretation: Oxford Amnesty Lectures 1992*. She is currently finishing a short book entitled *The Wake of Deconstruction*.

Joseph W. Lew is an assistant professor of English at the University of Hawaii at Manoa. Recent articles have appeared in *Studies in Romanticism, Eighteenth Century Studies,* and *Keats-Shelley Journal.* He is working on a book tentatively titled *Romantic Global Narratives.*

Laurie Langbauer is an associate professor of English at Swarthmore College. She published *Women and Romance: The Consolation of Gender in the English Novel* (Cornell, 1990). She is at work on a book about the everyday, the late-nineteenth-century English novel, and current cultural studies.

Anne K. Mellor is professor of English and Women's Studies at the University of California in Los Angeles. She recently edited *Romanticism and Feminism* (1988) and is the author of *Mary Shelley: Her Life, Her Fiction, Her Monsters* (1988) and *Romanticism and Gender* (1992), as well as numerous books and articles on English romanticism.

Barbara Jane O'Sullivan received an M.A. and an M.Phil from the University of York. Her M.Phil thesis was entitled "Cassandra (Un)bound: An Examination of the Fiction of Mary Shelley." She has also published "An English-woman in Italy: Mary Wollstonecraft Shelley and Mme de Stael's *Corinne*" in *The Canadian Journal of the Comparative Study of Civilizations*. She currently lives and works in Reading, U.K.

Morton D. Paley is a professor of English at the University of California, Berkeley, and is co-editor of *Blake: An Illustrated Quarterly*. His most recent book is an annotated edition and reproduction of Blake's *Jerusalem,* published for the William Blake Trust by the Tate Gallery. He is currently at work on *Apocalypse and Millennium in English Romantic Poetry.*

Alan Richardson, associate professor of English at Boston College, is the author of *A Mental Theater: Poetic Drama and Consciousness in the Romantic Age* and of essays on Romantic-era literature and culture in relation to gender, colonialism, and the social construction of childhood. He has recently completed a book-length study of literature, education, and ideology in late eighteenth and early nineteenth century Britain.

Esther H. Schor is assistant professor of English at Princeton University. With Pat C. Hoy and Robert DiYanni, she edited *Women's Voices: Visions and Perspectives* (1990), and is the author of *Bearing the Dead: The British Culture of Mourning from the Enlightenment to Victoria,* forthcoming from Princeton University Press.

Susan Wolfson is professor of English at Princeton University. She is the author of *The Questioning Presence: Wordsworth, Keats, and the Interrogative Modes of Romantic Poetry* (Cornell, 1986) and of numerous essays on Romantic writing. This article is part of a study in development provisionally titled: *Couples in Conversation: Romanticism and the Poetics of Gender.*

Index

Note: Mary Shelley is referred to as "Shelley." Her husband appears as "Percy Shelley."